The Story of *Webster's Third*

1/95

The Story
of *Webster's Third*

Philip Gove's Controversial
Dictionary and Its Critics

HERBERT C. MORTON

CAMBRIDGE
UNIVERSITY PRESS

Published by the Press Syndicate of the University of Cambridge
The Pitt Building, Trumpington Street, Cambridge CB2 1RP
40 West 20th Street, New York, NY 10011-4211, USA
10 Stamford Road, Oakleigh, Melbourne 3166, Australia

First published 1994

Printed in the United States of America

Library of Congress Cataloging-in-Publication Data
Morton, Herbert Charles
The story of *Webster's Third* : Philip Gove's controversial
dictionary and its critics / Herbert C. Morton.
p.   cm.
Includes bibliographical references and index.
ISBN 0-521-46146-4
1. *Webster's Third New International Dictionary of the English
Language*, unabridged.   2. English language – Lexicography.   3. Gove,
Philip Babcock, 1902– .   I. Title.
PE167.W4M67   1994
423 – dc20   94-5056
                                                            CIP

A catalog record for this book is available from the British Library.

ISBN 0-521-46146-4 Hardback

FOR BARBARA

Contents

Preface

This is a book for dictionary users, not dictionary makers. I write for readers who share my curiosity about what lexicographers do, how dictionaries are made, and why otherwise rather calm people so readily come to blows over disagreements about meaning, usage, pronunciation, and other matters that drive them to their dictionaries. It is my hope that at least a few linguists and lexicographers will also find this account of an extraordinary episode in cultural history and its consequences worth reading.

Up to now the war of words over *Webster's Third New International Dictionary* has remained a largely untold story, notwithstanding the blizzard of articles it provoked in newspapers and magazines more than thirty years ago. It has a middle – the crossfire of reviews and rejoinders during the early 1960s – but no beginning and no ending. Much has been left unreported or unexplored. A comprehensive and coherent account linking the controversy to the history of lexicography and to the decisions that shaped *Webster's Third* is long overdue.

My interest in the subject goes back three decades. When *Webster's Third* was published in September 1961, I was directing a scholarly publishing program. Like my friends in book publishing and journalism across the country, I was caught up in the debate. Before long, we found ourselves facing an editorial decision that was taking on unexpected significance. Should we adopt the new Merriam-Webster unabridged dictionary as the authority for spelling, meaning, usage, pronunciation, and so on or stand by the *Webster's Second* of 1934, long out of date but revered and unrivaled in its authority?

Establishment opinion seemed overwhelmingly in favor of rejecting *Webster's Third*, which was portrayed as a revolutionary document that would corrupt our speech and undermine our cultural traditions. The temper of the time and the hyperbole of the attacking forces fostered the impression that our decisions and those of other educated readers and writers might well determine the future of the English language, if not our national culture. Nonetheless, there were numerous estimable critics who favored the new work and saw nothing subversive in it. They argued, persuasively I thought, that language had changed greatly during the twenty-five years that had passed since the publication of the Second Edition; whether one liked the new edition in all of its particulars, it was a major achievement and the best guide available. When and precisely why I decided to select the Third Edition I do not recall, though I do remember that I was in the minority among my friends.

About fifteen years later, my memories of the controversy were revived by a splendid book about the *Oxford English Dictionary* and its editor, James A. H. Murray, entitled *Caught in the Web of Words*, by K. M. Elisabeth Murray. Many incidents that were described had a familiar ring, as if they had happened only yesterday, rather than nearly a century earlier, as if the setting were Springfield, Massachusetts, not Oxford, England, and as if the editor were Philip B. Gove, the embattled defender of *Webster's Third New International Dictionary*, not James Murray. Notwithstanding the great differences between the two editors and their dictionaries, there was an interesting commonality in many of their lexicographical problems. The idea for a book about Philip B. Gove and his dictionary began to take shape in my mind, though another decade would pass before I could begin working on it.

Acknowledgments

I am pleased to acknowledge my debts to working lexicographers, scholars, librarians, the Merriam-Webster Company, the Gove family, and many others who talked with me or gave me access to important files or commented on my manuscript.

Above all, I am deeply grateful to Henry Bosley Woolf, philologist and lexicographer, who was Gove's close associate and successor, and subsequently editor of the eighth edition of *Webster's New Collegiate Dictionary*. Woolf's comments on the task of dictionary making, his recollections of Gove, and the bridges he provided to many former colleagues and to the Gove family were indispensable. He read my first draft with a critical and discerning eye, and his continuing encouragement helped sustain my enthusiasm for the long project. He bears no responsibility, however, for what finally appears.

Gove's papers, deposited by his wife, Grace, at the American Heritage Center of the University of Wyoming, offered a rich source of information about his work and life. Emmett D. Chisum, research historian at the library, earned my thanks before and during my visit to the collection. I also thank the Regenstein Library at the University of Chicago for access to the papers of Raven I. McDavid, Jr., the Folger Library in Washington, the George Washington University Library, and especially the Georgetown University Library, whose excellent collection of journals and books on language and usage became my principal working library.

For recollections of their father and access to family correspondence, I am grateful to Norwood Gove and his wife, Ruth, Susan Gove Rudolph, and Doris Gove and her husband, Chauncey J. Mellor. Susan clarified and corrected many details in the manuscript.

My meeting with James Sledd was especially memorable and re-warding, and in my treatment of the controversy I drew heavily on his writings, published and unpublished. I also appreciated helpful inter-views with Robert Burchfield, Edmund Weiner, and Clarence Barn-hart. At an early stage in my planning, Sir Randolph Quirk, Gabriele Stein (Lady Quirk), and Robert Ilson listened sympathetically and made suggestions.

John Algeo offered generous encouragement all along and insight-ful suggestions on several chapters. For helpful comments on selected portions of my manuscript, I thank Robert L. Chapman, Thomas Creswell, and Virginia McDavid.

I am grateful to many editors who worked on the Third Edition for their willingness to discuss their recollections, including Hubert Kel-sey, Charles Sleeth, Henry Kratz, Sol Steinmetz, Frank Fletcher, and Grace Kellogg. Hazel Lord, secretary to Gove after the dictionary was completed, added another perspective on his work.

Crawford Lincoln, assistant to the president and later acting presi-dent of Merriam-Webster, was a splendid source of anecdotes about Gove and of leads to other information, for which I am grateful. I also thank Victor Weidman, former vice-president, and David Replogle, president when Gove retired, for their comments.

For additional perspectives, I thank two editors who received some of their early training from Gove after the Third Edition was pub-lished: Anne Soukhanov, executive editor of *The American Heritage Dictionary*, third edition, and Robert B. Costello, an editor on *The Random House Dictionary*, unabridged, first and second editions, and editor of *The Random House Webster's College Dictionary*.

At Merriam-Webster, Frederick Mish, editor in chief, arranged my access to the company correspondence and later discussed his own impression of the Gove legacy. Several staff members who knew Gove were gracious and helpful, especially E. Ward Gilman, who as a young editor learned his job on the Third Edition. He continued on the staff for more than thirty years, capping his career with a splendid book on English usage. Other staff members who talked with me were Julie A. Collier, Robert D. Copeland, James G. Lowe, and Robert W. Pease, Jr., who came to know Gove in his later years, after he had stepped down as editor and was spending much of his time advising and instructing new members of the editorial staff.

Several friends – editors, writers, and readers – commented on parts or all of the manuscript to good effect: Mark Carroll, Henry Lowenstern, Adam Stone, and Lawrence G. Weiss.

My introduction to lexicography was Sidney Landau's book, *Dictionaries: The Art and Craft of Lexicography.* I owe more to it than appears in my notes, for I can no longer sort out what I learned from Landau and what I learned from later reading and research. It was at his invitation that I submitted my manuscript to Cambridge University Press, and it was my good fortune that he decided to edit it himself. I could not have had more sympathetic and informed criticism and guidance. I am also grateful to Mary Racine, who prepared the manuscript for production with painstaking attention to editorial and production details.

I am indebted to the National Endowment for the Humanities for awarding me a year's research fellowship and the Rockefeller Center at Bellagio for giving me a place to work and support for several weeks of writing while my wife, Barbara, was a scholar in residence.

Finally, my loving thanks to Barbara for her support over the course of this project while she was hard at work on her own manuscript. She commented constructively on every chapter as I completed it and patiently reviewed my revisions with unflagging encouragement.

The Best of Times and the Worst: A Prologue

Every other authour may aspire to praise; the lexicographer can only hope to escape reproach, and even this negative recompense has been yet granted to very few.

Samuel Johnson, Preface to *A Dictionary of the English Language*

In the autumn of 1961 the publication of a new American dictionary touched off the stormiest controversy in the annals of lexicography. It was later described as "a literary scandal of the kind until then monopolized by Paris." It began quietly before the dictionary went on sale and gathered momentum in the press during the ensuing months. Lengthy indictments, derisive and angry, appeared later in the *Atlantic* and the *New Yorker* and were met with indignant point-by-point rejoinders. The debate went on for years in scholarly and professional journals, with occasional outcroppings in the media and books.[1]

At the center of the controversy was an unlikely target, *Webster's Third New International Dictionary of the English Language, Unabridged,* the eighth edition in a direct line of descent from Noah Webster's pioneering work of 1828, *An American Dictionary of the English Language.* The lineage was highly respectable, and though dictionaries are sometimes controversial, the subject matter was certainly not the stuff of the great publishing battles of the past, which were more often provoked by disputes over religious questions or freedom of speech. Furthermore, the work that it succeeded, the Second Edition of 1934, was the best-known and most widely used unabridged dictionary of the English language in the United States and perhaps the world. *Webster's Second,* as it was known, was more than respected. It was accepted as the ultimate authority on meaning and usage, and its preeminence was virtually unchallenged in the United States. It did not provoke controversies; it settled them.

What happened between the Second and Third Editions – in the making of dictionaries and the attitudes of dictionary users – to account for such a difference in reception? Even now it is difficult to disentangle all the factors – the lexicographical issues, the ideological antagonisms reflecting the cultural and social tensions of the early 1960s, the widespread ignorance about language and about dictionaries, the competence and fairness of the critics, and the misleading publicity material issued by the publisher to capture attention in the press. Moreover, it was the Merriam company's misfortune that the dictionary appeared at a critical time in the battle between linguists and humanists within university departments of English. Humanists resented what they regarded as the exaggerated claims of superiority by linguists; they had found philology comfortable, but structural linguistics seemed scientific and hostile. Linguists were offended by the refusal of literary scholars to recognize the contributions of linguistic research. It was clear, as the controversy grew in intensity, that the central issue was not merely the dictionary itself, though it was that primarily; it was also what the critics thought the dictionary symbolized. At stake, so it was made to appear, was the preservation of the English language and the survival of deeply rooted cultural traditions: *Webster's Third* was portrayed as a threat to both, and its editor, Philip Babcock Gove, bore the brunt of the attack.

PHILIP GOVE, like the dictionary itself, was an unlikely target. A New Englander by descent, upbringing, temperament, and choice, he was born in New Hampshire in 1902 and attended local schools and Dartmouth College. He was an enthusiastic outdoorsman from boyhood on. He was conservative in his political and social views and believed in hard work and the power of research and reason to solve problems. After graduate school, he taught college English for fifteen years and spent a year in London and Oxford on a scholarship; he served as a naval officer during World War II and returned to New England in 1946. He spent the last twenty-five years of his working life at the G. & C. Merriam Company in Springfield, Massachusetts, where he became editor in chief of Merriam-Webster dictionaries.

In coming to lexicography in midcareer, Gove at the age of forty-four was following a path taken by many dictionary editors before him. Noah Webster was forty-two in 1800 when he began working on his *Compendious Dictionary.* James A. H. Murray, editor of the *Oxford English Dictionary (OED)*, was forty-two when he changed course, and Samuel Johnson, the great eighteenth-century writer and lexicographer, was thirty-seven. All learned their craft on the job, as others have done since. Robert W. Burchfield recalls that he never wrote a definition before he became editor of the supplement to the *OED* in 1957. He had "glossarial experience," as he put it, and had assisted in the preparation of the *Oxford Dictionary of English Etymology,* but he felt totally at a loss about how to proceed with the making of a dictionary.[2]

Gove was hired as an assistant editor in 1946 on the strength of enthusiastic recommendations from his mentors at Harvard and Columbia universities, where he did his graduate work. He had been an outstanding student, and although his teaching career had been undistinguished, his strengths as a researcher and his interest in dictionaries made him a good prospect for the Merriam staff. He was painstaking, self-assured, and used to working things out on his own. Soon after his arrival at the Merriam company, he knew that the work suited him. He liked it and he was good at it. Five years after he joined the staff, he was put in charge of the making of *Webster's Third.*

He drove himself hard, with a firm sense of purpose, and was equally demanding of the staff. He combined a manager's grasp of the full picture with a scholar's attentiveness to detail. He put his faith in planning and rational decision making, perhaps to a fault; he sometimes seemed to assume that a good plan ensured a good outcome. Some professional staff members found him difficult to approach and autocratic, indifferent to the opinions and concerns of others. Thus, he had his critics. But he had admirers and supporters as well among the editors and company officers who recognized his capabilities and commitment. Secretaries and assistants usually thought him gentlemanly and considerate, though somewhat intimidating.

THE DICTIONARY – containing a hundred thousand new words or additional meanings of old words – required ten years to complete. When the first copies arrived from the venerable Riverside Press of

Cambridge, Massachusetts, in early September 1961, Gove looked them over with a great sense of relief, satisfaction, and pride. He had often told his family that he had the best job in the world, except for the presidency of Harvard. At this happy moment, with the "Big Book" at last in hand, he might not have conceded any exceptions.

For more than a century, successive editions, published and promoted after Webster's death by the G. & C. Merriam Company, fended off strong challenges from distinguished rivals in the highly competitive market for dictionaries. The Third Edition began as a reworking of the Second, which was getting out of date after an era of rapid change in the English language. Unprecedented advances in science and technology and changes wrought by the Depression and World War II had greatly expanded the vocabulary and introduced new patterns of expression. The editors were able to draw on the vastly enlarged Merriam citation files for additions to the vocabulary list and for evidence on which to base definitions and usage notes. More than 6 million examples of how words were used, four times as many as were available for the 1934 edition, were contained in the files. Along with other reference works available to the staff, they provided an unmatched inventory of the English language as it was being used in the United States in the mid-twentieth century.

The new edition was distinguished further, in Gove's view, by a more rigorous application of the policies that guided the Second Edition and by many innovations for which he could claim at least partial credit. Indeed, for a collective work, on which a staff of seventy collaborated and which drew on the knowledge of hundreds of consultants, it reflected his hand to a surprising extent.

IT WAS CLEAR even to a very private man like Philip Gove, who exercised his authority more by memo than by personal intervention and did not mix easily with his staff, that the publication of a new unabridged called for a staff celebration – not a perfunctory reception or public dinner but something more intimate. The logical site was his home, the Old Patrick farm, where he and his wife, Grace, had lived since moving to Massachusetts. It was located in the town of Warren, about twenty miles east of the Merriam offices in Springfield. The two-story wood frame Georgian house, with the only hipped roof in Warren, was recognized as a historic landmark.[3]

Philip and Grace had been delighted, at first sight, by the property itself and the view it afforded. Moreover, from Philip's perspective as a commuter, the location was ideal. For the drive from home to work in the morning, the sun would be at his back, and it would be at his back again for the return drive in the evening – a triumph of forethought over one of the small but vexing problems of life; it was a triumph that gave him particular satisfaction.

The farm was far enough from the office to offer Philip a sense of escape, yet not so distant that it made daily commuting a burden. After a tiring day at his desk, the scenic drive home and the prospect of unwinding on the farm revived him. Philip told visitors, who joined him in admiring the splendid view from his house, that this was what helped him keep his sense of balance.

THE ENTIRE EDITORIAL STAFF was invited to the publication party. Gordon J. Gallan, president of the Merriam company, was invited too, but he told Gove, "It's your day," and declined to attend.[4]

For most of the staff and their spouses, the trip to the farm was their first. A few had visited it when the Goves were new arrivals – in the days when Philip used to bring fresh eggs and vegetables to the office to sell. But the Goves did not entertain much after their children were grown. H. Bosley Woolf, Philip's closest associate (and later his successor), was an exception. He was an occasional weekend guest and usually spent the night at the farm after he and Philip returned from evening linguistic meetings at Yale University. Philip was generally viewed as a remote figure. Staff members found it hard to reconcile their impression of him as the proper and studious editor with the stories they heard of him as a working farmer who raised cattle and planted fields of corn and hay, whose farming methods, fastidiously sensitive to environmental concerns, won a state environmental prize, and who took his vacation every year during the haying season so that he could harvest and bale the crop himself to feed his cattle or to sell.

Arriving late on a lovely Saturday afternoon in September, the guests found their host atop the hay wagon, which was set up as a bar, jovially handing out drinks. He was dressed in overalls and a work shirt and seemed utterly at ease – a striking contrast to their reclusive boss in the staid environment of G. & C. Merriam Company. His son,

Norwood, a physicist, who had driven up from Oak Ridge, Tennessee, was on hand with his wife, Ruth, and their children. The Goves' youngest child, Doris, a high school senior, was also there. Susan Randolph, an older daughter, had been unable to attend with her family.

At dusk, dinner was served on the porch – chafing dishes with lobster Newburg, platters with hot vegetables, and a tomato and watercress salad. The vegetables and tomatoes, grown naturally without chemical fertilizers, had been freshly picked from Grace's garden. A puppet show followed, written by Grace, with taped music and lyrics by Norwood. Many of the insider jokes went over the heads of the guests, but the performance was in the spirit of the occasion. The evening ended on a high note with the presentation of a dictionary to every staff member, each copy inscribed by President Gallan in his crabbed, backslanted style.

NOTHING IN THE EVENTS of the splendid day, or of the preceding fifteen years, prepared Philip for the tempestuous intellectual and social controversy that was to follow. The battle preoccupied him for the next five years – and left him little peace for the rest of his life.

The dictionary was criticized for abandoning all recognized standards of grammar and usage – for "surrendering to the permissive school" that was the vogue in child rearing and was taking over the schools. It was attacked for eliminating biographical and geographical information and other encyclopedic material in order to make room for new words and examples. "Think if you can," thundered one critic, "of a dictionary from which you cannot learn who Mark Twain was . . . or what were the names of the apostles."[5] The Third Edition was ridiculed for quoting politicians, entertainers, and other nonliterary people to illustrate the meanings of words, instead of relying exclusively on great writers. "Three shows a day drain a girl" – a quotation attributed to Ethel Merman – was considered outrageous, though none of the critics argued that the quotation failed to make unmistakably clear the meaning of the word *drain* in this context; they merely objected to the quoting of a musical comedy star.

Among the more extravagant reactions was a charge that the dictionary was Communist-inspired; another was a scheme for buying out the Merriam company, junking the Third Edition, and beginning afresh on a fourth edition that would truly carry on the Webster tradition.

There were some well-founded criticisms; the dictionary had its faults. But the attacks that were most inflammatory and that gained greatest attention were usually facetious, mean-spirited, monstrous exaggerations, or wrong on their facts, mistakenly attributing to Gove the invention of policies that had guided the Second Edition and that had been established lexicographical practices for a century. Others treated a reasonable difference in judgment as evidence of anti-intellectualism or subversive intent. Nonetheless, underlying the arguments was a fundamental disagreement on the nature and role of dictionaries. It was summed up at the time as the difference between "descriptive" and "prescriptive" approaches to language.

Critics of the Third Edition believed that it was the responsibility of a dictionary to serve as a standard of correctness, to tell users what was right and what was wrong, according to principles that had been laid down by eighteenth- and nineteenth-century grammarians. Gove said that the job of the dictionary was to describe how people used language, not how they should use it, echoing the views expressed by Dean Richard Chenevix Trench in two famous papers on the deficiencies of English dictionaries. The papers (both read to the Philological Society in November 1857) greatly influenced the planning of the *Oxford English Dictionary* and English lexicography generally. Trench spelled out what the "true idea of what a dictionary is." He described it as "an inventory of the language . . . all the words good or bad." He called the lexicographer "an historian [of the language], not a critic" and explicitly warned his colleagues against repeating the mistake of the French Academy, which had sought to fix the language and prescribe a standard of correctness for the nation. Trench also expressed himself strongly on what a dictionary should contain and what it should omit, views that influenced Gove's approach to deciding what the scope of the Third Edition would be.

As a shorthand simplification, the disagreement could also be viewed as the difference between *dictionary makers*, who take their guidance from the way language is spoken and written, and *dictionary users*, who hanker for an authority to answer their questions according to rules governing the proper use of language. However it is perceived, the controversy over the descriptive and prescriptive points of view is still alive, though it is characterized by less polarized positions and more instructive discussions than it was in the 1960s.

GOVE TRIED TO ANSWER the attacks in the *New York Times* and elsewhere when they began to appear in the fall of 1961. His case was defended with particular effectiveness by two professors of English at Northwestern University, both Rhodes scholars – Bergen Evans and James Sledd – as described in Part III. Evans, a popular commentator on language and usage, was given equal space in the *Atlantic* to answer Wilson Follett's provocative attack, "Sabotage in Springfield," which set off a fresh outburst of hostile reviews of the dictionary when it appeared in January 1962. Sledd answered Dwight Macdonald's critique, which was published in March in the *New Yorker,* and he showed himself to be Macdonald's equal as a polemicist and his superior in his knowledge of dictionaries. But whereas Macdonald reached the large and influential audience of the *New Yorker,* Sledd could not find a comparable forum, and his reply appeared at last in the obscure proceedings of the Ethnology Association, which had given him a platform at its annual meeting. Later he was invited by Professor Randolph Quirk to University College, London, to explain to British linguists and grammarians why a dictionary that seemed such a splendid achievement to them was reviled in the United States. In late 1962, a year after the dictionary was published, Sledd and Wilma R. Ebbitt of the University of Chicago edited and published a harvest of news stories and reviews, pro and con, *Dictionaries and THAT Dictionary;* it included an exchange of views between Macdonald and Sledd and the articles by Follett and Evans.[6]

GOVE NEVER DOUBTED the merits of his work and was deeply troubled and hurt by the tone of the attacks. He had expected criticism from informed reviewers on matters where there were legitimate differences of opinion – and he encountered it, even from his strongest supporters. He had not expected to be judged primarily by detractors who had little understanding of the nature and history of dictionaries and who were intent on turning a debate about lexicography into an ideological war.

Had he lived a few years longer (he died at seventy in 1972), he might have felt vindicated. Although there are still editors, writers, and others who echo the attacks of the early 1960s, or who remain convinced that *Webster's Third* is a poor dictionary and that Gove was misguided, the place of the Third Edition as an important achievement in the history of lexicography is firmly established, notwithstanding its imperfections.

In some ways the controversy was a preposterous episode, as much a part of the sociology of human behavior as of the history of language and lexicography. But it is as a window on differing perceptions of the nature of language and the role of the dictionary that the episode, still largely unexamined, offers its greatest interest and most useful insights.

THREE MAJOR THEMES are intertwined in this account. One is biographical and historical – the role of Philip Gove and the traditions of the Merriam-Webster dictionaries that he inherited and on which his views were imposed. The second is the task of dictionary making – which is essentially a description of what the Third Edition was intended to achieve by recording the expansion of the language and changes in usage over more than twenty years and by revising the definitions, etymologies, pronunciations, and so on. It shows the similarities and differences between the Third Edition and the Second and the changes that were introduced to reflect developments in the language and in attitudes toward language. The story of dictionary making sets the stage for the blow-by-blow account of the controversy. Without some familiarity with these two underlying themes of historical change and the practice of lexicography, today's reader would be no better prepared to understand the dictionary war than were readers three decades ago.

The third theme is the chronicle of the controversy itself – a narrative of how the battle unfolded as it moved from the media accounts to the evaluations of practitioners and scholars. The battle lines are drawn over the role of the dictionary, the policies of *Webster's Third,* the ideological gulf between defenders of the dictionary and its detractors, the split in ranks of the once-united departments of English, and the commercial intrusions that affected the fortunes of the Merriam company. The story concludes with an effort to sort out the various themes and conclusions in the context of the 1960s and in the light of today's practices and attitudes.

In its full sweep, the story illuminates conflicting views about lexicographical practices and the role of dictionaries as does no other episode in the history of American lexicography. That is its enduring value. If some issues have faded away, others are as relevant as ever in the war of words that continues over dinner tables, in classrooms and the media, and in the writings of experts.

PART I

Philip Gove and the Genesis
of *Webster's Third*

2

Gove's Formative Years: The Road to Springfield

It is in the tradition of American life that a household cannot be regarded as adequately equipped for the business of the day without a Webster's Unabridged. The American child passed by natural progression from the spelling book to the dictionary, but the dictionary one never outgrew.

George Philip Krapp, *The English Language in America*

Philip Gove was a descendant of John Gove, a London dealer in brass, who came to the Massachusetts Bay Colony with two sons, John and Edward, and a daughter, Mary, in 1647. Over the next two centuries, the Gove family fanned out through New Hampshire and into Maine. They were farmers primarily, though some served in the militia and Philip's grandfather, Samuel Gove, also taught school.

Philip's father, John McClure Gove, however, broke with the farming tradition. John, one of Samuel Gove's six children, grew up in Raymond, New Hampshire, and attended Boston University, where he was captain of the university baseball team. After graduation he entered the university law school, but after a year changed his mind and decided to enroll in the Boston Institute of Osteopathy. He wrote his fiancée, Florence Babcock, that prospects for osteopaths looked very much brighter than those for lawyers and he had found the young men there to be "the most cultured and intellectual" he had ever met.[1]

John completed his studies in the spring of 1900 and became the first osteopath to establish a full-time practice in New Hampshire; after a decade of practice and additional study, he was awarded a doctor of osteopathy degree. John and Florence were married on June

25, 1900, and settled into a comfortable life in Concord, the state capital, on the Merrimack River in south central New Hampshire. Philip was born two years later, June 27, 1902, and his sister, Jean, in 1906.

EARLY DAYS

Philip had a rather typical New Hampshire boyhood. Hiking, swimming, skiing, hockey, and baseball filled much of his time outside the classroom. He had the usual chores at home and delivered newspapers to earn spending money. On holidays, there were often trips north to the Old Man in the Mountain and the Flume, a splendid gorge near Franconia Notch. The family spent summers at a rented house at Rye Beach. Philip became an excellent swimmer and learned to hunt and fish on outings with his father. For several summers, during college and after, he directed aquatic programs and taught Red Cross lifesaving methods at boys' camps in New Hampshire, New York, and Delaware. During winter vacations he shoveled snow on ten-hour shifts at the railroad yards or clerked for the Railway mail company. He made the most of his time and developed an aversion to idleness.

In high school Philip played hockey and baseball and went out for track. He was a good student and a member of the debating team. He also covered school news for the local newspaper, getting his first taste of what would become his principal extracurricular activity at college. During 1917 and 1918 he raised "vegetables for victory," the beginning of a lifelong interest in gardening and farming. From time to time during his high school years he accompanied his father on house calls, and during the influenza epidemic of 1918–19 he took time off from college to help deliver soup and medications to housebound patients in Concord.

Philip enrolled at Dartmouth College in September 1918, at the age of sixteen, along with two other youths from Concord. He intended to major in mathematics and then transfer to Dartmouth's Amos Tuck School of Business Administration, one of the earliest business schools in the country and one of the best. But he soon found literature and writing more to his liking. He majored in English, and in his sophomore year he was elected to the staff of *The Dartmouth*, the student newspaper.

Mementos among his papers for this period show that he shipped aboard the SS *St. Paul* to England as a seaman in the summer of 1920 shortly before his eighteenth birthday, earning fifty-six dollars for the twenty-four-day trip. He got a dock pass at Southampton, but to his great disappointment his ship headed back to New York before he could use it. Twenty years would pass before he saw London.

Back at Dartmouth in the fall, he began working part time as a stringer for several daily newspapers, and by his senior year he was doing professional work. A letter among his papers from the assistant city editor of the *Knoxville Journal and Tribune* refers to a check "covering your string for the past month, which totals about 5-1/2 columns. I wish to compliment you upon the good advance services you gave us."[2] During that year he also became a founding member of a new campus literary society. He was graduated in a class of 233 students on June 20, 1922, and was awarded the Joseph Story Prize for the best senior thesis on a subject in philosophy. He remained a loyal son of Dartmouth throughout his life. The award of an honorary doctor of letters at a Dartmouth commencement four decades later was a high moment in his career.

JOHN GOVE cherished the hope that his son would become a physician. When Philip decided that he would prefer to teach English literature, his father was deeply disappointed and refused to help finance Philip's graduate education. Philip went his own way, enrolling at Harvard for the fall term and supporting himself by managing an eating club and working nights as a proofreader and linotype operator. He obtained a master's degree in 1924. His teaching career began in the fall when, at age twenty-two, he took a job at Rice Institute in Houston, Texas. Although he apparently had no experience in acting or in theatrical productions, he directed the Rice Dramatic Society for two seasons, staging two plays each season.

He accepted a teaching job at New York University (NYU) in the fall of 1927. For most of the next fifteen years, he directed the freshman English program and developed strong views about how to teach students to write. He became increasingly skeptical about the value of the conventional curriculum, as he indicated years later in a letter to the director of the Dartmouth News Service, who had offered to send the Merriam company samples of student themes as illustrations of current usage:

There's an almost invariable rule that writing prepared under assignment and therefore artificially under pressure has certain forced awkwardnesses that make it quite different from genuine human utterances. Most of these writers, you will remember, didn't want to write the theme in the first place, didn't have anything they wanted to say in the second, and cared only about satisfying some artificial and quite likely false standards set up by their instructor. I know because I have assigned and read thousands of them.[3]

During the summer after moving to New York, Philip met the young woman he would marry, Grace Edna Potter of Worcester, Massachusetts. She was an office worker at the American Telephone and Telegraph Company, where he had taken a job during the vacation months. In the 1920s AT&T and other large corporations hired young English instructors in the summer to improve the clarity and effectiveness of company correspondence with stockholders. Philip went to work in the Treasurer's Department and soon took notice of Grace. The family version of the first encounter is that he told her he didn't think a proper young woman should expose her ankles while bending over the files "that way." No one remembers how she replied, but whatever she said, and however she said it, Philip and Grace were soon going out together regularly.

Grace was not a college graduate, but she was well read, intellectually curious, very outspoken, and not easily intimidated. Philip was several years older and very strong-minded, but he was rather chivalrous in an old-fashioned way. Grace held her own on most matters and increasingly asserted her independence. She expressed herself with verve and wit. She shared his interest in gardening and hiking and other outdoor activities. She later took up playwriting and acting as a hobby and became an activist in environmental affairs. From the beginning, theirs was a very close relationship. Long and affectionate letters when they were apart, especially during World War II and during much of Philip's fellowship year in England, reflect a growing devotion. When he was on naval duty at Pensacola, Florida, during the war, she was especially affected by one of his letters and wrote back:

I don't like to think of [our children] twenty years from now trying to piece together vaguely remembered impressions to find out what their parents thought of each other. I should like them to have the positive undoubted knowledge. . . . Some day . . . I want one of us to tell them that our love for each other didn't drop out of heaven, that it was something we had in mind and hopes when we married, that we worked for it, and that we strove deliberately to learn how to please each other. And that we were nice enough people so that it wasn't too difficult.[4]

Years after Philip's death, she typed up a selection of their wartime letters for each of her children. Grace's pride in Philip's work came naturally, and she stood by him staunchly during the dictionary controversy.

Their wedding was to have taken place in the spring of 1929, but it was delayed because Philip was hospitalized for fifty-six days with complications following an attack of scarlet fever; the count of days was recorded by his daily postcards, which had to be put through a decontamination process before they were mailed. By midsummer he had fully recovered. They were married on August 17, 1929, a month before the death of his mother from cancer.

The best man at the wedding was a colleague from NYU, Frank (Francis E.) Bowman, who later taught at the University of Rochester and at Duke University. They remained close friends, corresponding regularly about fishing, farming, and their families, as well as academic life. For many years Bowman's name appeared in Philip's will as executor. It was Bowman who reminded Philip to keep his teaching experiences and resolves in mind when he went to Merriam-Webster: "You won't forget, I hope, your difficulties with usage in freshman composition, and I am hoping that one of your collateral duties may be to shed some light on what we agree we ought to try to teach. I can't go so far as Marckwardt, but I am convinced that we are trying to impose an entirely artificial language on the freshman."[5]

FILE CARDS AND IMAGINARY VOYAGES

Philip began working toward a Ph.D. at Columbia University in 1930, but progress was slow because his teaching load at NYU was heavy and his family responsibilities were increasing. Norwood was born in 1932, and Susan in 1934. The family moved to Hawthorne and later to Yorktown Heights in Westchester County so that they could have a garden and keep animals. Norwood and Susan were given their own plots to tend. Philip worried a great deal about his father after Florence's death, and he usually returned to Concord for a week at the close of the school year and at other times if possible.

Although his course work went well, Philip was slow in deciding on a dissertation topic; he grew increasingly pessimistic about getting his doctorate. When Grace was away at commencement time one June, he wrote that his order for a cap and gown had gone astray, and he almost missed the annual ceremony. At the last minute, "an amply velveted doctor's gown" was found – "probably the first and last time I'll ever have the privilege of wearing one."[6] He was still toying with two research topics at the time. One eventually led, by a circuitous route, to his first scholarly journal article and the other to his dissertation.

Like many graduate students studying eighteenth-century English literature before and after, Philip found Samuel Johnson the most fascinating figure of the age, and Johnson's great achievement, *A Dictionary of the English Language* (1755), his most interesting work, especially in its use of illustrative quotations. Johnson had written in his preface to the dictionary that "the chief glory of every people arises from its authours," and his dictionary, in a sense, testified to that glory. He had selected more than a hundred thousand quotations to illustrate the meanings of words in context and to convey literary ideas and moral instruction.

Philip apparently saw the quotations as a key to understanding Johnson's mind, as well as an important development in dictionary making. A thorough study, he believed, would have to begin with the assembling of the quotations in a more convenient form, a formidable task in itself. He sought help from the Works Progress Administration (WPA), which had been established during the Depression of the 1930s to provide work for the unemployed. He received enough money to hire students part time to copy Johnson's quotations on file cards, but his budget was very tight. One of his economies was to have the quotations copied on the blank side of discarded three-by-five file cards from the NYU personnel records.

Fragmentary notes among his papers show substantial progress during the 1935–7 period – as measured by the increasing number of columns of the dictionary scanned under each letter of the alphabet and the names of the students who copied the quotations. Funds ran out before the project was completed, and the WPA told Philip to keep the cards himself. He stored them during World War II, and when he was hired by the Merriam company, he moved the cards to his barn at the farm in Warren. The cards were continually spilling out over the floor, much to the annoyance of his children, who had been given the responsibility of picking them up. He clung to the hope that he would get around to using them at some time in the future.

In early 1948 he found encouragement in an exchange of letters initiated by W. K. Wimsatt of Yale University proposing a joint project. During the previous spring, Wimsatt had completed a study of Johnson's use of philosophical and scientific words in the *Rambler* essays and the illustrative quotations in the *Dictionary*. The essays and the *Dictionary* were products of the same extraordinarily productive decade of Johnson's life, which ended in 1755 with the publication of the *Dictionary*, when Johnson was poor and obscure, before his emergence as a great literary figure. Wimsatt, who had learned of Gove's file from a mutual friend, James Clifford, wrote:

The thought that was uppermost in my mind as I came out of my own struggles with the thirty or so scientific sources on which I have concentrated was that it would be nice to have an accurate bibliography of the Dictionary sources, i.e. an identification of authors and books, down to exact editions where possible. . . . This kind of bibliography and sidelights will I think be a necessary preliminary to the eventual editing of Johnson's writings.

Without pretending that I am embarked or resolved on this long Dictionary job, let me say that I am interested in it, am nibbling at present on the letter A. . . . With the kind of file which I understand you have, you yourself would have a long start if you decided you wished to be the author of the definitive study.[7]

Wimsatt was impressed by Gove's reply, in which he described the work he had done, especially Gove's study of the surviving copies of Johnson's sources. Gove had, for example, purchased in England a copy of one volume of Robert South's *Sermons* of 1692, a major source of quotations for the *Dictionary*, and had copied into it all of the markings that Johnson had made in his own copy. Wimsatt mused at some length on the nature of the work to be done and the portion he himself might undertake and added, "This job looks to me less like a one- or two-man job than a committee job such as produced the *OED*," and suggested names of possible collaborators.[8]

Gove retained two other letters from Wimsatt in his files, but left no evidence of any further work on the project. Seven years later, when he was deeply immersed in the making of the Merriam-Webster Third Edition, he finally admitted to himself that he would never get around to writing the book he had envisioned. He had gone to New Haven in April 1955 to attend a celebration at Yale marking the 200th anniversary of the publication of Johnson's *Dictionary*. On that occasion, he became acquainted with Herman W. Liebert of the Yale library, a Johnsonian scholar who also became chairman of the Advisory Committee for the Yale edition of Johnson's complete works. Liebert expressed an interest in having the quotations for the Sterling Library. He arranged for Yale to pay the cost of shipping the cards to his home, where they would be sorted and indexed. In a letter confirming their talks, Liebert concluded, "I feel that our common efforts will bear fruit in this important area of Johnson research."[9]

A month later Gove responded that the cards would be shipped by railway express. He was apologetic about the possibility that he might have misled Liebert about the bulk. "The cards are in 54 tin boxes, packed solid, measuring 3 × 5 × 19-1/2," he wrote and went on to explain the odyssey of his collection with characteristic attention to detail:

These cards were collected first in one-thousand-card Oxford 3 × 5 boxes, then transferred to shoe boxes, then to larger and stronger shoe boxes and finally to tin boxes. They had been stored in seven different places with the result that they are in no kind of order. They are not only upside down but often backwards, and to make the matter slightly more complicated, many of the cards have irrelevant handwriting on one side, that is, they were secondhand cards, because I could not afford to buy new ones.[10]

Gove also explained the instructions he had given to his students to ensure consistency in their transcriptions and to make certain that specific irregularities in Johnson's procedures were taken into account. He concluded with expressions of thanks to Liebert for finding a home for the collection.

Liebert ordered sixty file drawers to accommodate the collection and arranged to hire a helper for the summer and a staff of three for the fall. But he cautioned Gove not to expect miracles. Indeed, as Liebert later recalled, the job took three or four years and was carried out largely by his wife.[11]

And so Gove's twenty-year affair with Johnson's quotations came to an end, not as he had planned but still with memorable satisfactions, the pleasurable associations with other Johnsonians, and the publication of his first scholarly articles. A half-century later, in the computer age, Gove's goal would be reached by others.

FOR HIS DISSERTATION, Gove chose his other topic, the imaginary voyage, a literary form that was especially popular in the eighteenth century but that had received little scholarly attention. Accounts of such voyages were sometimes written solely to amuse and at other times to convey social criticism or visions of an ideal society. To distinguish the genre from novels in general, he defined it as "a narrative of a voyage performed in the imagination, with the qualifications: that it must be oceanic, that it must extend beyond the limits of the Mediterranean, that its geography must not be merely abstract or allegorical, that where extraterrestrial or subterranean it must be conducted by physical means, that it may not be a mere dream voyage or journey to the land of the dead, and that where it does not comprise the whole it must occupy a considerable part of a work."

By early 1937 he had made enough progress to send a sample of the draft to his adviser, Professor Ernest H. Wright. Wright's reply reflected undisguised exasperation:

My failing eyes are aching and my entire head is swimming (I speak literally) from a perusal of your manuscript. Before you ever let anybody see another page of your typewriting I implore you to buy or somehow acquire a stock of ordinary paper and a ribbon still youthful enough to make what it prints distinguishable from anything that might be printed on the other side of the sheet.

Aside from this lamentable blemish I have a very good opinion indeed of the pages you have submitted. They represent good solid work, well digested, interesting, and informative.[12]

A year passed before Gove submitted the full manuscript, this time in appropriately readable form. The typing and retyping had been a nightmare. The typist, who had been recommended by the graduate school, had made numerous errors in the foreign language passages. Gove wrote a long letter illustrating the mistakes and indicating the amount of additional work his proofing had entailed and the retyping that would be required.

Wright was slow to comment on the revised draft because of ill health. In addition, he had an unusually large number of other dissertations to review.

While awaiting final word from Wright, Philip faced additional stress. His father had been hospitalized with leukemia since early January 1938; the disease had progressed to an advanced stage before it was diagnosed. Unable to visit Concord at this time, Philip depended on his sister, Jean, to take on a strong supportive role as she had done during her mother's terminal illness a decade earlier. Jean moved to Concord and wrote an almost daily account of John's ups and downs in mood, in physical condition, and in medical treatment, which she sent on to Philip and Grace.

On March 3 John summoned enough strength to write a letter to Grace, Philip, Norwood, and Susan. Referring to Philip's dissertation, he wrote, "It gave me a real thrill to hear you say 'It's done.'" Two weeks later Jean wrote "there is no doubt that Father is sinking rapidly." He died shortly before midnight on March 25, 1938.

Philip was caught up almost immediately in his father's affairs, paying bills, trying to collect delinquent accounts, and trying to establish the value of investments that had badly eroded during the Depression. Final disposition of John's affairs was not completed for more than a decade. Philip collected the last of the unpaid bills from his father's patients after he returned to civilian life following World War II.

In early April Philip received a progress report from Professor Wright, based on a reading of the early chapters of Philip's dissertation. It was Wright's view that, despite its scholarly merit, it needed additional work. It might pass the committee, but Wright thought a careful revision would lead to a much better manuscript.

Philip revised his paper during the next six months and submitted it shortly before the end of the year. This time he got a prompt reading; he was told to report on Friday morning, January 13, 1939, at the Low Law Library of Columbia University to take his oral examination. The next day he was officially notified by Dean George B. Pegram that he had passed. All requirements for the doctor of philosophy degree were completed except for the deposit of seventy-five printed copies of the dissertation in the library. If that were done by May 20, the degree would be conferred at spring commencement.

However, this time it was Philip who was not fully satisfied. He thought the dissertation could be improved by further research and decided to apply for a William Bayard Cutting Traveling Fellowship, a Columbia University award that would enable him to pursue his research in France and England. He decided that if he got the fellowship he would expand his dissertation into a book. If he was turned down, he would submit the required copies of the dissertation to fulfill the requirements for his degree. He wrote Wright on February

16, 1939, seeking support for his fellowship application: "I . . . have become unreservedly convinced that a superior and more conclusive book will result from an opportunity to study in the British Museum and Bibliotheque Nationale and that my time would be justifiably spent not only on this book but also on subsequent studies."

Ten days later he sent Wright a copy of his application, which stated that he intended to study rare books in French, German, and English which were available only in Europe and also "to study materials in England indispensable to my plans for a book on Samuel Johnson's *Dictionary* of 1755, on which I have been working for over three years. These materials include, as of first importance, a unique copy of the *Dictionary*, which has copious manuscript notes and additions, and the proof-sheets of the second edition."[13]

In early May Philip was notified that he had been awarded a fellowship for 1939–40, with a stipend of two thousand dollars. His request for a sabbatical year at half-pay was turned down, even though he had been on the NYU faculty for twelve years, because he did not have professional rank. Gove had to settle for a year's leave without pay, much to his disappointment and to the chagrin of his department chairman. The budget for his year abroad would be tight.

AMONG THE JOHNSONIANS IN LONDON
AND OXFORD

The Gove family sailed to England in June and continued on to the lovely south coast of Cornwall, some two hundred miles west of London. They rented a small bungalow for two months on the banks of the River Looe. Grace, Norwood, and Susan settled in for the summer, and Philip hurried back to London in search of more imaginary voyages.

The separation, which left both Philip and Grace in unfamiliar surroundings, was not easy for either of them, as their correspondence attests. They missed each other deeply, and Philip, perhaps feeling twinges of guilt at pursuing his projects while Grace and the children were isolated – albeit in beautiful environs – was especially solicitous. Much of their correspondence in succeeding weeks revolved around the children, Philip's work, the problems of finding a suitable school for the children in the fall and housing for them all in

London. The situation was more difficult for Grace than for Philip, since she was tied down with Norwood and Susan and, unlike Philip, had no particular reason for being where she was. Moreover, July and early August were unusually rainy. The morale at Looe varied with the weather and the arrival of letters from London. On July 27, a good day, Grace wrote:

You are wonderfully good to us. Nod [Norwood] came in from meeting the postman at the gate with a letter and three packages. He said, "This is a day, isn't it?" Susie was proud that she had a possession to share, and she and Nod became such good fellows over their games of dominoes that when Nod left to get the milk she insisted on accompanying him even though it was raining.[14]

From the beginning Philip's research bore fruit. He had no trouble getting a pass to the collections in the British Museum, and he was able to write within a month that he had found and written up eleven more voyages. He spent considerable time exploring London – close in and the outskirts – by bus, by underground, and on foot to see which part of the city offered the best prospects for decent, inexpensive housing with access to good schools. He learned that all residential areas were within a half-mile of a free school, and he was strongly advised to select one such school for his children. Fortunately, he could count on good instruction, since for a family on a very tight budget the costs of a private education seemed out of reach. Through July and early August his letters sounded in part like travelogues as he described the areas he visited and the forms of transportation he used.

After brief stays at two hotels in Bloomsbury, he found lodging at 2 Bedford Place in a boardinghouse much frequented by young scholars from the United States. It was inexpensive, a block from the British Museum, and congenial. Teatime often produced a bit of new information about London or interesting encounters worth passing along.

Among the later boarders were two old friends, both enthusiastic young Johnsonians, Ned (Edward T.) McAdam, Jr., and James Clifford. McAdam had been a colleague at NYU and later served on the Advisory Board of the Yale edition of Johnson's works. After a brief stop in London, McAdam went to Oxford. Philip visited him there a short time later, and after tea they called on Clifford, who was hoping to persuade Oxford University Press to publish his manuscript about Hester Lynch Piozzi (Mrs. Thrale), Johnson's close friend, admirer, and chronicler of much of his later life.

When Clifford came to London in early August on his way back to New York, he was able to report the good news that his manuscript had been accepted. (It was published in 1941, and a paperback reprint of a revised edition was published in 1987.) Philip, who had come to England with the hope that his manuscript on the imaginary voyage would interest the press, could applaud Clifford's good fortune enthusiastically. The next day Clifford took Philip on a whirlwind tour of literary London, even though he had left himself barely enough time in London to get ready for the return voyage to New York. As Philip recounted the occasion:

I quit the BM at teatime today to benefit from a personally conducted tour of the Johnson alleys and lanes and courts at the expense of Jim's time. . . . [H]e races through the streets . . . shouts back knowledge of the landmarks to all the busy people who will listen, and dashes on to his next objective. He bounded round a corner, suddenly stopped, ordered me to remove my hat as he was doing, and there we were almost stumbling over the grave of Goldsmith. I stood cowed and bareheaded until I felt the rain running about my scalp.[15]

Philip was preparing for a trip to Looe and invited McAdam to join him, but McAdam had just discovered twelve volumes of manuscripts that had not been known to exist and that would keep him busy for several days. Philip made the journey alone. In Looe he and Grace faced up to their choices on housing and schooling for the fall. They selected a boarding school near London – Cromwell House School, Gresham Road, in Staines, near the western edge of London, just south of where Heathrow Airport is now located. After the children were settled at Cromwell, Philip and Grace went back to Looe for a few quiet days, and visited Dartmoor and other nearby attractions.

By this time there was much talk of the imminence of war. Government public information leaflets from the Lord Privy Seal's office explained the meaning of air raid sirens, what to do in case of a gas attack, and how to black out windows. American tourists hurried to leave England. Transatlantic ships were booked solid for weeks. Train stations and ports were jammed. But Philip had a year's fellowship, and he was not going to be deterred from making the most of it. He and Grace, as outsiders, assumed the detached role of observers.

On August 31 they started out for London, but at the station they learned that London was to begin evacuating children to safer cities the next day, and they decided to get off at Reading, the last stop before London. When they arrived, the station was crowded and they had trouble finding a room. The city was preparing to welcome a contingent of eight thousand children the next day. That was to be the last night of street lighting in Reading until the end of the war.

The next morning, out of curiosity, they went ahead to London. They looked in at 2 Bedford Place, tried unsuccessfully to get into the hopelessly crowded American Express Office, and watched the crowds and preparations for defense. By dusk they felt the urge to get back to Reading and made their way through the blackout to Paddington Station, which was filled with refugees carrying household goods; many had been waiting for hours. Luckily a train pulled in after only a short wait, and they managed to get into a packed, poorly ventilated old coal car that had been put back into service for the emergency. In the blackness and with frequent stops, the trip took more than twice as long as usual.

The next day Philip and Grace left Reading for Oxford, where they found a room in a boardinghouse that had been recommended to them. On the morning of September 3, they went for a walk to visit a Norman church. Returning to their lodging, they were greeted by their landlady, who asked whether they had enjoyed their walk. Then she calmly announced, "Well, we are at war."[16]

GOVE'S FIRST FORAY

Despite the danger of the fellowship year being cut short, and the turmoil and other uncertainties of the next eight months, the stay in Oxford proved to be an unexpected stroke of good fortune. Oxford offered the Bodleian Library, distinguished scholars, and eager young faculty members and graduate students. Philip, like many other young Americans, found an ideal mentor in L. F. Powell, lexicographer, Johnsonian, and exemplar of scholarship at its best. Powell had worked on the staff of the *Oxford English Dictionary* for twenty years under William Craigie; his wife, Ethelwyn, had been a staff member for more than thirty years. Clifford, who had met Powell in 1935, arranged Philip's introduction, and Powell, with his customary generosity of spirit and concern for young scholars, took Philip under his wing. Being himself deeply engaged in bibliographic research, he was sympathetic to Philip's painstaking work on imaginary voyages, perhaps sensing in it a commitment to thoroughness and persistence similar to his own.

But it was not imaginary voyages that occupied Philip at Oxford; he had virtually completed that research in London. It was his revived interest in Johnson's *Dictionary.* With Powell's encouragement, he presented a paper at the December 1939 seminar of the Oxford Bibliographic Society on the serialization of the *Dictionary* that began two months after the first edition was published in April 1755. Published in 1940 in the Society's *Transactions,* Philip's article was the first of four he wrote during his fellowship year and his first scholarly publication.[17]

Johnson's *Dictionary* had been criticized because it cost too much. The serialization was intended to make available a less expensive edition on easy terms – six pence each for the weekly fascicles scheduled to appear in 165 installments. To the surprise of Johnson's publishers, a new edition of a famous dictionary first published three decades earlier by Johnson's precursor, Nathan Bailey, began to appear, installment by installment, in step with the serialization of Johnson's work. What was especially galling was that the revision of Bailey's *A New Universal Etymological Dictionary of the English Language* incorporated Johnson's definitions and illustrations either verbatim or only thinly disguised.

Gove traced the publishing history of the dictionaries with examples taken from the competitive advertising as well as the printing history and made a detailed comparison of the texts. The first advertisement announcing the serialization of Johnson's work appeared in Jackson's *Oxford Journal* for April 12, 1755. In early June a second ad appeared on page 3 of the *Oxford Journal.* But in the small world of English printers and publishers, it had been impossible for Johnson's publishers to keep secret their serialization plan, and their rivals were ready to move quickly. When the second advertisement appeared, the facing page carried an ad for the new serialization of Bailey's dictionary updated by Joseph Nicol Scott. Scott wrote a new preface and lent his prestigious name to the enterprise; additional new material was provided by others. Thereafter, it was easy for the Scott–Bailey publishers to keep up with the weekly installments, since the complete edition of Johnson's work had been available since April.

Gove's assessment was severe. He said that Johnson's history of the language had been reworked by "a servile but fully alert mind, too imitative to plan a reorganization of material . . . yet a mind active enough to draw occasionally upon its own background." Of the Scott–Bailey article on grammar, he said it could be called "downright copying with alterations."

His harshest judgment was reserved for the definitions: "A glance at any page of Bailey will reveal that line after line is rankly plagiarized from Johnson," a charge he substantiated by excerpts. Tracing the subsequent and rather bizarre printing history of Scott–Bailey, Gove showed the ways in which the serialized edition of Scott–Bailey was kept in print with new title pages and dates, but otherwise unchanged, until 1772, three years after Scott's death.

Gove's article attracted some attention and was discussed at some length a few years later by DeWitt T. Starnes and Gertrude E. Noyes in their classic study, *The English Dictionary from Cawdrey to Johnson, 1604–1755*.[18] They found no fault with the research. They thought that Gove's documentation of the copying of Johnson's definitions was persuasive, but they criticized the sharpness of the charge of plagiarism. No one familiar with the history of lexicography and the practice of borrowing, they argued, should have been either surprised or outraged by what Scott had done. Indeed, Johnson himself had borrowed from Bailey.

There was some basis for this criticism, but it did not take account of the unique aspect of the Scott–Bailey copying. During the century and a half after the first English dictionary, entitled *A Table Alphabeticall*, was published in 1604 by Robert Cawdrey, each of Cawdrey's successors had borrowed unabashedly from his predecessors. Usually, however, many years elapsed before the publication of the competing work, and thus there was little deleterious effect on the income of the author and publisher and little controversy over the practice of borrowing. In Johnson's case, however, the copying had been almost concurrent with original publication.

Whether Philip had been fully justified or too harsh may be arguable, but without doubt the Bailey–Johnson episode introduced him to the emerging history of dictionary controversies. The one in which he would be engaged would dwarf them all.

At the same time that Powell received the issue of *Transactions* with Philip's article, he also received his copy of *Library*, which contained another item by Philip. "They together make a very creditable performance, and you have every reason to be proud of them," he wrote. "Stick to it." He was equally complimentary and encouraging as the other articles appeared in print. "Let us have some more of this sort of thing." Of another piece, he wrote that he was pleased to read it and "glad to have fathered it."[19]

After Gove returned to the United States, he and Powell continued to write to each other on family and scholarly matters for some thirty years. Powell kept Gove informed of his progress on the index to his four-volume edition of Boswell's *Life of Johnson* and on a distinguished list of other works. When he died in 1975 at the age of ninety-three, revered both at Oxford and in the United States, an Oxford colleague wrote, "No one detail was too trivial to be verified, no failure of verbal usage was allowed to pass, no reference went unexamined, no quotation was accepted without careful collation with the original."[20]

Philip's search for Johnson's marked copies of his sources of quotations was assisted by the noted lexicographer C. T. Onions, an editor of the *OED* and later senior editor of the *Oxford Dictionary of English Etymology*. Philip had written to him to ask his help in gaining access to Johnson's copy of Mathew Hale's *Primitive Origination of Mankind*, published in 1677. Onions replied, "If you will be good enough to call at the Old Ashmolean Building on Friday next at 11:15, I shall be happy to show it to you and to arrange for its deposit in the Bodleian."[21]

Philip's work also interested the eminent editor and typographer Stanley Morison. In a letter on the *Times* letterhead, Printing House Square, E.C., Morison wrote, in his elegant calligraphy, "I hope you will persevere in your studies of this subject in newspaper history. I hope myself one of these days to produce MERCURIUS, a periodical devoted to the history of journalism in Britain. . . . What do you think of thinking of thinking [*sic*] of doing a paper for it? It might be wanted before 1944, the annus mirabilis that Churchill speaks of."[22]

By June 1940, Americans were being warned to catch "the last ship" before the threat of German submarines put an end to passenger travel. The Gove family would have to return earlier than they had planned. Moreover, Philip had received some discouraging news from his department chairman, Albert S. Borgman, who had written that Philip would not be teaching the course in eighteenth-century literature that he had been promised; a senior faculty member had exercised his prerogative to teach it, and Philip would be teaching freshman English again in 1940–1.

Still, it had been a successful and enjoyable year. After his return, Philip gave Dean Pegram an impressive summary of his fellowship studies. He reported that he had completed his work on *The Imaginary Voyage*, which would be published by Columbia University Press; Oxford University Press, which had provisionally accepted it, had to turn it down because of wartime constraints. He had continued his work on Johnson's *Dictionary*, gaining "access to several volumes annotated by him in its preparation" and taking sufficient notes to provide the basis for additional publications. He mentioned his paper on the Johnson and Bailey dictionaries, the other articles he completed, and his plan to edit at some future date the ledger books of William Strahan, founder of one of the largest and most successful eighteenth-century printing and publishing houses and publisher of Johnson's *Dictionary*.[23]

During the period when he was amassing and checking references for *The Imaginary Voyage*, Gove consistently demonstrated his thoroughness as a research scholar and editor. Hundreds of letters in his files for the period 1938–40 attest to the persistence of his research on the references. He tracked down specific editions of sourcebooks in several languages in libraries around the world. In some instances, his research in the Union catalog and others led to the identification of books that some librarians in major universities did not know they held. He was able to tell them where the book might be and how it might be listed. His doggedness in checking every detail and questioning every discrepancy showed a commitment to scholarship in the Powell style.

Columbia University Press had seen the dissertation before Philip went to Oxford and was prepared to proceed rapidly with publication. *The Imaginary Voyage in Prose Fiction* was published in early 1941. More than two years after the acceptance of his dissertation and the successful completion of his oral exams, Gove was awarded his Ph.D.

A detailed critical bibliography of the field, it was devoted primarily to an annotated list of 215 imaginary voyages published between 1700 and 1800. The reviews in the scholarly journals were essentially descriptive and modestly commendatory. "LF" (as Powell signed his letters) wrote his customary congratulatory note, complimenting Philip on "a reference book of high quality."[24] The book was reprinted in a British edition published by the Holland Press Ltd. in 1964. In the same year a contract was signed with Russell and Russell Inc. for a U.S. reprint edition.

TRAVELS WITH THE NAVY

Philip registered for the draft in February 1942. He was then nearly forty years old and had a wife and two children. In June he was classified 3A, but despite a deferment, he was eager to join in the war effort and applied for a commission to the navy. Physically fit, he was a wiry man 5 feet 10 inches tall and weighed 145 pounds. While waiting for the navy to act, he became an auxiliary policeman and helped to train hundreds of air wardens for the city of New York. During the summer of 1942 he also taught a preinduction course in English for draftees. On September 15, he received his commission and was sworn in as a lieutenant in the navy. After an eight-week training program at Ohio State University, he was assigned to the Naval Air Station in San Diego.

As he settled into his navy routine in early 1943, he had more time to think about his family, and he felt their absence keenly. It seemed likely that eighteen months to two years would pass before he would earn enough leave to return home. Grace was having the same thoughts; she saw little reason for her and the children to stay in Yorktown Heights.

On February 18, 1943, he wrote, "Darling, I want you in San Diego. . . . It looks as if I might stay here for a long time." In his typically systematic way, he laid out the pros and cons in nine numbered paragraphs dealing with food shortages, high rents, availability of jobs if she wanted to work (recalling her dissatisfaction with the lack of work in Oxford), the difficulty of the cross-country drive, entanglements in Yorktown Heights, and so on. There was also the problem of what to do with Brenda, their Newfoundland, and the pups she had recently delivered.

A few days later he followed up with more discussion and advice. Why not give Brenda to Dogs for Defense? If she survived, she would be returned to them after the war. (And, indeed, two years later she was returned to the family in Seattle with a medal on her collar. She spent several happy years on the farm in Warren, patrolling the twenty-acre hay field every day.)

Grace's response was prompt, succinct, and decisive. She and the children would leave on April 1 by car. That was only a month away. A flurry of correspondence followed about all the decisions that had to be made before the trip could begin. Philip had to arrange for travel allowances and find a place to live that they could afford.

About thirteen miles outside San Diego he found a small furnished house on a five-acre ranch (a ranch, he explained to Grace, was any plot of land a half-acre or more). The rent was low – forty-five dollars a month compared with seventy-five to a hundred dollars for places closer to the city; the owner was sensible and easy to deal with, the closest neighbor was friendly. The low rent encouraged Philip to talk "glibly of a horse, a cow, a bicycle, hens and ducks. As for pigs, there is a restriction that they must be clean." In an earlier letter he advised against bringing any gardening tools, but now he changed his mind and asked her to bring the long-handled ax, too.

On the ranch, Grace had no trouble keeping busy. Farming again became a major family activity. With a large garden, a cow, a goat, a calf, chickens, turkeys, and many rabbits, the Goves settled in comfortably – though not for as long as they had expected. Eight months later Philip was transferred to Seattle, where Grace and the children settled down until the war was over. He continued to move about – with assignments to gunnery training and duty in Pensacola and Jacksonville, Florida, and then to the Naval Air Station in Pasco, Washington. Philip often got weekend passes, but the long trips to the apartment in Seattle and back to Pasco were exhausting, and sometimes harrowing in the rain and fog. A third child, Doris, was born April 10, 1944.

Before the war ended in September 1945, Philip gave some thought to a career in the navy, to which he felt great loyalty. But that idea was rather short-lived. The disadvantages, including the prospect of continuing entanglements with bureaucratic prose, could not be shrugged off. On September 19 he wrote to Grace:

Dearest,
    . . . "With the effective utilization of meteorological advice" begins a report on some recent pre-peace action off Japan. The phrase has been running in my mind since I saw it this morning, and I wonder whether I could put up with it . . . or could I perhaps exert an ameliorating scintilla of effective coercion toward a more simple and direct manner of expression.[25]

A couple of weeks later he wrote that he had passed his physical and was a lieutenant commander, as of October 3 – at long last. "I think I feel better," he wrote in apparent reference to his disappointment when he was passed over for a promotion in August. That unexpected blow to his ambitions followed a disturbing fitness report by his commanding officer, who noted that although Philip had performed his duties satisfactorily, "he has rather definite convictions and at times is not tactful or diplomatic" (a comment not unlike some made later more bluntly by his critics at the Merriam company). Philip had been offended and asked for an explanation. The reply, which went into his personnel records at his request, explained that the remark was not intended to be unfavorable; Philip would doubtless be qualified for promotion as soon as he had spent sufficient time in rank.[26]

The promotion seemed like a vindication and a satisfying reward for all the hard work he had put into advancing his career. Whenever circumstances had permitted during his years of active duty, he had taken correspondence courses on ordnance and gunnery, communications, international law, investigation, commerce, and travel, foreign intelligence, coastal intelligence, and the like; without exception, he earned very high scores. He was proud of his wartime service and had a great affection for the navy, despite the many annoyances of military life. Returning to civilian life did not mean that he had to cut all of his ties. He served in the naval reserve for several years, achieving the rank of commander.

In November, Philip was detached from duty at Pasco and assigned to the Seattle Naval Air Station, where he would be near his family. He decided to stay in the navy until summer while he tested the academic job market and Norwood and Susan finished the school term. There would then be time for the family to take a vacation together before the fall semester began.

CHANGING COURSE

In early 1946 Philip began thinking seriously about employment possibilities for the next academic year. Though he had been on leave from NYU and could have returned to his former job, he began to explore other possibilities. Frank Bowman, who had taken a temporary appointment at Duke University, attended the midwinter meeting of the Modern Language Association and wrote him that there were plenty of jobs at the starting level of $2,400, up substantially from $1,800 before the war, but far fewer for midcareer men with families to support.

In his spare time he began writing to universities with widely differing characteristics – geographically and academically – including the University of Alaska. On February 12, he followed up at last on an idea that had been on his mind for a long time. He wrote to the G. & C. Merriam Company, publishers of the Merriam-Webster dictionaries, in Springfield, Massachusetts:

Sirs,

I should like to know whether there is an opportunity for me to go to work for your company in September of this year. . . .

I am not a linguist and have no claim to being a lexicographer but have done considerable research on 17th and 18th century dictionaries, have about as much knowledge as an outsider could acquire, I believe, of how dictionaries are made, and know something about printing and preparing Mss. for the printer.

I am not now asking for a job, but if there were a place for me in your organization, I should seriously consider applying for it rather than returning to my former teaching post because for several years I have wished that I were connected with the printing of Webster's Dictionary.[27]

A week later he received a letter from J. P. Bethel, general editor, expressing interest and requesting additional information and a list of references. Philip postponed his reply until May 7, when he received confirmation that he would be discharged July 1.

Bethel immediately sent letters of inquiry to four of the references mentioned by Philip. He could not afford to delay. The Merriam company, by this time, had become greatly concerned about the need to expand its staff for the preparation of a third edition of its unabridged dictionary, a project that would be more expensive and more time-consuming than any previous undertaking.

Philip's references responded promptly and enthusiastically, much to Bethel's relief. Professor Wright of Columbia University replied, "I know him intimately and can assure you that . . . he is just about an ideal man [for the job]. I know what editorial work is like, having done a good deal of it in my day, and I can recommend Gove for it unreservedly. I hope you can get him." Elliot V. K. Dobbie of Columbia called him "an extremely capable man in all respects. . . . I think he has the right temperament for dictionary work, and I think you would find him a congenial associate."

George Sherburn, chairman of the Department of English at Harvard, provided the strongest endorsement:

I know of only one fault in his career: he "settled down" for a time at New York University under the delusion that good teaching would bring advancement. Finding his error, he got busy, finished his thesis for the Ph.D. and was beginning a brilliant career in publication when the war got him.

His thesis I had the pleasure of reading when I was a member of the Columbia Department of English. It is one of the most learned works of its sort that I have ever supervised. Gove was able to quote at least a half-dozen languages effectively and correctly, and the work shows a considerable grasp of European languages. . . .

Gove's personality is a definite asset. He is clear headed, keen, wide-awake and all that. . . . He has a great many friends in the teaching profession, and I have never known of anyone who did not like and respect him.

I suppose I could say other good things about him, but if I go on you will suspect me of trying to help him to a job he wants very much to land. I rather hope you don't give it to him, because he is just the sort of man I want to see staying in the teaching of English. I have recently mentioned him for two good openings in universities, but I think he really wants to go into dictionary-making.[28]

Bowman, writing as a close friend, pointed out that even Gove's "informal style exhibits exceptional precision in the use of words." He said he could not write objectively about how well Gove would fit into a small group of editors, but "I should point out that he kept an even keel in one of the stormiest English departments I have known anywhere; the friends he made there are still his friends."[29]

On July 9, after telling Bethel he could be reached after mid-August, Philip hitched a trailer to the family car and headed east with Grace, the children, and Brenda. The six-week trip took them to Crater Lake National Park in Oregon, Banff in the Canadian Rockies, through the Dakotas to Mount Rushmore and the Badlands. They camped out in national parks and state parks, on baseball diamonds and empty fields.

When they arrived at the home of Grace's mother in Allendale, New Jersey, on August 20, Philip found a letter from Bethel proposing an interview. He wired Bethel promptly that he would be glad to meet with him on Monday, August 26. The interview was set for 3 p.m. in the Merriam offices. It went very well, Philip told his family. He said that he asked for more money than he had ever made and was informed that the annual salary that was agreed upon, $5,200, was more than the Merriam company had previously paid to a new assistant editor.

On Monday, September 16, 1946 – four years and a day after he had received his commission in the navy – Philip arrived in Springfield to begin a new career. A one-sentence note, signed by Lucius H. Holt, the managing editor, was delivered to the company president, Robert H. Munroe: "Mr. Gove reported for work in the Editorial Department this morning." In the paternal environment of the Merriam company – where each employee was given a turkey every Thanksgiving – even the arrival of a new assistant editor was a matter of presidential attention.

3

The Merriam and Webster Legacies

It is not only important but, in a degree necessary, that the people of this country should have *An American Dictionary of the English Language.*

Noah Webster, Preface to *An American Dictionary*

Dictionary making was viewed as a continuous process at the G. & C. Merriam Company; it went forward irrespective of the completion dates and printing schedules for successive editions. Publication signified a milestone, not a resting place. President Asa G. Baker emphasized this tradition in 1934 at the dinner celebrating the publication of *Webster's Second.* After a guest speaker expressed his satisfaction in knowing that work on a new dictionary would begin the next morning, Baker corrected him gently. Work on the Third Edition was already in progress, he said; there had been no break in the routine of the lexicographers between editions. In the company's scheme of things, it was assumed that the Third Edition would appear in 1959, twenty-five years after the Second Edition – which, in turn, had been published twenty-five years after the *New International Dictionary* of 1909.

The leadership of the Merriam company was also characterized by continuity; indeed, it could be called inbred. For six decades the Merriam brothers ran the business. Homer, the youngest of the three brothers, retired in 1904 at the age of ninety-one. He was succeeded by the first of the Bakers – Orlando M. Baker, who had worked at the firm for twenty-five years and then was president for ten. Orlando's son, Asa, was named president in 1922, following the term of H. Curtis Rowley. Asa Baker, in turn, yielded the presidency to Robert H. Munroe, a man in his mid-fifties, who had joined the company in 1898. It would be Munroe who would direct the early planning for the Third Edition.

Transitions in the editorial staff had proceeded almost as smoothly, beginning with the Merriams' appointment of Noah Webster's son-in-law, Chauncey A. Goodrich, professor of rhetoric at Yale University; he edited the 1847 revision. Goodrich, in turn, hired a colleague, Noah Porter (later president of Yale), who edited the 1864 and 1890 revisions. Thereafter, Yale and Harvard graduates continued to play prominent roles. When Gove was hired in 1946, the top two editorial positions were held by John P. Bethel, who had a doctorate from Harvard, and Lucius H. Holt, a Yale graduate. Both had worked on the Second Edition. Holt had also been an assistant editor for the 1909 dictionary.

THE MERRIAM TRADITION

Robert Munroe was in the tradition of the company's chief executive: an insider and a businessman with an instinct for salesmanship. He was hired as a shipping clerk when he was still in high school and after working for several years as a salesman was promoted to advertising manager. He was elected a member of the board in 1919 and president fifteen years later, in 1934. His two successors during the making of the Third Edition, Robert N. Fuller and Gordon J. Gallan, also came to the presidency after serving as advertising manager, though neither of them had previously been a longtime Merriam employee.

A cornerstone of company policy from the beginning had been a division of labor at the top. The president ran the business. The editor, typically a scholar, directed the making of the dictionary. An editorial board, chaired by the president and including members from the business side and the editorial side, gave final approval to basic policy decisions. Munroe honored this tradition. He showed a keen sense of responsibility to his stockholders; his voice was the voice of caution, and he had a long memory for slip-ups in earlier publications that had brought minor embarrassment to the company. Though the history of the company had taught that change was essential, he seemed concerned primarily about avoiding mistakes.

The long-range perspective that was reflected in the Merriams' emphasis on continuity – combined with an aggressive sales strategy

– is what gave the company its distinctive character. Alone among U.S. dictionary makers, the Merriam company sustained a commitment to periodic revisions decade after decade for well over a century. Every generation deserved a new dictionary to take account of changes in vocabulary and usage – and got it.

In contrast, the company's three chief nineteenth-century competitors faded from the scene because they wearied of the struggle or balked at the cost of keeping up to date, not because their dictionaries lacked merit. Joseph Worcester's dictionary of 1860, widely viewed upon publication as the best English dictionary in the world, was given only one perfunctory revision after Worcester's death five years later; by then it had been surpassed by the 1864 edition in the Webster series. Worcester's publisher backed away from the kind of competitive response that Worcester typically made during his long-running battle with Webster and his heirs. The great six-volume *Century Dictionary* of 1889–91 was given only one major updating. Edited by the distinguished philologist William Dwight Whitney of Yale University, who had been an associate editor of the 1864 Merriam-Webster unabridged, it was acclaimed by scholars and became immensely popular. In 1911 it was thoroughly revised and expanded to twelve volumes, but only minor updatings were made thereafter, and it was left behind. In 1913 a new edition of the 1893 Funk & Wagnalls *Standard Dictionary of the English Language,* unabridged, appeared. A one-volume work, it was the only true competitor of the Merriam unabridged. However, later printings incorporated only minor revisions and changes, not enough to keep the book abreast of the Merriam unabridged. By persevering with extensive revisions, the Merriam company won out over rivals who had temporarily bested it. The Second Edition of 1934 went unchallenged and dominated the market for unabridged dictionaries until the 1960s.

Thus, if the Webster name – made famous by the exceptionally popular and influential Blue-Backed Speller – helped to symbolize continuity in dictionary making, it was the institutional perspective of the management that achieved it. Management transcended personalities, so that long after Webster's death – and the deaths of the company founders, George and Charles Merriam – the dictionary continued to be improved; indeed, it was radically redone, within an established company tradition. A highly respected philologist, George Philip Krapp, asserted, rather extravagantly perhaps, that were it not "for elaborate publishers' revisions of Webster's work, revisions with which he had nothing to do but which nevertheless did retain what was genuinely good in the dictionary of 1828, Webster's name would probably now be unknown in the land."[1]

The Merriam company never lost an opportunity to identify itself with Webster and his work. In the community and among its employees, as well as in the book market, it cultivated the notion that its dictionaries were the true offspring of the nation's first great lexicographer. In 1940, when President Munroe had a new office built on Federal Street, overlooking downtown Springfield, he was given his choice of any odd number between 31 and 49 for the street address. He invoked the Webster connection by choosing 47 – 1847 was the year in which the first Merriam-Webster dictionary was published.

For the company's one hundredth anniversary in 1947, Munroe commissioned a company history, which was published in a handsome boxed edition that, despite its obviously self-serving purpose, set forth an informative and fair account of the record. It was entitled *Noah's Ark*. A sketch of Webster at the age of sixty-five by Samuel F. B. Morse appears opposite the opening page of Chapter One. Webster's photograph, a copy of his first great dictionary, and his desk still welcome the visitor to the Webster room off the entry hall of the building at 47 Federal Street.

NOAH WEBSTER

Noah Webster, who was born on October 16, 1758, on a farm in West Hartford, Connecticut, is generally described as a typical Yankee of the period: industrious, self-reliant, pious, frugal. He was also very ambitious and sustained by certitude. His detractors saw some of these qualities exaggerated to a fault. They considered him egotistical, opinionated, close-minded, and quarrelsome. There is much to say for both views. "All through life he was constantly, if unwittingly, alienating his best supporters, antagonizing political or sectional groups, rubbing audiences the wrong way."[2]

Before Webster turned his hand to lexicography in 1800 or thereabouts, he had been a schoolmaster, spelling reformer, lawyer, lecturer, journalist, crusader for copyright legislation, and the unlikely author of a two-volume work entitled the *History of Pestilential Diseases*, which was considered the standard work in the field. His advocacy of copyright protection, which reflected his own dismay at his inability to secure a copyright for his spelling book, took him to all the colonies when he was still in his twenties. He met Benjamin Franklin, with whom he corresponded for many years, George Washington, and other leaders of the time. These encounters strengthened his natural patriotic sentiments. He became an influential pamphleteer on behalf of a constitutional convention. His broader mission became the advancement of the new nation and the improvement of its schools.

In 1806, at the age of forty-eight, Webster published *A Compendious Dictionary of the English Language,* and he followed it two decades later with *An American Dictionary of the English Language,* a two-volume work that established his reputation as a lexicographer. It has been called "the most important dictionary between Johnson and the appearance of the first volume of the *Oxford English Dictionary,*" though it has been subjected to serious criticism.[3]

Estimates of Webster's lexicographical work are also marked by sharp differences of opinion, which largely reflect the relative weight to be given to his achievements, especially his skill in defining, compared with his shortcomings, especially in etymology.

His *Compendious Dictionary* contained a vocabulary of some 37,000 entries, including 5,000 words that Webster claimed were not included in any other English dictionary. The meaning of each was typically indicated by a synonym or series of synonyms. A smattering of etymological and usage information was included. An appendix, constituting 52 of the book's 408 pages, was "added for the benefit of the MERCHANT, the STUDENT and the TRAVELLER." It offered tables of the value of foreign money in sterling and dollars, weights and measures, a list of local post offices, state population figures, and "Chronological Tables of Remarkable Events and Discoveries." The "Remarkable" chronology begins with Webster's confident dating of "the creation of the world, and Adam and Eve 4004" B.C. and continues to A.D. 1805.[4]

The *Compendious* reflects Webster's longtime interest in lexicography, which dates back to his days as a schoolmaster after graduation from Yale University, and it marks his initial step toward the preparation of a more ambitious dictionary "which shall exhibit a far more correct state of the language than any work of this kind."[5]

One of his goals was to replace Johnson as the most influential dictionary maker. He admired Johnson greatly, citing him approvingly on many occasions; he used a quotation from Johnson's *Rasselas* on the title page of *An American Dictionary*. However, he was highly critical of Johnson's dictionary on a number of points – the limited scope of the vocabulary, the etymologies, and the pronunciations. Webster also attacked Johnson for using too many illustrative quotations. To some extent, he seems to have been torn later between his regard for Johnson's work and his resentment of the competition from the revised Johnson dictionaries that had been updated periodically by later lexicographers.

It took Webster two decades to complete the *American Dictionary*. During this period, he was supported mostly by royalties from his speller, which eventually sold some 100 million copies. Ten years of that time were spent on an ill-conceived and futile effort to work out an etymological theory that "would confirm in no small degree the scripture's account of the dispersion of men."[6] His quest led him to study, with various degrees of understanding and thoroughness, some twenty languages. He looked for signs of similarities among their vocabularies and for evidence of their common descent from the biblical Chaldee. His practice was to arrange the dictionaries of these languages around the walls of his study, open to passages to be compared, and to walk from one to another taking notes. It was a prodigious effort, conducted with diligence and scrupulous care. But it was misconceived. He had been carried away by his piety in accepting as a starting point the literal truth of the Bible. His stubborn belief in his own infallibility kept him from taking other views and research into account, the most important of which was the pioneering historical research by German linguists that was becoming known as his work neared completion.

Webster had expected that his etymologies would be his most glorious achievement, but they proved to be his most glaring failure – the most heavily criticized feature of the 1828 dictionary. Etymology had been Johnson's weak point, too, but whereas Johnson's shortcomings merely reflected a limited effort and the ignorance of his time, Webster's work was a tragic failure of good intentions and hard work wrongly channeled.

If his etymology was a fiasco, Webster's defining of words was his triumph, the achievement emphasized by those who rate him highly as a lexicographer. Webster regarded the definitions of words as the heart of a dictionary. He wrote in *An American Dictionary* that "the great and substantial merit . . . [of a dictionary] must lie in the copiousness of its vocabulary, and the accuracy and comprehensiveness of its definitions." And of all the tasks of dictionary making, defining was what he did best. Joseph Friend said Webster "wrote definitions that were more accurate, more comprehensive, and not less carefully divided and ordered than any previously done in English lexicography."[7]

In their notable study, *Dr. Johnson's Dictionary*, James Sledd and Gwin J. Kolb said of Webster that "in his definitions he met Johnson on his own ground and stood the comparison without dishonor." James A. H. Murray thought Webster a great man and called him "a born definer," an often-quoted characterization that clings to his name as a sobriquet in the history of dictionaries.[8]

Another of Webster's achievements was his expansion of the vocabulary in the 1828 edition to about seventy thousand entries, some twelve thousand more than in any earlier American dictionary. He added nouns in common use, such as *fracas, glacier, malpractice,* and *mammoth;* adjectives such as *dyspeptic, meteoric,* and *retaliatory;* verbs such as *explode, electioneer,* and *revolutionize;* and commonly used terms from mythology and history, such as *Augean* and *Punic.* He is credited with having coined one word, *jeopardized,* and he introduced, by his estimate, some four thousand technical terms such as *planetarium, polarize,* and *sulphate.* He added many legal words and improved on legal definitions.[9]

Because his definitions were much more detailed than Johnson's and often included verbal illustrations of his own devising to show how a word was commonly used, he seldom thought it necessary to include illustrative quotations. When he did so from time to time, he liked to draw on the Bible, as in his definition of *hunger,* under the sense "to long for": "Blessed are they that *hunger* and thirst after righteousness. *Matt v.*" He thought Johnson had grossly overdone the practice, thereby wasting space and adding unnecessarily to the cost of the work. Webster's scant attention to illustrative quotations damned his dictionary in the eyes of Richard Chenevix Trench, the British clergyman and philologist who greatly influenced the guidelines for the *Oxford English Dictionary.*

Webster took pride in the introduction of Americanisms – new words and new senses of old words that had arisen to meet the language needs of the new nation. He also called attention to American writers as authorities for his definitions even if he did not quote them and placed such works as *The Federalist Papers* and the writings of Franklin on a par with the British writers cited in earlier dictionaries. In doing so, he was expressing not only his patriotism but also his view of how language changes and why it is important for a nation to have a language that in some aspects is distinctly its own. In contrast to Johnson, who thought that language change, though inevitable, was undesirable and ought to be retarded, he welcomed the growth of English to meet new needs in new continents. He repeatedly emphasized that the North American English of his time must be different from Johnson's English. In Sledd and Kolb's words, "He never lost sight of the one great idea which governed his work."[10]

In the preface to the *American Dictionary* Webster expressed again ideas that he had begun espousing nearly three decades earlier:

It is not only important, but, in a degree necessary, that the people of this country should have an *American Dictionary* of the English language; for, although the body of the language is the same as in England, and it is desirable to perpetuate that sameness, yet some differences must exist. Language is the expression of ideas; and if the people of one country cannot preserve an identity of ideas, they cannot retain an identity of language. Now an identity of ideas depends materially upon a sameness of things or objects with which the people of the two countries are conversant. But in no two portions of the earth, remote from each other, can such identity be found. Even physical objects must be different. But the principal differences between the people of this country and of all others arise from different forms of government, different laws, institutions and customs. . . .

A great number of words in our languages require to be defined in a phraseology accommodated to the condition and institutions of the people in these states, and the people of England must look to an American Dictionary for a correct understanding of such terms.[11]

It is his guiding idea about the need for a dictionary to serve English-speaking people remote from England, his expansion of the vocabulary, and, above all, his skill as a definer that establish Webster's importance as a lexicographer.

His faults have not escaped the notice of later critics. Krapp, for example, thought that the dictionary was executed "with an inadequate scholarship and with a stubbornness of personal conviction that seriously impaired the noble design."[12] He drew attention to Webster's eccentricities, notably his overemphasis on New England examples and his neglect of pronunciations outside New England. He dwelled on the failure of the etymological research and argued that it was not until long after his death – with the publication of the highly regarded 1864 edition containing new etymologies – that the Webster dictionary become the authoritative and dominant dictionary of the English language and the basis for the modern editions of the Merriam-Webster dictionaries.

Although the failure of Webster's etymologies is mentioned about as frequently as his skill in defining is conceded, it can be argued that the attacks on his etymological misjudgments have been overdone. Allen Walker Read points out that until the beginning of the nineteenth century, French culture was dominant in American life and German influence was slight. Webster was working on his etymologies in the second and third decades of the century, many years before the achievements of European researchers, such as Jacob Grimm, Franz Bopp, and Rasmus Rask, reached the United States. His views had been formed largely by eighteenth-century perceptions, whose limitations he recognized. He sought to overcome these limitations on his own because he saw no alternative, and on his own, despite his mistakes, he advanced far beyond his precursors. On a visit to England in the late 1820s just before completing his dictionary, he found himself well ahead of the British, who were equally uninformed about the German advances. Taking into account that he was in his sixties, and fully engaged in a single-handed effort to prepare a new dictionary, Read concluded, "He has been censured too severely for not adopting the German learning, for at his advanced age he could not be expected to overturn his life's work."[13]

THE WAR OF THE DICTIONARIES

Critics dogged Webster during his lifetime as well, many of them preferring the dictionaries of his formidable rival, Joseph Worcester, who was a New Englander, Yale graduate, and schoolmaster, as Webster had been. The two became locked in a great controversy, known as the War of the Dictionaries, which continued long after Webster's death.

Worcester began his career as a lexicographer by editing *Johnson's English Dictionary, as Improved by Todd, and Abridged by Chalmers; with Walker's Pronouncing Dictionary, Combined.* Published in 1827, it was another of the many hybrids that had been assembled after Johnson's time, which attested to the continuing hold of Johnson's definitions and reputation on both dictionary makers and users. It also attested to the inadequacy of his treatment of pronunciation and other areas, which invited improvements by others.

Worcester's next publication was an abridged edition of Webster's two-volume *American Dictionary.* Published in 1829, it was more successful financially than the original 1828 edition and was reprinted several times. Nevertheless, Webster was not happy with it, and in 1830, when Worcester published his *Comprehensive Pronouncing and Explanatory Dictionary*, his first independent work, Webster's assessment of his former associate shifted from dissatisfaction to suspicion and anger.

The war began when Webster accused Worcester of plagiarism; it escalated later into a battle between their respective publishers and followers, which continued for two more decades. Webster had apparently sensed that Worcester would become a formidable competitor whose dictionary would cut into the sales of his own. His first accusatory and combative article appeared in the *Palladium* of Worcester, Massachusetts, which showed examples of similarities between his 1828 dictionary and Worcester's 1830 work. Worcester replied by emphasizing his own innovations and the differences between his book and Webster's. He noted that he had been working on his *Comprehensive Dictionary* before his association with Webster. He acknowledged some borrowing, but pointed out that Webster, too, had borrowed heavily from his predecessors. Beyond further estrangement between the two, not much came of this first exchange.

In an attempt to make a more effective response to Worcester's challenge, Webster – then in his early eighties – summoned up enough energy to prepare a revision of his *American Dictionary*, which he called the "2nd Edition, Corrected and Enlarged," published in 1841 (with an 1840 copyright). It included an additional five thousand words, but otherwise made no major changes. Priced at fifteen dollars, it was still too costly for the average reader, and it was no more successful commercially than its predecessor. It failed to dislodge Worcester from a share of the market.

Webster died in 1843, and for the next twenty years his fight with Worcester was carried on by the two brothers who became his publishers, George and Charles Merriam.

THE MERRIAM BROTHERS were printers and booksellers who had moved from West Brookfield, Massachusetts, to Springfield in 1831. They opened a book and stationery store and printed schoolbooks, law books, and Bibles. After Webster's death, they bought the unsold sheets of the 1841 revision of *An American Dictionary* from an Amherst firm and purchased from Webster's heirs the exclusive right to reprint and revise it. They saw the dictionary as a means of establishing themselves as publishers of reference books.

Well trained in all phases of book production, they also had an instinctive understanding of promotion and selling. Their first important publishing act was to prepare a revision of the dictionary that would be bound in a single volume and would sell for six dollars, less than half the original price. After Professor Goodrich was hired to edit this edition, several other Yale professors and Webster's son, William, who had helped his father with the 1841 revision, were added to the staff. The "New Revised Edition" of *An American Dictionary* was published on September 24, 1847, and it ushered in the Merriam-Webster series. It contained eighty-five thousand entries, ten thousand more than the preceding edition. The Webster family, which was to receive royalties from sales, was outraged at first by the cut in price, but was placated when the public responded so enthusiastically to the lower price that royalties greatly exceeded the family's expectations (more than $250,000 in twenty-five years).[14]

Meanwhile, Worcester had been busy with a new work, *A Universal and Critical Dictionary of the English Language*, which was published in 1846. He viewed it as more than a revision of his 1830 dictionary. It introduced twenty-seven thousand additional words, raising the total almost to the number in the 1847 Webster. A conservative dictionary, closer to English usage and less experimental than Webster's, it was similar in approach to Worcester's earlier work but introduced some etymologies, illustrative quotations, and notes. His handling of idiomatic verb phrases, such as *come about, come over, come to oneself, come upon,* was considered a clear advance.[15]

The new work was championed by scholars from Harvard and

much applauded in England. With the Worcester and Webster dictionaries appearing a year apart, the commercial phase of the War of the Dictionaries, as it was called in the press, was in full tilt (Figure 1). The rival publishers gathered testimonials from partisan supporters for their advertisements; debates over the relative merits of the two works raged on college campuses and in the press. The battle was enlivened briefly in 1853 by a British publisher who issued an English edition of Worcester's *Universal Dictionary* that contained on its title page the erroneous phrase "Compiled from the materials of Noah Webster, LL.D. by Joseph E. Worcester."[16]

A dozen years later two more competing editions were brought out by the rival publishers. Professor Goodrich, anticipating a new dictionary from Worcester, had scheduled a reprinting in 1859 that would contain additional words and an extensive collection of synonyms that he had prepared. When he learned of Worcester's intention to include illustrations, he hurriedly put together an eight-page section of pictorial illustrations that was inserted at the front of the book. This "New Revised Edition" was touted as the first illustrated American dictionary.

Despite this enterprising effort, the Goodrich revision was surpassed by Worcester's substantially new work, the *Dictionary of the English Language,* published in 1860. Acclaimed as his "masterpiece" by later critics, it soon became widely regarded as the best dictionary of English in England as well as in the United States. It not only cited authorities profusely but also included a generous selection of illustrative quotations. The etymologies were improved. On one matter, Worcester agreed with Webster. The definition, he said in his preface, "is the most important part of a dictionary." At the same time, still smarting from Webster's plagiarism charge in the 1830s, he explicitly kept his distance from his old rival, adhering to the rule "to take no word, no definition of a word, no citation, and no name as an authority from that work."

Worcester's triumph was short-lived, however. His dictionary was bettered by the Merriams in 1864 by what became popularly known as "the unabridged." Though this edition still carried Webster's name, it was largely the product of others brought in by the editor, Noah Porter. Thirty professors in scientific and humanistic fields served as editors, and other scholars and literary figures were encouraged to send in new words and citations. The vocabulary was en-

Figure 1. The War of the Dictionaries: Webster vs. Worcester. From *Vanity Fair*, March 10, 1860 – "Sporting Intelligence: The Battle of the Dictionaries." Reprinted with permission from Robert Keith Leavitt, *Noah's Ark: New England Yankees and the Endless Quest* (Springfield, Mass.: G. & C. Merriam Company, 1947), 55.

larged, fresh quotations were inserted, and three thousand pictorial illustrations were prepared for insertion in the main text. Most important was the reworking of the etymologies by Carl A. F. Mahn, a leading German linguist (see Chapter 6). So great was his contribution that the edition also became known as the "Webster-Mahn." The new work, a challenge to the printing technology of the day, was reputed to be the largest book to be printed in quantity in the United States.

The 1864 edition won not only praise in the press but also the endorsement of some literary figures who had previously favored Worcester over Webster. It became the preferred work in schools, courts, and printing plants across the nation, where editors and proofreaders were instructed to "follow Webster."

After Worcester's death in 1865, the War of the Dictionaries came to an end. The modest revision put out by Worcester's publisher in 1886 did not challenge the dominance of Webster, though it continued to be sold for many years.

If the Merriams were the victors in this conflict, the dictionary user was a beneficiary as well. Notwithstanding the nonsense that characterized some of the rival advertising claims, successive editions of the Webster and Worcester dictionaries over some three decades brought substantial improvements in both works. Lexicography in English took a notable step forward. At the same time there was an awakening of public interest in dictionaries, which was good for business. At the height of the War of the Dictionaries, as sales mounted, the Merriams were said to have commented, "Thank God for Worcester."[17] Thereafter, "What does Webster say?" became a common response when questions of meaning, pronunciation, and so on were raised.

In a new edition of 1890 – *Webster's International Dictionary* – Porter attempted to include the English of Australia and Canada as well as that of the United States and England. The dictionary claimed 175,000 entries, 59,000 more than the 1864 edition. The increase in coverage helped it hold its position against the newly published *Century* and the Funk & Wagnalls *Standard,* which followed three years later.

Another numbers game in the competitive saga of dictionary publishing was being played out. The *New International* of 1909 doubled the number of entries; Funk & Wagnalls topped that with its *New Standard* of 1913, which claimed 450,000 entries. In 1934, *Webster's*

Second New International claimed 600,000 entries, and the game was over. *Webster's Second* achieved the dominant position in lexicography and became the takeoff point for the Third Edition. During the rest of the 1930s and early 1940s, preliminary work on the next edition moved ahead along with several other editorial projects, including reprintings of the Second Edition with corrections, changes, and an addenda of new words to be bound into the front matter of the book. The fifth edition of the *Collegiate Dictionary,* published in 1936, also had to be kept up to date.

THE FRUSTRATING SEARCH FOR
LEADERSHIP

In late August 1945, President Munroe decided it was time to begin the search for new editors to direct the formidable task of preparing the Third Edition. He intended to follow the precedents of the 1909 and 1934 editions and hire a prominent public figure to serve as titular editor in chief and a scholarly general editor to manage the task of dictionary making. The hiring of a general editor was more urgent, since he was needed to recruit and train a staff in time to produce a new dictionary by the 1959 target date.

J. P. Bethel, who had succeeded Thomas A. Knott in 1935 as the general editor, had taken himself out of the running. He had become fully occupied supervising a family of specialized dictionaries that had been developed during the 1930s and early 1940s – the *Biographical Dictionary,* the *Dictionary of Synonyms,* and the *Geographical Dictionary,* which was nearing completion. He felt that he could not take on, in addition, the editorial responsibility for the Third Edition. He proposed hiring an associate general editor to direct work on the new edition while he continued to manage the other editorial projects. A new managing editor was also needed to replace Holt, who was ailing and nearing retirement. In time, the search would begin for a new editor in chief whose prestige as a scholar or public figure would add luster to the dictionary.

The search for an associate general editor began with deceptive ease, with no hint of the difficulties and delays that would follow. Bethel found a promising candidate at Harvard, Alexander Murray Fowler, and invited him to Springfield for an interview in the fall of

1945. Fowler impressed the company management, and he was attracted to the work. He joined the staff on January 2, 1946, for a one-year trial. During the next six months, he was introduced to lexical work by Bethel and others, wrote definitions, and interviewed prospective staff members. He helped establish procedures for cutting out and pasting up all the entries in the latest printing of the Second Edition on three-by-five slips so that they could be reviewed and revised for the Third – an enormous clerical task that took several years to complete.

In August, however, Fowler received a teaching offer from Harvard. He left Springfield on September 13, eight and a half months after his tryout began, and the search for an associate general editor was resumed.

The recruiting of staff editors proceeded with better results. Two assistant editors with strong academic backgrounds were hired during 1946, in addition to Gove. One was Donald W. Lee, who had recently received a Ph.D. in English from Columbia University; the other was Mairé Weir Kay, who had a Ph.D. in biology. Both became part of the small group of Gove's associate editors. Miss Kay, as she was always addressed, became a powerful figure in the making of the dictionary. She was known for rigorous attention to detail and her ability to get things done expeditiously and superbly. Her comments were often biting and intimidating, but she respected good work, and those who met her standards found her supportive and appreciative. If an oversight of her own was detected by an assistant, she could reply with a gracious note of thanks. She remained on the staff for nearly four decades, uncompromisingly individualistic in dress and manner, well ahead of her time. In her later years she brought out a new edition of the *Dictionary of Synonyms* and a new book, *Webster's Collegiate Thesaurus*. For a brief period before retirement, she shared the responsibility for the editorial direction of the company.

Meanwhile the search for leadership had taken on a new urgency because of the death of Dr. William Allan Neilson. Neilson had been a highly successful editor in chief of the Second Edition. A distinguished philologist, he was president of Smith College when President Asa Baker offered him the job in the mid-1920s. Springfield was only an hour away from the campus by train, and Neilson was able to schedule a half-day or all-day visit to the Merriam office every other Tuesday for editorial meetings without slighting his duties at Smith.

He was delighted to be engaged in important scholarly work again and sought to become more than a figurehead. He took on responsibility for Scottish words (he was a Scot by birth) and British universities. He wrote the definition for *pawky* – "possessed of a dry wit" – a term that had been applied to him as a young man.[18] As a philologist, he was able to contribute to substantive discussions; where he was less an authority, his experience as a scholarly administrator and the force of his presence enabled him to preside effectively over discussions that were often technical and heated.

From the company's point of view, Neilson's prominence as an educator was extremely important in gaining public acceptance of the dictionary as an authoritative work. His name and position were intended to provide reassurance that the dictionary work had been prepared under truly scholarly auspices. He continued to be helpful to the Merriam company long after the dictionary was completed. His advice continued to be solicited, and during the last year of his life he responded as well as he could to calls for help in identifying scholars who might be considered for staff openings. Thus, it was assumed that he would have to be replaced as promptly as possible by a scholar of comparable eminence as the titular head of the work on a new edition.

Munroe sought a successor in the same mold, who would be young enough and healthy enough to continue until the work was completed and a few years beyond – Neilson's association had lasted twenty years. The new editor would have to live close enough to Springfield to attend regular meetings without great inconvenience. Ideally, he should combine both roles as expert and figurehead, but if a choice had to be made between the two roles, it would be more important for the editor in chief to be an eminent man whose presence would lend credibility to the dictionary. The editor in chief of the 1909 edition had been William T. Harris, a philosopher, who had gained public prominence as head of the U.S. Office of Education. Although Harris knew nothing about lexicography, he faithfully attended editorial meetings over several years, and he served effectively as a figurehead, presider, and symbol of scholarly respectability.

During the early discussions after Neilson's death in February 1946, the list of candidates ranged over all fields. Suggestions came from former staff members and academic acquaintances, such as Percy W. Long, executive secretary of the Modern Language Association and former member of the dictionary staff, and Harold H. Bender of Princeton University, who had been chief etymologist for the Second Edition. Department chairmen at Harvard, Yale, and other universities offered suggestions.

Some thought a scientist might be a good choice, as long as he was not too specialized in his interests and had a breadth of experience. Such men as James B. Conant, president of Harvard, and Detlev W. Bronk, chairman of the National Research Council, were suggested. Over the next several months names of college presidents, linguists, and writers (Walter Lippmann, Archibald MacLeish) were put forth by members of the board and friends who tried to respond helpfully, if not always realistically, to Munroe's request for suggestions. At one point the board voted to offer the job to Dr. Conant. But there was opposition to the notion that a scientist would be suitable. As one former staff member noted, the dictionary was about language, not about science. Five years would pass before the issue was resolved.

THE SEARCH FOR A GENERAL EDITOR of the dictionary made little progress after Fowler's foreshortened tryout. Many leading scholars were considered over the next three years, including prominent professors of English or of languages – Albert H. Marckwardt, Norman E. Eliason, Robert A. Hall, and Frederic G. Cassidy, who later became chief editor of the *Dictionary of American Regional English*. Negotiations with Cassidy advanced to the point where he was offered the job, but he declined.

The lack of success in finding either an editor in chief or a general editor led to a change in management thinking. By the end of the 1940s there was growing support for a suggestion by Bethel to abandon the search for a titular editor in chief and hire a single full-time resident editor to take complete charge of the revision. Negotiations began with W. Freeman Twaddell, professor of German at Brown University. A graduate of Duke University, Twaddell had received his Ph.D. from Harvard, where he studied general linguistics, phonetics, and philology. He taught German at the University of Wisconsin from 1929 to 1946 and became chairman of the department before moving to Brown. He was active in the profession, serving as delegate of the Linguistic Society of America to the American Council of Learned Societies.

The talks with Twaddell went well, and in March 1950 the staff was told that he would join the Merriam company on July 1 as the editor of the Third Edition. Bethel would remain head of the editorial department and retain responsibility for other publications. Twaddell would come on a year's leave from Brown as a trial to see whether he wanted to leave academic life.

A change in the company's top management had taken place earlier in the year. Robert N. Fuller, the executive vice-president, who had come to the company as advertising manager in 1937, was named president in February 1950. Munroe became chairman of the board. Thus, in mid-1950, with a new president and a new editor for the Third Edition in place, the four-year search for new leadership to guide the company through the production of the next unabridged dictionary seemed to have been completed.

THE THIRD EDITION: ON TRACK AT LAST

If progress on the new edition had lagged because of the uncertainty over leadership and a shortage of staff, Twaddell found that considerable work had been done nonetheless. After sizing up the situation, he turned first to a new task. It was time, he said, to "begin to cast our nets for consultants." Identifying potential consultants and explaining the purpose and requirements of the consulting task required considerable tact. The company wanted to impress consultants with the need to complete their assignments promptly, but it also wanted to prevent competitors from finding out that work on the Third Edition was under way. Thus, Twaddell advised against mentioning plans for the Third Edition in preliminary inquiries. The work should be described as part of a continuing program of scrutiny, topic by topic, that included reviewing dictionary files and questions sent in by users in order to identify areas where changes should be made. The amount of work to be done and remuneration would be discussed at a personal interview.

In some situations, Twaddell directed house editors to prepare definitions that would be sent to specialists for confirmation, comment, and suggestions for revision. In other fields, consultants were asked to identify gaps in vocabulary and usage and propose definitions for the new terms. Where the work load was unusually heavy or the staff had little expertise, he suggested bringing in a consultant to the office for a year or so.

The task of finding highly competent people, preparing assignments, following up completion dates, and reviewing the work became increasingly burdensome, and it continued almost until the editing of the dictionary was finished. It was especially heavy in scientific and technical fields, where most of the extra load was picked up by Hubert P. Kelsey, editor for the physical sciences. He dealt not only with individual consultants but also with industry committees on nomenclature and standards. Kelsey had been hired on a temporary basis out of the University of Michigan in 1935, and his career with Merriam spanned some fifty years. He claimed that no one ever bothered to change his temporary status, an anomaly that amused him greatly. He retired once, but was called back during the early 1980s as an editorial adviser for the *Ninth New Collegiate Dictionary* and won great respect and affection from the younger staff members.

Mild-mannered in personal relations, Kelsey was a man of strong views about dictionary making and could "fulminate" when he was upset on the job or angry over a decision or policy. He found much to fulminate about during the making of the Third Edition. He thought that he and Gove got off to a bad start when Gove was placed under his tutelage. (All newcomers were assigned to a senior staff member for guidance.) Gove, then in his mid-forties, did not take kindly to instruction or advice, Kelsey said, and seemed to resent suggestions. Their relationship worsened over time, though Gove, who was never very sensitive to the attitudes of others, may not have been aware that he had offended Kelsey.

Kelsey disagreed with virtually all of the changes that Gove later introduced. He also regarded Gove as an incorrigible authoritarian. He never let anyone doubt that he much preferred the editorial policies of the Second. Years after the dictionary was published he recounted with considerable satisfaction his reply when he was asked by the advertising department to suggest which changes in the Third Edition made it better than its predecessors. "I told them I couldn't think of any." However, there was never any question about his commitment to his work and the high quality of what he did over his long career.[19]

To his search for consultants, Twaddell added the recruiting of junior staff editors and readers. In the past, the Merriam company

usually turned to nearby women's colleges to fill such positions, relying on friends and acquaintances to identify and recommend likely
candidates. But with placement offices well established on most campuses by the beginning of the 1950s and the need to move quickly,
Twaddell thought that form letters to guidance counselors throughout
New England would be more effective and efficient. He felt that
limiting recruitment to New England would not prove to be as provin-
cial as it might seem because the student bodies of leading schools
included students from all over the United States and Canada.

The reading and marking of books, newspapers, magazines, and
specialized publications for words and examples of usage to add to the
citation files had been proceeding at a modest but steady pace since
1936. It would have to be stepped up by the hiring and training of
additional readers. Staff editors would also have to devote some of
their time to reading and marking.

To advertise editorial jobs, Twaddell sent letters to graduate departments of leading universities throughout the country. A key early
recruit was Charles R. Sleeth, Rhodes scholar and Princeton Ph.D.,
who became chief etymologist. At Oxford, Sleeth's tutors had included J. R. R. Tolkien and C. T. Onions, the last surviving editor of
the *Oxford English Dictionary* and later principal editor of the *Oxford
Dictionary of English Etymology*. Sleeth received a B.A. degree in 1936
and a diploma in comparative philology (Greek and Germanic) in
1937 from Oxford. Then he took a Ph.D. in comparative philology
under Professor Bender at Princeton. After three years of military
service during World War II, he taught German at Princeton for five
years before he was interviewed by Twaddell and Bethel and hired by
the Merriam company.

By the spring of 1951, Twaddell had seen enough of the Merriam
company to reach a number of conclusions, which he put in a memo
to Bethel. In it, he finally laid to rest the assumption that had long
guided the management: the need to bring in outside leadership.
Twaddell saw no need for a titular editor to lend prestige to the Third
Edition or an outside expert to direct the staff's work on the dictionary. His message was clear: not only was a figurehead unnecessary,
but editors already on the staff could direct the work more effectively
than any outsider – including, by implication, himself. A job that at
one time seemed to require three people – an editor in chief, a
general editor in charge of the editorial department, and a general

editor of the unabridged – should, in fact, be the responsibility of one person. The tasks were too interrelated to be separated.

Nine months on the premises convinced Twaddell that the editorial department

is a force of the first order. . . . It is no longer necessary or even desirable to import or borrow the prestige of an eminent outsider for any product of the Editorial Department. . . . No one personage in scholarship combines high reputation and balanced versatility as the Merriam-Webster editorial staff does. The appearance of any one name on a title page as a warrant of quality is, from now on, unwise. . . .

Further, in all conscience, I don't know any figure now visible or likely to emerge within the next ten years who would command even moderate authority as an "outside" editor-in-chief. . . .

An eminent non-lexicographer is not what the Department needs. The massive machinery here works smoothly and effectively, within manpower limitations. . . . You have to make a lexicographer and a Merriam editor out of any newcomer before he can be of much use.

Twaddell warned against two evils: "(1) Lost motion, needless disturbance of the smoothly functioning machinery by the ignorance and inexperience of a newcomer; (2) the ever-present danger of being unself-critical, ingrown, tradition-bound."[20]

Two months after Twaddell wrote his memo, the first step was taken, apparently on the recommendations of Bethel and Twaddell. Munroe wrote Gove that "you have been selected to have full responsibility, under the Editorial Board, for the editing and production of the next edition of the Merriam-Webster Unabridged Dictionary. For the present your title will be Managing Editor." The salary was set at $8,000, plus a bonus if the company had a good year, and fringe benefits. At the end of six months his performance would be reviewed.

This solution to the leadership problem is not what Munroe expected in the late 1940s, and probably not what Twaddell or Bethel had anticipated a year earlier. But in 1951 it made sense to them all. Twaddell could return to Brown University in good conscience, and in Springfield work on the Third Edition could move ahead at full speed after a frustrating six-year search.

4

The New Editor Takes Hold

[An English dictionary] must everywhere preserve the line firm and distinct between itself and an encyclopedia.

Richard Chenevix Trench, *On Some Deficiencies in Our English Dictionaries*

Two issues were uppermost in Gove's mind when he met with the Editorial Board for the first time on November 20, 1951. One was how to make space for tens of thousands of new words in the Third Edition. The other was how to limit the role of the board, which was composed of key personnel from both the editorial and business sides of the company.[1] In Gove's opinion, it had been too intrusive during the preparation of the Second Edition. Chairman Munroe opened the meeting by pointing the way. The goals of the Third Edition, he said, were to maintain the traditions of the company, meet the needs of the 1960s, and succeed in the marketplace. He then turned the proceedings over to Gove.

Of Gove's two agenda items, the issue of space was more pressing, though less touchy. For the first time in the company's history, the editors could not make space for more entries simply by adding pages to the dictionary. At nearly 3,400 pages over all and five inches thick, the Second Edition had reached the physical limits of the one-volume format to which the company had long been committed. To bring the unabridged up to date, the editors would have to offset the additional entries by deleting an equivalent amount of material from the preceding edition. In the process, Gove noted, there would have to be "complete and detailed scrutiny of every feature," something Neilson had promised in making the Second Edition. "We can claim no less and do no less," he said. About 75 percent of the new work would be "scrupulously revised" material from the preceding edition, 10 percent would be accepted without revision, and 15 percent of the space would be allowed for new entries.

The need to expand the vocabulary without lengthening the book forced a reexamination of what a dictionary should include. For more than three centuries – beginning with the publication of Henry Cockeram's *English Dictionarie* of 1623 – the dominant trend in dictionary making had been toward greater inclusiveness. Cockeram introduced descriptions of living creatures and other things that were conventionally treated in encyclopedias – in contrast to Robert Cawdrey, whose first English dictionary two decades earlier had been limited to the definitions of words.[2]

Cockeram's successors, in turn, not only expanded the coverage of the standard vocabulary but also added other kinds of encyclopedic information in the belief that general reference material was popular with readers and helped to sell books. Almost every new work was expected to be bigger than its predecessors, and little thought was given to the criteria for selecting additional material. Dictionaries competed by offering "more" – more words, more information on etymology, pronunciation, and usage, and more encyclopedic information (which often had the advantage of being easier for editors to obtain and present than linguistic information). Improvements in quality and the touting of the editor's reputation were also important in the competitive struggle, but the easily measured factor of size remained an indispensable and unquestioned part of the selling effort.

The intense rivalry between the Worcester and Webster factions during the War of the Dictionaries greatly increased the incentive to add encyclopedic features. One revealing episode accounts for the biggest infusion of encyclopedic information into the Merriam dictionaries. It was supplied by William Wheeler, a writer and editor, who provided services for both publishers. First, Wheeler prepared an appendix entitled "Names of Men of Modern Times" for Worcester's 1860 dictionary. Later, he went to work for the Merriam company and produced a far more ambitious supplement for the 1864 unabridged dictionary. Wheeler's supplement included names of fictional characters and places in literature, as well as ten more appendixes presenting proper names in the Bible, names in Greek and Latin languages, modern biographical and geographical names, pictorial illustrations, foreign quotations, and the like. It filled 171 pages, about 10 percent of the 1864 edition.

Wheeler's list was incorporated almost in its entirety into the 1890 Merriam-Webster *International*, and additional entries of a similar nature were inserted at the same time. Both the 1909 and 1934 editions, in turn, picked up these compilations. To make room for new material in 1909, the editors introduced the device of the divided page – placing below a horizontal line near the bottom of the page less important, obsolete, or highly technical entries, which were more briefly treated and were printed in smaller type. As a result of this accretion and retention, Gove later observed, more than two-thirds of Wheeler's 1864 entries were still treated as "current allusions" in 1934, though they were, in fact, no longer current.[3]

With the publication of *Webster's Second* in 1934, the number of entries, including the encyclopedic materials, rose to more than 600,000. The publisher's proud claim was that this edition contained more entries than any other dictionary in any language.

This achievement also brought the company to a turning point. Either it would have to adopt a two-volume format for its next edition or, if it maintained the one-volume tradition, it would have to trim back some of the material in the Second Edition to make space for new entries. The publication of separate desk dictionaries of biographical and geographical information in 1943 and 1949, respectively, seemed to point toward a reduction of encyclopedic material in the next unabridged that would make possible the continuation of the one-volume format.

DECIDING WHAT TO OMIT

At first, board members had hoped that the space problem could be solved by modest adjustments, such as eliminating the lengthy biographical and geographical appendixes and incorporating the most important entries to the main vocabulary. But that possibility faded when Bethel presented his estimate that at least three hundred pages of material from the Second Edition would have to be dropped. Since the biographical and geographical appendixes totaled only two hundred pages, the editors would still have to identify deletions equal to one hundred additional pages of material even if they omitted the two appendixes in their entirety. Presumably, these further cuts would be made from encyclopedic material embedded in the main entries. The term *nonlexical* came to be used by the editorial staff for "all matter not accepted for inclusion in the Third Edition."[4]

The problem was more than a lack of space; it was a matter of substance as well. Successive editions of the unabridged had failed to keep the encyclopedic material up to date. Gove noted that in the 1934 edition hundreds of lines were given to titles and characters of Dickens but none to works and characters of Somerset Maugham, Thomas Mann, Oscar Wilde, or Eugene O'Neill. To bring Wheeler's design up to date would require adding several thousand entries. More space would be needed for nonlexical matter if it were to be held to the same standards as the vocabulary entries. This expansion not only would be costly but would be impossible to do in a one-volume edition.

Although board members could see the logic of the arguments of Bethel and Gove, several retained a protective feeling toward one feature or another – the names of the most important people and geographical features, the most popular given names, the most important mythological characters. Munroe and another board member, Walter Thwing (also a member of the Board of Directors), stubbornly pointed to the danger of ignoring user expectations; they warned against editorial judgments based on scholarly standards only. If the market for Merriam dictionaries was limited to scholars, the issue would be simpler, but it was essential to include information that interested the average reader. They believed it would be suicide to eliminate all encyclopedic matter.

Gove remained convinced, however, that "it is physically and financially impossible for the 3rd ed. to go on expanding in the same way. . . . A one-volume dictionary and encyclopedia combined is not feasible and not even sustainable without facilities now unavailable and a type of research not now being carried on." Therefore, he said the Third Edition would have to be "primarily a DICTIONARY OF THE STANDARD LANGUAGE as used throughout the English speaking world."[5]

At length, the board approved a recommendation permitting the editors to eliminate or greatly reduce several categories of nonlexical material. The categories were later revised in a memo distributed to

Table 1. *Summary of the types of material omitted or shortened in the making of* Webster's Third

Material omitted

The gazeteer and biographical appendixes; the "Abbreviations" and "Arbitrary Signs and Symbols" sections; the "Brief History of the English Language"

All foreign terms except those that had been anglicized or used as technical terms in such fields as law and music (*quid pro quo, da capo*)

Given names (*Jonathan, Louisa*) and nicknames and epithets (*Great Commoner, Keystone State*)

Names and titles of written works and works of art (*As You Like it, Sistine Madonna*); characters in fiction, drama, legend, folklore, and mythology (*Banquo, Robin Hood, Achilles*)

Names of persons in the Bible and saints (*Barabbas, Deborah, Saint Anthony*)

Names of cities and states as nouns (but included where treated as adjectives defined formulaically, for example, "of or from the city of Chicago, Ill.: of the kind or style prevalent in Chicago")

Names of rivers, lakes, currents (*Gulf Stream*)

Names of stars, constellations, comets

Names of districts, buildings, etc. (*Latin Quarter, Empire State Building*)

Names of battles and treaties; historical events; legislative acts; legal cases

Names of organizations – academic, social, religious

Mottoes, proverbs, famous sayings (*ad astra per aspera*)

The divided page and the pronunciation key at the bottom of each page

Material shortened

Rare, obsolete, and technical terms in special fields

Slang, dialect, and other nonstandard or substandard terms

The "Guide to Pronunciation" in the front matter (reduced by half)

Black and white illustrations (reduced by half)

Source: Adapted from the text of Philip B. Gove, "The Nonlexical and the Encyclopedic," *Names,* 13(June 1965):108–10.

the editorial staff in October 1954. The memo became part of the so-called Black Books – a guide for editors and assistants, which would eventually grow to more than six hundred pages of single-spaced instructions in black loose-leaf binders. (The list of omissions is summarized in Table 1.)

The difference between words omitted and words retained, Gove explained, was chiefly the difference between the proper noun and the common noun. "The proper noun as substantive noun is the only part of speech that is here to be considered nonlexical. Proper adjectives (*Canadian bacon*), attributive nouns (*Canada goose, macadam road*) and verbs (*Fletcherize*) . . . will be treated on the basis of usage."[6] Proper names that had extended meanings, such as *Judas, Quisling, Babbitt, Pyrrhic,* were to be retained. However, trademarks and brand names that had not become generic or that had not lost their brand identity were to be omitted as nonlexical.

His instructions to editors also listed examples contrasting lexical and nonlexical terms according to Third Edition criteria, such as

Nonlexical	Lexical
U.S. Coast Guard	coast guard
Missouri (state)	Missourian
Colosseum	coliseum

Gove also devised guidelines that were intended to save some explanatory material while adhering to the logic of a dictionary of the standard language. Though proper nouns would be omitted as entries, he said, many would appear in compounds (*achilles' heel*), or as adjectives, or as common nouns (*hercules* for any man of great strength).

Moreover, proper nouns might properly be included as part of a definition or etymology. Gove advised his staff that every deletion of a nonlexical term "imposes a responsibility for covering in 3d ed the constituent lexical terms. Because *Chinese Wall* is an entry in W34, the editor who approved it was not concerned whether the definition of *wall* could cover the specific use in *Chinese Wall,*" but it would be a consideration in revising the definition for the Third Edition.[7]

The Third Edition does in fact follow this admonition of 1954. The definition of *wall* includes the illustrative phrase "The Great Chinese ~ was 1500 miles long." The amount of information is much less than was included in the 1934 entry under *Chinese Wall,* but in Gove's view it was a useful illustration of a lexical term, however inadequate the description might be for an encyclopedia entry.

Gove offered a two-part rationale for his policy. He argued, first, that someone who wanted to know about the Chinese Wall should consult an encyclopedia. Second, he said that a person who turned to a dictionary for the meaning of *wall* would be helped to understand its many senses by the *Chinese Wall* citation, which illustrated the sense of *wall* as a strong fortification extending over some distance and serving as a boundary between territories or countries.

Gove wrote, "We need not hesitate to refer to a country of the world . . . a state of the U.S. . . . a city . . . or to George Washington or the U.S. Air Force if contextually appropriate in a definition proper, in a verbal illustration (as is now done in W34 at *declaration, n3* by mentioning the Declaration of Independence), or in a usage note."[8]

Gove conceded a point emphasized by Munroe, that there was a great risk in dropping material that had come to be expected by the users of the Merriam unabridged dictionaries, but he did not accept Munroe's contention that wholesale deletions would necessarily lead to "disaster." Gove thought they would be accepted if properly explained. Similar deletions had been made without incident in the past – such as the elimination of the separate section of pictorial illustrations by the editors of the Second Edition. That success could be repeated, he believed, if the editorial and sales staffs put forth explanations and sales messages that would make clear to buyers the reasons for the change in scope.

As demonstrated by the subsequent attacks on *Webster's Third* for omitting encyclopedic material, Munroe's fears were more prescient than Gove's optimism, in large part because of Gove's failure to publish the rationale for the omissions until 1965, and then only in a scholarly journal of very limited circulation. Explanations within the Third Edition itself or in the promotional material issued by the company proved inadequate to make clear to journalistic critics what had been omitted and why.

The preface to the Third Edition, for example, only begins to suggest the nature of the decision: "The demands for space have made necessary a fresh judgment on the claims of many parts of the old vocabulary. The dictionary is the result of a highly selective process in which discarding material of insubstantive or evanescent quality has gone hand in hand with adding terms that have obtained a place in the language. It confines itself strictly to generic words and their functions, forms, sounds, and meanings as distinguished from proper names that are not generic. Selection is guided by usefulness." As a summary, this is fair enough, but it leaves too much unsaid to be comprehensible to the average reader.

Although the decision to dispense with encyclopedic material was driven by practical considerations, the result was a policy consistent with an alternative tradition in lexicographical thinking associated with Johnson, Trench, and the *OED*. It did not reflect a new departure in dictionary making, but rather a shift from one tradition to another equally well established. In setting limits on what he would admit into his work, Johnson wrote: "As my design was a dictionary, common or appellative, I have omitted all words which have a relation to proper names . . . but have retained those of a more general nature, such as Heathen, Pagan."[9]

Dean Trench went further, making a sharp distinction between the role of the dictionary and the role of the encyclopedia. Trench criticized English dictionaries of earlier times because they "are not Dictionaries of words, but of persons, places, things; they are gazetteers, mythologies, scientific encyclopedias, and a hundred things more; all, of course, most imperfectly, even according to the standard of knowledge of their own time, and with a selection utterly capricious." He called for the expulsion of "these mere intruders and interlopers" to make room for the material needed to make a complete dictionary of words. Although he dwelled primarily on what was missing from dictionaries of the era, he pointed out that it was as necessary to know what to leave out as what to put in.[10]

This view is reflected in James A. H. Murray's exclusion of names of people and places from the *OED*, except when used attributively or as adjectives. That is, the *OED* had no biographical entry for *Shakespeare*, or *Shakspere*, but it had an entry for *Shakesperian*. It contained no geographical entry on the city of London, but it did enter and define the compounds in which London was used attributively, such as *London black* and *London clay*, as well as *Londoner* and *Londonize*. In short, what Trench advocated, and Johnson and Murray did as a matter of principle, Gove did according to a policy imposed by circumstances. It may have been his preference as well. But his practice was not understood by his detractors, who were not aware of the precedents he was following and thus attacked him unfairly for inconsistency and worse.

LIMITING THE BOARD'S ROLE

Gove's second major agenda item arose from his reading of the editorial board files for the Second Edition. The president during that period, Asa G. Baker, was the only president in company history who had a solid knowledge of both the business and editorial sides of the operation. An Amherst graduate, he had gained editorial experience on the editions of 1890 and 1909. That fact, plus the presence of a scholar of Dr. Neilson's stature as editor in chief, seems to have turned editorial board meetings into forums for unprecedented discussion of editorial matters that contrasted with the practices followed by the Merriam brothers and their immediate successors.

Gove's review of the record had persuaded him that the Editorial Board had meddled in editorial affairs. Its excessively detailed records indicated that it had intervened on matters that ought to have been left to the editors. He wanted the board's responsibilities clarified so that editorial decisions and procedures could be carried out in an orderly and efficient manner. Although the 1951 meeting was his first with the board since he had become managing editor, he did not hesitate to put the issues bluntly and press for a change in the board's work:

The minutes of the Editorial Board for [the] Second Edition occupy about 2000 typescript pages and fill eleven volumes. To me, that represents a stupendous, if not a stultifying, waste of time. I don't think we have the time to prepare these Editorial Board minutes from now until publication at the same fullness. What kind of material do you want? . . . I have a memo here which consists of thirty single-space pages on the subject "Repetition in Definitions." . . . Every point is itemized in clear detail, with all possible methods considered. . . . It is a scholarly piece of work. It would take anyone hours to digest and follow it. Do you want that sort of thing mimeographed and distributed before meetings? Can we afford the expense and the time of it?[11]

Gove acknowledged that he had implied his answer by the way he asked the question. These issues did not affect policy "in the larger sense of the term." They ought to be left to the editorial staff or summarized briefly for reference. He recognized that the board represented the company directors and had the responsibility for integrating editorial processes and publishing policies to prevent misunderstanding, but questioned how far it must go into detailed editorial decisions in order to fulfill its function without wasting time: "I understand that the Editorial Board for [the] Second Edition spent at least an hour discussing whether *hot dog* was to be entered. Just as soon as you get down to specific words rather than policy that type of thing is inevitable . . . and there is no reason to believe that differences of opinion in these matters will be clarified by bringing them before the board."[12]

Gove pointed out that preliminary memos on editorial policies governing etymology and several other editorial matters had been drafted by the staff and challenged the board on its need to see them. "We have taken the best means I know of to assure ourselves that we are doing the right things on these questions, and that is the hiring of editors competent in their fields. I should like to know if you agree with me that mimeographing and distributing such material is a waste of time."[13]

Differences between business policy and editorial policy were discussed at length, along with the scope of the editor's authority and responsibilities. In the end, the board concurred that the editor should have full control over editorial matters along with the clear responsibility to notify the board of editorial matters that impinged on business policy. In addition, memos on editorial policy would be put in a master book of editorial minutes, and digests of decisions would be provided to the board. "I don't want a vote," Gove said. "If there are any objections, the objection can be put on the record."[14]

Munroe went along reluctantly with the decision after noting some of the difficulties in distinguishing between editorial and business responsibilities. The company had learned from the preceding edition that even well-intentioned editorial decisions could backfire. Trademark entries had aroused protests from firms that feared that their product names might be jeopardized by wording in the dictionary. Minority and professional groups were offended by words and phrases that seemed innocuous to the editors. Even routine definitions had caused embarrassment, *journalistic,* for example, and *supersede.*

The definition of *journalistic* in the Second Edition, which had deeply angered newspaper and magazine writers and editors, resulted from an unusual slip, if not a unique one. It read, "characteristic of journalism or journalists; hence, of style, characterized by evidences of haste, superficiality of thought, inaccuracies of detail, colloquialisms and sensationalism; journalese." Only the five words before the first semicolon were appropriate. The rest, beginning with "hence," belonged with the definition of *journalese,* where, indeed, similar words were used.[15]

How had this mistake occurred? A check of the citation file for

Webster's Second turned up no helpful clues, only a surprise – there were no citations showing the use of *journalistic* in the file. A surmise, suggested by Bethel and Gove, was that the definition had been written in haste late in the project and had somehow escaped the required review by another editor. It was equally plausible that bias as well as haste had been to blame, given the disdain for journalistic writing often echoed in literary circles. Both Bethel and Gove saw the incident simply as evidence that human error was inescapable in so vast a book, despite the careful recruiting and hiring practices that were followed and the rigid requirements for editorial review and proofing; they saw no evidence of a failure in the system.

The row over *supersede,* however, arose not from an error but from an accurate statement that was perceived as a disparagement. The offending statement had appeared in a verbal illustration written to show the meaning of the word in context. It read, "gas has been *superseded* in large measure by electricity." The illustration was innocent in intention, but gas companies were infuriated by it. In later printings, a more bland example replaced the original on page 2533: "new methods have superseded those in use last year."

Trademark, however, was known to be a sensitive issue, one that might well call for consultation with the president or board. Ironically, despite this awareness and the precautions taken to avoid a recurrence of previous misunderstandings, it was the policy on trademarks that would lead to one of the sharpest confrontations following the publication of the Third Edition (see Chapter 12).

IN FULL COMMAND

Less than a week after the editorial board met, Bethel put into writing several recommendations that he had discussed with President R. N. Fuller over the preceding weeks about editorial leadership in the future. He had been in ill health for some time and wanted to step down as general editor, effective September 1, 1952. He recommended that Gove be appointed to succeed him and that he be given control over all editorial personnel to make sure that work on the Third Edition would enjoy the highest priority. In addition, Bethel argued that Gove be given the title editor in chief. Bethel believed that he himself should have received the title when the search for a figurehead editor had been abandoned, but he had not wanted to press the matter since it might appear to be self-serving. He felt no such hesitancy in urging the title for Gove.

Gove was given Bethel's job, as recommended, but the title of editor in chief was withheld until completion of the editorial work on the Third Edition. For Bethel, resignation after twenty-two satisfying years was very painful, but as he noted in a farewell memo to Fuller, the "distress of the occasion will be lessened a great deal by the knowledge that in my new domicile in Nassau, the Bahamas, I shall be able to continue as an employee of the company on a part-time basis."[16] Over the next few years, Bethel's job as a consultant was to review entries in the Second Edition and suggest how they should be revised for the Third Edition.

UPSTAIRS, DOWNSTAIRS

One of the problems that Gove inherited was a simmering hostility between the business staff and the editorial staff that had worsened during President Fuller's last months. The two staffs were physically isolated from each other. The president and the sales and business departments occupied the first floor of the building on Federal Street; the president and key executives had private offices. Editorial staff members occupied the second floor. Most of them sat at desks rather closely spaced in one large room that also contained banks of file cabinets filled with citations and other materials. There was a small room for science editors, another for typists, and one for proof-readers. The surroundings were Spartan, but not uncomfortable or inconvenient. Gove had a large office, which he later shared with H. Bosley Woolf, his eventual successor. The two of them continued to occupy the same room for five years after Gove stepped down as editor in chief in 1967 and became a consultant.

The allocation of space and the arrangement of desks were standard for offices at the time, and they functioned well. It was not physical separation that troubled the editors in the early 1950s, though it might have heightened a sense of isolation, but rather their belief that their work was undervalued and their status inferior to that of employees downstairs. They were, they felt, paid lower salaries and were accorded less recognition. In early 1953, shortly after Gordon J.

Gallan, the advertising manager, succeeded Fuller as president, Gove decided that the problem had to be addressed. At home, on the night of February 24, he wrote a bold memorandum to Gallan, covering three and a half double-spaced typed pages. The following excerpts indicate its tone and purpose:

May I presume upon the fact that I am older than you by a few months . . . and by a few years in service to the Company to make a proposal that I ask you to weigh and consider very carefully. I am typing this myself at home, which explains the necessity for numerous corrections, because I do not want anyone in the Company to know of its existence unless with your approval.

Our company has two chief jobs: selling dictionaries and making dictionaries. . . . They are dependent one upon the other; there would be no point in making dictionaries that could not be sold and we would be betraying our trust and undermining our responsibility . . . if were to sell dictionaries that were any less well made than the best of which we are capable. Obviously, cooperation and understanding between those in charge of these two jobs are essential. On this we have already agreed. . . .

As self-evident as these statements would seem to be, there is considerable evidence (which I need not go into) that their significance has often been disregarded, sometimes deliberately and sometimes unavoidably because of clash of temperament or incompatibility. . . . During the recent fall and winter months I have had occasional reasons for fearing that . . . the split was becoming more serious than ever.

Gove went on to explain, however, that he was encouraged by the signs of improvement during the short period since Gallan had become president. He now felt that the company could "rise to new heights in both editorial accomplishments and in sales accomplishments." He added:

To attain it, you need the help of all your staff, and particularly our editorial staff. We need a stimulus that will give us the feeling of cooperation. . . . My proposal for your consideration is that you symbolize our joint efforts by asking the directors to make your general editor also a Company vice president.

If this were done, I could at once inform members of my Department that the distinction had been conferred not upon me but upon them so that they grasp and share in the symbolized hope.

Gove disavowed any pursuit of personal gain: "To a scholar devoted to the English language and its lexicography no higher distinction could come than has already been given to me, the opportunity to be editor-in-chief of a major edition of *Webster's New International Dictionary*." He added that he had only scratched the surface of the situation – "the problems run very deep" – and he requested an opportunity to discuss the matter in person.[17]

The vice-presidency was never conferred, but the problems were apparently eased or resolved. Gove, who said the memo was written with "much hesitation and some courage," remained on good terms with Gallan.

GOVE'S MANAGERIAL STYLE had by this time – a year and a half after his promotion – established him as an aloof boss who worked tirelessly in his own office, eschewed meetings, and seldom conferred with others. He socialized only at lunch in the company dining room, and with a rather limited number of staff members. He trusted his own judgment and acted on his own except in areas of specialization where he placed great trust in his top associates. He delegated the responsibility for etymology to Charles Sleeth, for example, and for pronunciation to Edward Artin. The top definers, Mairé Weir Kay, Hubert Kelsey, and others, worked on their own. Administrative responsibilities were delegated to Anne Driscoll.

Nonetheless, Gove was always a formidable presence, and he put great pressure on his staff, has he did on himself, to get work done efficiently and rapidly. He left no doubt about his strong commitment to his job and deep loyalty to the Merriam company.

His promptness was legendary. He was at his desk before 8 a.m. every morning; he left at 5 p.m. Even after a heavy snowfall, when staff members who lived a mile or two away tended to arrive late, Gove, who had to drive some twenty-five miles from his farm in Warren to Springfield, arrived on time as usual. Grace would make a first pass down the driveway with the plow so that he could get through on his four-wheel-drive Scout.

Time wasting was anathema to him. On the job, he was impatient with the kind of easy talk and professional gossip that he associated with academic life in the prewar era. He imposed a virtual rule of silence. Editors were supposed to be able to work on their own and not interrupt one another with questions. When questions were necessary, they were generally written on pink slips and distributed to the appropriate desk, to be answered in writing or in person during a break or after work. Gove believed that interruptions were unsettling for both parties. Either one of two things would happen. The less likely was that the questioner would get a helpful answer to the query. More likely, both parties would simply waste time and would find it difficult to get back on track.

Even after the Third Edition was completed, the office environment and atmosphere remained much the same. Anne H. Soukhanov, who joined the Merriam staff in 1970 during the buildup for the eighth *New Collegiate*, recalls that what impressed her most when she was taken to see the working conditions on the second floor was the silence of the editorial room, which she likened to the main reading room of the Library of Congress. She said that when she became executive editor of *The American Heritage Dictionary* years later, she was strongly influenced in her managerial approach by her recollections of the work environment at the Merriam company.[18]

Gove was equally impatient with time wasting at home, according to his children; and his neighbors had the same impression of his attitude. When he became a member of the local school board, he was appalled by the dallying at evening meetings that sometimes ran on until almost midnight. After a couple of prolonged sessions, he said that there was no reason why all business could not be completed by 10 p.m. and that he would henceforth walk out at that time. The board soon fell into line.

He was a stickler for the rules, whether they pertained to office routine, such as the company's no-smoking regulations, or to editorial policy. But it was his stubbornness – or "rigidity," as some described it – in following the guidelines in the Black Books that struck staff members, especially those who were more used to a collegial environment.

Attempts to persuade him to be more flexible in dealing with unusual circumstances uniformly failed, and even if a request had little merit, Gove's rejection of it reinforced the assumption that he was simply being stubborn. A publicized disagreement over wine definitions described in the next chapter illustrates how even a reasonable exercise of authority was sometimes confused with authoritarianism by critical staff members. Nonetheless, sometimes Gove put greater emphasis on fidelity to principle than on the quality of the solution – and he acknowledged it to staff members and to outsiders. The impression was strengthened by Gove's brusque manner of expressing himself when he was in disagreement with something that had been said or written.

Gove disliked dealing face to face with staff members, which contributed to his apparent aloofness. He was more at ease in formal situations than in informal ones. Personnel matters made him uncomfortable, and he increasingly delegated them to others. In later years, Bosley Woolf took over most of the interviewing and hiring of editors, and it was to him that staff members turned when they had questions and encountered problems. Gove was usually content to set forth the guidelines and rules and check the results, with very little supervisory attention.

MOVING AHEAD

In response to the great measure of independence that had been given to him by the Editorial Board, Gove began submitting informal reports to the president of the company in mid-1952. The first covered his initial year as managing editor. The others followed at approximately six-month intervals. The final one – Number 18, dated January 10, 1961 – reported the shipment of the last page of copy to the compositor.

The first report struck the highly optimistic tone that became characteristic of Gove's outlook until the late 1950s. Addressing first the two most important needs that faced him when he took over, planning and hiring staff members, he wrote, "I can report confidently that both needs have been met."[19]

He described the planning process that had begun with a review of the eleven volumes of editorial minutes for the Second Edition and the directives issued by the general editor, Thomas A. Knott. Some preliminary notes had also been prepared for the Third Edition. With this information, it became possible to begin the preparation of an "editor's instruction book" (the Black Books) and to issue some miscellaneous directives. Early topics for the Black Books included instructions for marking editorial copy and for handling cross-references, typography, and style; some of these were revised later in the light of greater experience. Also prepared in preliminary form were notes on abbreviations, etymological style, the order of senses, and so on. Detailed memos on defining, etymology, pronunciation, and many less complicated matters followed over a period of some three years. Targets were also set for the completion of all the editorial and production steps, as well as for the remaining research tasks that would continue while work went forward on defining and other steps in the preparation of the new entries and revisions of the old ones.

An enormous clerical task, which required some five years to accomplish, was also nearly finished that year. Every definition and every sense in the 1947 printing of the Second Edition was clipped and placed on three-by-five slips, which were sorted into 107 categories from aeronautics to zoology; many slips might be required to accommodate the definitions of a single word. All etymologies were divided into 18 groups according to linguistic lineages or affiliations, a task that alone required more than a year.

In the next decade, millions of three-by-five slips would go through several hands before they were assembled for transmittal to the printer. Essentially, the system was an old one in the field of lexicography that had been refined over two hundred years. That it was carried out virtually without error in both the Second and Third Editions was an extraordinary feat.

Gove reported that after interviewing more than a hundred candidates, he had hired twenty-six new staff members: assistant editors, editorial assistants, and readers for the gathering of citations, in addition to typists and file clerks. Among the assistant editors were two who played key roles and became associate editors. Howard G. Rhoads, who obtained his doctorate at the University of Pennsylvania and had taught at several universities, began work on March 31, 1952; he was the first of the group to arrive. Philip H. Goepp, a Johns Hopkins University Ph.D., who had been on the faculty at the City College of New York and the University of Rochester, followed on May 26. Goepp and Rhoads stayed until the dictionary was finished – providing stability amid the turnover that marked the rest of the decade.[20]

By the time Gove submitted his second report in November 1952, he was able to state that more than sixty-nine full-time and five part-time staff members had been hired; only two positions remained unfilled, those of illustrations editor and reader. More than two-thirds of the full-time newcomers were editors and readers; most of the others were typists.

Gove said that his target was to begin sending copy to the printer at the beginning of 1957 with the objective of publication in mid-1959. He estimated that there would be 400,000 entries in the volume, which would total 3,400 pages.

The citation files were growing steadily. About 1.5 million examples of usage had been gathered since the completion of the Second Edition. With the hiring of additional readers to search a wide range of periodicals and books for examples of current usage, Gove estimated that 500,000 citations would be added each year through 1955. These would become the basis for writing definitions of new words and new senses of old words, along with the updating of the illustrative quotations used in earlier Merriam dictionaries to show the meaning of words in context. He also reported that some 50,000 definitions had been drafted and were ready for review and approval – approximately 12 percent of the estimated total to be prepared.

If work proceeded according to plan, he concluded, "there is reason to feel assured that the assumption at the beginning of this report will be realized and that the 3d edition can be successfully published in 1959 as planned."[21]

The optimism was excessive. It rested on the assumption that the editorial and production schedules could be substantially speeded up by careful planning, improvements in efficiency, and greater effort. But the work, which was expected to require ten years, was already two years behind schedule when Gove became managing editor in 1951.

PART II

The Making of the Dictionary: Gove's Aims and Practices

5

The Meaning of Words: Definers at Work

For all practical purposes, the defining part of a dictionary is by far the most important.

Noah Webster, Preface to An American Dictionary

It was to the task of defining that Gove devoted his greatest attention. He held strong convictions about how definitions should be written and how illustrative quotations should be selected. Troubled by lapses in objectivity in some Second Edition definitions, he was determined to prevent editorializing in the new edition. He also had some personal ideas about editorial style.

Having delegated the chief responsibility for etymology to Sleeth and for pronunciation to Artin, he took the leading role himself in preparing the guidelines for definers. Shortly after becoming managing editor, he began meeting periodically with three senior associates – Edward F. Oakes, who had worked on the Second Edition, Sleeth, and Anne Driscoll. From these meetings emerged his first tentative memorandum on defining – "jottings" he called it – which was distributed to the staff in April 1952. During the ensuing years, other editors were consulted on special topics.

THE SEPARATION OF SENSES

Among the most daunting of these topics was one that lies at the heart of the definer's task: the separation of senses – identifying the different meanings a word may convey in different contexts and capturing new meanings when they appear in speech and writing. The little word *set* offers a striking example of how complicated this work can become. Samuel Johnson, the first master of the art of discriminating senses, devoted five pages of his great dictionary of 1755 to the definition of *set* and its compounds, for which he identified more than ninety senses. Two centuries later, *Webster's Third* listed about twice that number, arranged as follows:

- forty numbered senses as a transitive verb (*set* the table, *set* pen to paper, *set* a record),
- sixteen senses as an intransitive verb (the sun *sets*, how long will it take for the cement to *set?*),
- eleven senses as an adjective (*set* in his ways, all *set* to stay),
- forty-seven senses as a noun (a *set* of dishes, the younger *set*, a stage *set*),
- scores of compound forms of *set* used to convey other meanings, some included as run-ons to the main listing, others (such as *set back, set down,* and *set up*) entered in their alphabetical places.

Although *set* is an exceptional word, proliferation of meanings and versatility of function are apparent on every page of an unabridged dictionary. Many other words bear heavy semantic burdens – such as *do, go, make, open, shake* – and in functioning as a verb, noun, and adjective, *set* is overshadowed by other words that almost run the gamut of parts of speech. *Like,* for example, serves as a verb (they *like* each other), noun (he has many *likes*), adjective (a *like* number), adverb (more *like* a dozen), preposition (she looks *like* her sister), and conjunction (*like* a duck takes to water – a use that has been much disputed though it has a long history).[1]

Native speakers of English take the great variety of senses in stride. No conscious sorting and selecting are required. The context of an utterance (or writing) makes clear the sense that fits the occasion. They are not aware of having to decide when *magazine* means reading matter and when it means storehouse. C. S. Lewis refers to this as "the insulating power of context"; that is, "the sense of a word is governed by the context and this sense normally excludes all others from the mind."[2]

However, the definer, working from a file of citations, must consider every one consciously and decide whether it is another example of an established sense or connotes a new and distinctive sense that should be recorded separately. A noted lexicographer, J. R. Hulbert, commented that "the difficulty of discerning the different meanings and determining their logical arrangement and the time and energy which they require are inconceivable to anyone who has not worked on an historical dictionary."[3] Though not a historical dictionary, *Webster's Third* presented a challenge to definers that was no less formidable since it was to be an unabridged dictionary of the contemporary vocabulary as it had evolved over the past two hundred years.

Aware of the difficulties, Gove asked Donald Lee to explore the matter during the early 1950s and develop criteria for coping more effectively with the separation of senses. Since the Merriam company employed a large staff that was subject to considerable turnover, it was important to establish criteria that would lead to greater uniformity in judgment among definers. Lee made a painstaking search through the work and papers of earlier lexicographers and the writings of linguists and semanticists, but came away disappointed. He concluded: "Rather grotesquely, after centuries of lexicography and language study of one sort or another, it appears that no one has answered the question of how we may know with sharp clarity and definitive exactness when a word has one meaning alone . . . and when it has two or more quite discrete meanings." There was no choice, he added, but to proceed by rule-of-thumb guidelines.[4]

In his speculative moments, Gove thought about practical ways to deal with the problem. The key to greater consistency, he thought, might lie in matching words and definers. Work could be assigned with that end in mind, since most definers seemed to fall into one of two groups. Some were "meaning-finders" and some were "meaning-losers." Crawford Lincoln, assistant to the president, recalls Gove's musings as follows:

Imagine someone lying out in a field on a sunny day looking up at the white puffy clouds overhead and seeing a cloud in the shape that resembled a dog. He would exclaim, "See the dog up there in the sky." The meaning-finder would want to write a sense under the word *dog*, "a cloud in the shape of a dog." The meaning-finder would be forever searching for nuances and seeking out additional senses almost to the point of absurdity.

The meaning-loser, on the other hand, confronted by an overabundance of citational evidence for a great number of senses, would suggest a grouping and coalescing of meanings under fewer senses. What Phil envisioned was assigning words like *run* and *set* to the meaning-losers and words with narrower applications to the meaning-finders.[5]

Inescapably, the definer's separation of meaning into senses retained an aspect of the arbitrariness that characterizes much of lexicography, from the selection of words to be included to the choice of sources for reading and marking, and much more. As Gove was fond of saying, "Lexicography is an art as well as a science."

Not only do senses have to be differentiated from one another, but they must also be arranged in a way that seems logical to the user. In Merriam-Webster dictionaries, the pattern was well established. Senses were arranged in historical order, as far as it could be determined, the oldest meaning appearing first. After World War II, there was increasing support among commercial dictionary makers for an alternative arrangement of senses – listing the most common ones first. This practice had been a prominent feature of Funk & Wagnalls' unabridged *Standard Dictionary* of 1893, and it was adopted by the popular *American College Dictionary* of 1947; *Webster's New World* followed suit.

During the 1950s, the Merriam company felt the pressure for change from the sales staff, which reported that many university faculty members thought the arrangement of senses by frequency of use was preferable for their students. The issue was not one that provoked discussion among Third Edition editors, however. The historical order was a practical organizational guide and was thought to have the additional advantage of displaying the development of a word's meaning and thereby of contributing to the reader's understanding of the word. Merriam editors also argued that the advantage claimed for the alternative rested on the assumption that the sense most commonly used was also the one most commonly looked up in the dictionary. The opposite could be argued with equal plausibility – the most common use might be among the least likely to be looked up. Both views continue to have adherents.

CHANGES IN MEANING

The increase in the number of senses a word may signify is one aspect of the broader problem of change that besets the dictionary maker. Historically, new senses have emerged in response to changes needing to be expressed – changes in technology and ideas and in the way a society organizes and conducts itself. Where new senses do not suffice, new words are introduced, commonly made from the available

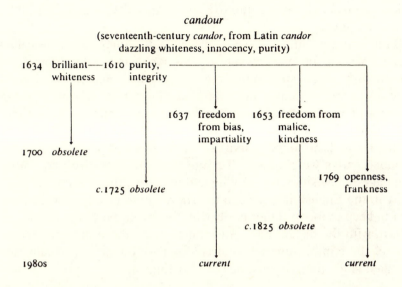

candour

(seventeenth-century *candor*, from Latin *candor*
dazzling whiteness, innocency, purity)

Figure 2. Changes in the meaning of *candor* since the seventeenth century. From Robert Burchfield, *The English Language*, 119. Copyright 1986, Oxford University Press. Reprinted with permission.

parts – roots of words, prefixes, suffixes, and so on or a simple blending of two words. Words "are capable of expansion fore and aft, as it were, to modify the meaning of the base word," as Robert Burchfield put it.[6]

In his book, *The English Language*, Burchfield drew on his experience in editing the supplement to the *OED* to illustrate how meaning changes over time. Among the examples he cites is *candor*, a Latin word that originally meant "dazzling whiteness" and that later took on the added senses of "innocence" and "purity." Its origin can be traced to the Latin *candidus*, meaning "white."

Candor entered English in the early 1600s and underwent successive changes in meaning over the next century and a half. It soon acquired two additional senses, "impartiality" and "kindliness," but not until the 1760s did it take on its most common current meaning, "frankness." Today, "frankness" and "impartiality" are the only senses still in use. The other meanings have become obsolete, as shown in Burchfield's diagram (Figure 2). (*Webster's Third*, however, also gives a twentieth-century citation for "whiteness," suggesting that this sense persisted longer in the United States.) Over time, the adjective *candid* also came into use, as did the adverb *candidly* and the noun *candidness.*

This is not an unusual word history, but neither can it be called typical. Many patterns of change are observable in the development of the English vocabulary. Sometimes the original meaning of a word survives as the principal meaning after new senses appear; at other times, a new sense takes over, but the old one continues to be used. Sometimes the current meaning bears no apparent relationship to the original, which no longer survives. The number of senses added and dropped varies widely. English is not peculiar in this respect; other languages show similar instability. Nonetheless, there is enough stability in the English language in the short run to enable each generation to keep in touch rather easily with the recent past and, to a lesser extent, with the distant past. And some words, those denoting members of the family, numbers, and colors, have remained virtually unchanged since their appearance in Old English.

TENDENCIES IN THE DRIFT OF MEANING

Who or what accounts for the use of *candor* in the sense of "impartiality" or "kindliness"? Why did one meaning catch on and retain its place in speech and writing while the other did not? Were the originators of a new sense searching for a metaphor, confusing *candor* with a different word, or groping for a word to express a sense they could not find in the recognized vocabulary? Though the answers to such questions can often be guessed at when new words and new senses are examined, for the most part they remain unanswerable.

More informative are generalizations inferred from changes in groups of words. It has been observed that words tend to drift toward either broader meanings or narrower ones, and toward either more pleasant connotations (amelioration) or increasingly negative ones (pejoration). The definer's task is to identify these changes and determine whether a new sense is distinctive and sufficiently widespread to warrant inclusion.

The tendency toward the generalization of meaning can be illustrated by the verb *go.* Originally *go* meant *walk,* but over time it came to mean motion from place to place by any means, not only by people and animals but by vehicles (Where are you going today? Does this bus go downtown? Are you going by ship?). The verb *discard,* which originally meant to put aside a playing card from one's hand, was expanded to mean any act of getting rid of things that have become superfluous or unpleasant. One can *discard* old clothes or old ideas.

The opposite trend toward specialization can also be observed. The noun *deer* was once a general term for animals; now the term applies only to a single animal family. *Meat* usually meant food of any kind (as in the phrase "meat and drink"); now it refers most commonly to animal flesh.

Shifts in connotation are apparent in the words *urbane, fond, villain,* and *hussy. Urbane* no longer means characteristic of a city, or relating to it, but rather very polite or polished. It has taken on a more elevated status. *Fond* originally meant foolish, but now means affectionate or loving, a similar improvement in connotation. In contrast, some words have become pejorative. In the feudal age a *villain* was a free peasant; today he is scoundrel. A *hussy,* once a housewife, is now a brazen woman.[7]

An obvious practical conclusion is that dictionaries must be revised periodically to reflect shifts in meaning, as well as to define new words. Another is that meaning depends on usage. It is the daily speech and writing of those who use the language that determine the current meaning of most English words – not etymology, nor philosophy, or a pronouncement by a noted linguist or editorial board. As a practical matter, the editor who defines a word for a dictionary today works from the evidence at hand – citations gathered from books, newspapers, and other periodicals, as well as earlier dictionaries. The first task of the definer is to find out what a word means. Then work can begin on composing a clear, concise, and complete definition.

But what seems so self-evident to lexicographers – that meaning depends on usage – makes many teachers, editors, and commentators on language uncomfortable. It strikes them as circular reasoning, dangerously close to the Wonderland assertion that a word "means just what I choose it to mean." They are reluctant to give up the notion that there is a "true" meaning of a word and that the lexicographer's job is to find it. Although they may acknowledge that many words in good standing today do not mean what they used to mean or perform a different function (or additional functions), they tend to regard such changes with suspicion, especially those that occur in their lifetime. Even Johnson and others who acknowledged the inevitability of change urged resistance to it in the hope of slowing it down. Change was viewed in the eighteenth century not as a process of adaptation but as a decline in the expressiveness and usefulness of the language. Johnson felt this strongly, and though he recognized the futility of trying to regulate language ("to enchain syllables, and to lash the wind are equally the undertakings of pride," he wrote in the preface to his dictionary), he still clung to the belief that it was reasonable to try to slow down the pace of change – a view that still attracts a wide following, for whom the poet John Ciardi, for example, has been an eloquent spokesman.

It was not uncommon, however, for writers and grammarians to look to etymology as the key to true meaning; some also argued that a word could properly have only one meaning, the etymological one.[8] Ambrose Bierce, an early-twentieth-century American author, confidently stated in a book on writing that the word *dilapidated* should be applied only to rundown *stone* structures, and not to deteriorating buildings made of wood or other materials, because etymology shows that the root word *lapis* means "stone" in Latin. It was also widely believed that the original sense of a word reflected a divine intent or a natural link between the word itself and the thing or idea it signified – between "what is" and the name for it – an issue that Plato explored nearly 2,400 years ago in the dialogue between Socrates and Cratylus.

Today, the view that a word may have several meanings is generally accepted by lexicographers and linguists, though the notion of one-word, one-meaning has not died out. A linguist, Charles Ruhl, contends that the differences in meaning attributed to such general verbs as *go, come,* and *take,* or the prepositions *of, in, out,* and *over,* as well as many other words, are not attributable to the word itself but to other words with which it is associated.[9] In popular discussions, moreover, the notion persists that the etymological or original meaning of a word is the correct one, even if it has been modified or superseded in common parlance. It is not unusual for spirited arguments over current meaning to be settled by recourse to etymology.

But even if etymology is not the authoritative source on *current* meaning, it can play a useful role in deepening one's understanding. Mitford Mathews considered it to be the "most fruitful way to approach meanings." He wrote, "Many times the etymology will illuminate not only a particular meaning but all the meanings a word has, and will show the way to related words and their meanings."

Among his many examples is the word *nausea*, "a classical Greek word in English dress. It is based upon another Greek word meaning a ship. The Greeks were acquainted with the miseries of sea-sickness, which their word *nausia* meant, but in thinking of this distress they focused attention on a ship rather than on the sea. Dictionaries in their etymologies point out that *nausea* is closely related to *nave* (of a church or cathedral), *nautical, naval,* each of them having this basic idea of a ship."[10] Etymology, in short, can be an aid to understanding and to memory, not a determiner of meaning, though the original meaning sometimes persists.

A NEW STYLE OF DEFINING

Gove's most distinctive innovation was a defining style that was intended to achieve precision and objectivity, and he drew attention to it with satisfaction in his preface to the Third Edition. It was also one of his most controversial ideas. It was opposed by some staff members who found it difficult to apply, and it was later singled out for attack by his detractors. His critics on the staff were primarily those who had been trained in the tradition of the Second Edition. Those who were recruited to work on the Third Edition adjusted to the new approach more readily. Gove wanted definitions to be expressed in good expository prose. He insisted that essential information be logically organized in a single coherent and clearly expressed phrase that needed no punctuation except where commas were essential to separate words or groups of words in a series. A comparison of the Second Edition's entry on *aardvark* with the entry in the Third Edition illustrates the change in approach introduced by Gove.

The Second Edition definition reads as follows: "Either of two African mammals of the genus *Orycteropus*. They attain the length of five feet, including the tail. They burrow in the ground, feeding entirely on ants, which they catch with the long slimy tongue. They constitute the order Tubilidentata."

Third Edition defines *aardvark* as "a burrowing nocturnal African mammal about five feet long that feeds on ants, has a long snout, a snakelike tongue, large ears, and a heavy tapering tail, and is usu. considered to form a single variable species (*Orycteropus afer*) that is the sole recent representative of the obscure mammalian order Tubilidentata – called also *ant bear, ant eater, earth pig.*"

The revision replaces a loose series of sentences with a structured statement in which key information appears first and related material is grouped logically. It offers more information about habits (nocturnal) and about appearance (long snout, etc.); it indicates the aardvark's uniqueness as a species; and it lists the other names by which it is known (ant eater, etc). There are no superfluous words or phrases such as "They attain the length of." One need only compare the first five words in the two entries to sense the sharper focus of the later definition.

The example also shows the danger inherent in the single-statement rule – it sometimes requires the defining phrase to run on to an unnatural length. Keeping a statement going and coherent until all the necessary information is imparted was a demanding requirement that not all definers adjusted to with equal ease. When difficulties arose, they did so in the definition of nouns; the critics later pounced on *door* and *groan*. Gove recognized the difficulties but considered strict adherence to the single statement to be more important than avoiding occasional instances of awkward and unnatural prose by relaxing the rule. In response to a criticism from James Sledd, he wrote:

I am well aware of the difficulties connected with our new defining technique, and I have recognized it frequently by use of the phrase "lexicographic license" to cover a style sometimes a little more involved than good rhetoric allows. Some of our best definers worked on this problem, but maybe the results are not as felicitous as possible. One thing I am sure of though: I'd dislike mightily to have to return to the loose style of the Second Edition. If I were to teach freshman English again I would require students, at least as an experiment, to write a few paragraphs with no commas. I would expect to see their style clarify and sharpen itself under such rigid restriction (as did that of most definers), which would be good even if they were allowed to return to normal afterwards.[11]

Sledd, though one of Gove's staunchest defenders in the controversy over the Third Edition, had stated, in the course of a generally supportive letter, that "your technique of definition seems to me to create some difficulty when you're defining nouns because a long stream of post-modifiers – prepositional phrases, participial phrases, relative clauses and the like – can quickly grow confusing in a language with so few inflections as English."[12]

Among the staff members, Hubert Kelsey was one of the most outspoken critics of Gove's approach to defining. He thought the single-statement formula unsuited to the scientific definitions with which he was concerned, and he was upset by the elimination of the subject labels that had been used in the past to highlight the field to which particular senses applied. They had been a very visible feature of the Second Edition, and Kelsey thought them very helpful to readers who were searching for the sense that applied to their particular field. They were italicized and frequently abbreviated – *Anat.*, *Law*, *Meteorol.*, and so on. Gove thought the practice unnecessary and sometime misleading, since a sense originating in a special field often came into general use in an unrelated context. Definers were still left with a number of labels to use – such as *slang, nonstandard,* and other status or stylistic labels, labels for regional and British expressions, and chronological labels (see Chapter 8).

THE SINGLE-STATEMENT DEFINING STYLE was superimposed on several well-established defining practices explained in the guidelines. The most important was the classic pattern of defining that emerges from elementary rules of logic and consists of two familiar steps: It classifies what is being defined – for example, "a hammer is a *tool*." Then it adds the distinguishing words indicating how a hammer differs from other tools: "A hammer is a *hand* tool *used for pounding*." The two parts of the analytic definition are the *genus* (tool) and the *differentiae* (everything else). Depending on the guidelines for the dictionary, additional differentiating information might be included to describe, for example, the head of the hammer and the handle.

Ideally, the genus word should be one that is more commonly used and more likely to be understood than the word being defined (the "definiendum"), though this goal is not always attainable, especially in the treatment of scientific words. The genus word must be neither too broad nor too specific. It is also susceptible to change as technology and society change. One can speculate, for example, on what is likely to be the genus word for *dictionary* ten or twenty years from now if electronic dictionaries become as common as printed ones. Today a "dictionary is a reference *book* containing words usu. alphabetically arranged along with information about their forms, pronunciations, functions, etymologies, meanings, and syntactical and idiomatic uses." Given the pace of technological change, one can imagine a future definition beginning more appropriately as follows: "The dictionary is a *reference work* in electronic or printed form. . . ."

THE DEFINERS

H. Bosley Woolf, who joined the staff in 1955, was the last of the top editors to be hired for the Third Edition. A professor of English from Louisiana State University, he had studied English philology at Johns Hopkins University, where he was elected to Phi Beta Kappa and awarded a Ph.D. degree. He did his graduate work under Kemp Malone, a prominent philologist, who took an active interest in lexicography; Malone had been in charge of etymology for the *American College Dictionary.*

Temperamentally as well as intellectually, Woolf was well suited to the austere Merriam-Webster environment. He was disciplined and well organized. He felt comfortable working on his own. After a brief tutoring in the methods and art of defining by Daniel Cook, who had joined the staff in 1952, he rapidly became recognized for the excellence and preciseness of his definitions and his administrative competence. His first assignment had been to rewrite the definition of *aardvark,* cited earlier, according to the new defining style. Later he handled many of the most important verbs under the letters *g* and *s* – *get, give,* and *go,* and *shake, smoke,* and *strike* – which called for careful distinctions among numerous senses.

The entry for *strike,* a long and complex one, also tapped his enthusiasm for baseball. (Woolf was a Red Sox fan. In the 1960s when he visited the Goves on weekends during the baseball season, he and Philip often watched Red Sox games on television, to the exasperation of Grace, who thought they ought to be outside enjoying the sunshine.)

The Second Edition's definition of the noun *strike* as applied to baseball was awkwardly expressed and hopelessly vague. That it escaped criticism is a measure of the acceptance accorded *Webster's Second* by reviewers and editors who later showed their appalling lack of knowledge of its contents – its policies as well as its practices.

Sense 12 of the noun *strike* reads as follows: "*Baseball.* Any actual or constructive striking at the pitched ball, three of which, if the ball is not hit fairly, cause the batter to be put out; hence any of the various acts or events which are ruled as equivalent to it, as failing to strike at a ball so pitched that the batter should have struck at it."

It was expanded and clarified in the Third Edition as follows: "12 a: a pitched ball (as in baseball) recorded against a batter ⟨it's one–two–three ~s, you're out at the old ball game – Jack Norworth ⟩ (1): a pitch at which a batter swings and misses (2): a pitch passing through the strike zone at which a batter does not swing (3): a foul bunt not caught on the fly (4): a foul ball hit with less than two strikes on the batter and not caught on the fly (5): a foul tip caught by the catcher before it hits the ground." The detail and precision of this definition exact a price in concentration, but the entry is far more informative than its predecessor.

As generalists, definers were expected to cope with whatever words or sections of the word list were next in line. It was a matter of luck when they encountered a word or a sense in which they had a special interest or competency. There were exceptions: highly specialized or technical terms that were assigned to experts, many of whom were outside consultants, and groups of words that were related in meaning or function.

To achieve a measure of consistency, related words were assigned to a single editor. The definition of April as "the fourth month of the Gregorian calendar" was written first and set the pattern for the others. Sleeth recalls handling the pronouns, perhaps because they originated in Old Norse and Old English and were related to his etymological interests. The function words – such as articles, prepositions, and conjunctions – were handled as a group, because they are identifiably different from other entries. Generally, they show how a word is used to indicate relationships among other words in a sentence. They also acquire lexical meaning in particular senses that require a conventional definition. Thus, the entry on *at* at sense (2b) in the Second Edition included a definition that was exemplified by the phrase ⟨creditors are *at* him again⟩. Gove wanted to make sure that such lexical meanings were not overlooked.[13]

Another set of words that had to be handled as a group were the colors, which were redefined by an editor in accord with the recently developed international system of standards. With the help of the

Munsell Company of Baltimore, a pioneer in the field of color standards, guidelines were established for defining each color systematically in relation to the adjacent ones. The adjectives used in each
definition were based on a three-dimensional system of *hue, lightness*
(light, medium, dark), and *saturation* (dull, strong, vivid). The speci-
ficity and uniformity of the results were impressive, though the definitions were difficult for the average reader to comprehend. Thus, *taupe*
is defined as "a brownish gray that is paler and slightly yellower than
chocolate, duller and slightly redder than mouse gray, and duller and
slightly redder than castor." Two color charts and a page of text at the
entry *color* illustrate and explain the system for determined readers.[14]

LAUDS AND SNEERS AND MORE
DOS AND DON'TS

Gove was especially determined to root out the gratuitous editorializing that had crept into earlier editions, especially in the treatment of
minority groups. He often used as an example the definition of *Maori:*
"one of the aborigines of New Zealand. . . . They are vigorous and
athletic, tall in stature, and *pleasing in features, and brave and warlike*"
(my emphasis). "Pleasing to whom?" he would say. "Presumably to
Maoris and to certain West Europeans, but what would a Hottentot
think?"

He objected strongly to the definition of *Holi Hinduism:* "a licentious spring festival." He asked, "To whom is the Hindu spring festival licentious? Not to the Hindu himself." The Apache were defined
as "nomads, of warlike disposition and relatively low culture." He
commented, "These lauds and sneers are subjective and ethno-
centric. . . . Even made-up verbal illustrations though they may be
defended as illustrations should avoid gratuitous value judgments."
Among his examples: "*cure* vt 4: to restore from something objectionable or abnormal; as to *cure* girls of running after officers." He hardly
needed to remind the staff about the phrase "electricity has superseded gas," which had to be revised soon after publication of the
Second Edition at the insistence of irate gas producers.[15]

Even though Gove was on firm ground in alerting the staff to the
dangers of unintentional bias, some members of the staff thought he
went too far in his insistence on objectivity. They saw it as another

instance of his tendency to be too rigid, which he had shown in defending his defining technique. On that matter, as he indicated in a letter to Sledd, he was willing to sacrifice clarity to preserve his rules.

One attack on his strictures against editorializing attained some notoriety years after the dictionary appeared with the publication of an exchange of views that had taken place between Gove and an unidentified editor who had been asked to prepare guidelines for wine definitions. The editor urged Gove to relax his rules against editorializing and proposed that such descriptive phrases as "the best known wine of [name of district]" be permitted to distinguish among wines that could not be differentiated by taste, color, and strength. The memo, written in 1955, appeared a dozen years later in *American Speech* (February 1967) in the Miscellany Department edited by Edward A. Stephenson.

In a rejoinder (published on the following page), Gove rejected the request "flatly and unequivocally"; he saw it as an invitation to such definitions as "caviar: the most famous food of the Russians." He said the definer seemed to want to involve the dictionary "too deeply in varietal types of wines all out of proportion to the rigid exclusion policy faced in larger and more important subjects (e.g. Botany)." He said the Third Edition "is not a wine list." Furthermore, if differentiating characteristics are needed, "why is there almost never any information in our definitions about the kind of grapes used. . . . That could be *definitive*."[16]

This exchange has been cited as conclusive evidence of Gove's rigidity, but it seems less an example of mindless inflexibility than a good illustration of the acerbic tone he used when he was annoyed – a tone that offended some staff members. The proposal he rejected seemed of questionable merit even to the editor's colleagues. As the memo shows, the proposal had been shown to two top editors, and they had disagreed. Hubert Kelsey, Gove's most outspoken critic, said he would *not* use the kind of definition proposed by the memo writer. Edward F. Oakes favored it, however. Gove's reputation for rigidity, well supported though it often is, was also exaggerated by uninformed gossip.

A better case was made by those who were put off by Gove's inclusion of the definition of *wood duck* among his examples of gratuitous editorializing in the Second Edition. The definition included the phrase a "handsome American duck," a description that seemed reasonable, harmless, and certainly not worth making a fuss about. But to Gove it represented an unnecessary subjective judgment. It had to go. The Third Edition's definition, which used the phrase "a showy duck," cannot easily be faulted as a description of a duck noted for its "large crest and plumage varied with green, purple, black, white and chestnut." But did "handsome duck" belong on the list of gratuitous judgments with"licentious festival"?

THE ROLE OF CITATIONS

Definers at the Merriam company worked from two sources of information. One was the file of citations produced by the reading and marking program. It provided evidence that would indicate whether the senses that appeared in the Second Edition were still current, whether new senses had to be added, and whether there were new words that ought to be included in the new dictionary.

The other source was a file of buff-colored three-by-five slips on which the individual entries contained in *Webster's Second* had been pasted. In effect, these slips became a preliminary working copy of the manuscript for the Third Edition. Their long journey through the editorial process took several years, with stops along the way for the insertion of not only revised and new definitions, but also the etymology, pronunciation, cross-references, editorial styling, and production instructions. After they had been corrected and merged with additional slips for new words, new senses, and new verbal illustrations, they were mounted on $8\frac{1}{2}$-by-11 sheets of heavy manila paper, which constituted the final manuscript. After a final reading by Gove, these pages were sent to the R. R. Donnelley company in Chicago for typesetting.

Precisely when the collection of citations for dictionary making became a systematic activity at the Merriam company is not clear, but the launching of the big historical dictionaries by Jacob and Wilhelm Grimm in Germany and the Philological Society in England made the gathering of citations a much more significant activity during the second half of the nineteenth century than ever before. The goal of preparing an inventory of the language turned lexicographers into researchers and greatly increased the scale of their efforts. Editors could not rely simply on their memory and their own reading habits for information, as Johnson had done, for example, when he established the importance of illustrative quotations in English dictionaries.

Because their funds were limited, the Grimms and, later, the Philological Society turned to volunteers for assistance. At Oxford, James A. H. Murray recruited hundreds of volunteers from both England and the United States who eventually contributed more than a million citations to his files. Among Murray's chief problems with the volunteers was one that Gove encountered later – readers collected too many citations of unusual words and too few of ordinary words. Murray wrote that he or his assistants had "to search for precious hours for examples of common words, which readers passed by. . . . Thus of *Abusion* we found in the slips about 50 instances: of *Abuse* not five."[17] Gove dealt with the problem by requiring a random sampling of pages from works read to obtain quotations containing common words.

Even though it was preparing dictionaries of the current language rather than a historical dictionary, the Merriam company faced comparable pressure to gather evidence of how the language was being used, and it built up its files rapidly during the preparation of the Second Edition. It drew primarily on its own staff for citations instead of relying on volunteers. Since it envisioned producing dictionaries on a regular schedule, it included the expense of "reading and marking" in the budgeting of its annual operations. It also hired additional readers periodically in anticipation of a new edition that would demand fresh evidence for definers.

By the time the Second Edition was completed in 1934, the staff had assembled what Dr. William Neilson proudly called "a storehouse" of evidence – 1,665,000 citations to assist definers. These had been gathered with an eye to the current uses of the language – "contemporary authors particularly having been widely read for new words and for new meanings of older words," as explained in the Preface. The Second Edition definers also had access to 2 million citations from other dictionaries, principally the *OED*. To identify and define new scientific and technical terms they consulted more than two hundred experts, a practice established by management many decades earlier.

These practices were continued for the gathering of evidence for the Third Edition. There were, however, questions about the ways in which some citations had been gathered and about the looseness in the practices that had emerged over the decades. For example, how authoritative and representative were the citations? Gove was well aware that a million citations, or 10 million, did not necessarily portray how the language was used; they were only illustrative. There were no grounds for assuming that the samples collected for the preceding unabridged edition fully and accurately reflected the universe of speech and writing from which they were drawn; nor was there any practical way to do so for the Third Edition. "The usable evidence lies buried in the zillions of words that surround us," he later wrote, and, ideally, one should be able to draw on everything written and spoken, "who used [the words], how they were used, and what the circumstances apparently were."[18] But the task was obviously impossible, as was a statistically sound process limited to sampling only the written language.

Nevertheless, there was no alternative to sampling in some fashion. Standard statistical procedures for drawing samples seemed neither appropriate nor feasible, but sensible and consistent guidelines could be adopted to promote greater comprehensiveness and reduce biases. Gove stated the goal in broad terms and then supplied details:

[Editors] must read continuously all the printed matter they can absorb: books of all kinds but mostly contemporary prose that is expository, descriptive, or factually narrative; newspapers and periodicals including numerous learned and technical journals – a few of them regularly as issued, most of them by sampling from time to time; house organs for both insiders and outsiders; annual reports from industry; mail order catalogs, especially those with pictures; college catalogs; transportation schedules; notices on bulletin boards; menus; theater programs; instructions on food containers and in operator's manuals and rules for games – wherever the native language is genuinely at work. The usual exceptions are translations, conversation in fiction and most poetry. Citations must be sought from all English-speaking places of the world, not just from the United States.[19]

Gove did not believe that the language was "genuinely at work" in the vocabulary of fictional conversation, most poetry, and advertising; in these modes, it was often "contrived" for special purposes, a position that became controversial. Burchfield disagreed; he favored inclusion of good poetic uses, even if they showed up only once. John Willinsky considered the term *contrived* to be offensive and accused

Gove of downgrading poetry.[20] But that was not Gove's intent; he sought rather to deny poetry special status. Gove believed that until new words and special senses – whether they originated in poetry, science, or special circumstances – showed up in general discourse they were not appropriate for the dictionary. New words from whatever source had to meet several criteria, notably a minimum number of citations (no fixed number specified but often taken to be about a dozen), evidence of use beyond a narrow geographical area or constituency, and continued use over an extended period – a barrier to the acceptance of transitory words and fad expressions.

Thus, if new words or senses expressed in a poem were taken up by other writers, they would be entered in the dictionary on the basis of their broader acceptance. Such secondary appearances of Shakespearian and biblical words and phrases account in large part for their frequency as dictionary headwords.

The single appearance of a word in a highly reputable publication has never ensured its appearance in a Merriam dictionary. A lag between the first citation of a word and its appearance in a dictionary is commonplace. The term *atomic bomb*, for example, languished among the unused citation slips for years before it was thought to be of sufficient interest to the general public to warrant space in *Webster's Second*. It entered the Merriam files in January 1917 when a member of the staff, Col. A. W. Chilton, clipped a reference to it from the *Yale Review*. He added the notations "fanciful" and "chem. explosion of an atom." The word was added to the "New Words Section" of the Second Edition after the explosion at Hiroshima three decades after the original notation.[21]

Instructions for reading and marking citations were among the first of the Third Edition guidelines to be completed and were distributed to the staff in late August 1952. Later they were supplemented on such topics as nonstandard words and examples from English-speaking areas outside the United States. Readers were advised not only to look for new words but to note the guidelines shown, in abridged and paraphrased form, in Table 2.

Editors were expected to spend an hour or two each day reading selected publications; some concentrated on particular subjects, and others read periodicals in chosen fields. From time to time particular gaps in the files were noted, such as the discovery in mid-1953 that

Table 2. *Gove's guidelines for reading and marking*

Mark for all *new senses* of words in the Second Edition.

Mark good definitive and quotable illustrative citations and citations showing analogous and contrasted meanings for all words and senses *now in* the Second Edition.

Emphasize the text, but also scan legends accompanying illustrations, footnotes, and bibliographies.

Concentrate on marking terminology pertaining to the topic of the book or article.

Mark all trademarks and copyrighted terms in advertising and general discourse when they appear in lowercase, especially in derivative and inflected forms (two *cokes*, *simonizing* cars) or "unmistakably" in reference to products serving the same purpose as the protected product (*thermos, dictaphone, kleenex*).

Mark nonstandard words – slang, vulgar, derogatory, facetious, informal, colloquial, dialect, illiterate, and so on – when the labeling, etymology, definition, or pronunciation is contrary to their treatment in the Second Edition. Include extensive context and information on the writer's occupational and social level where pertinent. Distinguish dialogue from ordinary text.

Mark spelling and syntax in special cases, such as spelling variants and the writing of compounds as one word, two words, or with hyphenation.

Source: Adapted from "Marking Instructions," Memo to staff, Aug. 8, 1952, 1–3, AHC.

there was a great need for examples of nonstandard uses – slang, derogatory and vulgar terms, jargon, and illiteracies. Gove himself was an avid collector of citations, mostly at home. He marked passages in newspapers and magazines that were delivered to the farm. Most of the books in his library bore penciled evidence of his zeal. Stacks of three by five slips were always arranged in readiness on the table next to his reading chair facing the fireplace.

Years later when Burchfield visited Merriam-Webster in search of citations for the period following the completion of the original edition of the *OED*, it was the breadth of the staff effort to build the citation file that especially impressed him, along with the emphasis on science and technology, which had been virtually neglected in the original *OED*. Burchfield subsequently allotted some staff time to reading and marking, but continued to rely on volunteers, as did his successors.[22]

CLARIFYING MEANING

A definition is a snapshot of a word at rest.[23] An illustrative quotation and a verbal illustration show it at work. In the context of a phrase or sentence, the word conveys a distinctive sense – much as a musical note, placed in a series of other notes, becomes part of a distinctive melody. Gove set as one of the goals of the Third Edition a large increase in the use of both illustrative quotations and verbal illustrations and as he wrote to Bethel, his predecessor, in 1954, the criteria for selecting and using illustrative quotations would be stricter than in the past.

Gove's criteria can be summarized as follows, largely in his own words.[24] An illustrative quotation must be free of ambiguity and easy to understand if it is to help a reader grasp the meaning of a definition and distinguish one sense from another. Where appropriate, it should be current. It should avoid irony, which could lead to misinterpretation. It should not be merely decorative. "The hard truth is that literary flavor in a dictionary quotation represents a luxury of a bygone age," though he acknowledged that there might be "an extra pleasure of recognition" if the author's name meant something to the reader, but that was not the criterion for selection.

Since a quotation is selected not for literary flavor or for lending authority to a definition, it follows that "it doesn't much matter who is quoted . . . the quotation is illustrating a word, not citing an author." Mickey Spillane, Polly Adler, Fred Allen, Al Capp "all use standard English, some of them rather profitably, and are often quite quotable." (In practice, he made one exception: living members of the full-time Merriam-Webster staff, past or present, were not to be quoted.)

Gove thus took a wholly utilitarian view of the illustrative quotation. What mattered was its usefulness in "clarifying meaning," not its source or any other purpose. *Webster's Third*, like its predecessors in the Merriam series, was intended to be a dictionary of the language of its time, not a record of the historical development of English. It did not seek to emulate the *OED* or the *Vocabolario* of the Accademia della Crusca of Florence, which first used illustrative quotations extensively two centuries earlier with exemplary scholarly commitment, identifying the source and page meticulously if from "well-printed books" and the name of the owner if from a manuscript. For *Webster's*

Third, the full name of the person quoted would suffice (or the name of the work, if more appropriate). Nor was there any reason to display the usage of the best authors or impart moral instruction, two of Johnson's goals that had become irrelevant in modern lexicography.

If no suitable quotation is available, a carefully composed verbal illustration is preferable. It should reflect the same utilitarian criteria as the illustrative quotation. There is no reason in principle, Gove believed, why one would necessarily be better than the other. Indeed, the task of supplying well-formulated examples constitutes "the most exacting test that the defining process can impose." Whereas most defining skills are teachable, devising good verbal illustrations calls on a special talent that not all definers possess. To succeed, verbal illustrations have to be not only precisely focused but also "as easy and natural as possible and should seem to have come from native speech." Familiarity rather than novelty is the key to their usefulness.

Under Gove's guidelines, a quotation that appeared in the Second Edition was to be replaced if it was merely decorative or highly metaphorical. The following examples, in his judgment, contributed nothing to the clarification of the definition:

> death, keeping his circuit by the *slicing* edge – Marlowe.
>
> whitest honey in fairy gardens *culled* – Tennyson.
>
> I will encounter darkness as a bride and *hug* it in mine arms. – Shak.

Also, because of the pressure to keep within the established length of the dictionary, it was necessary to shorten or eliminate excessively long quotations, such as the following from Galsworthy: "Originally, perhaps members of some *primitive* sect, they were now, in the natural course of things members of the Church of England."

At the other extreme, some quotations in the Second Edition were unacceptable because they were so abridged they served no purpose other than to show that the word had been used: "Her *candid* fame" – Browning. "Pen looked uncommonly *wicked*" – Thackeray. "Be of good *cheer*" – *Matt. ix.* 2. None included enough context to clarify the meaning of the entry.

Gove also pointed to the need for greater emphasis on modern examples. He noted that a user who found in the 1934 edition at the word *wrath* four quotations from before 1611 might think it was time for the editors to climb out of the Dark Ages. Where updating was necessary, a definer would be justified in substituting Sinclair Lewis for Milton if doing so would clarify a meaning.[25]

Nonetheless, Gove explicitly cautioned against replacing a Second Edition quotation just for the sake of change. Good illustrations should be retained. Consequently, even after the infusion of thousands of new quotations into the Third Edition, Shakespeare continued to be the most frequently cited author, with 2,143 quotations, and Milton was second, with 446. Other great writers of the past were also well represented. The Bible was quoted 780 times.[26]

It is clear, however, that in some entries the balance clearly shifted, particularly when it was necessary to take account of many new senses. For example, some thirty sources were quoted to illustrate the senses of the transitive verb *shake*. The Bible and Shakespeare were quoted, as were Tennyson and Addison, but twentieth-century examples dominated – chosen not for the reputation of the author but for the aptness of what was said. Polly Adler, the madam who wrote the best-seller *A House Is Not a Home,* appeared at sense 5b: "There was no shaking off the press." She was in unusually good company. The writer quoted two lines above her was Elmer Davis, noted journalist and Rhodes scholar; immediately below, at sense 6a, the quotation was from Virginia Woolf. The choice of quotations was left to the definer, who could turn to the best writers or to a contemporary popular figure as long as the quotation succeeded in clarifying the intended meaning.

Among the modern American writers whose quotations were chosen for the Third Edition were Lewis Mumford, cited 252 times, Edmund Wilson, 193, and H. L. Mencken, 118; at the lower end of the scale, at 10 each, were such well-known figures as J. M. Cain, John Kenneth Galbraith, and George Gamow. Political and military leaders, including Douglas MacArthur, Dwight D. Eisenhower, and John F. Kennedy, were quoted, as were such athletes as Willie Mays and Ted Williams. Musical comedy star Ethel Merman was quoted twice.

In short, Gove's interest in clarifying meaning by example led to an overhauling of previous Merriam practices and to a great increase in the use of both illustrative quotations and editorially devised verbal illustrations. When it was completed, the Third Edition contained about 100,000 quotations and an equal number of verbal illustrations.

6

The Origins of Words: The Etymologist's Task

[Sanskrit bears to Greek and Latin] a stronger affinity . . . than could possibly have been produced by accident; . . . no philologer could examine them all three without believing them to have sprung from some common source, which, perhaps, no longer exists.

Sir William Jones

When Charles Sleeth became chief etymologist in 1951, he inherited a notable tradition that had begun nearly a century earlier with the reworking of Noah Webster's etymologies by Carl A. F. Mahn for the 1864 unabridged dictionary. Mahn's work was carried forward for three more editions by two prominent philologists, Edward S. Sheldon of Harvard University and Harold Bender of Princeton. Sheldon worked on the 1890 education and was chief etymologist for the 1909 *New International Dictionary;* Bender revised the etymologies for the 1934 Second Edition. "Because of the foundations laid by Mahn and Sheldon," wrote a prominent lexicographer in 1955, "the etymologies in late *Merriam-Websters* are the best to be found in any one dictionary."[1]

THE ROOTS AND PRACTICES OF
MODERN ETYMOLOGY

The approach that Mahn introduced was based on the early-nineteenth-century historical research by German and Scandinavian philologists who revolutionized scholarly understanding of the origin and development of language. Before them, it was not widely recognized that the Germanic languages (English, German, the Scandinavian tongues, Dutch, Flemish, and others) had developed from a common source, though the similarities among them had been noted. Nor was it known that other Western European languages (Celtic, Greek, and Latin among them) had evolved from that same source.

What the nineteenth-century researchers demonstrated was that these tongues developed from a prehistoric language dating back to 3000 B.C. or earlier, which is now called Proto-Indo-European (Figure 3). They showed, moreover, that Indo-European was also the source of many languages in Eastern Europe and Asia, including the Balto-Slavic languages, Albanian, Armenian, Anatolian, Tocharian, and Indo-Iranian. These languages of Eastern Europe and Asia not only bore a close relationship to one another, but had identifiable similarities with languages in Western Europe, including English. No written record of Indo-European has been found. What is known about it has been inferred (or "reconstructed") from the characteristics of the languages that developed from it.

The key insight that opened the way for these discoveries came from an English linguist, jurist, and polymath, Sir William Jones. While serving as a judge in India in the late eighteenth century, Jones studied Sanskrit, which had a literature older than that of any European language. He was struck by its strong similarities to Latin and Greek and became convinced that such close resemblances could not have occurred by accident. Confirmation of his insights and further findings were produced during the early decades of the nineteenth century by Rasmus Rask, a Danish philologist, and two German philologists, Franz Bopp and Jacob Grimm.[2] Their research placed English in the larger constellation of Germanic and other Indo-European languages and established the foundation for modern etymological practices.

THE TASK OF TODAY'S DICTIONARY ETYMOLOGIST, as Sleeth describes it, is to determine the earliest recorded occurrence of a word in English – and its written form and meaning – and then to trace it back to its ultimate source. This requires presenting evidence of its descent from the native stock of the Germanic and Indo-European languages or showing its adoption from a foreign tongue, such as

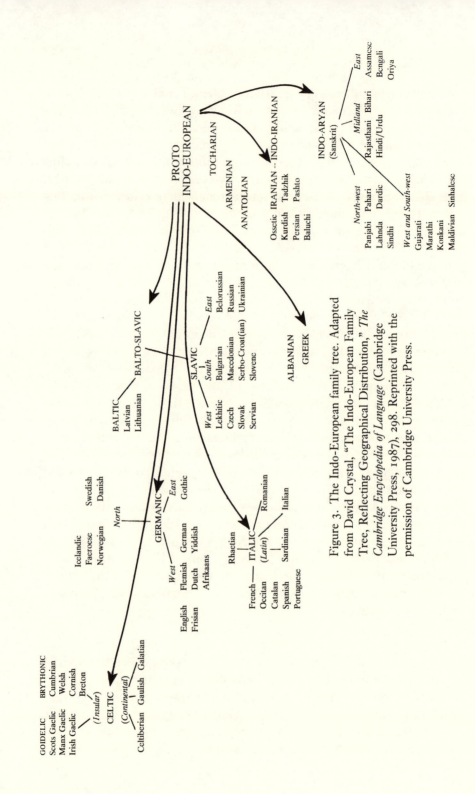

Figure 3: The Indo-European family tree. Adapted from David Crystal, "The Indo-European Family Tree, Reflecting Geographical Distribution," *The Cambridge Encyclopedia of Language* (Cambridge University Press, 1987), 298. Reprinted with the permission of Cambridge University Press.

Latin. In short, it is etymological research that points to when and where a word originated, when it entered the English language, and how its form and meaning changed over the centuries.[3]

If, for example, an occurrence is found in Middle English, the next step is to try to trace the word back to Old English. If it is found to be of Old English origin, the search turns to cognates, words of similar form and meaning in related languages that developed from a common ancestry. A word in Old English, Sleeth notes, will almost always have cognates in Old High German or Gothic or Old Norse. The search next turns to cognates in other Indo-European languages. Generally, Latin, Greek, and Sanskrit are chosen.

A key requirement for a correct etymology is to account for differences in the sound and form of a word and its cognates by the phonetic laws established by the nineteenth-century philologists. A knowledge of the Germanic "consonant shift," for example, is essential for differentiating Germanic from other Indo-European languages, such as Latin. Otto Jespersen, noted Danish philologist, stated it succinctly: "Any *p* was changed to *f* " in Germanic languages – thus *father* corresponds to *pater* in Latin; any *t* was changed to *th* (designated by the symbol thorn), and *tres* in Latin is the equivalent of English *three;* any *k* became *h,* and *cornu* is the equivalent of *horn.* With these and other shifts "there were comparatively few words that were not altered past recognition."[4]

Another requirement is that a word can be designated or a loan-word adopted from a foreign language only if it can be shown that there was historical contact between speakers of the two languages. As Walter W. Skeat, the English etymologist, noted, Old English did not borrow words from Prussian or Coptic.[5]

GUIDELINES FOR *WEBSTER'S THIRD*

Sleeth, who had a skeptical turn of mind and high scholarly standards, took nothing for granted as he prepared plans and guidelines for his staff. He required that all etymologies from the Second Edition be checked for accuracy, completeness, and conformity to the revisions in style he was developing for the Black Books. He revised or rewrote entries when his research uncovered more convincing evidence and expected his staff to do the same. He modified editorial procedures in his guidelines where it seemed advisable to do so for clarity and consistency, or for updating in accord with refinements in linguistic terminology – for example, the abbreviation *Teut.* became *Gmc,* for Germanic, as the name of the language family; *Anglo-Saxon* became *Old English;* cognates in other languages were introduced by the phrase *akin to* rather than the cross-reference abbreviation *cf.* used in the Second Edition.

Gove's exclusion of nonlexical material introduced an additional challenge. The Second Edition had included valuable information outside the formal etymology about the transmission of words through other languages before they reached English. Sleeth's solution was to put some of this material into the new etymological form – much as definers saved relevant encyclopedic material by putting it into illustrative examples. Thus, in showing the derivation of the word *cannibal* in the etymology, he cited the Arawakan forms "*caniba* and *carib,* that had been recorded by Christopher Columbus in Cuba and Haiti, respectively – and Carib cognates that meant 'strong men, brave men.'"

In following Gove's rule to save space, Sleeth required detailed etymologies for words of the core vocabulary of English and a system of cross-references to these "ultimate goal" etymologies from related words. This, he believed, was "the most economical way of giving rich information about Indo-European cognates" without excessive repetition.

At such entries as *hell, wit, heart,* and *care,* he would give a rather full display of cognates in other Indo-European languages, ideally including Old English, Old High German, Old Norse, Gothic, Latin, Greek, and Sanskrit. "If I found no Sanskrit cognate, I would, if possible, substitute for it a cognate in one of the other satem languages, such as Lithuanian or Old Church Slavonic," in accord with the work of Julius Pokorny.

Next, Sleeth said, he would make cross-references to these "ultimate goal" etymologies from other words that came into current English by different routes: "Thus from *conceal* a cross-reference to *hell,* from *vision* a cross-reference to *wit,* from *cordial* and *cardi-* a cross-reference to *heart,* from *garrulous* a cross-reference to *care,* and so on."[6]

Loanwords presented a special problem because of their great number and because of the frequent possibility that they entered English from more than one language.

THE TREATMENT OF LOANWORDS

The English language has been especially hospitable to words borrowed from early invaders who overran the British Isles, immigrants, and people encountered in other lands. After Old English was established in the fifth century by the invading Angles, Saxons, and Jutes from Europe, the door was open. During the next thousand years there was a great infusion of Scandinavian and French words taken from the speech of the Viking and Norman conquerors. Latin and Greek words entered English from the vocabulary of Christianity and the revival of classical learning. After 1500 the borrowing was extended to other tongues through trade, colonization, travel, and the flow of refugees and immigrants into English-speaking countries. As dictionary etymologies attest, the English vocabulary became the great lexical melting pot of the world, and the process continues. By the early 1990s, Japanese appeared to have overtaken Spanish as the second most important source of new borrowings, though it still ranked far behind French.[7]

Old English words still constitute the core of the language. The one hundred words most frequently used today, and the great majority of the thousand most used, are from Old English. They include indispensable little function words, such as *the, of, and*, and the verbs, nouns, pronouns, adjectives, and adverbs that are relied on in the ordinary business of life: *come, do, drink, go, help, ride, sleep; foot, friend, man, wife, father, brother, tooth, water, cow; hard, good, better, best, more, most, strong; I, me, mine, we, us, our, who*, and so on.

The words that were borrowed from the Scandinavian tongues were common ones, much like the native Old English stock. Most of them came into English during the tenth and eleventh centuries after a Dane, King Canute, became the ruler of England in 1016. The borrowings included *law, husband, fellow, wrong, call*, and the verb *egg* in the sense of "incite," as well as the following examples from a recent list of about four hundred words used in "modern literary English": expressions about the weather, *fog* and *muggy;* parts of the body, *leg, calf,*and *skin;* nouns we now know as *bag, bark*, and *bole* (of a tree), *knife, reef, sky*, and *window;* the adjectives *flat, low, meek, loose, rotten, seemly*, and *ugly;* such verbs as *crawl, droop, get, guess, hit, lift, ransack, take*, and *thrive.*[8]

Scandinavian words were readily borrowed because they fit in especially well with native words. They shared a common ancestry. Of particular importance were the Scandinavian pronouns that became *they, them,* and *their,* which are more distinctive than the Old English forms; they also fit well with the system of words that began with the same sound, such as *the, that,* and *this.* There were other instances in which the Scandinavian won out over the Old English, such as the noun *egg,* which replaced the native *ey,* or in which Old English words survived but took on the Scandinavian meaning. For example, *dream* meant "joy" in English until it acquired the current meaning from Old Norse during the Middle English period.[9]

Some Old English and Old Norse words survive side by side as synonyms. These include *no* (Old English) and *nay; hide* and *skin; sick* and *ill.* Other pairs of words in these languages have different meanings today despite their common origin in an older Germanic tongue – *shirt* and *skirt,* for example. In Old English the Germanic word became *scyrte* (with the *sc* pronounced like the *sh* in *shirt*). In Old Norse it was *skyrta,* pronounced with the hard *k* sound. As a rule, Scandinavian words of Germanic origin retained the *sk* pronunciation (as in *skin* and *sky*), while Old English regularly changed the pronunciation to *sh.*

The effects of the eleventh-century Norman conquest on English were much more dramatic. The invaders brought with them a different culture and a distinctive Norman-French dialect and vocabulary. A sampling of familiar borrowings from the French vocabulary in several fields is given in Table 3.

The French synonyms were often longer and more literary than the English words, as illustrated by the following pairs noted by Jespersen: *begin, commence; hide, conceal; feed, nourish; inner, interior;* and *outer, exterior.*[10]

Many of the borrowed French words originated in Latin, and some became Latinized in their spelling when they entered English or later under the influence of the revival of learning. For example, the letter *c* was sometimes inserted to conform with the Latin spelling, as in the change from *verdit* to *verdict* and *perfet* to *perfect;* the Latin *ad* replaced the French *a,* as illustrated by the change from *aventure* to *adventure* and from *avantage* to *advantage.*[11]

In the handling of loanwords, Sleeth often turned to the *OED* – not to the etymologies, though he often found them helpful, but to the earliest quotations that are cited. These indicated, for example, whether a word came in from French or directly from Latin. The

Table 3. *A sampling of French loanwords, by subject*

Words pertaining to government (itself a word of French origin): *authority, country, chancellor, parliament, people, realm, reign, state;* to political and social institutions: *fief, vassal, duke, baron;* to court life: *courteous, fine, glory, heraldry, honor*

Legal terms: *attorney, defendant, judge, jury, justice, plaintiff, sue, traitor;* military terms: *assault, siege, lieutenant, sergeant, soldier*

French cuisine: *sauce, boil, fry, roast, toast, soup, sausage, jelly, dainty* (Sir Walter Scott observed in an often-quoted comparison in *Ivanhoe* that the names of prepared meats were French [*beef, veal, mutton, pork, bacon*], whereas the names of animals were English [*cow, sheep, swine*])

Words pertaining to the lighter side of life: *joy, pleasure, delight, ease, comfort, leisure, sport, cards, dice* (and *ace, deuce*); to clothing: *apparel, dress, costume, garment*

The word *art*, along with *beauty, color, image, design, ornament;* the vocabulary of architecture: *arch, pillar, vault, porch, column, aisle, choir, cloister, palace, castle*

Source: Otto Jespersen, *Growth and Structure of the English Language, 1905* (New York: Doubleday/Anchor, 1956), 88–104.

choice was often very difficult. "If you find the first appearance of a word in English in a translation from French, then it probably came in from French. Then you can trace the French back to the Latin and then to the other Indo-European languages. If the word first occurs in Chaucer's translation of Boethius, for example, it probably came in directly from Latin, though you can't always tell from its form in English whether it came from one language or another."[12]

The word *philosophy,* for example, illustrates the form for indicating a Latin word that was borrowed from a Greek word and reached English via the French. It first appeared in Middle English as *philosophie,* the same as it was in French. The etymology in *Webster's Third* is shown as follows: "[ME *philosophie,* fr. OF, fr. L *philosophia,* fr. Gk, fr. *phil-* + *sophia* wisdom, fr. *sophos* wise + *-ia -y*]."

DRAWING ON ETYMOLOGY AND USAGE:
AN EXAMPLE

Sleeth's correspondence with readers illustrates how an etymologist can answer not only questions of word origin but also practical questions of why certain spellings and usages have to prevail. Something of Sleeth's thoroughness, patience, and cast of mind can also be seen in his letters. Along with the other top editors, including Bethel and Gove, he answered his share of queries from dictionary users. The editorial staff took this responsibility very seriously. Letters were answered thoughtfully by the most qualified staff member. Sleeth was especially conscientious. Letters pertaining to etymology or the history of language were generally referred to him, and he welcomed the work as a pleasant diversion.

A characteristic letter was his reply in late 1951 to the president of a commercial college in Detroit, who asked a very simple question: why is *defense* spelled with an *s* and *fence* with a *c?* The response illustrates how an etymologist blends his or her knowledge of other languages, the history of how language changes, and scholarly judgment.

Sleeth replied that his answer would be rather complicated, "involving as it does no less than three factors – derivation, usage and the methodology of making dictionary entries." It is quoted here almost in its entirety. Beginning with derivation and usage, he wrote:

The English word is derived from Old French, where the principal recorded forms are *defense* and *defens*, derived respectively, from the Latin, *defensa* and *defensum*. On this score alone, therefore, only the spelling with an "s" would appear to be warranted, but actually in English usage the spelling *defence* had become quite common by the time America was colonized, though without entirely supplanting the older *defense*. In the centuries since that time, the spelling *defence* has achieved in British English a virtually complete triumph. In the United States the spelling *defense* has maintained its ground much better, accounting for two thirds of American citations used in the preparation of *Webster's New International Dictionary, Second Edition.*

To mirror this state of affairs in our entries, we first entered *defence* in its own alphabetical position, calling it "the British spelling" of the words in question. The phraseology, including the use of the definite article, implied correctly that no other spelling of this word is acceptable in British usage. Then in the alphabetical position of *defense* we made the double entry, *defense, defence* with no geographic or limiting label attached to either variant. This means that in the English language as a whole . . . the spellings with the *s* and *c* are both so abundantly attested that both must be considered acceptable.

Turning now to the related problem of *fence*, we find that *defense* is not derived from the word *fence* by the addition of a prefix, but the other way around. *Fence* is derived from *defense* – that is, *ce* from *se* – by the dropping of the first syllable. This shortening occurred in Middle English at a time when both the "s" and "c" spellings of *defense* were freely current. Accordingly, we find both spellings of *fence* or *fense* in its early occurrences, the latter variant not dying out until the sixteenth century. Unlike *defense*, however, *fense* did disappear completely from standard written English and therefore can no longer serve as a dictionary entry despite its past existence, history, and derivation.

To put the whole matter more briefly, it is usage which requires the dictionary maker to enter *fence* as an invariable spelling and *defense/defence* as variants. If we attempted to set up etymology as the criterion instead, we would have to prescribe that both words be spelled invariably with "s" and this would be clearly unjustifiable.[13]

THE VOCABULARY OF SCIENCE

Sleeth took particular pride in two achievements. One was the introduction of the label *International Scientific Vocabulary*, or ISV, and the other was his written systemization and clarification of Merriam-Webster etymological practices, which eventually filled more than eighty pages in the Black Books. These guidelines were completed in 1955 after four years of preparation and refining. They were published by Gove a decade later.[14]

The ISV is a useful device for identifying with greater consistency and fairness the origin of new scientific terms that have been coined in several languages, mostly from Latin or Greek words. It avoids the misleading and erroneous information that had crept into the etymologies for such terms and the false implication that these Latin-derived forms had existed in Latin. It is the kind of refinement that appeals to the lexicographer and specialist in a field of inquiry rather than to the average reader. It illustrates an etymologist's effort to deal with a practical lexicographical problem where full knowledge is missing.

Mahn had begun dealing with the origins of the scientific vocabulary by introducing the abbreviation *N. Lat.* for "New Latin," which he defined in the explanatory notes as the Latin that developed after A.D. 1500. In the notes to the 1909 edition, Sheldon added the clarification that New Latin in an etymology "amounts to saying . . . *not* that a word was taken into English from modern Latin . . . *but* that a word is composed in a form befitting modern Latin rather than

English." That is, unlike modern Greek, which is the language of the modern Greek nation, New Latin was not a spoken language.

An entry in the text of the dictionary finally appeared in the Second Edition as a run-on entry under *Latin,* as follows:

New Latin, the Latin of modern times, since the Revival of Learning, employed chiefly in scientific description and classification and especially in scientific names coined in Latin form from Latin, Greek, or modern elements; – often styled Modern Latin.[15]

While the *New Latin* designation was a step forward, it left many ambiguities and often led to the inclusion of misleading information. Percy Long, a distinguished staff member on the 1909 and 1934 editions, singled out the need to improve the scientific etymologies as a major task for the Third Edition.

Sleeth recalls that his own awareness of the problem underlying his ISV innovation developed when he was preparing etymologies of the names of minerals. Working from a standard reference book, he discovered that many mineral names often appeared in other languages before they appeared in English, but that wasn't what the Second Edition showed. There the constituents of the compound were given as if the word had originated in English, whether it had or not.

"It seemed to me that we really ought not to claim English origin for some things that didn't originate in English," he said. "I went through the entire book [on mineralogy] and treated all the names on the basis of the language in which they first appeared. Then Freeman Anderson, who was also working on etymologies at that time, mentioned handling the entries on cytology in the same way, since his source also supplied full information on the first appearance of the modern word."

Sleeth said it became clear to him and Anderson, however, that reference books that would enable them to do the same in every branch of knowledge were not available in the Merriam library, if they existed at all, "and even if we had them, it would have taken us a century" to do the job.[16]

Sleeth's solution was to work out a procedure for dealing with scientific terms in three situations: first, when the source language was not known; second, when the word first appeared in a language other than English; and third, when the source language was English. If the source language was unknown, Sleeth used the ISV label plus the elements from which the word was formed. Thus, for *hydroelectric,* which is *hydroelektrisch* in German and *hydro-électrique* in French, the etymology is [ISV *hydr-* + *electric*]. This formulation showed that the term was part of the International Scientific Vocabulary and in each language was given a form appropriate to the borrowing language.

If the term was known to have originated in a language other than English, as in the following example, the format was modified. The etymology for *colloidopexy* shows that the term entered English from French and was made up of word elements that were ultimately derived from Greek: *colloidopexy* [ISV *colloid* + *-o-* + *pexy;* orig. formed as F. *colloidopexie*].[17]

If the term was known to have been coined in English, neither an ISV label nor another language was given. Thus, the etymology for *chromosphere* is [*chrom-* + *sphere*], indicating that it was put together in English from components that were already in the English vocabulary and that the etymologies of the components appear in separate entries showing their derivation from the Greek *chroma* (color) and *sphaira* (ball).

ISV did not wholly replace the use of New Latin, which continued to be used for terms that entered several languages unchanged from the Latin. Gove later cited three successive entries in the Third Edition to illustrate the distinctions that were made possible by the introduction of the ISV formulation:

> homoplasia [NL, fr. *hom-* + *plasia*]
> homoplastic [ISV *hom-* + *plastic*]
> homoplasy [hom- + *-plasy*]

. . . the first has latinate endings, the second has English form and is known to have cognates in at least one other language [but the source language is not known], and the third (with neither the NL or ISV label) is known to have been coined in English. It was, in fact, coined in 1870 by the English scientist Ray Lankester.[18]

Gove estimated that there were between five thousand and ten thousand ISV etymologies in the Third Edition.

DEALING WITH UNCERTAINTY

From time to time an etymological search runs into a dead end or leads to a number of possibilities. Many words that entered English during the preceding one or two hundred years often proved more troublesome than Old and Middle English words and early borrowings, especially informal and slang expressions.

As a general rule, Sleeth preferred to suggest an etymology, if a plausible one could be deduced, and to indicate the likelihood of its being correct. Etymologies of doubtful reliability were to be given the qualifying label *prob.* or *perh.* The former meant that the etymology was more likely than not to be true, the latter that the chances of its being true were less than 50 percent (but this distinction is not made clear in the explanatory notes).

But if there was no evidence, he required that the phrase *origin unknown* be inserted to avoid ambiguity. This was a slight modification of the Second Edition policy, which allowed such entries to stand without any reference to etymology, thereby leaving the reader guessing whether the omission had been unintentional or the result of a lack of information (the phrase *origin uncertain* was also sometimes used in the Second Edition).

For example, Sleeth could find no convincing support for an old etymology for *schooner*, introduced by Noah Webster. As given in the Second Edition, it read, "from *scoon* to skim or slip," and was followed by this extended note: "The first *schooner* is said to have been built in Gloucester, Massachusetts about 1713 by Captain Andrew Robinson. When the vessel was launched, a bystander cried out, 'Oh how she *scoons.*' Robinson replied, 'A scooner let her be'; whence the name. . . . In the New England records the name appears to have originally been written scooner." (A reader who checked the etymology for *scoon* would have found that the word was probably of Scandinavian origin, probably akin to the Old Norse word for hurry.)

Some other American dictionaries give the origin as *scun*, which is a Scots dialect word meaning "to skim across the water." The *Oxford Dictionary of English Etymology* (1962) notes this possibility, which had also appeared in the *OED*, but the *OED* added, "The anecdote, first recorded on the authority of tradition in a letter of 1790, looks like an invention . . . [though it] is not at all improbable." Sleeth could not find any evidence linking *scun* to the ship or for the schooner story, and he thought it was farfetched. Thus, *Webster's Third* gives the etymology as "[origin unknown]," and that is the way it has appeared in succeeding editions of the Merriam *Collegiate* dictionaries, through the tenth edition of 1993.[19]

Frequently when the evidence is persuasive but not conclusive, an editor is forced to choose among plausible but not definitive explanations. Sleeth admits he probably introduced some "risky etymologies" in following his policy of using plausible etymologies with the qualifying abbreviations *prob.* and *perh.* He recalls, for example, his original decision to base the etymology for *OK* on a persuasive article by Allen Walker Read, who found that the expression gained currency during the 1840 presidential campaign between Martin Van Buren and William Henry Harrison. Read attributed its origin to the O.K. Club, which was formed by supporters of Van Buren, who was also known as Old Kinderhook, or O.K., after his birthplace, Kinderhook, New York. This explanation seemed more convincing to Sleeth than the Second Edition's guess that the term was from the Choctaw *oke, hoke,* meaning "yes, it is." However, further research led to the discovery that "O.K." had appeared in the *Baltimore Sun* on February 24, 1840, before the O.K. Club was formed. Read found an earlier occurrence in the *Boston Morning Post* of March 23, 1839, as a facetious abbreviation for "oll korrect," an alteration of "all correct." The use of "O.K." in the 1840 political campaign helped fix the abbreviation in the language. The "oll korrect" version appeared in a later printing of the Third Edition.[20]

Sleeth was also uncertain about his etymology for *panhandler.* Earlier etymologies had suggested that it was from "a handler of pans." But he was "never able to visualize a panhandler as 'handling pans' and found it much easier to guess that a panhandler's extended forearm could be compared to the handle of a pan. The etymology "fr. the extended forearm" continues to appear in the *Collegiate,* tenth edition of 1993.[21]

"PRODUCE, PRODUCE"

By the time the Black Books were put into final form in 1955, the etymological work was lagging behind Gove's schedule. Sleeth had set ambitious research goals and was guided almost entirely by scholarly considerations, with much less attention to production goals. The etymological guidelines themselves had required a great commitment of time. Gove was slow to realize "Sleeth's lack of practical acumen," according to Henry Kratz, who joined the staff in 1955 and was later given some responsibility for "pushing the work through." Kratz admired Sleeth's erudition – "intellectually he was the best in the place" – and liked him personally, but felt he didn't fully appreciate the practical necessity of completing the etymological work promptly so as not to delay publication of the Third Edition.[22]

Sleeth later came to accept the need to make compromises. Time spent on research was reduced, and ultimately Sleeth had to give up his original intention to review every etymology personally. In the latter part of the alphabet, a few erroneous etymologies ("probably not many") crept into the first printing of *Webster's Third* and had to be corrected in later printings. The etymology of *tympani*, for example, was given as "L. pl. of *tympanum* drum," whereas it should have been "It. pl. of *timpano* kettledrum, fr. L. *tympanum* drum," since Latin words in *-um* form the plural in *-a*, not *-i*.

What Sol Steinmetz felt most strongly when he arrived in 1958 to join the etymology staff was the intense pressure "to produce, produce." It never let up. The work seemed simple at first, he said, but after about six months "it dawned on me that the task is difficult, because the more you knew the more you wanted to check. So I started checking. My etymologies improved, and Sleeth was pleased. He said he had not wanted to press me, and preferred to let me learn my way: 'I just watched what you were doing,' he told me. 'First you just followed the rules. Now you are grasping what it is all about.'"[23]

It was Steinmetz's first job, and he looks back on it with great pleasure; he had come from Columbia University, where he had completed all of his graduate work except the dissertation. With a knowledge of six languages, he proved to be a ready pupil and became a highly productive worker.

He was deeply impressed by the high morale of the staff and the standards of scholarship. He had expected a much more conventional business atmosphere: "We were idealistic, concerned with scholarship, facts, accuracy. We were not working just for money. We were there because of our love of the work. There was no goldbricking."

Steinmetz said that it was Sleeth's knowledge and scholarly commitment that remained uppermost in his memory. He loved working with him and especially admired the "clean design" of Sleeth's etymologies. "First you gave the immediate form, then you traced it back to where it came from. Then you started giving the cognates and all the other terms related to it. It had a texture, like a weaving of a fabric." Steinmetz considers the etymologies in *Webster's Third* to be "infinitely superior not only in accuracy but in presentation" to others up to that time, "a model of what a dictionary etymology ought to be . . . a masterpiece of concision and accuracy."

During the 1980s, as the managing editor of a new book on etymology, Steinmetz went over the Third Edition etymologies again and found himself "constantly amazed" by the coverage and accuracy of what he found. "About 90 percent of the research we did matched the information in the Third Edition, but of course," he added, "we also had newer information based on later research." The superiority of the Third Edition etymologies over those of the Second Edition was also stressed by I. Willis Russell, whose review focused on the difference between the two editions.[24]

BUT WHATEVER IMPROVEMENTS WERE MADE in clarity, consistency, and accuracy, the etymologies in the Third Edition were still bound by the lexicographer's traditional shorthand presentation, which relies heavily on abbreviations and symbols. It is a format not readily understood by the average user, who consults the dictionary primarily for answers to questions about spelling, meaning, and pronunciation. By and large, a user knows little about the purpose and potential usefulness of etymologies and finds them difficult to read. Thus, after a century of great progress in the scholarship of Merriam-Webster etymologies, the beauty of the work remains apparent much more to specialists than to typical users. Gove used to say that what one gets from an unabridged dictionary depends upon how much one brings to it, a dictum that seems especially applicable to etymologies. The best educated and most experienced readers are the best served.

Nonetheless, the early lexicographers were not wrong in believing that there was great public curiosity about the lore of word origins. For nearly a century this has been confirmed by the ready market for popular articles and books on the subject. The books are highly selective, presenting only a small fraction of the known etymologies, and they dwell on the most unusual and striking examples – Greek and Latin myths, historical occurrences, and names of people. All these lend themselves to extended anecdotal treatment.

Shortly after publishing its 1909 unabridged, for example, the Merriam company issued an illustrated pamphlet called *Surprising Origins of English Words from Webster's New International Dictionary,* which suggests the genre that was developing, both in its selection of words and its storybook treatment. The words that lent themselves to this treatment in the Merriam pamphlet included *assassin, bonfire, bedlam,* and *yuletide;* all of them had interesting and memorable stories. A highly popular book of 1950, *Word Origins and Their Romantic Stories,* by Wilfred Funk, was indicative of the literature that developed. Such volumes have continued to appear – for example, Stuart Flexner's *I Hear America Talking* (1976) and *Listening to America* (1982). In 1989 the Merriam company itself published a large selection of about 1,500 such items from its files under the title *Webster's Word Histories.* In a departure from this pattern of offering popular treatments of word origins outside dictionary covers, *The American Heritage Dictionary* introduced 400 paragraphs of unusual word histories into its third edition (1992).

Etymological dictionaries have also been published in recent years building on the pioneering work of Walter Skeat in 1882. *Origins,* by Eric Partridge, was published shortly before *Webster's Third;* the *Oxford Dictionary of English Etymology,* by C. T. Onions and others, followed several years later. The *Barnhart Dictionary of Etymology,* edited by Robert K. Barnhart and Sol Steinmetz, represented a major effort to be user friendly, as one reviewer put it. It is marked by "studious avoidance of abbreviations, special symbols and . . . shorthand jargon. . . . Entries verge on the chatty."[25]

Dictionaries, however, deal with tens of thousands of words whose origin and development do not invite historical and anecdotal digression. The large unabridged editions help to establish the record from which the popular books select their materials. In the unabridged editions, etymology has been less a sales feature intended to enlarge the dictionary market than a fulfillment of a scholarly obligation to complete the vocabulary entry by helping to illuminate the origin and historical changes in words.[26]

ETYMOLOGY AND THE WORD
THAT WASN'T

When the guidelines for etymology in *Webster's Third* were nearing completion, Gove took time out to add the story of *dord* to the lore of how things can go wrong in dictionary making. *Dord* was a word that

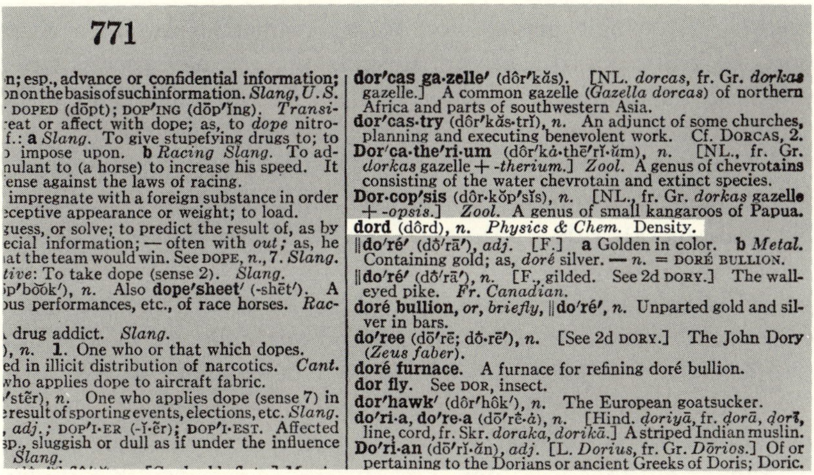

771

n; esp., advance or confidential information; on the basis of such information. *Slang, U.S.* • DOPED (dōpt); DOP'ING (dōp'ĭng). *Transi-* -eat or affect with dope; as, to *dope* nitro- f.: a *Slang.* To give stupefying drugs to; to ɔ impose upon. **b** *Racing Slang.* To ad- nulant to (a horse) to increase his speed. It 'ense against the laws of racing. impregnate with a foreign substance in order ɔceptive appearance or weight; to load. ꜰuess, or solve; to predict the result of, as by ecial information; — often with *out*; as, he ꞁat the team would win. See DOPE, *n.*, 7. *Slang.* *tive:* To take dope (sense 2). *Slang.* ꞁp'bŏŏk'), *n.* Also **dope'sheet'** (-shēt'). A ꞁus performances, etc., of race horses. *Rac-*

ꞁ drug addict. *Slang.*), *n.* **1.** One who or that which dopes. ed in illicit distribution of narcotics. *Cant.* ꟷho applies dope to aircraft fabric. ꞁstēr), *n.* One who applies dope (sense 7) in ꞁresult of sporting events, elections, etc. *Slang.* , *adj.*; DOP'I·ER (-ĭ-ẽr); DOP'I·EST. Affected ꞁsp., sluggish or dull as if under the influence ꞁ *Slang.*

dor'cas ga·zelle' (dôr'kăs). [NL. *dorcas*, fr. Gr. *dorkas* gazelle.] A common gazelle (*Gazella dorcas*) of northern Africa and parts of southwestern Asia. **dor'cas·try** (dôr'kăs·trĭ), *n.* An adjunct of some churches, planning and executing benevolent work. Cf. DORCAS, 2. **Dor'ca·the'ri·um** (dôr'kà·thē'rĭ·ŭm), *n.* [NL., fr. Gr. *dorkas* gazelle + *-therium*.] *Zool.* A genus of chevrotains consisting of the water chevrotain and extinct species. **Dor·cop'sis** (dôr·kŏp'sĭs), *n.* [NL., fr. Gr. *dorkas* gazelle + *-opsis*.] *Zool.* A genus of small kangaroos of Papua. **dord** (dôrd), *n. Physics & Chem.* Density. ‖**do're'** (dō'rā'), *adj.* [F.] **a** Golden in color. **b** *Metal.* Containing gold; as, *doré* silver. — *n.* = DORÉ BULLION. ‖**do're'** (dō'rā'), *n.* [F., gilded. See 2d DORY.] The wall- eyed pike. *Fr. Canadian.* **doré bullion**, *or, briefly,* ‖**do're'**, *n.* Unparted gold and sil- ver in bars. **do'ree** (dō'rē; dō·rē'), *n.* [See 2d DORY.] The John Dory (*Zeus faber*). **doré furnace.** A furnace for refining doré bullion. **dor fly.** See DOR, insect. **dor'hawk'** (dôr'hôk'), *n.* The European goatsucker. **do'ri·a, do're·a** (dō'rē·à), *n.* [Hind. *doriyā*, fr. *dorā*, *dorꞁ*, line, cord, fr. Skr. *doraka*, *dorikā*.] A striped Indian muslin. **Do'ri·an** (dō'rĭ·ăn), *adj.* [L. *Dorius*, fr. Gr. *Dōrios*.] Of or pertaining to the Dorians or ancient Greeks of Doris; Doric.

Figure 4. The ghost word *dord* as it appeared in *Webster's Second;* it was not caught and corrected until 1940. From *Webster's Second New International Dictionary,* 1934.

had appeared spontaneously and had found a quiet niche in the English language two decades earlier. It was recorded in *Webster's Second* in 1934 on page 1171 (Figure 4), where it remained unde- tected for five years. It disappeared from the dictionary a year later without ever having entered common parlance. The facts, which had been established years earlier through a search of company files, were as follows, as abridged from Gove's explanation.[27]

The lack of an etymology for *dord*, meaning "density," was noted by an editor on February 28, 1939, when he was perusing the dictionary. Startled by the omission, he went to the files to track down what had happened and what needed to be done. There, he found, first, a three-by-five white slip that had been sent to the company by a consultant in chemistry on July 31, 1931, bearing the notation "D or d, cont/density." It was intended to be the basis for entering an additional abbreviation at the letter *D* in the next edition. The nota- tion "cont," short for "continued," was to alert the typist to the fact that there would be several such entries for abbreviations at *D*.

A change in the organization of the dictionary possibly added to the confusion that followed. For the 1934 edition, all abbreviations were to be assembled in a separate "Abbreviations" section at the back of the book; in the previous edition words and abbreviations appeared together in a single alphabetical listing (which is how they again appeared in the Third Edition). But after the original slip was typed for editorial handling, it was misdirected. Eventually, it came to be treated with the words rather than with the abbreviations.

The editorial stylist who received the first typed version should have marked "or" to be set in italics to indicate that the letters were abbreviations (D *or* d). But instead, she drew a continuous wavy line underneath to signify that "D or d" should be set in boldface in the manner of an entry word, and a label was added, "Physics & Chem." Since entry words were to be typed with a space between letters, the editorial stylist may have inferred that the typist had intended to write **d o r d**; the mysterious "cont" was ignored. These errors should have been caught when the word was retyped on a different color slip for the printer, but they were not. The stylist who received this version crossed out the "cont" and added the part-of-speech label *n* for noun.

"As soon as someone else entered the pronunciation," Gove wrote, "*dord* was given the slap on the back that sent breath into its being. Whether the etymologist ever got a chance to stifle it, there is no evidence. It simply has no etymology. Thereafter, only a proofreader had final opportunity at the word, but as the proof passed under his scrutiny he was at the moment not so alert and suspicious as usual."

The last slip in the file – added in 1939 – was marked "plate change imperative/urgent." The entry was deleted, and the space was closed up by lengthening the entry that followed. In 1940 bound books began appearing without the ghost word but with a new abbreviation. In the list of meanings for the abbreviation **"D *or* d"** appeared the phrase "density, *Physics.*" Probably too bad, Gove added, "for why shouldn't *dord* mean density?"

7

The Sound of Words and Other Matters

It must be admitted that on pronunciation dictionaries are less satisfactory than on spelling, meaning, and etymology.

J. R. Hulbert, *Dictionaries: British and American*

Although speech preceded writing in the history of communication, it was the other way around in lexicography. English dictionary makers did not introduce guidance on pronunciation until long after spelling, defining, and etymology were well established. Cawdrey's dictionary of 1604 ignored pronunciation (as well as most of the other features that are common in today's dictionaries), and his successors paid no attention to the way words were spoken for more than a century – perhaps underestimating the relevance of pronunciation or over-estimating the obstacles to showing it in print.

Certainly the difficulties were daunting. Pronunciations in England varied from one locale to another and among social groups, with additional variants arising from differences among individuals. Whose pronunciation should be depicted? And what was the best way to represent sounds in print in a comprehensible fashion?

The first small step toward providing answers to such questions was taken by Samuel Johnson's precursor, Nathan Bailey. In his 1727 supplement to the *Universal Etymological English Dictionary*, Bailey marked where the stress should fall in the pronunciation of a word.[1] Johnson followed Bailey's practice. In his 1755 dictionary, he showed the stress mark in the main entry following the vowel in the syllable to be stressed, as in FO'RMAL and INFO'RMAL.

Representations of the sounds of vowels and consonants did not appear until much later in the century with the publication of dictionaries by Thomas Sheridan and John Walker. Sheridan and Walker worked independently, each taking the spellings and definitions from Johnson's work and adding his own pronunciations. Sheridan, who completed his book (*A General Dictionary of the English Language*) in 1780 shortly before Johnson's death, made pronunciation a distinctive element of the entry in the modern fashion. He respelled the head-word and showed the diacritical marks and accents on the respelled word. His intent was to capture the pronunciations prevailing among educated speakers. His work was said to have "commanded more attention as a pronouncing dictionary than any other of the kind that preceded it."[2]

In 1791 Walker published a competing volume that became even more popular, influential, and long-lived – staying in print for more than a century. Walker's dictionary, *A Critical Pronouncing Dictionary and an Expositor of the English Language*, established pronunciation as "an expected feature of English language dictionaries."[3] Unlike Sheridan, Walker did not hesitate to correct the pronunciations he disliked when he believed that prevailing usage was mistaken – a practice that tied in with the growing emphasis during that period on correctness in grammar and usage (see Chapter 8).

Despite the great influence of Walker, the representation of pronunciation did not become standardized during the ensuing century. Noah Webster claimed on the title page of his 1828 dictionary that he "intended to exhibit . . . the genuine . . . pronunciation of words," but he failed to take advantage of the contributions of Sheridan and Walker. He marked the stressed syllable in the entry word itself and he used diacritics to indicate sound, but critics found his system cumbersome and inconsistent – "crude, indefinite, and old fashioned" and of dubious value to dictionary users.[4]

James A. H. Murray complained a half-century later that when he sought advice on how to indicate pronunciation in the *Oxford English Dictionary*, he encountered a different view from everyone he consulted. He was advised by Henry Sweet (the noted phonetician who was thought to have inspired George Bernard Shaw's creation of Henry Higgins in *Pygmalion*) that the situation was virtually hopeless. It would be better to leave pronunciation out of the dictionary, Sweet advised, especially since Murray already had too much to handle. But Murray disagreed. He feared that the argument that too little was known about the subject could be used against nearly every part of the dictionary.

For three more years Murray continued to experiment before settling on a system of his own, which reached the public in 1884 when Part I (A–ANT) was published. It served his purposes but did not contribute much to the field. Lacking the careful historical research that characterized the rest of the dictionary and based largely on his own introspection, his treatment of pronunciation has been called the weakest part of his dictionary.

Yet Murray's attitude toward pronunciation is noteworthy, especially in the context of *Webster's Third* and the debate over whether a dictionary should be prescriptive or descriptive. According to his biographer, "The one thing of which he was certain was that it was not the function of the Dictionary to establish a standard of 'right' or 'wrong.' It was to record facts, and the fact was that usage differs for reasons to be found in the history of the language."

It is not surprising, therefore, that he decided to show several pronunciations where more than one was well established. In his words: "Language is mobile and liable to change, and . . . a very large number of words have two or more pronunciations current . . . and give life and variety to language . . . it is a free country, and a man may call a *vase* a *vawse*, a *vahse*, a *vaze*, or *vase* as he pleases. And why should he not? We do not all think alike, walk alike, dress alike, write alike or dine alike: why should we not use our liberty in speech also so long as the purpose of speech, to be intelligible, and its graces are not interfered with?"[5]

FROM *WEBSTER'S SECOND* TO THE *THIRD*

One of the major distinctions of *Webster's Second* was its treatment of pronunciation under the guidance of John S. Kenyon, a professor of English language at Hiram College and a leading American scholar in the field. Kenyon believed that the task of the dictionary was to record pronunciation rather than to dictate what it should be. His views were set forth in the Second Edition's "Guide to Pronunciation," which was far more than a guide to the pronunciation system used in the dictionary; it was a landmark statement in the field. Its key points are summarized here, because they also guided the approach to pronunciation in *Webster's Third*.

English, like other languages, Kenyon began, "is in the process of constant change." Notwithstanding past efforts to fix pronunciation, it is "no more fixed than it was in Shakepeare's day." A pronunciation that is widely accepted may in time turn out to be only transitional; it may be supplanted or augmented by another that becomes equally acceptable.

Spelling, however, has become increasingly standardized, and as a consequence there has developed a divergence between pronunciation and spelling. Vowels like *a* have come to stand for several different sounds (as in *date, at, father, banana*). At the same time, several different spellings have developed for a single sound (*ate, bait, eight,* for example, and *brought, taught, law*).

This divergence was not generally appreciated, however, and Kenyon was much troubled by one misconception that seemed to be "almost ineradicable . . . that the spelling of a word is the word itself, which should be pronounced accordingly." In fact, the relationship is the other way around. "We are constantly tempted to forget that speech is primary and reading and writing secondary." Murray made a similar comment in the "General Explanation" to Volume 1 of the *OED:* "The living word is *sound* cognizable by the ear, and must therefore be itself symbolized . . . to reach the understanding through the eye."

What can be said about "correctness" under these circumstances? "It is perhaps as accurate a definition as can be made to say that a pronunciation is correct when it is in actual use by a sufficient number of cultivated speakers," Kenyon wrote. The frequent assumption that one pronunciation "should be looked upon as wholly standard is not the prevailing view of those who are familiar with the essential facts." In support of this view he quoted several leading British and American authorities on the question. (One of them pointed out that in a thousand words from the *Legend of Sleepy Hollow* as pronounced by a native of Rochester, New York, and by a Londoner, twelve words differed in the usage of *r*, thirty-six in the sound of the short *o*, and eleven in the sound of *a* in *ask*.)

In short, Kenyon concluded that there was no uniformity in pronunciation among English speakers, although there was a sufficiently "practical uniformity" to enable English speakers to understand one another. The standard pronunciation of English "so far as a standard may be said to exist is the usage that now prevails among the educated and cultured people to whom the language is now vernacular."

Kenyon also explained that for practical reasons the Second Edition had to treat each word in isolation, artificially as "an unrelated entity" without indicating emphasis and pitch or "the countless minor variations to which the pronunciation of a word is susceptible under the influence of other words." It was impossible to show how pronunciation varies in "running speech." Moreover, because of changes in pronunciation over time, new and old forms persist, with the result that "there are hundreds of words pronounced two or more ways by the persons on whose speech the standard of pronunciation of the dictionary is based."

Kenyon's statements are carried over, often word for word, in Artin's essay on pronunciation in the Third Edition and are echoed in Gove's preface, as they had been echoed in Neilson's introduction to the Second Edition. Indeed, the similarity of the lexicographical approaches of the Second and Third Editions to the subject of pronunciation – as opposed to the treatment, which changed substantially – is striking. Perhaps nowhere else is the affinity between the Second and Third Editions so apparent as in the Kenyon and Artin essays dealing with the notion of correctness in pronunciation, language change, and the descriptive role of the dictionary.

There is one major difference in approach, however, between the two editions. The style of speech represented in the Second Edition is "formal platform speech," not that used in casual conversation. Kenyon recognized that other pronunciations were used by educated speakers, but pointed out that it was not possible to represent them in a work such as *Webster's Second.*

After publication of *Webster's Second,* Kenyon continued his research in collaboration with Thomas A. Knott, general editor of the Second Edition. They sought to break away from "platform speech" and to record colloquial English pronunciation "of the everyday unconscious speech of cultivated people." Following their lead, Artin abandoned the "platform style" as the model for the Third Edition and based his judgments on the pronunciations as revealed by his prodigious sampling of speech in a wide variety of circumstances and regions.

The work of Kenyon and Knott was published in 1944 by the Merriam company. Entitled *A Pronouncing Dictionary of American English,* it won critical acclaim, and forty years later it was still the "only major pronouncing dictionary of this century to appear in the United States."[6] Many years after the publication of *Webster's Third,* Artin drew up a proposal to revise the Kenyon and Knott work, but neither the Merriam company nor other publishers who were approached thought there was a large enough market to warrant a new edition.

THE GREAT EAVESDROPPER

Edward Artin joined the Merriam staff in 1930. He had dropped out of Harvard after making Phi Beta Kappa in his junior year. He had studied the classics but became preoccupied with words. On the strength of a long list of typographical errors in the latest unabridged that he sent to the Merriam company, he was hired as a proofreader. Later he became part of the pronunciation staff headed by Paul W. Carhart, pronunciation editor and managing editor of the Second Edition and earlier pronunciation editor for the *New International Dictionary* of 1909.

When Artin began thinking about how pronunciation should be indicated in *Webster's Third*, he hunted through the files to find out how decisions had been made in the past. His findings were slim but included the results of a survey of 125 prominent public figures during the preparation of the *New International* of 1909. The questionnaire offered the respondent two to five ways of pronouncing a word, along with the option of suggesting another. The surviving evidence was fragmentary, and respondents were typically identified by number rather than by name, so that the identity of the participants was a mystery. Artin found one memorable exception, "the familiar big bold signature of Woodrow Wilson" on a questionnaire filled out in 1907 when he was president of Princeton University. Wilson had checked off the pronunciation of *mayonnaise* with the accent on the final syllable and *cantonment* with the accent on the first. Wilson's slip also suggested confirmation of a story that Artin had heard. Wilson had "once rebuked Secretary of War [Newton D.] Baker at a cabinet meeting for saying [the word] *cantonment* with an accent on the second syllable, reminding him icily that "in cabinet meetings we use the dictionary pronunciations."[7]

Questionnaires were also used to gather evidence for the Second Edition, and staff members were polled on their views. But there were no slips in the files of the 1909 and 1934 editions indicating that actual speech had been recorded. The evidence consisted solely of written notes by listeners of what they had heard and notes on how the pronunciation of words had been treated in other dictionaries. Artin recalled that as a neophyte in the early 1930s he saw the pronunciation editor leaning back in his chair and pronouncing words to himself, testing out their acceptability on the basis of his own taste.

It was the inadequacy of the historical files and a lack of confidence in the research underlying some of the Second Edition pronunciations that led Artin to embark on his extraordinary effort to record as completely and as systematically as he could the actual pronunciations prevailing in different parts of the country and different English-speaking nations from the 1930s through the 1960s. He was probably the most single-minded eavesdropper of his time. His wife Dorothy L. Artin, an editorial assistant for the Second Edition, recalls that "we were married in 1931, and I soon learned that much, indeed most, of our 'free' time was to be dedicated" to his consuming interest in recording how people pronounce words. "During the ensuing forty-three years . . . evening after evening, weekend after weekend, holiday after holiday, he listened to representative speakers, on radio, television, or face-to-face, all the while making . . . citations on three-by-five slips."

She recalls that "on a vacation (more truly a fact-finding mission) he stopped to talk with some loungers on the street of a small town. He asked them, 'What town is this' (Not 'How do you pronounce the name of this Town?' which might have made them self-conscious and distorted their answer). As he got back in the car he heard one of them say, 'That poor guy must be illiterate. There's the sign. Right there!'"

When not absorbed by the world of words, he devoted himself to his garden, which he cultivated enthusiastically with chemical fertilizers and modern technology in private rivalry with Grace Gove, the outspoken believer in nature's way. But "mostly he just listened and made a record of what he heard," Mrs. Artin said.[8]

In recording his own research, Artin used the symbols of the International Phonetic Alphabet (IPA) that had been devised in the late nineteenth century as a standard for all researchers in the field of pronunciation. But a simpler guide was needed for users of a general dictionary. The system of diacritics that had been used in Merriam dictionaries was also complicated, however, and management was troubled enough about its acceptability to suggest a survey of user attitudes. Should the Third Edition continue to use the same symbols that had been used for *Webster's Second?* Should the symbols be modified or replaced by the symbols favored by the IPA?

Artin leaned toward the IPA system or a modification of it. He was convinced that in the long run IPA would become the standard. Others in the company were worried primarily about reader reaction. The old Webster system was well entrenched. It ought not to be radically changed or replaced unless there were very convincing reasons to do so. There was no objection to tinkering with the old pronunciation key, especially for the purpose of simplifying it, but no support for abandoning it.

In early 1953 a series of brief surveys was conducted by the staff to find out whether scholars, editors, and other users were satisfied with the existing system or favored changes. The results were difficult to interpret and frequently inconclusive. But there was clearly a wide range of preferences and no mistaking the opposition to the traditional Webster system of diacritics.

Textbook publishers were the most critical. They thought the Webster system too complicated. They relied instead on "pronunciation-at-sight" systems that used respellings with familiar letters to suggest familiar sounds – for example, Chaucer: CHAW-sur; Disraeli: Diz-RAY-lih; Aeschylus: ES-kuh-luhs. They recognized the limitations of this approach but opposed any kind of pronunciation key.

Teachers who were interviewed on campuses from the East Coast to Chicago favored simplification two to one. Of the alternatives discussed, Artin's adaptation of an IPA system seemed to enjoy the most support. One teacher pointed out, however, that "it was not a symbol problem but a teaching problem." Students would not learn an IPA-like system more readily than they had learned the diacritics, but respondents conceded that, with Merriam's prestige, whatever it decided would be accepted.[9]

THE COMPROMISE

The system that was finally devised for the Third Edition was a modified diacritical system. It introduced several changes that were intended to achieve simplification and make possible a more thorough and accurate representation of pronunciation than was presented in any earlier dictionary.[10] Experts generally found the new approach to be one of the most impressive features of *Webster's Third*. Users were often baffled (see Chapter 14).

There were two major features of the new system. First, in line with the recommendation of the IPA, the stress mark was placed before the stressed syllable, not after it, as in the past, on the logical grounds that the syllable cannot be pronounced before the stress is known – that is, *a'bout* in the Third Edition rather than *about'*.

Second, the representation of vowel sounds was simplified. Several diacritical marks were eliminated, and only three were used: the macron \ā\, as in d*a*y; a single raised dot \ȧ\, as in f*a*ther; and two raised dots, or diaeresis, \ä\, as in c*o*t or b*o*ther. The *schwa* \ə\ was introduced to replace several ways of representing the same unstressed or stressed vowel sound, as in *a*bando*n*, b*u*tt*e*r, and penc*i*l. (A superscript schwa was used to indicate the unexpressed or expressed vowel between such consonants as *t* and *n*, as in *mittᵊn*.)

A comparison of the pronunciation keys in the Second and Third Editions shows that the Third simplifies the representation of vowel sounds but lengthens the pronunciation portion of the entry by showing a wider range of variant speech patterns and introducing a number of unfamiliar symbols to save space. In addition, a number of familiar and less familiar symbols were used for several new purposes. For example, to indicate a division of opinion, the *obelus* \÷\ was used before pronunciations that were common in educated speech but that often met with strong objections from educated speakers. Parentheses were used around letters within a word to indicate sounds spoken by some educated speakers but not by all – as in *numerous, n(y)üm(ə)rəs*. A vertical light face bar \|\ was used to separate variant pronunciations; slanted double hyphens \⫽\ were used to signify the repetition of syllable sounds in the transcription of successive variants. This system of representing variant pronunciations, though troublesome to the average user, efficiently conveyed a great deal of information to experts.

The essence of Artin's approach was clear enough. He attempted to represent the normal conversational speech of educated users. To the extent possible, he took account of how the pronunciation of a word was changed by the sounds of the preceding and following words. A full transcription of pronunciation in running speech remained beyond reach, as Gove explained in the preface to the Third

Edition. Changes in pitch, pauses, emphasis, and the relative length of syllables could not be shown, but Artin made great progress in indicating actual pronunciation. He left an unprecedented body of information on how English was spoken in the United States, as well as in some other English-speaking countries, which was highly valued by fellow students of pronunciation.

Notwithstanding President Munroe's desire for a system that would appeal to the average dictionary user, Artin prepared his pronunciations with the expert in mind. He viewed the unabridged as a scholar's dictionary as well as one that would be accessible to the average reader. Much of the criticism that his pronunciations later attracted was based on the expectations of reviewers who, like Munroe, were looking for a pronunciation system that would be appropriate for a desk dictionary.

SIGNS OF SLIPPAGE

In mid-1955 Gove reported to President Gallan that more than half of the definitions had been written and that the gathering of quotations under an expanded reading and marking program was exceeding expectations. It was the seventh of his semiannual reports, and it continued to reflect the confidence and optimism that had characterized his outlook since his first report in 1952. The rate of progress, as he gauged it, made him eager to see sample entries in type so that the typography and layout of the dictionary could be fully tested before the start of typesetting two years hence. The specifications for *Webster's Third* would have to take into account the need to save space and to devise typographic innovations to meet unusual editorial requirements.

The logistics of the editing and production processes were formidable – the routing of hundreds of thousands of three-by-five slips from one editor to another and then to editorial assistants for checking and marking for the printer. The task of monitoring progress was also burdensome. In the beginning, definitions were counted one at a time as they were completed, a tedious, time-consuming process. Gove simplified it by measuring the number of inches of completed copy and calculating the number of entries from the measurements.

Then he sought to improve the accuracy of his progress reports to management by taking into account definitions in the pipeline, including those assigned to consultants. By mid-1955 more than seventy consultants had been hired since Twaddell began recruiting them in 1950. Each was assigned from a few hundred to several thousand definitions and was given a target date for completion. Their progress was estimated on the basis of the time elapsed since the assignments were made. Eventually the number of consultants would be about the same as were required for the Second Edition – some two hundred – not counting scores of other experts who offered advice on specific points.[11]

The consultants for *Webster's Third* worked on nearly a hundred thousand words and senses, all told. They wrote new definitions for some entries, reviewed new and revised entries prepared by the staff, and suggested new entries in the fields of their expertise. A dozen consultants had completed their assignments by late 1955, including Harvard University law professor Erwin N. Griswold, who reviewed eight hundred legal terms. Many others were scheduled to complete their assignments before the end of that year, but failed to meet their deadlines. Some lagged behind in their work almost from the beginning and had to be replaced. In some technical and industrial fields, definitions had to be worked out in consultation with industry committees on nomenclature and standards, often a very time-consuming process.

The work of the consultants dragged on longer than expected. Not until the early months of 1960 did the most remarkable performer, Charles D. Hurd, complete his work.

Hurd, research professor of chemistry at Northwestern University, was given the task in 1952 of reviewing "12,790 terms in all branches of chemistry," and it took him the rest of the decade to complete it. When he sent his final slips to Springfield in May 1960, he felt compelled to enclose an explanatory note. He wrote that the count of terms given to him "did not even remotely carry the inference of the magnitude of the 200,000–250,000 slips in the 60 boxes that I ultimately processed. It took me 6-1/4 years to do it here but that involved evenings, week ends, vacation periods, as well as much regular time. I doubt that I could have done it in less than 4 years even if I had been working on it full time (but without overtime) at Springfield."[12]

For five years there had also been a full-time resident editor for chemistry, Janet D. Scott. The work of the consultants left resident editors with many follow-up tasks – such as styling definitions in accord with the Black Books and integrating technical senses into the treatment of multisense words.

As time passed, evidence began to accumulate that consultants were by no means the only ones falling behind. Gove's projections of what would be produced by the average staff member were colored by what he hoped could be produced. His earliest schedules were based on the assumption that the dictionary would be finished in 1959 (the original target date). The total amount of work to be completed by that time was divided by the number of months remaining before the deadline, with little weight given to the current rate of production. He apparently assumed that improvements in efficiency or the hiring of additional staff members could bring the rate of production up to the target figure. During 1956, however, staff turnover started to become a problem, and the gap between planning targets and production achievements widened. Keeping the staff at full strength became a major preoccupation and a losing struggle until the book was printed. Belatedly and reluctantly, Gove revised his projected completion date to reflect the actual rate of progress.

GETTING INTO TYPE

The good news in early 1957 was the successful testing of the plans for producing the Third Edition. In a pilot run during the first half of the year, more than two thousand sheets of final copy ($8\frac{1}{2}$- by 11-inch pages on which three-by-five slips had been mounted) were sent to the R. R. Donnelley's Lakeside Press in Chicago in monthly installments for typesetting, proofing, correcting, and page makeup. Some thirty dictionary pages were produced from the two thousand sheets, and Gove and the press found themselves in agreement on what had to be done. A contract was signed that called for production to begin by July 1.

The key to the arrangement had been the Donnelley company's ingenuity in devising an efficient way to handle the enormous number of special characters that the Third Edition required and its decision to train a group of young apprentices especially for the task, instead of relying on journeyman printers, who might be resistant to the special demands.

Webster's Third was printed during the waning years of the great typesetting technology introduced in the 1880s and high-speed presses that had revolutionized printing. But even in 1961 the old system proved it could still adjust to new demands. It was able to fulfill the Merriam company's search for high legibility and a pleasing appearance while achieving maximum efficiency in the use of space through the appropriate choice of typeface and page layout.

The versatility required for the task was available on Monotype typesetting machines, which offered an unusually large number of special characters, letters, and symbols. Normally, the Monotype machine – so named because it cast letters and symbols one at a time, unlike a Linotype, which cast a line of type on a single metal slug – had the capacity to handle 225 different letters or other characters in its so-called mat case. Merriam needed twice as many. The contract was awarded to the Donnelley company on the basis of a proposed customization of Monotype technology devised by Charles Singer, a printer whose inventiveness and prowess as a problem solver earned him a reputation as a genius among his colleagues. Donnelley also had an enormous typesetting capacity, which would not be swamped by the heavy burden imposed by the Third Edition.

Singer expanded the versatility of the Monotype machine by increasing the capacity of its mat case – that is, the number of characters accessible in normal operation – from 225 to 375. He provided for even greater flexibility by an innovative system for inserting additional characters as needed with minimal interruption of normal keyboarding and typecasting. As described by John Babrick – who administered Donnelley's typesetting of the dictionary and communications with the Merriam company – Singer devised a system of *stop codes* that gave access to additional characters contained in special mat case setups. "Whenever the keyboarder encountered a special character that was not in the mat case at that time, he keyed in a *stop code* and indicated which character was to be inserted. . . . He would resume keyboarding until he encountered another special character etc."

In the casting room, "the machine would cast the lines, one character at a time, in justified lines, stopping whenever it was told to do so. The caster man would insert the proper character into the spot indicated by the keyboarder and start the machine again." At that time, Babrick explained, the only alternative was "to set bogus characters [to hold the place for the desired characters] and replace them by hand with the correct characters, a very expensive operation in both money and time."[13]

Singer also decided that by using $5\frac{1}{2}$-point body type, rather than 6 point as originally planned, he could get thirty-six additional lines (twelve per column) on each page, resulting in the saving of 224 pages. This decision largely accounted for the fact that the Third Edition had far fewer pages than originally estimated. Gove's editorial plan called for a dictionary that would be no longer than the Second Edition, about 3,300 pages. Its actual length was only 2,726 pages. (Some reviewers mistakenly, though not unreasonably, later interpreted the reduction in the number of pages as a reduction in content. However, if the typographical specifications had been the same for both works, the length of the two editions would have been about the same.)

After typesetting began, Gove visited the Lakeside Press to observe the production process and made a tour of the plant. He stopped at several places to meet members of the staff, mostly young compositors recruited as apprentices and trained for the distinctive demands of the dictionary. Later he described one encounter with obvious relish. His handwriting was notoriously bad, and when he was introduced to a group of compositors as the man responsible for all the radical typographical requirements, one young typesetter looked up from his keyboard and asked, "Are you the son of a bitch who writes with the red pencil?"[14]

8

Usage and Final Tasks

The cold fact about usage in natural languages is that it is diverse and is subject to change. Essentially, in the usage of native speakers, whatever is, is right, but some usages may be more appropriate than others, at least socially.

Raven I. McDavid, Jr., "Usage, Dialects, and
Functional Varieties"

The most striking of Gove's policies on usage was his decision to cut back on the use of the slang label, eliminate the label *colloquial* entirely, and put greater reliance on illustrative quotations and usage notes to indicate the status of words that were on the borderline of standard English. As he frequently stated, good English is the English that is appropriate to the occasion. Words that are often frowned upon by speakers and writers are not invariably "incorrect" or nonstandard. The context is crucial. Thus, labels could often be inadequate or misleading indicators of usage, especially when applied to words and expressions whose "correctness" or appropriateness were matters of dispute among the experts. Gove, in effect, reserved the label for clear-cut deviations from standard English. When the question was in doubt, he preferred to provide illustrative quotations, examples of usage, and explanatory notes – leaving the decision to the user. His rationale was that the unabridged was not intended for children or adults who were learning English; it was intended primarily for those with a serious interest in language, though it had been management's hope that it would appeal to the average family.

The concept of slang that guided the editors of *Webster's Third* was conventional: a nonstandard vocabulary characterized by extreme informality, coined words (*palooka,* for example), clipped and shortened forms (*psycho*), extravagant or facetious figures of speech (*screwy, square*), and some of the cant, argot, and jargon of special groups. Slang terms are often short-lived, but some win acceptance in the standard vocabulary, and others go out of vogue but continue to be used (such as *duds,* used for clothes since the sixteenth century).

What was distinctive about Gove's guidelines was the emphasis on citations as the basis for decisions on usage. What did the evidence show? Did it indicate that the word in question was used mostly in standard or nonstandard contexts? Decisions on the status of questionable words – as on pronunciations and definitions – were to be based on the facts of usage, not on personal opinion about what usage should be. Words listed as *slang* or *colloquial* in the Second Edition were to be reevaluated on the basis of evidence of recent decades (especially in the light of the marked trend toward informality in speech following World War II) to determine whether a change in their status had occurred or whether an illustrative quotation or a usage note would be more appropriate than a label. Several pages of examples indicating how words and senses were to be handled were prepared to help definers make their decisions. A borderline term associated with certain activities – such as *big time,* which was customarily associated with sports, crime, and the theater – was not labeled when it appeared in its usual contexts; instead, its status was illustrated by quotations. Such examples, Gove thought, would convey to educated users what might be inappropriate in formal situations.[1]

Distinguishing between slang words and standard English was not a new challenge for Merriam editors. It had long been a troublesome problem for lexicographers generally, and differences in their judgment and inconsistencies in their practice had frequently been cited. James B. McMillan, a prominent linguist, wrote a classic article in 1949 showing the sharp disagreements among five college dictionaries in the treatment of *movie, plug, razz,* and *tycoon* and questioned the criteria for the conflicting judgments. In the opinion of the lexicographer J. R. Hulbert, the affixing of labels "is governed by nothing except the judgment of the editor and his advisers; there is no absolute criterion."[2]

Given the inevitable subjectivity of labeling and the inconsistency of past practices by lexicographers, it is not surprising that Gove attempted to guard against labeling based on casual inspection or hunch and to look for alternative ways to indicate reservations about the acceptability of a word. Implicit in the approach was the view that slang had its uses as well as its drawbacks. If it was socially risky when used at the wrong time and place, it also required no apology when used appropriately – and indeed, in the right context the rewards of slang were clear both to the user and to the reader or listener.

Gove's reluctance to label a word *slang* when its status was uncertain was at odds with the general practice. When in doubt, dictionary editors typically attached a label to a questionable word. There was little evidence in general dictionaries of the affection for slang that infuses books on the subject. In a preface to a dictionary of American slang, for example, Robert L. Chapman quotes Walt Whitman, who called slang "an attempt of common humanity to escape from bald literalism, and express itself illimitably." Chapman writes that "slang shares misty boundaries with a relaxed register usually called informal or colloquial. . . . [It] also shares a boundary with a stylistic register we might call figurative idiom." These qualities account not only for its appeal but also for the difficulty of deciding what is standard English and what is not.[3]

Unfortunately, Gove did not present a convincing rationale for reducing the use of the slang label, either in the Third Edition itself or in explanatory material about the dictionary. As a result, many reviewers did not recognize the full significance of the examples or usage notes and mistakenly assumed that there were no restrictions on the use of any word that did not carry a label – that it was standard in all situations. At least part of the furor over the treatment of slang described in Part III can be attributed to Gove's oversight.

Gove's position on the colloquial label was an even greater departure from conventional practice. He gave several reasons for dropping the label from the Third Edition: readers generally misinterpreted what *colloquial* meant; the status of a word could often be conveyed more informatively and precisely by an illustrative quotation or a usage note than by a label; and it was often too difficult to tell whether a word was colloquial or slang when it stood alone rather than in a particular context. Sledd was to find these reasons inconsistent and unconvincing.

The ambiguity of the colloquial label was not a matter of dispute; it had been widely recognized for many years. Fifteen years before the Third Edition was published, for example, the influential linguist

C. C. Fries wrote that "even teachers of English frequently misunderstand the application of the label *Colloquial*. Some confuse it with *localism* and think of the words and constructions marked 'colloquial' as peculiarities of speaking which are characteristic of a particular locality. Others feel that some stigma attaches to the label '*Colloquial*' and would strive to avoid as incorrect (or as of a low level) all words so marked."[4]

Gove saw no need for a substitute label since "colloquial" speech was standard English, unlike slang; it was part of the vocabulary that most Americans used most of the time. Quotations and usage notes could help users decide when such speech was appropriate.

Other stylistic labels that had appeared in the Second Edition were also discarded such as *correct* and *incorrect*, and *proper, improper,* and *erroneous*. The labels *humorous, jocular, ludicrous, gallicism, poetic,* and *contemptuous* were also dropped. Alternative ways were suggested for handling words previously labeled *euphemism, popular,* or *loosely.*

However, Gove did use labels – though much less frequently than his predecessor – contrary to the erroneous charge that he had abandoned them entirely. He used *nonstandard* and *substandard* to identify words that were not standard English, and temporal labels to indicate *obsolete* and *archaic* words that were no longer in common use but were still important to readers of early works in English. Regional expressions were also labeled, as were words common in England or other English-speaking areas.[5]

CORRECTNESS AND THE PURISTS

Thus, Gove's views about labels, grammar, and the status of words were of a piece with his views on lexicographical matters. He believed that the status of words, like their meaning and pronunciation, depended on usage. However, the powerful role of usage in dictionary making, which had been established for a century or more, differed from the prevailing views of most grammarians, teachers, and others.

During the years when Gove was teaching English composition, the prescriptive rules on grammar and usage that had been developed during the eighteenth and nineteenth centuries still dominated the schools and colleges. At the same time, a growing literature testified to the biases and limitations of the traditional texts on grammar and usage and challenged the grounds on which many of the prescriptions had been based. Gove's own experience persuaded him of their inadequacy in helping students learn to speak and write with greater clarity and effectiveness.

Fries, considered to have had a major influence on the views that guided *Webster's Third,* contrasted the traditional and empirical points of view as follows: "The conventional point of view" assumes that "there is a correctness in English language as absolute as that in elementary mathematics" and that there are "very definite rules" that measure correctness. It denies the role of usage, as indicated in the comment by a traditional grammarian, Richard Grant White: "There is a misuse of words which can be justified by no authority, however great, and by no usage however general."

Fries contrasted this with the "scientific point of view" held by outstanding scholars of language for a hundred years. The British grammarian and phonetician Henry Sweet, for example, had written a half-century earlier that "the rules of grammar have no value except as statements of facts: whatever is in general use in a language is for that very reason grammatically correct." This, Fries noted, was consistent with the *OED*, which based its meanings on use or practice.[6]

The origins and development of the traditional perspective during the eighteenth and nineteenth centuries by Bishop Robert Lowth and such followers as Lindley Murray were severely criticized in a landmark historical study by Sterling Leonard. The "logical grammarians" who promulgated this prescriptive view, Leonard wrote, put their emphasis on "matters of correctness and precision, with only minor attention to merely utilitarian questions of clarity or force in the communication of ideas." They sought to use reason and philosophical ideas about the origin and nature of language to make English fully consistent and orderly, but with little attention to how the language was being used. The focus of Leonard's study was to explain why there had been such a "flood of English grammars" during the second half of the eighteenth century, why the prescriptivism that they promoted became so popular, what assumptions about the English language they were based on, and the consequences of their efforts.[7]

Despite the dominance of their views in teaching for two centuries, Leonard found little evidence that the prescriptive grammarians achieved much beyond fostering an interest in the study of language. His concluding chapter is an unrelenting and somewhat contentious attack on their theories, their rules, and their legacy. Two quotations from Noah Webster helped him to establish the mood: "Lowth . . . has criticized away more phrases of good English than he has corrected of bad." And ". . . of the doubtful points [in grammar] not half of them have been correctly settled by Lowth and his followers . . . the grammars now taught in our schools, introduce more errors that they correct."[8]

Leonard found the efforts of the grammarians largely counterproductive. "Their activities appear in perspective to have been a prodigious raising of issues already laid, and of points irrelevant and insignificant." He noted that of more than three hundred grammatical and logical issues listed in his appendix, fewer than a dozen "are regarded as illiterate or popular usage today." He continued:

Of the forms effectually banned, a number, already long dead were exhumed in the eighteenth century solely for critical obloquy. . . . In certain formal aspects of literary revision such as precise parallelism in sentence structure and sequence of tenses, and in printers' forms like the apostrophe in the possessive plural, a few more points were established. All this makes no creditable total record for the century of laborious grammatical criticism, and it illustrates well the useless precaution of purists.[9]

Matters worsened under the nineteenth-century grammarians. Leonard wrote that "whole heaps of the prejudices, taboos, and prescriptions of eighteenth-century writers were carried entire into the books of writers who followed them, so that a majority of their ideas . . . [may] be found today earnestly and convincingly taught in our schools." Before any progress could be made in the teaching of composition, he concluded, "a cleaning out of this ancient purist muddle" was essential.

Leonard subsequently conducted a survey of opinions on usage under the sponsorship of the National Council of Teachers of English (NCTE). By polling representatives of several groups – prominent linguists, NCTE members, writers, editors, businessmen, and others – he sought to find out whether a list of controversial expressions appeared to be acceptable in the discourse of educated speakers and writers or only among the less cultivated or illiterate. Respondents were to report the actual use of language as they had observed it, not their opinions of the propriety of the items. The results led him to conclude that the grammars and usage books were much more conservative than the practices of educated users. Many disputed expressions rejected by traditionalists were widely accepted in reputable circles, and thus it seemed to him that it was a waste of time for teachers to try to"eradicate" them.[10]

Criticisms of the limitations and shortcomings of Leonard's work, which was both highly influential and sharply attacked, led the NCTE to sponsor additional surveys. The first, by Albert Marckwardt and Fred Walcott, sought to gather evidence of the actual use of the items Leonard had submitted to his survey respondents. They took their examples of usage primarily from the *OED*, and they reclassified Leonard's results into different usage categories. Their findings were contrary to those of Leonard in many respects, but on Leonard's central conclusion there was no disagreement; they found that "textbooks are too conservative in matters of usage."[11]

Fries was also highly critical of the effects of Bishop Lowth's views on the teaching of English and spoke out strongly for the superiority of usage as "the basis of all the *correctness* there can be in language." He wrote that in the United States "a kind of standard English has evolved that is based on an older London English modified by the American experience. It is standard not because it is any more correct or more beautiful or more capable than other varieties of English; it is 'standard' solely because it is the particular type of English which is used in the conduct of the important affairs of our people. . . . It is also the type of English used by the socially acceptable of most of our communities."

The goal of the schools, in a society opposed to artificial restraints to an individual's advancement, is to train all pupils to learn standard English so that their speech will not be a handicap to them. What has impeded the achievement of this goal (which some think unrealistic) is that the schools have tried to teach a 'make-believe' correctness which included forms that were not used outside the classroom instead of the prevailing usage.[12]

One of the by-products of the attacks on eighteenth- and nineteenth-century grammarians and their continuing influence was a heightened estrangement of linguists from traditional grammarians and literary scholars. The controversy over *Webster's Third* derived much of its intensity from this bitter and long-standing quarrel.

THE LOOM OF COMPETITION

During the late 1950s Gove periodically received reminders from President Gallan about the growing competition in the college dictionary market that began after World War II. The Third Edition figured in Gallan's plans to defend the company's position in the college market. A new unabridged edition opened up a once-in-a-generation opportunity to promote the Merriam-Webster name and other Merriam dictionaries in the marketplace.

The first major postwar challenge to the company had come from the *American College Dictionary (ACD)*, published by Random House in 1947, shortly after Gove arrived in Springfield. Produced under the direction of Clarence Barnhart, it achieved both critical and sales success. It offered several features that set it apart from the Merriam-Webster *Collegiate:* the ordering of senses by frequency of use, the combining of encyclopedic information and the generic vocabulary in a single alphabetical list, and the use of the schwa in the pronunciation key. Barnhart had added prestige to his work by recruiting some of the nation's most eminent scholars to serve as contributing editors and advisers.

A decade later new challengers were in the market. In December 1958 Gallan wrote, "I can report with what I believe to be reasonable accuracy that competition has strengthened during the past year and has evidently become more determined to grasp a larger share of the total volume. With the future in mind it would seem only fair for me to be perfectly frank at this time."[13]

Two years later, with the publication of the Third Edition only months away, Gallan cautioned Gove against complacency: "We know of at least three publishers who are determined to go after the potential dictionary market and who have announced plans for issuing new desk dictionaries during 1961 and 1962."[14]

The problem was not unfamiliar to Gove. He had been keenly aware of it since early in his tenure as editor. The emerging rival at that time was *Webster's New World Dictionary,* published in 1953, a very good dictionary that had arisen from the ashes of a series of potboilers published by a firm that had been condemned only a few years earlier by the Federal Trade Commission for unfair business practices (see Chapter 12). The episode illustrates Gove's defensiveness on the subject of competition.

He was drawn into it in early 1955 when he learned of correspondence between Edward Artin and Raven I. McDavid, Jr., of Western Reserve University regarding McDavid's work on the Linguistic Atlas of the United States. In a letter devoted mostly to pronunciation questions, McDavid alluded to faculty discussions about the appropriate order of senses in a college dictionary. There was considerable support for an ordering based on frequency of use, McDavid said, and he asked for Artin's views. Artin responded on February 7, 1953, with an enclosure written by a colleague, who expressed doubt primarily on two grounds: that the "commonest" sense could not be readily determined for most entries and that there was no evidence that the commonest sense was the one most likely to send a reader to the dictionary in the first place.

For instance, for the word *film* the order of commonness will require giving first a sense that would very seldom be sought by a generation that has been seeing movies since shortly before they stopped wearing diapers. . . . The sense desired is as likely as not to be in the middle of the conglomerate . . . [and] then the consultant has to read through senses he already knows and may find boring before he reaches the desideratum. If the historical order is followed, then the consultant may not only read through no more senses than in the other case, but at the end he may pick up some information on semantic development that may be of some use to him.

Two weeks later Gove wrote a follow-up to Artin's letter addressed to "Dear Dr. McDavid" in which he commented on a second issue that had emerged in the correspondence, the decision by the Western Reserve English Department to allow students to choose any of three leading dictionaries for their personal use instead of recommending only the Merriam-Webster *Collegiate* as in the past. (The other two were the *New World* and the *American College Dictionary.*) He was annoyed that competing dictionaries were accorded equal standing with the *Collegiate.*[15]

Whenever I hear about a committee on freshman English at a first-rate university, whose members are reputable scholars and linguists coming up with a decision that all of the competing college dictionaries should be put on an equal basis (in alphabetical order) I am baffled . . . over the question of how and where there has been a breakdown in communication. . . . Apparently you or your committee feel certain observations about pronunciation and historical order . . . are sufficient reasons for overlooking the comparative methods that have produced the competing dictionaries. Is there any doubt about the difference between a dictionary that is put together on the basis of citations drawn from the real language of people communicating as distinguished from a dictionary compiled by a few people working at a desk with dictionaries already in existence and with little in the way of original observation to go on? The implication seems of overwhelming significance to us, and we are all the time underlining its importance to justify it all. We can only wonder why there can be any hesitation.

McDavid replied a month later that both Artin's letter and Gove's letter were circulating to the faculty. On April 5 he wrote that "there's a small teapot tempest around here" over the Artin and Gove letters to the faculty, especially references to the *New World Dictionary,* which was edited by Joseph Friend, head of the department (a fact that Gove may not have known, McDavid added). "But the reactions to [Gove's letter] . . . were definitely not good."

He said he could not give an official reason for the department's decision, but he could say that "no one denies the tremendous amount of work the Merriam company has done to provide good dictionaries. There is a feeling, as I said before, that a frequency ordering of senses might be better for a college dictionary, with the historical approach kept for the bigger ones."

McDavid also noted that the tactics of a Merriam salesman on a recent visit to the department were unfortunate in two respects: "They were bad in themselves, especially since there are friendly personal relationships between the department and many in the World Company, and, second, they gave the impression that the Merriam Company seems so worried about the new competition that it would stop at nothing to try to hurt the *New World Dictionary.* I know this is not true, but some salesmen can make very powerful and lasting impressions."[16]

THE BUMPY ROAD TO THE FINISH LINE

Typesetting for the Third Edition moved ahead auspiciously at Lakeside Press in mid-1957. Enough edited copy arrived each week from Springfield during July and August to make fifteen typeset pages in the three-column format of the new dictionary. The compositors were soon turning out twenty-five pages a week in response to a speedup in editorial production. The typesetting rate had reached the target anticipated in the printing contract. Had it been sustained, the dictionary would have been typeset, made up into pages, and made ready for printing in mid-1959. However, the Merriam editors could not sustain the faster pace. In November the preparation of edited copy began to decline because of disruptions caused by the resignation of experienced editors at the Merriam company and the recruitment and training of replacements. By the end of the year, typesetting had fallen behind schedule and was running at about half the desired rate. Gove remained hopeful that the lost time could be made up, but the slippage continued.

The semiannual progress reports to the president and Board of Directors after 1956 reflected the swings in productivity and mood that characterized the final years of the dictionary's preparation – achievements and setbacks, optimistic forecasts and missed deadlines, reassurances, and acknowledgments of new difficulties. In 1956 – when seven editors and nine editorial assistants resigned – Gove believed that the experience was atypical and would not recur. After replacements were hired, it was expected that in a few months they could be trained and that normal production would be resumed after only a minor setback.

During the following spring, however, three more editors resigned, including two associate editors whom Gove had counted on to carry a heavy load during the final phase of production. One of them, who was troubled by ill health, found the pressure to meet deadlines too much to bear. He had been convinced since 1955 that Gove's expectations were unrealistic and that the 1959 target date was unattainable. Gove urged him to stay, explaining the importance of the editor's contribution to the completion of the work, but to no avail. By the end of 1957, staff losses for the year totaled six editors and ten editorial assistants – no improvement over 1956. The company was partly responsible for the problem because of the low salaries it paid – a frequent complaint of staff members. Employees in the lower ranks found it rather easy to find higher-paying jobs. Moreover, Gove's personnel selections were often poor. He was not a good judge of applicants, often too impressed by academic credentials and insufficiently attentive to the experience and the suitability of applicants to the kind of work they would be doing.

In the twelfth report to the board, in January 1958, Gove wrote that "the job of getting out the 3d edition on schedule (as revised) is neither impossible nor hopeless. But we have to rebuild our staff to the productive potential it had in the spring of 1957 when we signed in good faith our contract with the Lakeside Press."

Gove continued to foster the belief that the original publication date of 1959 could probably be met, almost until the deadline was upon him. As a man who took pride in efficiency and in keeping commitments, he was reluctant to concede that the dictionary would be published a year or two behind schedule. That the major delay had occurred before he became editor was little consolation. He had accepted the original deadline when he accepted his promotion and had expressed confidence that the lost time could be made up.

In his June 1958 update, Gove reported that, after nearly a year of typesetting, about 700 pages were in type, only a fourth of the Third Edition. There was also more bad news: "We are 180 pages behind [and] we are planning to increase the copy flow . . . by two pages per week. On this basis we could make up a deficit of 20 pages by April 1960." He reiterated what he had noted in previous reports: "Our most difficult problem, and the chief cause of slow progress is finding, training, and keeping qualified editors and assistants." At this time the "weakest and slowest link" was etymology. The appointment of F. Stuart Crawford in 1959 soon helped to bring the work on etymologies up to schedule.

At midyear, when the compositors began setting the entries under the letter *H,* a total of 968 pages were in type (39 percent), but production was 110 pages behind the revised schedule established six months earlier. The probable publication date was not indicated. Unable to find enough suitable replacements in the vicinity of Springfield, the company acquired three editors by advertising in Boston and New York newspapers.

In June 1959 Gove reported an improvement in the staffing picture (only two assistant editors and two editorial assistants had been lost), but he finally acknowledged the seriousness of the situation: "I have become aware during the past six months of a new factor that worries me and seems too important to be passed over in silence. Many staff members have been pushed to the limit of their capacities, and even some beyond. They are tired. I set this down as a fact with no analysis of its possible significance to our work."

Resignations reached "an all-time high" of five assistant editors and thirteen editorial assistants during the last six months of 1959, Gove noted in his next report. "In addition to the scars left in the wake of such a turnover, we begin the new year with one of our pronunciation editors planning to be out at least four weeks – if not permanently – for a serious eye operation, one definer in the hospital with a broken right arm, and another definer snatched away from us by the government." Despite these difficulties, there continued to be some progress; about two-thirds of the dictionary had been typeset and half of the pages had been made up by January 1960. Over the next six months, to Gove's relief, production met the revised schedule. After that, the final year had its ups and downs but no major surprises.

ZYZZOGETON AT LAST

Gove's final progress report, dated January 10, 1961, echoed a familiar theme: "During the period of the report we lost by resignation four assistant editors and ten editorial assistants and employed five new editorial assistants." But it was not accompanied by the usual laments and portents of disaster. The job was done, Gove reported succinctly:

1. The final definition (for the word *zyzzogeton*) was written on October 17, 1960.
2. The final etymology was inserted on October 26, 1960.
3. The final pronunciation was inserted on November 9, 1960.
4. The last sheet of the final copy of the vocabulary was given its final reading on November 29, 1960.
5. The last sheet of final copy was checked by cross reference on December 2, 1960.
6. This last sheet of final copy was shipped to the compositor on December 2, 1960.[17]

The time-consuming process of getting the book ready for printing – the proofing, correcting, and reproofing at Donnelley, then the proofing and correcting by Merriam, and finally the page makeup, checking, and correction by Donnelley – took three and a half years. Final approval to print was not readily granted. Merriam "insisted on correcting and recorrecting final page proofs," Babrick noted. "Final" came to mean what the Merriam company wanted it to mean. "I remember we had to throw away 163 pages of final OK's because new 'final' OK's with corrections came in."[18]

For the last act in the production of the dictionary, the scene shifted from Chicago to Cambridge, Massachusetts, where the book was printed by the Riverside Press of H. O. Houghton Company, printer of the Second Edition and other earlier Merriam dictionaries – another example of the continuity in the Merriam tradition.

Gove was on his own during the late summer of 1961 while the dictionary was being printed and final publicity and marketing plans were being worked out. Grace and Norwood's wife, Ruth, had gone to Russia again. They often traveled together after Philip decided that he preferred to spend his vacations at home or nearby. Ruth remembers sitting on the porch with Philip at the farm before the departure for Russia and his saying very intently, "Don't say anything or do anything that would spoil her trip." Besides his usual solicitousness about Grace's welfare, Philip's interest in the trip was characteristically in the planning of it. Grace had written Ruth (June 9, 1961): "Actually, Philip will get more pleasure out of our trip if he does our thinking for us than if he went himself."

WILL IT SELL?

As management turned its full attention to publicity and marketing in mid-1961, it faced the challenge of matching the success of the Second Edition when it was launched in 1934. That had been a triumphant occasion. Journalists and critics had treated the arrival of *Webster's Second* as a notable succession in established order. It was an event to be celebrated rather than assessed, the kind of reception the publishers of the Third Edition hoped would be repeated upon publication of their edition. *Time* magazine caught the mood in its issue of July 9, 1934. After paying appropriate tribute to the *OED*, the *Century Dictionary*, and the Funk & Wagnalls, it offered its judgment. "Most Americans," it said, "still settle their bets by looking at the Merriam-Webster."

The *Christian Herald* echoed the tone of acceptance a few months later: The "book event of 1934 was unquestionably the appearance of the *Webster's New International Dictionary* . . . supreme authority on all matters applying to the language." It called the definitions in the Second Edition "magnificent," singling out for special praise the definitions of religious terms. The review in *Science* magazine paid its respects as well. It said the new edition deserved to be considered a botanical reference book, not just an ordinary dictionary. "It is the one work which is generally accessible to all readers, to which they may turn for the spelling, meaning, and derivation of hundreds of botanical terms or for brief information about thousands of different plants." The reviewer, H. A. Gleason, a botanist at the New York Botanical Garden, said that the list of vernacular plants "surpasses any preceding list in any language," while the list of genera is second only to the leading handbook in its general utility.

The *New Yorker* took the virtues of the new dictionary for granted and dug into the lesser-known details. In "Talk of the Town" for October 6, 1934, it reported that "we had one of our scouts who was at the yacht races return via Springfield to investigate" the publication of the new dictionary, since the company name was so well known. What the scout discovered, among the history of the Merriam company and the facts about the dictionary, was that no Merriams owned the company any more — its ownership was secret — and that millions of words were left out, most of them names of the 500,000 possible carbon compounds and some 600,000 zoological species.

It was the treatment of pronunciation that the *Christian Science Monitor* chose to applaud in its review. "The new book reaches down to the streets and backyards" and meets the people on their own level, in contrast to the exacting and artificial notion of the so-called best pronunciation in the 1909 edition that was alien to most people. On definitions and the treatment of particular words, the reviewer acknowledged some disagreements and perplexities, but bowed to the Second Edition's conception of its role: "After all, a dictionary records usage."

There was little evidence of serious and independent assessment. Trade publications of all kinds joined in with either sympathetic descriptions or laudatory reviews. A rare, faintly dissonant note was sounded in the *Subscription Books Bulletin* review of October 1934, which said the dictionary was not easy to use because the type was small and crowded. *Library Journal*, however, called it "up-to-date, clear and accurate." And William Lyons Phelps, professor of English at Yale University and a widely known popularizer, solved the Christmas gift problem for readers of *Scribner's* by writing in his column in the December issue: "For a man or woman, boy or girl, it is a noble, beautiful, useful and valuable gift."

There was support, too, from the scholarly community, as evidenced in a review by Louise Pound, a professor of English at the University of Nebraska. She called it "the most comprehensive yet practical and up-to-date dictionary of our mother tongue now available" in either England or the United States, "a work in which we may well take pride."[19] With the passage of time, the reputation of the Second Edition continued to grow.

The launching of *Webster's Second* had also been a social and cultural success in Springfield. More than three hundred people, including leading scholars, publishers, and staff members, had attended a dinner at the Hotel Kimball on June 25, 1934, to welcome the new edition. Professor Albert B. Hart of Harvard echoed an old Merriam theme: "A dictionary," he said, "is not a definitive record or body of facts but rather a continuous register of thought and a changing guide to the expression of thought."[20]

In 1961 the question facing President Gallan was whether to follow the 1934 precedent or attempt something more ambitious. He decided to forgo the traditional banquet and concentrate on a more aggressive promotional strategy instead. He approved a major publicity campaign under the direction of a New York public relations firm, Ruth Mallard Associates. Ruth Mallard was properly cautious about the prospects for making news, but found reason for optimism. There were enough good story angles to catch the attention of newspaper and magazine editors – solid news such as the introduction of a hundred thousand new words and senses, the authoritativeness imparted by Merriam's unmatched file of citations, the new etymologies, and the Webster and Merriam tradition. Moreover, lively quotations from well-known public figures in the press, politics, entertainment, sports, and so on would warrant the enclosure of photographs to illustrate the story.

Though their hopes were high, the public relations firm and the company were prepared for indifference from the press. What never occurred to them was that a great publicity success might offend a major constituency and bring on a war over words.

PART III

The War over Words

9

Early Returns: The Fuse
Is Lit

Everyone who knows enough to know he speaks English can assert an inalienable
right to correct the speech of his fellow man and to throw stones at his dictionary.
Philip B. Gove, Speech at the English Lunch Club,
Boston, February 10, 1962

On September 7, 1961, three weeks before publication day, the Third
Edition made news across the country, as the Merriam publicity strat-
egists hoped it would. In New York, the *Times* ran a breezy headline –
"Webster Soups Up Its Big Dictionary" – over a story by McCandlish
Phillips. The new edition, Phillips wrote, was "entirely renewed in
content and radically altered in style." It was a popularization that
would be authoritative for scholars and also "interesting," and "even
entertaining, for 'average families'" to read.

Phillips took due note of the key publishing statistics – the length
of the book, 2,726 pages; the number of entries, 450,000; weight,
$13\frac{1}{2}$ pounds; the total cost, $3.5 million; and the list price, $47.50.
He called attention to the new style "of definitions written in single
phrases" and the liberal use of quotations from contemporary sources
to illustrate meanings – including quotations from former President
Eisenhower (on *goof*), popular authors such as James T. Farrell and
Corey Ford, and the Trans-World Airlines timetable. Gove was quoted on the increasing informality of English usage. Phillips concluded
by noting that *ain't* was "defended as used orally in most parts of the
U.S. by cultivated speakers."

The story was a fair and accurate reflection of the publicity material
that was distributed by the Merriam company, if not quite true to the
dictionary itself. It was respectful and complimentary – almost every-

thing a publisher could wish for in a news story in the nation's most prestigious newspaper. It even included the exaggeration inspired by the publicists that the dictionary would be "entertaining" reading for the whole family.[1] The prepublication phase of the company's ambitious public relations and marketing campaign seemed to be off to a good start.[2]

THE WORD SPREADS

In other cities across the country, most of the stories that appeared on September 7 were written and distributed by the Associated Press (AP) or United Press International (UPI). They set a jocular tone that characterized much of the prepublication press coverage. What had been almost an afterthought in the article by Phillips – the treatment of *ain't* – became the lead. The UPI story began: "You may have been taught it is uncouth to say 'ain't.' But it ain't."

An additional twist appeared in another UPI lead carried by two competing Chicago newspapers, the *Tribune* and *Sun-Times:*

The word "ain't" ain't a grammatical mistake any more. And there are some prepositions you can end a sentence with.

If anyone disagrees, look it up in the dictionary – the forthcoming *Webster's Third New International Dictionary.*

After the lead sentence, the UPI story kept to the facts without further facetiousness, mentioning an important fact that the *Times* had overlooked: the new edition contained one hundred thousand new words and senses.

The AP story was in the same vein: "The word 'ain't' at long last has come into its own. It is officially recognized as acceptable usage by *Webster's Third New International Dictionary* to be published September 28 by G. & C. Merriam Company, of Springfield" (*Los Angeles Herald-Express*).

Many modest-sized and small newspapers – in Watertown, New York; Mason City, Iowa; and elsewhere – went their own way. Drawing on press kit material, they wrote accounts that were generally longer and better balanced than the wire service stories. They included a larger sampling of the new words, from *astronaut* and *beatnik* to *ugrug* (bearded seal), a greater number of illustrative quotations, and a great deal more about Noah Webster and the history of the Merriam dictionaries. The *Mason City Globe-Gazette* published its story a day before the release date, and its editor, a dictionary and usage buff, continued to comment on the controversy through spring 1962.[3]

Among columnists and editorial writers, the accent on *ain't* and the growing informality of English usage provoked the greatest reaction. Over the following weeks, variations on the obvious were played out in the headlines: "It Either Is or It Ain't" (*Boston Herald*), "Ain't Nothing Wrong with Use of 'Ain't'" (*Louisville Times*), "With Area Educators, 'Ain't' Still Has Taint" (*Binghamton Sunday Press*), "Good English Ain't What We Thought" (*Chicago Daily News*), "There's Them as Ain't Using 'Ain't,' Mr. Webster" (*Jacksonville* [Fla.] *Journal*), "'Ain't' Is In, Raviolis Ain't (*New York Times Book Review*), "Say It Ain't So" (*Science*).

Months later a sports columnist, Charles McCabe, rose above the mass of predictable variations on the theme with an article entitled "Why Ain't 'Slud' in the Dictionary?"[4] Like other sports writers, McCabe rejoiced in the Third Edition's handling of sports lingo and cited approvingly the inclusion of *screwball, foot-in-the-bucket, Bronx cheer, red dog* (as a verb), and others.

But missing from the dictionary, McCabe complained, was Dizzy Dean's inspired contribution – *slud* – as in "he 'slud' into third base." Dean had become a sportscaster after an extraordinary career as a pitcher for the St. Louis Cardinals and delighted baseball fans with his inventive expressions. Schoolteachers and others were not amused, but even the *New York Times*, which was later to express its horror over the treatment of *ain't* and of usage generally in the Third Edition, was said to have defended *slud* in the sports pages. As for himself, McCabe concluded, "Ain't is good, but 'slud' is better." McCabe also happily echoed a familiar refrain among language observers: "More language is made in saloons than salons. Academies for the preservation of the idiom never get anywhere anyhow."

Another sports columnist, Oscar Fraley of UPI, commented on the "tremendous impact" of sports on the language. Football coaches and writers were being quoted in a dictionary for the first time. Among the new entries he cited were "broken field, mousetrap, . . . screen pass,

"Sorry. Dr. Gove ain't in."

Figure 5. *New Yorker* cartoon by Alan Dunn; copyright 1962, 1990, New Yorker Magazine, Inc. Reprinted with permission.

Statue of Liberty, tally and skull practice . . . nothing on point spread" (December 2).

Cartoonists were slower to join in, but a drawing by Alan Dunn in the *New Yorker* several months later was widely reprinted (Figure 5). Gove could never see any humor in it, but it was the gentlest gibe that he was to receive from the *New Yorker*.[5]

Some journalists made sure their readers knew that they or their papers had been quoted in the new unabridged. Herb Caen, columnist for the *San Francisco Chronicle,* took credit for *beatnik.* He wrote: "'Beatnik,' a term I coined four years ago, is in the new Merriam-

Webster Unabridged Dictionary. I've never been particularly proud of the word, but it's nice to see it in such good company." John Ferris, a staff writer for the *New York World-Telegram*, noted that the paper and two of its columnists, Inez Robb and Robert Ruark, were among the people whose writings were quoted to illustrate the meaning of *snide, just, spade* (slang), and *infiltree*.[6]

While the news stories generally presented the facts in a favorable light – once they got by the hurdle of *ain't* in the headline or lead paragraph – the early editorials expressed reservations or dismay. The *Chicago Daily News* went along with the Third Edition's tolerance for ending a sentence with a preposition, but it disputed the assertion that *ain't* was used orally by cultivated speakers. "Cultivated, our foot. 'Ain't' still makes its user stand out like Simple Simon." Nonetheless, despite its reservations, the *Daily News* concluded on a positive note: "But in the main we believe it the function of an unabridged dictionary to deal realistically with a world that has, after all, buried John Dryden and Alexander Pope and elevated Mickey Spillane and Miss Adler to best-sellerdom."[7]

However, the *Toronto Globe and Mail* quickly registered unqualified disapproval and righteous indignation. Its editorial on September 8 predicted – correctly – that the dictionary's more tolerant treatment of *ain't* "would become the subject for humorous news stories and editorials," and then went on the attack: "Yet just how funny is it? Webster's to the contrary, 'ain't' is not acceptable except when used ironically, in any educated conversation. What Webster's has done is to cast the mantle of its approval over another example of corrupted English." The editorial portrayed this as another stage in the discouraging trend set in motion by advertising slogans, sports jargon, lazy educators, and the overuse of euphemisms (*casket* for *coffin, emotionally disturbed* for *insane,* and so on) by "special pleaders." It concluded:

A dictionary's embrace of the word "ain't" will comfort the ignorant, confer approval upon the mediocre, and subtly imply that proper English is the tool only of the snob; but it will not assist men to speak true to other men. It may, however, prepare us for that future which it could help to hasten. In the caves, no doubt, a grunt will do.[8]

Toronto was ahead of the pack in its scorn and vehemence, but within a few weeks it found itself in good company.

THE QUAGMIRE OF *AIN'T*

The Merriam company was taken aback by the prominence given to the entry on *ain't.* Jocular or not, the press treatment was embarrassing and conveyed a misleading impression – that the dictionary had omitted all caveats in the entry when, in fact, it contained important qualifying words and called it *substandard* except when used orally in sense 1. Some press accounts also included gratuitous words for emphasis. The *Times*, for example, said the dictionary *defended* the use of *ain't*, though the intent was only to *describe* it – a major distinction.

About a week after the first stories appeared, the Merriam company decided to issue a clarifying statement. Apparently drafted by Gove, it pointed out that the dictionary's treatment of *ain't* was not what the press interpreted it to be. *Ain't* was not a newcomer to the dictionary; it had been in the Webster dictionaries since 1890, and evidence of widespread use of the word went back to the seventeenth century. Moreover, it was not true, he said, that the word was accepted without qualification. Sense 1 began with a qualifying usage comment, and sense 2 carried the label *substandard*. The full definition, which was written by Gove himself, was reproduced in the statement to show the differences between the press accounts and the dictionary entry. (The dictionary's style was to use a swung dash [~] rather than repeat the headword, which in this instance was *ain't*.)

1a: are not <you ~ going> <they ~ here> <things ~ what they used to be> **b:** is not <it ~ raining> <he's here, ~ he?> **c:** am not <I ~ ready > —though disapproved by many and more common in less educated speech, used orally in most parts of the U.S. by many cultivated speakers esp. in the phrase *ain't I* **2** *substand* **a:** have not <I ~ seen him> <you ~ told us> **b:** has not <he ~ got the time> <~ the doctor come yet>.

Gove was quoted as saying:

This entry does not seem to us to constitute acceptance or approval of 'ain't.' Its frequent occurrence, in fact, is severely restricted to less educated speech, and when 'ain't' is the equivalent of *have not* . . . it is clearly labeled *substandard.*

The dictionary merely recognizes a linguistic fact which cannot be disputed no matter how objectionable: There are many speech areas of the United States in which cultivated speakers do use "ain't," although even among such speakers it is likely to be restricted to the interrogative tag phrase, "ain't I?"[9]

The shortcomings in the news accounts on *ain't* could not be blamed on the press, however. They reflected errors in the company's press release, which had drastically curtailed the entry to the point of distorting its meaning. The release failed to include the qualifying comment at the beginning, "Though disapproved by many. . . ." It left out the qualifier *many* in the phrase "used orally . . . by many cultivated speakers." It also omitted the distinction between sense 1, which was unlabeled, and sense 2, which was labeled *substandard* in the dictionary, as Gove pointed out in his press release. Moreover, it commented that "'ain't' gets official recognition at last, as 'Used orally in most parts of the U.S. by cultivated speakers,'" an unfortunate statement that invited the inference that *ain't* was appearing in a Merriam dictionary for the first time and that the dictionary was in the business of conferring official recognition on what was and was not acceptable usage.

The follow-up statement did little to help Gove's cause. Though it presented the definition accurately, it did not point out explicitly the list of omissions just noted or explain why examples and usage notes were used in preference to labels. Moreover, it was ignored by most of the press, which typically paid little attention to minor clarifications. Journalists who did report Gove's clarification were puzzled by it and wondered whether Gove was retreating from the position expressed in the original release. When he denied that the dictionary registered either acceptance or approval, was he referring to this particular entry only or to the general proposition that only lexicographers would be likely to appreciate – that a descriptive dictionary is not in the business of expressing approval or acceptance; it merely records the language?

Syndicated columnist Charles McDowell, Jr., had been troubled because none of the early news stories and editorials that he had seen reported exactly what the definition said, and he was still puzzled after seeing the clarification. "This may or may not leave 'ain't' in a more or less acceptable position when it means 'are not,' although we can't tell. Our own hope has been that 'ain't' would some day be accepted in the sense of 'am I not?' – that is, 'ain't I?' which is at least better than 'aren't I?'"

A story in the *Wilmington* (Delaware) *News* (September 16) described Gove's reaction as touchy and defensive. It said the company's pain from the press reaction "was showing through its typewriter."[10]

If the new treatment of *ain't* did not seem to the Merriam editors to constitute acceptance, neither did it clearly suggest disapproval or rejection to others like McDowell who found it equivocal. Thus, even if Gove's follow-up statement had been widely reported, it probably would not have done much to clarify the dictionary's position for the average reader.

Two years later Gove gave virtually the same explanation in an article for schoolteachers, except for a slight elaboration. He wrote that the phrase *disapproved by many* "reflects the dominating influence of traditional grammars and implies that no one who wishes to be accepted by those who pass judgment should use 'ain't' in situations where it is disapproved." He added, "Surely this amplification of the complete entry leaves no basis for saying that our dictionaries accept or approve *ain't*. I know of no more careful analysis in such succinct form to reflect faithfully the facts of usage about this word."[11] However accurate he may have been, Gove never successfully faced up to the problems of readers who were still mystified by the close reasoning and fine distinctions that lay behind the usage comment in sense 1 and the label in sense 2. Without the prominence given to them in recent years by American dictionaries, usage comments written into Third Edition definitions apparently had little impact.[12]

This minor misadventure in clarification was of little concern outside the Merriam company. Only a few reporters took note of it, and it proved to be of little consequence in the unfolding controversy. It is interesting chiefly for the glimpse it affords of the confusion arising from the press release and the company's – or Gove's – defensiveness and inexperience in dealing with the press. It also seems to have marked Gove's emergence as company spokesman on the contents of the dictionary. It was Gove, not President Gallan, who would answer the attacks that followed in the *New York Times, Life* magazine, and other newspapers and magazines. His written performance improved in these situations, and he gradually developed an effective style of responding without seeming too defensive. At the same time, he grew increasingly pessimistic about the usefulness of responding to questions from reporters and criticisms in the press.

THE RELEVANCE OF FOWLER

In defining *ain't*, Gove characteristically looked to the evidence. As he explained later, however, he depended in this instance not only on the

Merriam citation file but also on his own observations and the surveys being conducted for a large cooperative study of regional variations in English, the Linguistic Atlas of the United States and Canada, which had been launched in the 1930s by Hans Kurath of the University of Michigan.[13] He saw the status of *ain't* as an empirical question – was it in reputable use? The decisive issue was how *ain't* was used and by whom, not what grammarians thought about its correctness or acceptability. Thus, neither Gove nor his defenders sought to bolster their argument by pointing to the growing tolerance of *ain't* in the writings of highly regarded authors and grammarians.

In 1926, for example, the most widely known and influential writer on English usage, Henry W. Fowler, discussed the matter almost wistfully and conceded that *ain't* had its virtues. After noting that the use of *ain't* for *isn't* was a blunder, he wrote: "But it is a pity that *a(i)n't* for *am not*, being a natural contraction & supplying a real want, should shock us as though tarred with the same brush. . . . there is no abbreviation but *a(i)n't* I? for *am I not?* or *am not I?*; and the shamefaced reluctance with which these full forms are often brought out betrays the speaker's sneaking affection for the *ain't I* that he (or still more she) fears will convict him of low breeding: (*Well, I'm doing it already, ain't I; Yes ain't I a lucky man? I'm next, ain't I?*)"[14]

Thirty-five years later, Sir Ernest Gowers inserted a reference to the more common *aren't I* when he edited the second edition of *Modern English Usage* (and at the same time deleted Fowler's engaging phrase, the "speaker's sneaking affection for 'ain't I'"). Gowers wrote: "The shamefaced reluctance with which these full forms are often brought out betray the *speaker's sneaking fear* that the colloquially respectable and indeed almost universal 'aren't I' is bad grammar and that 'ain't I' will convict him of low breeding" (my emphasis).

Fowler's observation apparently had little effect on the attitudes of writers and editors. Was Fowler less read than celebrated? Or was the unacceptability of *ain't* too deeply rooted to be shaken even by his opinion? There was no large constituency for legitimizing the word; indeed, to the contrary, since it was one of the rare usage rules that is widely remembered, both the barely literate and the highly cultivated had a stake in preserving its pejorative status.

A Canadian journalist who did mention Fowler's statement found it merely uncharacteristically indecisive: "The forthright Fowler dipsydoodles around the decision in a most unseemly manner. He won't say Yes, and he won't say No." As for himself, the columnist said his mind was made up: "It's one of the ugliest words in the English language, and I want no part of it."[15]

Schoolteachers whose opinions were sampled by local newspapers in several communities displayed no enthusiasm for accepting *ain't* as standard English. For example, in Binghamton, New York, most said they would not use the term themselves, though some "would let the children know it has been accepted as proper English."[16]

Still, had he chosen to do so, Gove could have used Fowler's entry to demonstrate that he was not pronouncing a wholly new doctrine in the Third Edition, as critics implied. He had merely extended Fowler's rationale by accepting the legitimacy of *ain't* in all forms of the present tense, not just the first person. He could also have cited others who had urged the acceptability of *ain't* – H. L. Mencken among them. Even Jacques Barzun, who later turned angrily against the Third Edition, had pronounced himself on the verge of accepting *ain't*. Taking his cue from Mencken, Barzun wrote in 1946:

I am ready to applaud his [Mencken's] attack on the conservatism that refuses to sanction well-established popular usages in grammar. Vernacular grammar not only simplifies; its reasoned acceptance would teach us something about the genius of the language that is obscured by our shoddy and excessive wordmaking. For example, preferring *ain't I?* to the prissy *am I not?;* getting rid of *whom*, which is now omitted where it belongs and where it does not; accepting *he don't* (with no apostrophe in this or similar contractions) would really be "modernizing" in a fashion tolerably practical and democratic.[17]

Gove's reluctance to cite the writings of Fowler, Mencken, and Barzun to support his case was consistent with his preference for a purely empirical approach. To have fallen back on another line of defense might have seemed a resort to convenience rather than a reliance on principle. Moreover, he objected to much of Fowler's work because of its prescriptivism. When Kemp Malone condemned Fowler's *Modern English Usage* as "a brilliant and vicious book," Gove indicated his agreement.[18]

Yet one wonders whether citing Fowler and Barzun, as well as Mencken, would have been a helpful strategy. It would have made clear, in terms that his critics could not dismiss, that *Webster's Third* had not been guilty of an arbitrary and unprecedented judgment and that the definition had nothing to do with the so-called permissiveness of American culture in the 1960s. But if citing respectable precedents may have softened the criticism, it was not likely to have changed public opinion: the country wasn't ready to modify its disdain for *ain't,* and shows no inclination to do so more than three decades later.

SYMPATHETIC ASSESSMENTS

The major news weeklies shaped their stories to their readership; most ignored *ain't* and focused on more relevant matters. *Business Week* looked at the dictionary sympathetically from a managerial perspective. "How's this for a businessman's nightmare," it began. "A company that pours millions into research but brings out a new model only about four times each century" comes out with a product "that could easily prove 20 years ahead of its market."

Aside from its reference to buyer resistance to the new edition, the article was upbeat and respectful. It gave most of the space to information about the new edition and to Gordon Gallan's hopes for reaching a larger market. It quoted the admiring comments of a competitor who said that what Merriam did in its new edition was right, though it was ahead of the market in some of its policies, and that the company's scholarship and scholarly resources were unmatched.[19]

Publisher's Weekly carried the news of the Third Edition to the book trade, emphasizing the company's ambitious advertising and marketing campaign, which would be costlier than any previous campaign for a comparable reference work. The article included photos of President Gallan with the dictionary and a close-up of the brass promotional display rack available to booksellers. It filled a page and a half and was free of disparaging innuendoes; it was clearly a good plug for the book. But it did take note of the complaints of booksellers who were angered by the company's refusal to accept the return of unsold stock for credit. Dealers were mollified later when the Second Edition began selling at a premium in the wake of the early hostility toward the new work.[20]

Time magazine put the Third Edition into historical context with references to Johnson and Webster, and it described how the citation file was built and used. The story was a long one, and as the following excerpt indicates, the style was vintage *Time:*

The dictionary nowadays is more a *Social Register* of language than a Supreme Court of language. In the 27 years since . . . the Second Edition . . . thousands of new words have clamored to be listed. Last week, . . . Merriam responded with a brand new edition. . . . the most radical version yet of the nation's most famous dictionary.

. . . from *A* to *zyzzogeton* (a genus of South American leaf hoppers) Merriam Webster's Third Edition is lighter and brighter than its immediate predecessor. . . . Gone are the gazetteer, the biographical dictionary and 100,000 obsolete or non-lexical terms. . . . In are about 100,000 brand-new terms from *astronaut* to . . . *zip gun*. . . .

. . . *wordwise*, science by far outdoes slang in supplying neologisms. . . . Medicine yields the longest word (45 letters). . . . Conversely, one of the shortest words, *set*, requires the longest definition – more than a full page.

The most conspicuous change . . . is that every definition is really new. Instead of thumbnail essays, they run to single phrases. To illustrate new shades of meaning, they include 200,000 quotations that draw on sources as diverse as *Variety, Lingerie Merchandising,* and TIME (probably the most frequently quoted magazine).

Ain't was mentioned only incidentally in a paragraph that listed some changes that might "pain purists," such as additional four-letter words "usu. considered vulgar" and other questionable new words, such as *snide, just* (in the sense of merely), and the slang term *in spades*.[21]

Television viewers were given a brief, lively, and sympathetic introduction to the Third Edition by Stuart Novins on September 9 over the CBS network.

In England, where the British edition was to be published by George Bell & Sons, publisher of Merriam dictionaries for a hundred years, the *Bookseller* printed the first of many consistently favorable reviews that would appear in British periodicals. Half of the *Bookseller*'s long and supportive review was devoted to the key features of the new work, especially the gathering and use of citations, and half to Noah Webster's life and work.[22]

The *St. Louis Globe-Democrat* presented a favorable interpretation of the company's goals and achievements. It was written by Sumner Ives, a professor of English at Syracuse University, who had prepared "An Outline Commentary" on the Third Edition at the behest of the Merriam company; Merriam used it in its book promotion. Ives called it a dictionary "made by scholars [and] addressed to laymen." What set it apart, he said, were its huge file of citations that provided a cross section of how English is used; the drawing of conclusions from the raw materials of language in a rigorous, objective, and inductive procedure; the professionalism of its staff of skilled lexicographers; and its focus on the words in the language, in contrast to dictionaries that include encyclopedic information.[23]

AN EARLY BALANCE SHEET

At this point in the history of the Third Edition, the Merriam company and its public relations consultant could still conclude justifiably that the prepublication campaign had been a success. It attracted attention across the country, thereby paving the way for the sales campaign to follow. For the most part the publicity was favorable, though it offended some readers. Where reservations or criticisms were expressed, they were usually offset by positive comments about the coverage of new words and favorable references to the Merriam-Webster tradition. The minor embarrassment over Gove's clarification of *ain't* was momentary. The sharp attack in the *Toronto Globe and Mail* seemed to be an exception. The *New York Times* indicated its irritation in a short editorial that caricatured the dictionary's acceptance of seven words that the newspaper's editors did not consider to be standard English – *orientate, upsurge, hipster, dig, jazz, beef up*, and *finalize*. But the full implications of this brief item were not obvious at the time.[24]

Years later, Raven I. McDavid, Jr., wrote a detailed assessment of the prepublication publicity and came to a more pessimistic conclusion. He thought the early press clippings showed that even before the Third Edition was published it "was going to get a working over" from the press. He felt it never had a chance for a fair hearing.[25]

As a linguist, McDavid thought that four themes in the early stories boded ill for the dictionary among serious dictionary users: the claim that the Third Edition would provide entertaining reading for the average family; the emphasis on novelty; the trend toward informality in usage; and the apparent acceptance of *ain't* used orally as standard English. His article – which begins with a superb and succinct sketch of the background of the controversy and is heavily documented by quotations from scores of press accounts – supplies ample evidence of the pervasiveness of these themes in the prepublication period and their troublemaking potential. None of them were likely to appeal to devoted users of the Second Edition, however much they may have titillated the press.

However, there is no evidence that most journalists were prejudiced against the dictionary from the beginning and were bent on undermining it. They merely made the most of what they found in the company's publicity kit. The early stories reveal more about journalistic practices in popularizing scholarly and unfamiliar material than about the attitudes of journalists toward *Webster's Third*. They showed the susceptibility of the press to publicity handouts that are well crafted and the difficulty of striking a balance between serious reporting and the temptation to strain for cleverness. McDavid interpreted the headline on the story by McCandlish Phillips – "Webster Soups Up Its Big Dictionary" – as evidence that the *New York Times* had "tipped its hand." This is highly unlikely. This was day one in the story; the *Times* had not yet decided to take a stand. There was no hint of bias in the news story by Phillips, and it is much more plausible to infer that the editor who wrote the headline was only enlivening the message to catch the attention of readers; it was not his job to bring news coverage into line with the views of the editorial page staff.

Similarly, there was indeed an emphasis on newness in press reports, but too much was made of it as an expression of journalistic bias. What else would a newspaper story emphasize other than what was new? Gove himself emphasized newness in his own writings. The opening lines of his preface said, "Webster's Third New International Dictionary is an entirely new work. . . . Every line of it is new." The preface to the Second Edition had said almost as much, but not as emphatically. Sumner Ives emphasized newness in his commentary and his review, and so did the press release. The problem was not newness but the inference by critics in later stories that the past had been neglected. Instead of inspiring curiosity and excitement, newness came to suggest to writers and editors the abandonment of tradition.

The description of the Third Edition as entertaining reading for the whole family utterly misrepresented it to the general public, and as McDavid noted, it suggested to editors and teachers a different kind of work than the scholarly guide they had leaned on for so long. However, like all the other themes that boded ill for the Third Edition, this one was not conjured up by a biased press bent on giving the dictionary a "working over." It appeared first in the Merriam company's publicity kit. The top heading on the release read, "New Merriam-Webster Unabridged Dictionary, Breaking Sharply with Tradition, Is First Specifically Planned to be Read and Enjoyed by Students, Housewives and Business Men as well as Scholars."

The rest of the release, in keeping with the opening hyperbole and misstatements of fact, seemed more suited to the promotion of a circus or the sale of patent medicines. It boasted of "revolutionary" achievements, such as the use of quotations from "contemporary notables . . . in a revolutionary break with tradition." It cited as a "revolutionary defining technique" the use of "precise single phrases to define 450,000 entries." It added that "a third [revolutionary achievement] is the simplified system of sound symbols which make all subtle nuances of pronunciation clear for the first time, even to students of English."

These statements were either demonstrably wrong or highly misleading, though such exaggeration was not unusual in the highly competitive business of dictionary publishing. Nothing in the deliberations of the Editorial Board or in Gove's Black Books suggested that the Third Edition was planned for the enjoyment of the average family; indeed, the material most likely to be popular with the average person was thrown out when the decision was made to include only lexical material. Gove edited the dictionary to exacting lexicographical standards as he saw them. He did not cater to the preferences and pleasure of readers. He hoped the dictionary would attract a large audience and prove useful to any reader who took the trouble to read it carefully, but his policies and practices were not guided by this hope.

The use of illustrative quotations from contemporary sources was hardly "revolutionary," since it had been done in the Second Edition. Indeed, even James Murray had included contemporary quotations in the *OED* – thereby provoking an outcry from his peers.[26] Gove greatly expanded the practice, but not for the purpose of entertaining readers or trading on the fame or notoriety of the source quoted. The presentation in the press release was completely at odds with the views on illustrative quotations he expressed in a paper delivered in 1961 at Georgetown University (discussed in Chapter 6).

The new defining technique by Gove could be called an admirable new approach, but hardly revolutionary. The new pronunciation system used fewer symbols than its predecessor, but it included many new ones and, if perhaps technically superior, was harder to master. Though it sought to make subtle nuances of pronunciation clear, it was designed for experts, not students.

All of these misrepresentations appeared on the first page of the release. Additional errors in fact and judgment occurred on the ensuing pages. The entry on *ain't* was seriously misquoted. The publicist's grammar was sometimes shaky: "There are less differences in the use of English." It was a surprisingly poor piece of work in all respects but one: it succeeded in generating heavy press coverage.[27] Moreover, the press kit contained more than the press release. It included other historical information and several photographs. A pinup of movie star Betty Grable, who had been quoted in an illustrative quotation, struck at least one editor as bizarre.

In short, the publicity campaign, as many linguists noted at the time, was based on a huge miscalculation and proved to be a serious blunder. The company and its public relations consultant failed to understand the nature of their new dictionary and its market, and they were out of touch with their traditional constituency. Gallan promoted the kind of dictionary that he thought the market wanted and that he had hoped the company would publish, not the dictionary that Gove had produced.

A CLOSER LOOK AT THE PUBLICITY STRATEGY

How could such a miscalculation have been made? Some predisposing factors can be identified. Long before the Third Edition appeared, there had been a clear difference between the nature of the dictionary as the editors saw it and as it was portrayed in the company's promotion and advertising programs. Over many decades, the company had advertised its unabridged dictionary as the "supreme authority." It solicited, quoted, and disseminated the opinions of jurists and educators who said they looked to the Merriam dictionaries for the best answers to questions of meaning and usage. It invited the inference that Merriam editors and consultants were arbiters of what was correct and incorrect in the use of the English language.

The editors saw their product in a quite different light. They made no claims to being authorities. The dictionary was *authoritative* because it was based on the largest and best collection of citations showing how the English language was being used and because it was produced by an experienced and highly trained staff of scholars and editors. The Merriam company had not been designated by a higher authority – nor had it appointed itself – to decide what was good or correct usage.

This difference in perspective was tolerated within the company rather than challenged. Just as the business office let the editorial department manage its own affairs, so presumably did the editors go along with publicity that would help sell books as long as the integrity of the dictionary was not compromised. To the extent that Ruth Mallard, the public relations consultant, maintained the convenient distinction between marketing and editorial responsibility, she was doing nothing unprecedented in proclaiming qualities for the product that the editors did not assert. In avoiding the "supreme authority" slogan, apparently on the recommendation of the editorial staff, she was perhaps more modest than some of her predecessors. Little is recalled about the roles played by the consultant and company executives in the planning of the publicity campaign, except that Mallard warned that the outcome was uncertain, especially when a release date was set well in advance of the event. A major news break might well crowd out a story about a new dictionary.

Mallard must have had some assistance from the marketing and editorial departments, however. It would have been difficult for an outsider to ferret out the details that appeared in the press release, and it is difficult to believe that Gove and his top editors would have been completely ignored in the planning of the final publicity. Gallan could have been only of limited help, since he knew little about the substance of the dictionary and deferred to Gove on editorial matters. But if personally consulted, Gove is not likely to have become seriously involved. He "wasn't really interested in such details, and I doubt that he saw the press release before it was sent out."[28] Moreover, since he was to express his own views in the company publication *Word Study* in October (see Chapter 11), he may have been less concerned about what appeared in the publicity release.

A more likely source of help may have been the commentary by Professor Ives, which ran more than forty typewritten pages and explained the features of the dictionary clearly and in considerable detail. The opening part of it appeared under his byline in the *St. Louis Globe-Democrat* for September 25. An abridged version of the commentary was published in the December 1961 issue of Merriam's *Word Study.* Copies of the full commentary were also distributed with review copies of the book.

An article that appeared in the *St. Louis Post-Dispatch* several years later suggests that neither Gove nor Gallan had a say in the final draft of the press release or in selecting the rest of the material in the press kit. "One of the ironies . . . is that the aspects of [the dictionary's] content that were used for their news value in the early publicity releases were *settled upon* by a promotion firm [my emphasis] and not by the dictionary publishers. Presumably they themselves would have known enough about popular attitudes toward language and dictionaries to have played down the fact that they had been lenient toward 'ain't' and had quoted people like Art Linkletter and Ethel Merman."[29]

Gove reprinted this review a year later in his book on the role of the dictionary, lending credence to its authenticity.[30] If the interpretation was unfounded, Gove would probably not have chosen to reprint it. The ambiguous phrase "settled upon" leaves open the possibility that Gove and others were in fact consulted in the preparation of the release – and may have agreed to most of the contents in principle – but had no opportunity to check the "final form" of the release with its errors and misrepresentations.

THE PREPUBLICATION PUBLICITY CAMPAIGN set the stage for the ensuing controversy. It alerted the press to the publication of an important new dictionary, and the early news stories and editorials aroused the critics, helped shape their agenda, and built an audience for the battle over the Third Edition. But neither the publicity tactics – misguided as they were – nor the prepublication stories can fully account for the intensity of the criticism that erupted during the last months of 1961 and that reached a climax during 1962. Why didn't the controversy simply fade away after the fun over *ain't* was over? It is when the debate moves beyond *ain't* and becomes entangled with deeply held views about language and society that the unusual conjunction of the dictionary and the times becomes understandable.

10

The Controversy Heats Up

I find righteous denunciations of the present state of the language no less dismaying than the present state of the language.

Lionel Trilling

A shift in the wind was detectable when the first major review appeared on September 30, 1961, in the *Saturday Review* under the byline of David M. Glixon, a New York editor and reviewer. Glixon likened *Webster's Third* to the *New English Bible,* which had outraged admirers of the King James Version a decade earlier and had led to a memorable controversy. The appearance of the new dictionary, he noted, "is equally important, for the adherents of a given dictionary defend their choice with all the fervor of religious devotees" – an assessment that was to be repeatedly confirmed.

Glixon noted that "fresh criteria" governed the making of the Third Edition, leading to a narrower concept of what a dictionary should include and a less traditional view of what constitutes standard English. He lamented the decision to narrow the scope by eliminating rare words, obsolete meanings, and the historical and literary information that made the Second edition a "virtual one-volume encyclopedia." He found it especially strange that while proper nouns were left out, adjectives derived from them were included (*dickensian* was in but *Dickens* was not). There was no suggestion in his assessment of the estimable precedents for this change in the practices of the *OED* or in Johnson's omission of proper nouns.

He interpreted the use of illustrative quotations "from all levels of culture" and the omission of the colloquial label as a relaxation of raditional standards. "For under the new dispensation the editors do ₁ot pretend to rule on what is correct; they merely record the words and pronunciations now prevailing 'among the educated and cultural people to whom the language is vernacular.'" In his comments on *ain't*, he cited the Third Edition more accurately than the press had done, having apparently read the actual entry, but he was no less derisive. "It is good to be told that although when used in place of *hasn't* or *haven't*, *ain't* is considered 'substandard,' you may feel free to use it for *aren't*, *isn't* and *am not*. . . . It would seem that permissiveness, now on the wane in child-rearing, has caught up with the dictionary makers. Having descended from God's throne of supreme authority, the Merriam folks are now seated around the city desk, recording like mad."

Numerous editorial practices annoyed him, such as the elimination of the pronunciation guide on the text pages and the omission of the initial capital letter in entry words that were customarily capitalized: "And if the *Shorter Oxford Dictionary* exasperates the user by beginning every entry with a capital, the Third International fiendishly echoes a certain modern poet" by replacing the capitals with the notes *cap*, *usu cap*, and so on. Overall, the "deficiencies" of the Third Edition, Glixon wrote, overshadowed the "solid virtues" of its greater scientific accuracy. "Let us grant the Third New International scientifically arrays before us our present-day world of words – but don't throw out your copy of the Second Edition unabridged."[1]

Compared with some of the criticisms that appeared later, Glixon's style was low-key, but his review left little doubt about his dismay. Two of his themes in particular resonated with the feelings of Gove's critics: one was the use of the term *permissiveness* as a symbol of what was wrong with the new edition; the other was his concluding tag, "Don't throw out your copy of the Second Edition." Both were echoed repeatedly in the ensuing months.

THUNDER FROM THE *TIMES*

Unfavorable reviews in the following weeks took on a more hostile and uncompromising tone. On October 12 the *New York Times* set the new style. It published a stinging rebuke that began with a derisive parody of the dictionary's policies and ended with a startling call for a "new start" on a dictionary based on the Second Edition that could replace the unacceptable Third Edition. The article began as follows:

A passel of double-domes at the G.&C. Merriam Company joint in Springfield, Mass., have been confabbing and yakking for twenty seven years – which is not intended to infer that they have not been doing plenty work – and now they have finalized Webster's Third New International Dictionary, Unabridged, a new edition of that swell and esteemed word book.

Those who regard the foregoing paragraph as acceptable English prose will find that the new Webster's is just the dictionary for them. The words in that paragraph all are listed in the new work with no suggestion that they are anything but standard.

Webster's has, it is apparent, surrendered to the permissive school that has been busily extending its beachhead on English instruction in the schools.

The new dictionary, it continued, was a disaster because it "reinforced the notion that good English is whatever is popular." Such a "say-as-you-go dictionary," it said, "can only accelerate the deterioration" already apparent among college students. Webster's had established itself as "a peerless authority" on American English, becoming "almost a public institution. Its editors therefore have to some degree a public responsibility. In issuing the Third New International they have not lived up to it."[2]

A few days later, Sydney J. Harris, the popular columnist of the *Chicago Daily News*, echoed the *Times*'s parody: "Lemme recommend a swell new book that has been in the works for 27 years and has just been finalized – no kidding – by the G.&C. Merriam Co." He continued with an attack on "relativism . . . the reigning philosophy of our day in all fields. . . . There is no right and wrong – it is all merely custom and superstition to believe so." He concluded by elaborating on Glixon's theme of permissiveness with a far broader generalization: "Our attitude toward language merely reflects our attitude toward more basic matters. It is not terribly important whether we use 'ain't,' or 'like' instead of 'as' – except as symptoms of a general decay in values."[3]

Gove was astonished and appalled by the article in the *Times* and its echoes in other publications. As he saw it, a dictionary presenting up-to-date information on some 450,000 words had been damned largely on the basis of a few disputed usages – such words as *ain't* and *finalize*, a comparative handful of quotations attributed to popular politicians, athletes, and entertainers, and the elimination of nonlexical information (for which there was ample precedent). It seemed that the criticisms of the dictionary rested less on lexicographical criteria than on judgments about the social status of words and the fear that by readily accepting changes in usage, the Third Edition would corrupt the mother tongue and contribute to the widespread decay already at work in American society.

Gove drafted a detailed reply to the *Times* that was buttressed by quotations showing extensive use of the disputed words by established writers and other prominent people. He was dissuaded from mailing it, however, because others at the Merriam company thought it was too long and too strongly worded to be accepted by the *Times*. Instead, he sent a shorter and more restrained version, which was published as a letter to the editor on November 5. Referring to the editorial's opening paragraph, "in which you pounce on nine words out of 450,000 to announce that we have been confabbing and yakking . . . for twenty-seven years to finalize a new dictionary," he wrote:

This paragraph is, of course, a monstrosity totally removed from possible occurrence in connection with any genuine attempt to use words in normally expected context. It hits no mark at all. A similar monstrosity could be contrived by jumbling together inappropriate words from formal literary language, or from the Second Edition.

He explained that there were many degrees of standard usage that could not be distinguished by status labels but that could be suggested by illustrative quotations. The ridiculed words were all standard in the appropriate context. As for *finalize*, it had appeared without a usage label in the Second Edition, and it "turns up all over the English speaking world from the Nineteen Twenties through the Nineteen Fifties in highly reputable places like *Current History*, . . . *The New Republic* and *The Times* itself."

Regarding *double-dome*, he wrote, "I could quote from some of your respected peers like John Mason Brown in the *Saturday Review;* the *New Yorker;* . . . Clifton Fadiman in *Holiday* . . . and Alistair Cooke in the *BBC Listener.*"

Webster's Third New International Dictionary quotes the *Times* at more than 700 entries. This figure does not include several hundred other quotations attributed to such *Times* byliners as C. L. Sulzberger, James Reston, Arthur Krock and Brooks Atkinson. . . .

In this way we get the kind of evidence we need and rely on to keep up with our changing standard language. . . .

Whether you or I or others who fixed our linguistic notions several decades ago like it or not, the contemporary English language of the Nineteen Sixties – the language we have to live with, the only language we have to survive with – is not the language of the Nineteen Twenties and Thirties.[4]

Gove also sent letters to editors of the newspapers that reprinted or quoted from the editorial in the *Times*. The version printed in the *St. Louis Post-Dispatch* of November 10 noted that "the basic responsibility of a dictionary is to record language, not set its style. For us to attempt to proscribe the language would be like the *Post-Dispatch* reporting the news as your editors would prefer it to happen. . . . the social and professional consequences of using a wrong word in wrong circumstances remain as serious as ever."[5]

The *Times* also received an indignant letter from an innocent bystander, Art Linkletter, who objected to being "linked with a notorious 'madam,' Polly Adler," in the editorial attacking the Third Edition's illustrative quotations. He said he had a master's degree in English, had written "several fairly creditable books," and took pride in his use of English. In his daily program for a mass television audience, he had not been "slangy, sloppy or trite" in his phraseology. "I have been good to my mother, raised a fine family, and have never kicked a newspaper man even when I found one under my table. . . . Why blast me? . . . This is irresponsible writing, and not what one would expect to find in the world's most responsible newspaper."[6]

The editorial in the *Times* also provoked a letter from Bergen Evans who wrote Gove that he thought "the editorial in the *Times* last week was contemptible." He added that he was doing an article on new words for the *Times* in December in which he intended to call the Third Edition "*the* word news of 1961." He congratulated Gove "on the great work you have accomplished. I am awestruck. . . . I have a light book on words coming out soon (Random House) and in the course of it I have discussed a dozen or more words whose meanings have changed so recently that no dictionary has yet taken cognizance of the change. I will not deny that I was mightily pleased with myself. After an hour with the Third International I had to pull every one of those statements in page proof. You had caught every last one of my words."[7]

Gove expressed his thanks promptly. Among the many letters of congratulations he had received, he wrote, "yours rises right to the top." Nonetheless, he had come to a rather gloomy conclusion: "We look for many other supporters, but the forces of uninformed traditionalism are so strong that I expect to struggle against them for the rest of my life with success only here or there."[8]

MIXED REPORTS

The *Times* rapidly picked up allies in the press and among other writers and editors in its opposition to *Webster's Third*. In style and substance its editorial became the prototype for many of the most outspoken attacks that followed. Moreover, the *Times's* startling proposal that the Third Edition be thrown out and work begun on a replacement was not mere bravado. Within months the Merriam company would be fending off well-financed efforts by outsiders to buy out the company for precisely that purpose.

Still, the picture was not wholly bleak. On the very day the *Times* ran its parody, the *Wall Street Journal* published a review by John Chamberlain, its conservative economic and political commentator, who took quite a different tack. He was impressed by the Third Edition's portrayal of the enormous growth and change in the language since Noah Webster's day, both good and bad. Among his examples was the word *Aesopian*, which the new edition first defined in the traditional sense, "in the manner of Aesop or his beast fables." But he also noted with displeasure the widespread acceptance of the second sense, its use as a synonym for "dissembling," as in "Aesopian language only understood by those indoctrinated in such verbiage." This he considered to be the kind of distortion of meaning that Orwell had warned against. Chamberlain's target was the propagandist and obfuscator who intentionally misused the language, not the dictionary that reported what was going on. He urged writers and speakers to learn more about the origin and development of language. "If you know where your language comes from, you will recognize Big Brother's Newspeak for what it is."[9]

There was much more good and bad news for the Merriam company as the reviews and comments continued to flow in during the year. A few encouraging words appeared even in the *Times*. The Sunday *Book Review,* separately edited, published a review ten days after the editorial attack in the daily *Times*. It was written by Mario Pei, professor of romance philology at Columbia University and author of the highly popular book *The Story of Language* and other works. Pei was sympathetic to the lexicographer's view of language change. He called the growth of the English vocabulary a matter for rejoicing and an intellectual achievement, not a cause for alarm, and he found that "there are many commendable features in this latest of vocabulary offerings."

Still, he doubted that the so-called revolutionary techniques of defining made "words meaningful to everyone." He noted that if the dictionary's authority was based on usage, it wasn't clear "whose usage" was to be followed. Yet when he came to the treatment of *ain't* and the dropping of the colloquial label, he commented, "This is all to the good, but it leaves me wondering how far the process of informality can go before it incurs the charge of outright vulgarism." In the next paragraph he took the Third Edition to task for inconsistency in failing to include all the four-letter words. If usage was the criterion, "why this residual prudishness?"

He cited several inconsistencies in treatment – the plural *s* on *spaghettis*, but not on *ravioli* or *rigatoni*. He expressed regret at the omission of specialized tables that had appeared in the Second Edition, the lack of etymologies of names, and the inclusion of personal and place names "only in their adjectival" role. "Are personal and place names not as much a part of the language as some of the common nouns that receive satisfactory attention?"

He found that "the expansion in meaning of the word [*shake*] is little short of astonishing" and that the definitions "are exemplified by an impressive series of quotes from Polly Adler to Virginia Woolf." His comment on *shake* was based on a comparison of sample pages from Webster's 1828 dictionary and the Third Edition, which were sent with the commentary by Sumner Ives to reviewers.

His review concluded on a positive though guarded note: "Despite these and other criticisms that could and will be made, 'Webster's Third New International Dictionary' will enjoy a healthy life, even if not too prolonged. It is the closest we can get, in America, to the Voice of Authority."[10]

Pei's review is noteworthy not only for its acceptance of *ain't* and the use of illustrative quotations from nonliterary sources, two of the matters most heavily attacked by the press, but because it focused on the dictionary itself rather than on the ideological issue of permissiveness. In time, however, Pei would reverse his position, and his would become a major voice in the chorus protesting the Third Edition's alleged permissiveness.

At about the same time, Gove was buoyed by a congratulatory letter from Professor Bernard Bloch of Yale University, who was in Seattle on a year's leave at the University of Washington:

> Today came your magnificent new dictionary. . . . After spending the better part of the evening leafing through [it], dipping into it at odd places, browsing here and there, reading a little in the Guide to Pronunciation, . . . I want to drop you this line of thanks and congratulations. The qualities that strike me most forcibly in the new work are boldness and courage . . . the scrapping of the hallowed "Webster Key," with all its confusion and redundancy . . . the disappearance of the limbo at the foot of the page – the words beneath the line; the often spritely and even witty tone of your definitions (as at *wolf* 2a (4), which make it an active pleasure to read this dictionary . . . the defiant realism of the pronunciation . . . the striking use of lower case for all entries, with its implication in many cases that the use of capitals for every so-called proper noun or adjective is beginning to pall – I could go on for pages. I am thoroughly in favor also of your decision to minimize the encyclopedic character of the work.
>
> My sincere thanks. . . . It's a lovely dictionary.[11]

A few days later *Life* magazine picked up on the themes of Glixon and the *Times:* "Webster's, joining the say-as-you-go school of permissive English, has now all but abandoned any effort to distinguish between good and bad usage. . . . Thus, the most monstrous of all non-words – 'irregardless' – is included in the dictionary. So is Madison Avenue's abomination of adding '-wise' to those nouns." *Life* nonetheless welcomed new words like *beatnik* and *litterbug*. Like Pei, it went along with *ain't* as a justifiable contraction. "We're not opposed to progress, but we'll just keep the Second Edition around awhile for little matters of style, good English, winning at Scrabble and suchwise."[12]

Life's misrepresentations and mistakes in its comments on the treatment of usage were so flagrant that Gove drafted a strong rejoinder. In his response, he suggested that the editor take another look at the Second and Third Editions. "You will find that *irregardless* is in Second and that Third calls it 'nonstandard'; *enormity* is not 'approved' (nor even listed) in Third as a synonym for 'enormous-

ness;' *normalcy, concretize* and *finalize* are in the Second as well as in
Third, and *wisdomwise* and *governmentwise* are in neither edition." He
added that "the social and professional consequences of using a
wrong word in wrong circumstances remain as serious as ever."[13]

Bergen Evans was equally annoyed by the *Life* editorial and wrote
Gove another supportive letter:

I happened to be in the hospital when I read their statement, and having
some time on my hands amused myself by reading their entire issue, not the
ads, marking the words that are not in the Second International or that are
used with meanings not in the Second International. I came up with 44.[14]

Meanwhile, the assistant managing editor of the *New York Times*,
Theodore M. Bernstein, stepped up the attack on *Webster's Third* in
the *Bulletin of the American Society of Newspaper Editors*. In an article
discussing the spreading misuse of the language, he coined the word
delinguancy to describe the spreading corruption of the language. He
said he had identified its most common forms "while serving as the
self-appointed cop on the delinguancy patrol" for the *New York Times*.

Bernstein's comments on *Webster's Third* appeared under the title
"Permissiveness Gone Mad" in a separate story that was inserted
within a box on the second page of his article. He said that the new
dictionary, "a complete revision of the generally respected Second
Edition, has methodically removed all guideposts to usage except for
an infinitesimal number labeling the most obvious pieces of slang and
vulgarity and has turned the dictionary into a bewildering wilderness
of words. It is all things to all words. It is permissiveness gone mad."

Bernstein acted on his objections two months later. On January 4,
he issued a directive to the newspaper's staff stating that the *Times*
would continue to use the Second Edition for spelling and usage and
would refer to the Third Edition only for "new, principally scientific,
words. Two copies of that edition are available in the news department."[15] Later, the *Times* selected *Webster's New World Dictionary* as
its desk dictionary.

The attack continued in an editorial in *Science*, the prestigious
journal of the American Association for the Advancement of Science.
The editor conceded that the Third Edition paid its "debt to science
more fully than to general culture," handling technical terms better
than English in general. But outside his area of expertise, he was
content to repeat the typical criticisms – objecting to the dropping of

the colloquial label and the treatment of *ain't;* he echoed the charge that distinctions between pairs of words, such as *imply* and *infer,* had been blurred. Following the lead of *Life,* he mistakenly interpreted the label *nonstandard* to mean that *irregardless* was accepted usage.[16]

FRIENDLY CRITICS IN THE PRESS

Outside New York, Washington, and Chicago, *Webster's Third* received a much more favorable reception than has been commonly recognized. Several highly regarded newspapers gave strong support to the new edition – notably the *St. Louis Post-Dispatch, Christian Science Monitor, Louisville Times,* and *Cleveland Plain Dealer.* In addition, the leading magazine of the newspaper business, *Editor & Publisher,* welcomed it and rebuked the press for its uninformed and silly treatment of the new work. When these reviews are added to the sympathetic accounts in the New York weeklies – *Business Week, Time,* and *Publisher's Weekly* – the journalistic reception of the Third Edition in late 1961 appears to be far less one-sided than the dictionary's critics made it out to be. The weight of opinion, however, as contrasted with the number of reviews, was probably against the dictionary, given the visibility and influence of the *New York Times.*

Among the most knowledgeable of the sympathetic reviewers was Roy H. Copperud, whose column on newspaper style had been published regularly in *Editor & Publisher* for many years. Copperud was favorably impressed by the Third Edition and called the attacks on it "a flurry of nitwitted commentary."

Twenty minutes spent on the conclusions of any reputable linguist in the last 25 years should convince even the most obtuse that the business of a dictionary is to report how words are used, and not to prescribe or proscribe meanings. . . .

. . . there is no resisting new usages if they gain acceptance, nor is there any evidence that discouragement has had any effect. Let us remember that *blizzard* was once slang. . . . Nor is it true that lexicographers agree that once a misuse has occurred, it must be accepted. On the contrary, their conclusions represent a consensus based upon millions of examples culled from a tremendous variety of reputable sources.

Far from introducing a new era of permissiveness, he continued, "Webster editors are conforming with scholarly conclusions that have developed over the last half-century and are now so firmly established as to be beyond question." He referred readers to *Webster's New World Dictionary* and *The American College Dictionary*, major competitors of the Merriam-Webster *Collegiate*, to illustrate the consensus among lexicographers that usage determines correctness. "These principles are fairly well known among those who use language professionally, with the notorious exception of newspapermen, whose typical use of the tools of their trade has even been damned by a name, *journalese*."

There remained a place for judgments on usage, he asserted. Like others, he had personal prejudices against many uses that had crept into the language, including the word *finalize*. He was also critical of some of the Third Edition's innovations: the new system of pronunciation would baffle readers; the historical order of senses could be challenged; he, too, wondered at the failure to include the four-letter word "for *copulate with*," when all the other words omitted in the "prudish" Second Edition had been included.

But all in all, he said, the new dictionary "recognizes as standard the informal style that is now everywhere current – in books, newspapers, the casual conversation of the educated, speeches, and what have you." By contrast, the earlier Webster, like its contemporary grammars and works on usage, took its cue "from the 'formal style,' which has now passed out of existence, except perhaps in mayors' proclamations and news editorials and even a generation ago did not represent a cultivated consensus."[17]

David Horne, executive editor of Yale University Press, took a rather bemused view of the controversy. He noted that an editor cannot depend on any single dictionary or book on usage, though he may consult them occasionally, especially for the meaning of an unfamiliar word. Sometimes he will be editing the work of a writer whose style is formal and proper and sometimes the work of an easygoing informal writer. "A book editor should not himself be rigid. . . . His job is to see that what an author says is right . . . namely, that which is fitting and proper in its context." Convinced that the power of the dictionary to regulate language was greatly overrated, Horne saw no danger of the Third Edition corrupting the use of English or subverting the nation.[18]

Norman E. Isaacs, the widely respected editor of the *Louisville Times*, chided the New York critics for their views and pretensions. Isaacs found it "most unlikely that the erudite gentlemen of the New York *Times* can win the argument. . . . traditionalists in language have always lost these debates. For language is a living thing. No language remains constant from one generation to another. . . . The net is that we have a new dictionary and it will become the accepted authority, despite all the literary hassles that will ensue."

On specifics, Isaacs observed that if such terms as *teaching fellow, carbon 14, traffic island,* and *crop duster* were accepted, why object to *litterbug, double domes, yakking, finalize, two-way stretch, greasy spoon,* and others? "Are these not also part of the language?" He noted with approval the elimination of editorial comments that had appeared in Second Edition definitions, such as the pejorative one on *journalistic,* which had enraged the profession.[19]

Rudolf Flesch, whose books on clear writing and clear thinking were best-sellers during the late 1940s and the 1950s, greeted the Third Edition with great enthusiasm in his newspaper column, "Conversation Piece." He called it a "breakthrough in the field of English" and cited approvingly the Third Edition's notes on the wider acceptance among educated speakers of such usages as *it's me* and *who do you know,* even though they were "disapproved by some grammarians."[20]

In the *Christian Science Monitor,* Millicent Taylor, education editor, guided readers through the major features of the new dictionary sympathetically and explained its contribution in considerable detail. She thought the format made "the entries more difficult to read" than those in the Second Edition, and she was put off by the lack of capitalization. But overall, she found it to be "an intensely interesting and distinguished scholarly work, an important milestone in the history of a particularly living, flexible and beautiful language."[21]

The *New York Times* resumed its heckling on November 30, when President Kennedy used *finalize* during his news conference. Seizing the opportunity to taunt the Third Edition once again, it commented under the heading "Finalized?": "Mr. President, are you sure you gave the old place a thorough housecleaning after you moved in? It seems that your predecessor left a few loose words behind that you may have inadvertently picked up." It compared his usage to Eisenhower's "as quoted in Webster's Third (or Bolshevik) International," and suggested inviting in the cleaners. "They'll have the know-how to get the job finishized."

In a second item on the same day, it quoted the words of an anonymous "grieving linguist" that "Eisenhower began the process, and Kennedy is finalizing it."[22]

It might all have been seen as just good fun had it not been for the suggestion of a subversive link between *Webster's Third International Dictionary* and the Communist Third International, the bogey of the day, which added an inflammatory irrelevancy to the debate. In straining for cleverness, the *Times* writer had gotten the facts wrong: it was the *Second* (or non-Bolshevik) *International* of 1934, not the Third, that had first recognized *finalized* as standard English. But that mattered little. The seed had been planted. A Detroit newspaper later put it more bluntly by charging that the influence of the "bolshevik spirit" could be seen in the Third Edition's willingness to "abandon standards and judgments." It added (paraphrasing Dean Inge of St. Paul's Church, London): "Wherever men believe that what is, is right; wherever they discard discipline for an easy short-cut, there is bolshevism. It is a spirit that corrupts everything it touches."[23]

The *Times* made no effort to answer the essential question: Why should *finalize* carry a stigmatizing label? Why was it less acceptable as a dictionary entry than verbs formed in the same fashion from other adjectives (*formalize, legalize, secularize*) or from nouns (*capitalize, terrorize, winterize, subsidize*), and verbs (*pressurize, flavorize*)? Derision was substituted for evidence and logic; and the question was evaded.

The *Times*'s objections to the *-ize* words were nothing new. Such words had been criticized since the seventeenth century as "barbarous" combinations of a Greek suffix and words from Latin and other languages. The criticism had little effect on the development of the language, however. Over the ensuing centuries – as the English vocabulary was enriched by words borrowed from other languages, anglicized, and combined with prefixes, suffixes, and so on – the *-ize* suffix proved to be highly useful. Webster used it in forming the only word he claimed to have coined, *demoralize,* and was criticized by some contemporaries for including it and *Americanize* in his dictionary. Among all the *-ize* words that gained acceptance during the nineteenth century, *jeopardize* was singled out for attack before attention shifted to *finalize.*

Although *finalize* appears without a warning label in leading American desk dictionaries today, some recent books on usage warn writers to be aware that the prejudice against it persists; one doggedly extended the warning to *-ize* words generally and used as an example of questionable usage the word *theorize,* which has appeared in the writings of the best writers since 1638.[24]

The attacks on the Third Edition suggested a puzzling "cultural lag" to Ethel Strainchamps. "Our writers are more modern in what they do than in what they think," she wrote in the *St. Louis Post-Dispatch*. "They don't, in short, approve of their own uninhibited practice." She had reviewed the contents of the new dictionary favorably two months earlier, and in her follow-up story on December 17 she turned to the criticisms that had been directed at it. She expressed surprise at how little the critics knew about either the Second or Third Edition. As for relying on the Second Edition, she commented that the *Life* editor "can hardly have been serious. For *Life* to conform even to W-III standards would change its whole personality." The issue carrying the editorial contained "some thirty easily spotted usages that were not unequivocally sanctioned" by the editorial writer's style guide – including "three nonwords (heister, low-key, boyfriend), one archaism (erstwhile); five slang words (fussing, jinx-plagued, stash, kicked out, whiz), three dialect or regional terms (maverick, raise [for rear], douse), three colloquialisms . . . and four old words in unapproved meanings: liquidate (a person); sleazy (of an idea), faceless (of people); and cliché (of an act)." Strainchamps noted that "a foreigner, or even a native speaker of English, who has been taught formal English and has held his reading to the classical works in the tongue, would have a hard time understanding all of almost any article in any issue of the *Saturday Review*, the *New York Times* or *Life*, and his 1934 Webster would be of little help to him on the very words that would puzzle him the most."[25]

Two days later, a significant endorsement of the Third Edition appeared in the *Cleveland Plain Dealer*. It was written by Joseph H. Friend of Western Reserve University, the general editor of one of Merriam's rivals in the college dictionary market, *Webster's New World Dictionary of the American Language*. His highly favorable comments on the dictionary and criticisms of Gove's detractors were reprinted by the *Plain Dealer*'s columnist Wes Lawrence:

After reading some of the more inane, misinformed, and wrongheaded reviews and comments that have followed the publication of the *Third New International Dictionary*, the latest and best of the Merriam Company's Webster's, it is a pleasure to come upon an enlightened note such as yours in the *Plain Dealer*. . . .

People who are shocked at the attitude toward language that underlies the treatment of locutions like *ain't, it's me, hassle, finalize* etc. in both the new dictionary . . . and the *WNWD*, simply do not understand some elementary facts about the relations between language and its cultural matrix. They seem to think of "the dictionary" as something apocalyptically manifested, like the Tables of the Law, forever good and forever the same. This ingenuous view implies an equally innocent – and equally uninformed – set of notions about good usage. . . .

The fact that lexicographers record disputed expressions should obviously not be taken by anyone as in itself a "sanction" of the indiscriminate use of these in all contexts and situations. I imagine that Mr. Gove, like me, perhaps you, and certainly a great many other educated people, says "ain't I" in familiar conversation, but I would be much surprised to find him writing it in a formal scholarly paper or even uttering it in, say, an address to a university seminar. What is involved here is the doctrine of appropriate usage, about which dictionaries cannot possibly give all the relevant data.[26]

YEAR-END ASSESSMENT

At the end of 1961, the Merriam company could still take an optimistic view of its prospects for the new year. It could argue that the worst of the newspaper barrage was probably over, that most of the important papers and critics had been heard from, and that only desultory pro and con exchanges lay ahead. If that were true, the debate was at worst a standoff, notwithstanding the sharp and influential attacks in the *Saturday Review* and *New York Times*. Meanwhile, the dictionary had been given unprecedented publicity, including some strongly supportive reviews, which could be put to good use by the sales force.

So it seemed from the public record. But much more was going on behind the scenes. The battle in the media – far from fading away after reaching a peak – was just getting under way. Writers, editors, and publishers, primarily in the East, were determined to undo the work of the Merriam staff. They considered the Third Edition a bad dictionary that would have a pernicious influence on the future development of American English. The *New York Times* editorial of October 12 was not a climactic statement; it was merely the warning hiss from the buildup of underground pressure soon to erupt.

11

Calamity or Calumny?

[Dictionaries] cannot stop change, nor can they cause changes disapproved of, or not accepted by, the user. They can and do stabilize the usage, particularly in the written language . . . they do clarify meanings and make them more systematic, particularly in . . . scientific and other technical registers.

Ladislav Zgusta, "The Role of Dictionaries in the Genesis and Development of the Standard"

During the last week of December 1961, word of Wilson Follett's forthcoming attack on the Third Edition spread through the annual meeting of the Modern Language Association in Chicago. Merriam staff members, lulled by congratulatory comments from friends on the publication of *Webster's Third,* took the rumors in stride.[1] The warning from Bergen Evans had alerted them to the appearance of a hostile review in the January *Atlantic.* But even so, they were not fully prepared for the intensity of Follett's indictment when they saw it in print after returning home. The title was the tipoff: "Sabotage in Springfield."

The four-thousand-word article dwarfed everything previously published by the dictionary's critics. Earlier reviews and editorials had usually run under a thousand words. Follett lengthened the bill of particulars against the Third Edition and developed the arguments at greater length and with greater destructiveness than earlier critics had done. He established the agenda and the tone for another phase of the controversy, showing the way for a new wave of attacks by like-minded writers. He set the stage, too, for the grand assault on the dictionary that would follow in early March – an article by Dwight

Macdonald in the *New Yorker* that would be more than twice as long. On every point, Follett would eventually be challenged by formidable rejoinders written by defenders of the dictionary, chiefly Bergen Evans and James Sledd. As Gove later wrote, "How come Northwestern has not one but two eloquent attackers of the nitwitted commentators?"[2] But Follett during the early months of 1962 commanded the stage.

"SABOTAGE IN SPRINGFIELD"

Follett described the Third Edition in the *Atlantic* as "a scandal and a disaster" and dramatized his case by attacking the motives of the editors as much as the dictionary itself. He acknowledged that it would take years of use "to fully discover" the merits of such a work, but "it costs only a few minutes to find out that . . . [it] is in many crucial particulars a very great calamity. . . . All of us may without brashness form summary judgments about the treatment of what belongs to all of us – the standard, staple, traditional language of general reading and speaking . . . in short, fundamental English. And it is precisely in this provenance that Webster III has thrust upon us a dismaying assortment of the questionable, the perverse, the unworthy, and the downright outrageous."[3]

He was equally indignant about what had been left out: "Think – if you can – of a dictionary from which you cannot learn who Mark Twain was . . . or what were the names of the apostles . . . or what and where the District of Columbia is." The "disappointment and shock" are greater when the Third is compared with the Second Edition."

We have seen a century and a third of illustrious history largely jettisoned; we have seen a novel dictionary formula improvised, in great part out of snap judgments and the sort of theoretical improvement that in practice impairs; and we have seen the gates propped wide open in enthusiastic hospitality to miscellaneous confusions and corruptions. . . . Worse yet, it plumes itself on its faults and parades assiduously cultivated sins as virtues without precedent.

. . . Webster III, behind its front of passionless objectivity, is in truth a fighting document. And the enemy it is out to destroy is every obstinate vestige of linguistic punctilio, every surviving influence that makes for the upholding of standards, every criterion for distinguishing between better usages and worse. In other words, it has gone over bodily to the school that construes traditions as enslaving, the rudimentary principles of syntax as crippling, and taste as irrelevant. . . . The Third New International is at once a resounding tribute of lip service to the Second and a wholesale repudiation of it – a sweeping act of apology, contrition, and reform.

The editors at Merriam-Webster were appalled by the rhetorical hyperbole and innuendoes that filled much of the first third of the article. They were especially angered by the subversive intentions attributed to them. Follett charged that "to convert the language into a confusion of unchanneled, incalculable williwaws, a capricious wind blowing whithersoever it listeth . . . is exactly what is wanted by the patient and dedicated saboteurs in Springfield."

After the sweeping denunciation, Follett turned to a long list of particulars, beginning with his objections to the "unreserved acceptance as standard" or a list of expressions including *wise up, ants in one's pants,* and *one for the book* – some of which were not main entries but phrases that happened to be included in quotations that showed the context in which particular entries appeared. These words "and a swarm of their kind," Follett continued, were admitted "to full canonical standing by the suppression of such qualifying status labels as *colloquial, slang, cant, facetious* and *substandard.* The classification *colloquial* it abolishes outright."

The Third Edition's reservations about the use of *slang* and other labels suggested to him "a large scale abrogation of one major responsibility of the lexicographer . . . on the curious ground that helpful discriminations are so far beyond his professional competence that he is obliged to leave them to those who . . . have vainly turned to him for guidance."

Turning to the grammatical judgments in the entries, Follett noted that "under the distributive pronoun *each* we find, side by side: '(each of them is to pay his own fine) (each of them are to pay their own fine).' Where could anyone look for a neater, more succinct way to outlaw the dusty dogma that a pronoun should agree in number with its antecedent?"

To illustrate the "more common solecisms," Follett began with the acceptance of *center around* or *about* for *center on* or *in* or *at,* and criticized the "manufacture of a composite preposition, *due to,* solely to extenuate such abominations as 'The event was canceled due to inclement weather.'" He discussed at length the use of *like* for *as* and *as if.* He acknowledged this early use of *like,* but added that *like* had virtually disappeared as a conjunction "until our Third New International Dictionary decided to exert its leverage." Follett summed up his comments on grammar by charging that "the latest Webster whittles away at one after another of the traditionary controls until there is little or nothing left of them."

The definitions themselves came in for close scrutiny and severe criticism. Echoing earlier critics, Follett said that Gove's formula for definitions results in "some of the oddest prose ever concocted by pundits. . . . [When the idea is not simple, it results in] a great unmanageable and unpunctuated blob of words strung out beyond the retentive powers of most minds that would need the definition at all."

To illustrate the problem, he selected the definitions of the nouns *groan* and *kymograph* (one word familiar and the other technical) and contrasted them with the definitions in the Second Edition. The Third Edition definition of the noun *groan* makes the point: "1: a deep usu. inarticulate and involuntary often strangled sound typically abruptly begun and ended and usu. indicative of pain or grief or tension or desire or sometimes disapproval or annoyance." He concluded that "in practice the one-phrase design without further expository predication lacks all the asserted advantages over a competently written definition of the free conventional sort; it is merely more difficult to write, often impossible to write well, and tougher to take in."

He ridiculed the choice of illustrative quotations from so many (fourteen thousand) authors not all of whom could have been worth citing. Like most reviewers before and after him, Follett expressed puzzlement over the listing of all entries in lowercase with capitalization indicated by the terms *cap, usu cap,* and so on, which he called another "curious abrogation of authority in a work extolled as 'more useful and authoritative than any previous dictionary.'" In his closing peroration, he wrote:

The rock-bottom practical truth is that the lexicographer cannot abrogate his authority if he wants to. He may think of himself as a detached scientist reporting the facts of language, declining to recommend use of anything or abstention from anything; but the myriad consultants of his work are not going to see him so . . . the work itself by virtue of its inclusions and exclusions, its mere existence, is a whole universe of judgments, received by millions as the Word from on high.[4]

After Follett's attack, journalists and literary critics rallied to the cause, echoing his views and quoting from his article. The *Richmond News-Leader* noted admiringly that Follett "rips into Webster's III with a savagery not encountered in the academic world since A. E. Housman demolished the German Latinists for their blunders in Manilius." Follett was not alone, it reported: "Across the country, scholars and critics who reverence the English language are outraged at Webster's almost incredible surrender to the forces of anything-goes." The *News-Leader* quoted Follett on the beauties of the Second Edition and condemned the "saboteurs." Its enthusiasm – unspoiled by any direct acquaintance with the dictionary – carried it astray in its discussion of usage: "Nothing in the new Webster's is 'substandard.'" The *News-Leader* proclaimed, "We enlist willingly on the side of those who believe in high standards of English usage, and we feel certain that the defenders of linguistic purity will win this war in the end."[5]

The *Washington Post* picked up on David Glixon's theme, advising its readers that even if their copy of the Second Edition was "battered and dog-eared, don't throw it away. . . . Hang on to it." It called the Third Edition a "monstrosity" and said Follett was "apoplectic" over its "sins of commission and omission," the worst being its "complete abdication of authority." It also criticized "pretentious and obscure verbosity," which it illustrated by "its definition of so simple an object as a door: 'a movable piece of firm material or a structure supported usually along one side and swinging on pivots or hinges, sliding along a groove, rolling up and down, revolving as one of four leaves, or folding like an accordion by means of which an opening may be closed or kept open for passage into or out of a building, room, or other covered enclosure or a car, airplane, elevator or other vehicle.'"[6]

The *New York Times*, whose October editorial had been widely cited by others, returned the favor in early February by quoting comments from the *Library Journal*, the American Bar Association (ABA) *Journal*, and the *Atlantic* that supported its position.[7]

The ABA *Journal* article drew heavily on the editorials in the *Times* and *Life* magazine and stressed the "importance in our profession of the use of words." It charged that *Webster's Third* had struck "a serious blow" to the cause of good English when "it utterly abdicated any role as judge of what is good English usage." It cited "perhaps as the most flagrant example of lexicographic irresponsibility . . . the undiscriminating listing of that most monstrous of all non-words *irregardless.*"[8]

The "irresponsibility" in this case was not Merriam's but the ABA's own. As Gove pointed out in a reply to the editor, the ABA had relied entirely on the editorials in the *Times* and *Life* magazine, and in doing so had repeated the error of *Life,* which said the Third Edition had treated *irregardless* as standard when it was clearly labeled "nonstandard."[9] Indeed, *irregardless* was used in the explanatory section of the dictionary to illustrate the label *nonstandard* as opposed to standard English. This was not the only blunder that Gove would seek to correct in the ensuing weeks as it became increasingly clear that some of the loudest critics had never looked at the dictionary itself. Equally erroneous, he found, were the critics' notions of what was contained in the Second Edition.

Moreover, the *Library Journal*'s review in the January 15 issue was not simply a one-sided attack as it was reported to be by the *Times*. It found much to commend as well as to criticize. It called the Third Edition "indispensable for its new (and revised old) material, deplorable for its wholesale *abridgements* – as well as its obfuscations of the boundaries between prestige and non-prestige uses." It commended the liberal use of quotations from current sources, the cross-references ("which achieve new levels of thoroughness"), the revision of tables and illustrations, and the more legible type. It noted approvingly that "all definitions (not to say etymologies) were reexamined and appropriately revised (characteristically in a refreshingly lucid and succinct idiom)." But it found that other changes largely offset the improvements, particularly the announced premise that "a dictionary were better *de*scriptive than *pre*scriptive." It was highly critical of the new pronunciation system. It concluded, "The deed is done, however, and to serve their users adequately most libraries will need both 2d and 3d editions."[10]

The *New York Times Book Review* published a severely critical article on February 11 that was in line with the paper's editorial position but out of step with the earlier review by Mario Pei. It appeared in a column by J. Donald Adams, who quoted extensively from Follett's article and emphasized the charge that the Third Edition had repudiated its heritage and abdicated its responsibility. He likened the authority of the dictionary to that of the Bible "as an unfailing fountain of truth." He concluded: "For my own part, after the examination I have given it, I shall never turn again to the new Merriam-Webster. . . . As a source of information, it strikes me as a gigantic flop, and you may decide for yourself whether the use of that word is a descriptive term or a colloquialism."[11]

Other attacks in early 1962 included a review in the *National Review* by Garry Wills, who wrote: "The large new Merriam-Webster has all the modern virtues. It is big, expensive and ugly. It should be a great success." Its principal sin, as he caricatured it, was that it "has only one standard – inclusiveness." Any word that slips into print will automatically be included. The task of keeping up with language change is the only task recognized "by the editors of this wondrous stew [who] do not feel they have any duty toward their own language, any job of defense or purgation or clarification, any even minimally normative function."

He derided the choice of new words, pointing with disdain to *Time* as a source. He called attention to some "weird intruders" in the word list – sixteen abbreviations consisting of two or three capital letters ("RB, RBC, RBH, RBI," etc.), which he found scattered on a single page. But, in fact, most of them were not new intruders but old friends from the Second Edition or substitutes for them. Seventeen such abbreviations appeared in the Second over the same range of the alphabet (RB to RE). Five appeared in both editions (RC, RCM, RD, RDY, and RE). The others in the Third Edition were replacements for obsolete, obscure, or less frequently used terms.[12]

"BUT WHAT'S A DICTIONARY FOR?"

Follett's criticisms, echoed by many writers, reached a growing audience without a serious challenge from any review of comparable visibility and weight for several months; Gove's morale was sustained largely by comments from scholars who shared his views.[13] It was a bleak period for him, a letdown after the closing weeks of 1961 when the dictionary was being lauded in newspaper reviews. He found some comfort in the prospect that Evans's review would appear in the spring, and he was buoyed by favorable reviews in the British press and letters of support from sympathetic scholars. Among the letter writers was Evans's colleague James Sledd, who had recently published a book on English grammar and whose earlier book on Johnson's dictionary Gove had reviewed. A superb scholar, Sledd was also known for his strong convictions and a willingness to defend them. He was a fierce polemicist as well, and eventually he became the key figure in the counterattack against the dictionary's attackers.

Sledd did not approve of the Third Edition uncritically – he had reservations about and objections to some of its features – but he was deeply offended by the unfairness of the attacks on the dictionary and its staff, as well as by the ignorance displayed by the critics and the misrepresentations that were readily apparent to one who had given thought to the subject of dictionaries. He was especially angered by the obvious lack of respect for serious scholarly work and the arrogance of amateur commentators who thought their offhand judgments were superior to those arrived at by dedicated scholars who had devoted years of work to the subject.

Sledd, who did not know Gove personally, wrote twice to him in February, first to request copies of all the reviews that had appeared and later to comment on the criticisms by Follett and others. The reviews that he received became the starting point for the collection of articles and reviews about the dictionary that he was preparing in collaboration with Wilma R. Ebbitt.[14]

Sledd wrote: "So far most of the attacks seem to be of the predictable variety – anyway I can cite lots of parallels from 18th and 19th century attacks on Johnson, Webster, etc. The ideas aren't new, and the critics generally don't seem to know much about the history of lexicography in general or even about the history of Webster's. It's all fairly depressing, since one would hope that the serious work of serious scholars would be seriously judged. . . . It must be depressing to see the breathless condemnation of the incompetent." He continued on a more encouraging note: "Sooner or later the experts will have their say, and thoughtful laymen will judge your book only after using it thoughtfully. I'm confident, as I'm sure you are, that these considered judgments will be more favorable."

In March, Gove received an advance copy of Evans's article for the *Atlantic* and replied that "the only dark shadows across [it] are that it won't be before the public until the May issue and that the circulation of the *Atlantic* doesn't equal *Life*'s. It shines like polished silver."[15]

Evans began the article, "But What's a Dictionary For?", as follows: "The storm of abuse in the popular press that greeted the appearance of *Webster's Third New International Dictionary* is a curious phenomenon. Never has a scholarly work of this stature been attacked with such unbridled fury and contempt."[16] He then set out to explain "the monstrous discrepancy" between the nature of the dictionary as depicted in its pages and the picture of it conveyed by the critics who condemned it as a "flagrant example of lexicographic irresponsibility" and a work that "would accelerate the deterioration" of the language.

A new dictionary was needed, Evans pointed out, because great changes had taken place in the English vocabulary and English usage in response to technological and social developments, two world wars, mass education, and the spread of democracy. With the increased use of written English, "the language has become more utilitarian and more informal." Every American publication "includes pages that would appear, to the purist of forty years ago, unbuttoned gibberish. Not that they are; they simply show that you can't hold the language of one generation up as a model for the next. He continued: "It's not that you mustn't. You *can't*. For example, in the issue in which *Life* stated editorially that it would follow the Second International, there were over forty words, constructions and meanings which are in the Third International, but not in the Second," echoing part of what he wrote from his hospital bed to Gove.

The *New York Times*, he said, used "one hundred and fifty-three separate words, phrases, and constructions which are listed in the Third International, but not in the Second, and nineteen others which are condemned in the Second" in the issue that carried its editorial attack on the Third Edition. The *Washington Post*, which advised its readers to "keep your old Webster's," said in the first sentence of the editorial, "'don't throw it away,' and . . . the second, 'hang on to it.' But the old Webster's labels *don't* 'colloquial' and *doesn't* include 'hang on to' in this sense at all."

In short, all of these publications are written in the language that the Third International describes, even the very editorials which scorn it. And this is no coincidence, because the Third International isn't setting up any new standards at all; it is simply describing what *Life*, the *Washington Post*, and the *New York Times* are doing.

Turning to his central question, "What's a dictionary for?", Evans said its purpose was to give the reader help on spelling, pronunciation, and the meaning and proper use of words. The reader wants to know "what is current and respectable. But he wants – and has a right to – the truth, the full truth. And the full truth about any language . . . is that there are many areas in which certainty is impossible and simplification is misleading."

A dictionary cannot always be absolute even about "so settled a matter as spelling. *Theater* is correct, but so is *theatre;* and so are *traveled* and *travelled . . . catalog* and *catalogue,* and scores of other variants."

He noted that James B. Conant (then president of Harvard), Bernard Baruch, and Dwight D. Eisenhower pronounced "economics as ECKuhnomiks," while A. Whitney Griswold (then president of Yale), Adlai Stevenson, and Herbert Hoover pronounced it "EEKuhnomiks." "The reader looks in the dictionary and finds both pronunciations."

Has the dictionary abdicated its responsibility? Should it say that one must speak like the president of Harvard or like the president of Yale, like the thirty-first President of the United States or like the thirty-fourth? . . . So widespread and conspicuous a use of two pronunciations among people of this elevation shows that there are two pronunciations. Their speaking establishes the fact which the dictionary must record.

On usage, Evans turned to "the ultimate" of permissiveness, the Third Edition's inclusion of *finalize.* If the *Times* writer had looked at the Second Edition, he would have found it there, too, without a label.

And why shouldn't it be there? . . . It has been recorded for two generations. Millions employ it every day. . . . To list it as *substandard* would be to imply that it is used solely by the ignorant and illiterate. But . . . President Kennedy and U Thant are highly educated men, and both are articulate and literate. It isn't even a freak form. On the contrary it is a classic example of a regular process of development in English, a process which has given us such thoroughly accepted words as "generalize" . . . and "verbalize." One is free to dislike the word. I don't like it. But the editor of a dictionary has to examine the evidence for a word's existence and seek it in context to get, as clearly and closely as he can, the exact meaning that it conveys. . . . He is not compiling a volume of his own prejudices.

Evans challenged the assumption that simple labels could indicate the status of a word or a grammatical construction. He cited as an

example the word *fetch*, which used to be "a standard word full of
dignity . . . [but has become] the kind of word that conscientious
people look up in the dictionary."

Will they find it labeled "good" or "bad"? Neither, of course, because either
applied indiscriminately would be untrue. The Third International lists
nineteen different meanings of the verb *to fetch*. Of these some are labeled
"dialectical," some "chiefly dialectical," some "obsolete," one "chiefly Scottish," and two "not in formal use." The primary meaning – to go after and
bring back – is not labeled and hence can be accepted as standard, *accepted
with the more assurance because the many shades of labeling show us that the word's
status has been carefully considered.* (My emphasis)

Evans cited similar evidence on grammatical questions where the
Third International carried such comments as "used by speakers and
writers on all educational levels, though disapproved by some grammarians" or "less often in standard than in substandard speech" or
simply "dial." Evans did not mention the furor over *ain't*, but the
parallel was clear. There was nothing unusual in judging senses of the
same word separately and treating some as standard and others as
slang or substandard. The problem, he noted, was partly that there
was "no standard for standard" because of the rapid change in views
of what was proper written and spoken usage in various situations.
But the dictionary's role was no more "to oppose this process than to
speed it up."

Evans said he was troubled by the obvious "hostility" evinced by the
Third Edition's critics and their inability to use a dictionary. "Most of
the reviewers seem unable to read the Third International and unwilling to read the Second."

Shortly after the Evans article appeared, the Merriam company
received a letter from George S. Noss, professor of philosophy and
religion at Berea College in Kentucky. Gove tucked away a copy
among his papers. Noss wrote that after reading the articles by Follett
and Evans, he wanted to join in the defense.

I bought a copy as soon as it was available, and went right through it,
beginning at the first page, and going from entry to entry until I was finished. . . . Of course, most of the entries were passed over, but every time I
came to one that attracted my interested attention I read both definition and
examples with pleasure and profit. This edition is for me much better than
the second, and the measure of its excellence is partly to be explained by the

amount of abuse heaped upon it. New things usually arouse rage in the minds of the conservatives. I admit that at first the different treatment of some words puzzled me, and it was a little while before I learned how to make proper use of your aids to pronunciation, but it was not long before I was 'sold.' . . .

I hope that, after I am probably dead, and your firm issues a fourth edition, it will be advanced enough to reap another harvest of abuse.[17]

THE WORD FROM BRITAIN

British assessments of *Webster's Third* were so different from those by American critics that one might wonder whether they dealt with the same dictionary. Reviews appeared in at least ten major British publications during early 1962, including the *New Statesman, Times Literary Supplement, Observer, Manchester Guardian, Glasgow Herald,* and *Nature.* They all treated the new edition respectfully, and most were written by scholars who praised it. Any reservations or criticisms were substantive and professionally argued in the context of the dictionary's overall achievement. Failures or shortcomings were attributed to differences in judgment or purpose, or to inconsistencies in performance, and not to disreputable motives or hidden ideological objectives. None of the reviewers found *Webster's Third* subversive, even where they disagreed with it.

Writing at length in the *New Statesman,* Randolph Quirk called the Third Edition a "magnificent and meticulously complete register of English vocabulary," which had "many palpable advantages over any other dictionary in existence." He pointed to the "very genuine newness" of its vocabulary and the definitions that rest squarely upon reputable, up-to-date documentation. He noted that "relatively new words like *turbo-prop* and *radar* [are] not merely included but splendidly defined."[18]

Regarding the "far more difficult" task of identifying and defining new senses of old words, Quirk found the new edition equally good. He welcomed the illustration "of particular uses of words on a lavish scale from contemporary writers."

However, he considered the failure to provide dates for the "earliest recorded references," as provided by the *OED,* a shortcoming, as it had been for the Second Edition. But to the Merriam staff, there was no reason to provide the dates, since the Merriam-Webster books were not historical dictionaries. Quirk gave a mixed assessment of the effort to make the Third Edition a truly international dictionary: "The coverage of specific British and Commonwealth words is fairly good (*windscreen, trafficator, roundabout* and the like) but the editor seems not to have grasped that for international use it is equally necessary to label as American the words and uses that are restricted in this way too." He found "rather regrettable," particularly for international readers, the lack of a label to indicate colloquial or informal use. This omission meant that for the word *awful* the senses "ugly" and "great" were put "on the same footing as the sense 'inspiring awe.'"

With a bow to the impossibility of doing justice to "a large and noble book of this kind in a short review," he said, "The fairest epitome would be that it is difficult to imagine in so compact a form so vast, so authoritative and so up-to-date a body of information on what Dr. Gove describes as 'the most important language on earth.'"

The flavor of the other British reviews is suggested by the following brief excerpts. In the *Scotsman* Morey McLaren was moved "to chronicle with gratitude that Webster includes in their own right, and not as dialect, a number of Scottish words neglected by the [Oxford English] Dictionary. There is less provincialism, it would appear, in America than in Oxford." The *Sydney Daily Telegraph* was similarly pleased by the coverage of the Australian vocabulary, noting that 688 Australian entries were included in the Third Edition, more than shown for Scottish, Cockney, Irish, and so on. "Aussie slang, for the first time in the history of lexicography really gets its foot in the door." But it disagreed with the view that the dictionary's mission was to describe the language as it is spoken, and it echoed the theme that the Third Edition "frankly abdicated all authority."

The British *Law Times,* concerned like the ABA *Journal* with the importance of words to the legal profession, came to a different conclusion about the value of *Webster's Third:* "It would be difficult to praise too highly the erudition, skill and industry which have gone to the production of this outstanding volume." The *Times Literary Supplement,* in the usual unsigned review, gave a sympathetic description of the new edition's principal features.

At the British publisher's invitation, several prominent British writers and scientists wrote comments on the dictionary for the company's newsletter. One of them, Sir Lawrence Bragg, Nobel laureate, gave a lesson on how an expert in any field of knowledge could contribute to the assessment of a dictionary. He turned first to the subjects in his own field of interest, "the words beginning [with] 'electr . . . and as a specialist in x-ray crystallography to the entries under 'crystal'. I am impressed with their clarity and accuracy and with the balance that has been attained in covering the main points while at the same time keeping to a reasonable length."

D. W. Brogan, frequent contributor to American periodicals and commentator on the American scene, wrote that for those whose work forced them to keep up with the "new words that technology, science and innovation in the arts pour over us, the new edition of Webster is indispensable." The illustrative quotations "from famous and obscure authors," he added, "not only make the meaning clearer but start off trains of thought as well as providing interest and amusement. Geoffrey Tillotson, professor of English at the University of London, said, "An Englishman cannot but be impressed by the conciseness and clarity of the definitions."[19]

The contrast between the British reviews and the attacks in the American press reflects a striking difference between expectations in Britain and the United States. The British were interested in the new words, changes in meaning and usage of old words, quality of the definitions, usefulness of the book for readers outside the United States, and other matters of lexicographical scholarship. No one referred to the descriptive–prescriptive dichotomy or took seriously the American belief that a dictionary could alter the course of the English language – either by preserving it from corruption or by undermining it.

Yet Americans are said to be unsure of their speech and want to be told what is correct. As Allen Walker Read put it, there was a "yearning for certainty" in the United States that developed from the nation's early reliance on "a book standard to learn what they thought prevailed in England. This linguistic colonialism lasted a long time and set the pattern of accepting the dictionary as a 'lawgiver.'"

Rather than observe the language around them, as Englishmen do, Americans give up their autonomy and fly to a dictionary to settle questions of language. This call for dogmatic prescription has been a source of uneasiness to lexicographers, most of whom now argue that all they can do legitimately is to describe how the language has been used.[20]

After months of unrelenting criticism, the *New York Times* sent a more detached observer to interview Gove. Brooks Atkinson, the paper's noted theater critic and writer on the arts, came to Springfield late in February. His article – "Webster Editor Disputes Critics, Says New Dictionary Is Sound" – appeared on March 1.[21]

Atkinson presented a thoughtful, wide-ranging account of the interview, reporting Gove's replies to the criticisms that had been made by Follett and others and quoting an upbeat comment on sales by Crawford Lincoln: "More copies were shipped out in the first fifteen weeks after publication than in many of the best years of the 1934 dictionary." He also reported his conversations with book dealers who said the Third Edition appeared to be selling well.

Atkinson cited Gove's distinction between his dual roles – as a lexicographer and as a rhetorician. As a linguist, Gove said, he must be guided by the Merriam citation file in making the dictionary, but as a rhetorician he personally used the language more critically. "'I am not a vulgarian,' he said, 'and it is not true that anything goes' in the Third Edition."

The interview covered specific questions on grammar and usage, including the words *ain't, irregardless,* and *finalize.* Gove also defended his definition of *door,* one of the definitions attacked by critics: "Where can you find a better definition?" He called it "compact" and "complete" and written so that it would be intelligible to a reader who had never seen a door, Atkinson wrote. "In his opinion that is the function of a public dictionary."

Gove was pleased by the treatment he received from Atkinson and wrote to him the next day: "I want you to know that I, as well as everyone here, liked yesterday's special very much. It is a model of objective factual reporting, notable for its considerate fairness. Its appearance in the *Times* with your name on it should do a lot to calm down the journalistic controversy as it goes on and on."[22]

As fair-minded as Atkinson's story was intended to be – and as satisfied as Gove professed himself to be with it – the article perpetuated a practice that had crept into most press reports and editorials. They typically cited and quoted only the negative reviews when referring to the controversy; favorable reviews in major publications were neither quoted nor mentioned. Atkinson, for example, listed the attacks in the *Atlantic, New York Times, Washington Post, Saturday Review, Life,* ABA *Journal,* and *Library Journal.* He did not list any of the publications carrying the favorable stories, such as *Time* and *Business Week,* or the favorable reviews in the *St. Louis Post-Dispatch, Christian Science Monitor, Editor & Publisher,* or *Publisher's Weekly.* Nevertheless, he did make an unusual concession, inserting a parenthetical expression, "(a lot has been favorable)," in a sentence dealing with the unfavorable reviews.

To be sure, Atkinson quoted Gove, so that there was the appearance of a reasonable balance, but the effect was not the same as quoting favorable comments by independent reviewers, which would have indicated the split in critical opinion. The practice of citing and quoting only the hostile critics reinforced the mistaken impression that virtually all the reviews, or at least all the ones that mattered, were harshly critical. It was this treatment that helped to establish the prevailing view that the Third Edition stood almost alone against the critics during the controversy. In recent years a disparaging reference to *Webster's Third* has been almost de rigueur in popular articles about dictionaries and disputes over usage. A way of showing sophistication is to toss off the comment, when an opportunity arises, "Of course, I use *Webster's Second.*"

MACDONALD AND SLEDD FACE OFF

Gove had known since the early autumn of 1961 that the *New Yorker* was going to publish a review of the Third Edition by one its most popular writers, Dwight Macdonald. The prospect could hardly have pleased him. He did not think much either of the *New Yorker* or of Macdonald, as he had indicated years earlier in responding to a letter from J. P. Bethel, who had been offended by a review that Macdonald had written. A letter from Macdonald in early October apprised Gove of the *New Yorker*'s intent to carry a review, and it posed nine probing questions, some with unsettling implications.

The first three questions dealt with the sales of the Second and Third Editions and the competition the two editions had faced from other publishers. The fourth noted that the Second Edition had 600,000 entries and the Third 450,000 (of which 100,000 were new ones). Thus, 250,000 words had been dropped from the Second. He asked Gove: "Could you give me some statistical ideas as to what kinds of words these 250,000 are? And what kind the 100,000 new ones are?"

Questions 5 through 8 requested examples of borderline cases of "comparatively useless" words, to which "your literature" refers, asked why the gazetteer and biographical appendixes had been dropped, asked why the dictionary was called "International," and queried the legal status of the word *Webster's*. Introducing the ninth and final question he said he was puzzled by the dictionary's discriminations on usage, especially slang, and asked, "Why is 'boiled' for 'drunk' *slang* while 'tight' is not?" Macdonald said he was "less interested in specific reasons than in general principles."[23]

Gove invited Macdonald to Springfield to discuss not only the questions but "also the procedures and lexicographical principles" that guided the editors. Macdonald accepted the invitation but requested an immediate answer to questions 1 through 4 and 8. Gove provided them on October 10. Regarding question 4, he listed the following deletions: 15,000 biographical entries, 20,000 geographical entries "with the balance made up of rare and obsolete words plus a great many nonlexical items such as the names of characters in Dickens, names of paintings, treaties, battles etc. which had no generic significance."[24]

After Macdonald's visit, Gove replied to a question about how many words were interjections. About 300, he estimated, "more than I supposed when you were here," excluding words that were sometimes used as interjections, such as *thunder* and *goodness*.[25]

Macdonald's questions and his visit could have left little doubt in Gove's mind that the review would be unfavorable. Gove was familiar enough with Macdonald's style – as exemplified by his review of the Revised Standard Version of the Bible – to anticipate the tone. A few days before the article appeared he also received a warning from James Sledd, who mentioned "a rumor that the *New Yorker* will soon run a long article by Dwight Macdonald about the dictionary. May I predict the next accusation? You guys planted the attacks just to get free advertising."[26]

Sledd's reference to Macdonald was an afterthought. The purpose of Sledd's letter was to reassure Gove that "the tide is clearly turning in your favor now." He cited the Evans article in the *Atlantic* and a paper he was working on for the spring meeting of the American Ethnological Society in Washington.

But that optimism proved premature. Macdonald's article in the March 10 *New Yorker*, "The String Untuned," was devastating. Macdonald had warmed to the subject and was at his rhetorical best. Armed with examples from the new edition to back his argument, he developed his case carefully, gradually shifting from a tone of reasonable disagreement – which included concessions to some features of the new work – to an unrestrained condemnation of the dictionary. His readers were delighted. For the foes of the Third Edition, this became the definitive review. Later Macdonald observed that he received more letters on this review (and about 98 percent of them against Webster) than for anything else he had ever written – and "about twice as many as I got even on my reviews of the 1952 R.S.V. Bible. . . . I concluded that language arouses even more passion than religion."[27]

But as the dictionary's defenders saw it, the article revealed a surprising ignorance of lexicographical practices and misrepresented the contents of both the Second and Third Editions. That, plus its condescending and insulting tone, outraged them. Evans wrote Gove: "You must have moments of wondering if the *whole* world isn't maliciously mad. . . . Speaking of mad, I ran into Sledd the other day and he was quivering with indignation over the Macdonald review."[28] Of the leading "alarmists" from Glixon to Macdonald, Sledd observed later, "Macdonald is the most alarming because he is the most eloquently mistaken."[29]

Most of Macdonald's criticisms can be grouped under three related themes: (1) the Third Edition had abandoned the principles embodied in the Second; (2) it went wrong because it was based on the new ideas of structural linguistics; (3) its emphasis on citations from contemporary sources reflected a bias against the tradition of the language. These themes led Macdonald to believe that the way to escape the corrupting effect of the Third Edition in the short run was to keep using the Second. Eventually, a dictionary based on a different approach would have to be prepared. Sledd disputed each of these charges, in addition to numerous other criticisms put forth by Macdonald. The battle was joined.

THE CLASH OF VIEWS

Macdonald acknowledged that the new edition had some good points, and Sledd, from his perspective, recognized that the Third Edition was open to reasonable objections, but beyond these perfunctory mutual concessions, they were hopelessly at odds. The major arguments, Macdonald's charges, and Sledd's rejoinders are summarized in the following pages.

Gove and Neilson

Macdonald's attack depended heavily on his view that Gove's approach to lexicography repudiated that of his predecessor, William Allen Neilson. He wrote that Neilson

followed lexical practice that had obtained since Dr. Johnson's day and assumed there was such a thing as correct English and that it was his job to decide what it was. When he felt he had to include a sub-standard word because of its common use, he put it in, but with a warning label. . . . Dr. Gove, while as dedicated a scholar as Dr. Neilson, has quite a different approach. A dictionary, he writes, should have no traffic with . . . artificial notions of correctness or superiority. It must be descriptive and not prescriptive.

When one compares 2 and 3 [Macdonald's shorthand for *Webster's Second* and *Third*], the first difference that strikes one is that 2 is a work of traditional scholarship and hence oriented toward the past, while 3 – though in many ways more scholarly, or at least more academic than 2 – exhales the breezy air of the present.[30]

The views attributed here to Neilson are Macdonald's, however, not Neilson's. Sledd put it this way: "The *Second International* appears to be 'oriented toward the past' merely because we are looking at it from its future. Its editors thought otherwise."

Indeed, Neilson had written in his preface: "Once more the editors have had to make a new book. Traditional features that have stood the test have been retained, so that the book is still a Webster, but more important than the retaining of time-honored methods or conventions has been the task of making the dictionary serve as an interpreter of the culture and civilization of today, as Noah Webster made the first edition serve for the America of 1828."[31]

When Gove addressed the needs of the present, he consciously followed in Neilson's footsteps, as he stated explicitly at his first Editorial Board meeting in 1952 (see Chapter 4). Neilson had written of the "highly selective process in which the problem of discarding was second only to that of adding." Where the choice "lay between a word used last by an obscure writer of the sixteenth century and an essential term in aviation," the latter was chosen. The same perspective guided the gathering of citations, "contemporary authors particularly having been widely read for new words and for new meanings of older words."[32]

Far from paying mere "lip service" to the Second Edition or repudiating it, as Follett had charged, Gove had followed its lead. The Second Edition had its roots in the past, but it was cultivated and pruned and nurtured to meet the needs of the present, and where choices had to be made, the present was served. On this matter, Gove could make no claim to originality in his approach.

As for lexicographical practice since Johnson's day, Macdonald had that wrong, too. It had typically eschewed prescriptivism, not embraced it. The dictionary's critics, Sledd wrote, "seem to believe that the idea of lexicography as history, not law, is a peculiarly modern aberration of structural linguists and Philip Gove. . . . Nothing would awaken them more roughly from their fantasy than a course of reading in the great lexicographers." He quoted from Johnson, Webster, Trench, the Philological Society, and *Webster's Second* to support his case. Johnson, who had hoped at first to "fix the language," slowly came to recognize that "neither reason nor experience can justify" that expectation and eventually concluded that it was foolish for a lexicographer to think it was in his power to secure his dictionary from "corruption and decay."[33]

Noah Webster wrote that the lexicographer had no concern "with the use of words in writing. . . . [The] business of the lexicographer is to collect, arrange, and define, as far as possible, *all* the words that belong to a language, and leave the author to select from them at his pleasure and according to his own taste and judgment." And in another context he said: "The man who undertakes to censure others for the use of certain words and to decide what is or is not correct in language seems to arrogate to himself a dictatorial authority, the legitimacy of which will always be denied."[34]

Thus, what Glixon had derided as the "new dispensation" to pretend not "to rule on what is correct" was not new at all. It had been a common practice since Johnson, who had said, "I do not form but register the language." The responsibility that Gove had supposedly abrogated had never been accepted by his predecessors. They expressly disclaimed it. But the journalistic and literary critics of the dictionary had not done their homework. They accepted the judgments of Glixon, the *New York Times* editorial writers, Follett, and Macdonald. The myths were widely disseminated and perpetuated.

The Bugaboo of Linguistics

Macdonald believed that the Merriam editors had taken the wrong road because of their sympathy for "the school of language study that has become dominant since 1934 . . . sometimes called Structural Linguistics." Gove had written a lengthy article entitled "Linguistic Advances and Lexicography" for the October 1961 issue of the Merriam publication *Word Study*, and it was this article that Macdonald cited as evidence that linguistics was the corrupting source of the Third Edition's misguided policies.

Gove had cited five precepts from a 1952 statement entitled the *English Language Arts* published by the National Council of Teachers of English (NCTE) and Macdonald quoted them:

1. Language changes constantly.
2. Change is normal.
3. Spoken language is the language.
4. Correctness rests upon usage.
5. All usage is relative.[35]

The precepts were correctly quoted by Macdonald, but they were wrongly interpreted. First, as Sledd explained, these precepts were neither new nor descriptive of what linguistics was about. They were commonplace views about language that were widely shared by students of language and teachers of English. They had, in fact, been expressed in the Second Edition.

Second, contrary to Macdonald's assertion, Gove's article did not show the influence of structural linguistics on the preparation of the Third Edition, but rather the opposite. Up to the 1960s, Gove explained, linguists had paid little attention to the making of dictionaries and lexicographers had found little in linguistics that was helpful to dictionary making, except for the treatment of pronunciation. Gove's purpose was to indicate that though linguistics had made no specific contributions to the Third Edition – or to other dictionaries in the past – it might do so in the future. Where "linguistics as a science" had already made an impression, he said, was in the classroom, in the study and teaching of English over the preceding three decades.

Looking at Gove's article today, one wonders how its meaning could have been so utterly misunderstood and why the misinterpretation gained credence. Any reasonably attentive reading makes his argument unmistakably clear. One by one he had gone through the principal tasks of the dictionary maker to answer the question, What did linguistics contribute "specifically to new Merriam Webster dictionaries?"

Linguistics, he said, had no appreciable effect on spelling, which had been fixed since the eighteenth century, or on etymology, because "not enough linguistic study has been directed toward problems facing the etymologist to have any noticeable effect." As for definitions, the major business of dictionaries, "linguistics has had . . . hardly any effect on meaning and vocabulary." It had "much to say about grammatical function and syntax" but not in ways that were directly applicable to lexicography. In the realm of pronunciation, where the effect of linguistic study had been "profound and exciting," Gove said it had been anticipated in Merriam-Webster dictionaries and made "explicit in the 'Guide to Pronunciation' of Webster's Second International Dictionary, which was written by John S. Kenyon before 1934 and before linguistics was recognized as a science" (see Chapter 7).

Not until a decade later did Gove himself make a passing and regretful reference to the misreading of his article. He conceded that the title was partly to blame for the misreading. "Unfortunately," he wrote, "the article seemed to the uninformed, and even to some of the informed, to establish a relationship between W3 and linguistics that invited critics to condemn the dictionary, the science, structural linguists, and me all in the same vituperative breath. It would have been fatuous to try to explain that the word linguistic in my title phrase 'linguistic advances' was really broad and probably somewhat obsolescent. It became clear only after an unhappy year or two that W3 had . . . taken over the role of spokesman for linguistics or linguists. If only I had written 'grammatical advances.'" Perhaps he should also have stated, "if only I had published an immediate clarification."[36]

Neglect of the Past in Citations

Macdonald approached the use of illustrative quotations in the Third Edition as a question of the proportion between the old and the new.

The most important aspect of 3, the rock on which it has been erected, is the hundred thousand illustrative quotations – professionally "citations" or "cites" – drawn from fourteen thousand writers and publications. . . . Most . . . are from living writers or speakers.

One may think as I do that 3 has dropped far too many of the old writers, that it has overemphasized its duty of recording the current state of the language and skimped its duty of recording the past that is still alive. . . . A decent compromise would have been to include both, but the editors of 3 don't go in for compromises. They seem imperfectly aware of the fact that the past of a language is a part of its present, that tradition is as much a fact as the violation of tradition.[37]

But among Gove's papers is a tally of the quotations that gives a different picture. It indicates that a "decent compromise" was indeed achieved. Great writers from Shakespeare's time onward were strongly represented to illustrate the vocabulary of their time, as the tabulation below indicates. But for the hundred thousand new words and new senses that came into use after 1934, Shakespeare offered no help. The Merriam editors had nowhere to turn for illustrative examples other than contemporary writings and utterances, as Murray had done for the *OED* and Neilson for the Second Edition. It is not surprising that anyone examining the new dictionary for new words and senses will inevitably be struck by the new quotations more than the old ones. It was precisely this flavor of contemporary usage that appealed to other reviewers.

The three most frequently cited sources in the Third Edition are Shakespeare, by a large margin, the Bible, and John Milton. In Gove's list of fifty-six people who were quoted more than a hundred times, only five had been born in the twentieth century (none later than 1915). The fifteen sources most often quoted are listed below, with the number of times each is cited. It hardly reflects a "skimping of the past that is still alive" or a failure to recognize "the fact that the past of a language is a part of its present."

William Shakespeare   2,143
Bible (all versions)   778
John Milton (1608–74), English poet   446
Ellen Glasgow (1874–1945), American novelist   424
John Buchan (1875–1940), Scottish author and governor general of Canada   416

George Bernard Shaw (1856–1950), British playwright   394

Arnold Bennett (1876–1931), English novelist and drama-
tist   376
Vernon Louis Parrington (1871–1929), American educa-
tor   352
Morris R. Cohen (1880–1947), Russian-American philoso-
pher   306
George Meredith (1828–1909), English novelist   303
Charles Dickens (1812–70), English novelist   282
Thomas Babington Macaulay (1800–59), English histo-
rian   282
Willa Cather (1873–1947), American novelist   281
Sir Walter Scott (1771–1832), Scottish novelist   269
Jane Austen (1775–1817), English novelist   266[38]

This list of sources was compiled after the work was completed. As
pointed out in Chapter 6, the quotations were selected because of
their usefulness in clarifying meaning, not with the intent of filling a
quota for Shakespeare, the Bible, Dickens, or others. The test of the
illustrative quotations was not their representativeness as examples of
English letters in earlier historical eras but their usefulness for the
task of definition. Gove had instructed that quotations in the Second
Edition were to be replaced only where they failed in their principal
function of clarifying meaning or were ludicrous as outdated examples of current usage.

But the vintage of the quotations, however selected, would be a
poor indicator of the new edition's concern for the past of the English
language. It does not take account of the dictionary's 140,000 etymologies or the carefully drawn distinctions among senses that
emerged over time and are listed in chronological order (as far as they
can be determined from the *OED* and other sources, which Gove
gratefully acknowledged). Moreover, even after the great cutback in
the number of old words that had not been used since 1755 (the date
of Johnson's dictionary), the Third Edition retained nearly 20,000
archaic and obsolete terms because they appear in literature that is
still read.

The Second Edition's Heresies

To avert the disaster that he was certain would follow general
acceptance of the Third Edition, Macdonald, like others before him,

urged continued reliance on the Second Edition. But Sledd noted that the sins of the Third permeated the Second.

- The policy on pronunciation. The Third Edition closely followed the Second, which read as follows: "to record as far as possible the pronunciations prevailing in the best present usage rather than to dictate what that usage should be. . . . In the case of diverse usages, of extensive prevalence, the dictionary must recognize each of them."
- Use of the schwa as a pronunciation symbol, which Macdonald called a "catastrophic innovation." No innovation, it was used in the "Guide to Pronunciation" in the Second Edition and, being an established symbol of the International Phonetic Alphabet, "was in use before Macdonald was born." It had also been introduced into desk dictionaries by the *American College Dictionary* fifteen years before *Webster's Third* was published.
- The definition of *Stalinism* as "the theories of Joseph Stalin." Macdonald called this definition ridiculous "since Stalin never had a theory in his life," but the same definition had appeared in the Second Edition's "Addendum of New Words."
- Derivatives and compound words, including *nooky* and *night clothes*, that Macdonald ridiculed. These had appeared in *Webster's Second*. Contrary to Macdonald's charge, Sledd pointed out, "not all the *night-words* are self-explanatory. *Night clothes* once meant informal evening dress; and how could a foreigner know that an *evening gown* and a *nightgown*, *night dress* and *evening dress*, are such very different things?"
- The thirty-four pages of words beginning with *un-*. Such words filled forty pages in the Second Edition, Sledd noted.

But these examples merely illustrated some of the errors resulting from Macdonald's unfamiliarity with the Second Edition. A more basic argument could be made, Sledd wrote:

The most solid proof that Macdonald cannot really accept the authority of the *Second International* is that "Dr. Gove's five little precepts" of "Modern Linguistic Science" are there too. . . . [T]he essential conclusion [is] that the *Second Edition* is not what he thinks it is. It's poison too!

Regarding the first two precepts, that "language changes constant-ly" and "change is normal," Sledd quoted Kenyon's statement that "English like other living languages is in a process of constant change" and noted that Professor E. S. Sheldon of Harvard had made the same point more than a half-century earlier; it was conventional wisdom even then. "Horace might just as well have been quoted as Professor Sheldon," Sledd noted.

On the third precept, "Spoken language is the language," Sledd quoted Kenyon again: "Spoken language is more important in every-day life than written or printed. . . . In the observation of language we are constantly tempted to forget that speech is primary, and reading and writing secondary."

The fourth precept, "Correctness rests upon usage," had led Mac-donald to charge that "the permissive approach of the Structural Linguists . . . impoverishes the language by not objecting to errors if they are common enough . . . and pretty soon *biweekly* gets two differ-ent meanings and anybody who wants to can pretend that he doesn't know who means which."

But this notion was also part of the tradition that Gove inherited and not a product of structural linguistics. Sledd noted that this pre-cept can be found on the first page of the introduction to the Second Edition, which states that definitions and pronunciations "must be written only after an analysis of citations" showing actual usage. Thus, the Second Edition had also listed two meanings for *biweekly* (every two weeks and semiweekly without a label), as had the *OED*.

"The fifth and last of the . . . heresies is that 'all usage is relative.'" This, said Sledd, "amounts to the not very exciting statement that people talk differently in different ages, at different places, and on different occasions, so that there can be no absolute and unchanging correctness in language." Kenyon had noted that standard spoken English and standard written English are not the same, "and indeed there is no single standard of cultivated speech. There are instead 'extensive regional types of cultivated English, each of which is cor-rect in its own area.'" Sledd concluded, "Macdonald must therefore strike out both editions from his lexicographic honor roll."

Other Parries by Sledd

Although Macdonald built his argument around large themes, he also marshaled detailed evidence from the dictionary to support a number of miscellaneous criticisms. In doing so he gave credence to Sledd's charge that "some reviewers are too unfamiliar with unabridged dictionaries to use them skillfully."[39]

Macdonald appears, for example, to have been stumped by the Third Edition's practice of indicating cross-references by printing the referenced word in small capital letters (as they had appeared in the Second Edition). Consequently, he concluded wrongly that the Third Edition failed to include the special meanings of important Marxist and Freudian terms, *masses* and *ego*, respectively. Commenting on the entry for *masses*, he said that the dictionary's "full entry is 'pl. of mass.'" But he failed to notice and to tell his readers that the word *mass* appeared in small capitals. As Sledd pointed out, that should have led him to the definition at *mass* – "the great body of the people as contrasted with the upper classes," and to the synonym *proletariat* (also in small capitals), where the Marxist definition appeared: "the class of wage earners who lack their own means of production and hence sell their labor to live."

He criticized the entry for *ego* because it was "defined as Fichte, Kant, and Hume used it but not as Freud did." Here his problem was a failure to look down the list of senses. The psychoanalytic meaning appears under sense 3: "the large conscious part of the personality that is derived from the id through contacts with reality and that mediates the demands of the id, of the superego, and of external everyday reality in the interest of preserving the organism." It is even labeled *psychoanalysis*, a rare instance of the use of a field label in the Third Edition.

One of the practices of the Third Edition (for the convenience of the reader) was to list some dialect word forms as separate entries in small capital letters when they were more than five inches away from the main entry – a practice also followed with plurals and inflections of verbs. Thus, the dialect form *knowed*, "past of *know*," is printed in small capitals to indicate that it is a cross-reference, but Macdonald took it to be an entry for a standard word. In the main entry of the verb *know*, as Sledd pointed out, *knowed* is labeled *dialect*.[40]

In support of his views, Macdonald followed the pattern of selectively citing only the critical comments: "The reviews of 3 in the lay press have not been enthusiastic. *Life* and the *Times* have both attacked it editorially as a 'say-as-you-go' dictionary."

Macdonald concluded his article by returning to the theme of the

"permissiveness that permeates 3" and the question of standard usage, its importance, and how it was to be determined:

Counting cite slips is simply not the way to go about the delicate business of
deciding these matters. If nine-tenths of the citizens of the United States,
including a recent President, were to use *inviduous* the one-tenth who clung
to *invidious* would still be right, and they would be doing a favor to the
majority if they continued to maintain the point. . . . The decision, I think,
must be left to the teachers, the professional writers, and the lexicographers.[41]

But which members of these groups, and in what proportions? How
would a representative panel of experts – say, one hundred or five
hundred – be assembled and how would they go about the great
business of deciding meanings, spellings, pronunciations, and usage
for hundreds of thousands of words? Macdonald concludes his article
without addressing such questions. In any case, not all members of
these groups would be eligible to participate, since so many had been
disqualified by Macdonald in the course of his argument: not "the
teachers who have learned anything lately about language," Sledd
wrote, not the writers who deny Macdonald's standards, and not the
lexicographers like Gove and others since Johnson who have defined
their job as recording the language and have refused the role that
Macdonald wished on them. "What Macdonald really means," Sledd
suggested, "is that he approves the judgment of teachers, writers and
lexicographers who think as he does."[42]

Sledd considered Macdonald guilty of ignorance and misrepresen-
tation in discussing the Second and Third Editions, and guilty also of
the "familiar tricks of petty sophistry." He said that "Macdonald's
technique is not to assert directly but to imagine and suspect. When
the dictionary labels some uses of *ain't* substandard, he imagines the
label was applied 'reluctantly'; since the label *slang* is used rather
sparingly, he suspects 'Doctor Gove' would have liked to drop the
label entirely."[43]

Sledd characterized the espousal of traditionalism by the dictionary's critics, beginning with Glixon, as "phony." "They are really not
traditionalists at all," he said, "but revolutionaries who believe that
professional lexicographers have been moving in the wrong direction
for two centuries and that in two hours an amateur can set them right.
One would welcome some concrete demonstration of their ability, just

as one would welcome a real argument for their quaint belief that the English language is being corrupted, that the *Third International* has hastened the process of corruption, and that right-minded scholars and men of taste must retard the process by using only *Webster II*."

In June, Sledd looked back over the events of the preceding months and wrote Gove another reassuring letter:

It must have been a rough year, to say the understated least but you're still smiling. For that, congratulations. I don't think I'd have that much fortitude. . . .

The one thing that's angered me in this whole affair is the irresponsibility of the attacks on the dictionary. A man who publishes a book expects criticism. If his book is worth printing at all, it is worth examination. Chomsky and his colleagues and followers have shown that my own little grammar has lots of weaknesses, and though I don't enjoy admitting that I was wrong, in many ways I was. I'd be silly to deny it or to be angry at a fair statement of my mistakes.

You do have a good reason to be hopping mad, because you haven't had a fair trial. Most of the attacks that I have seen have been ignorant and unjust. Very few of them have contained anything constructive. Yet Macdonald reaches hundreds of thousands, while a reviewer for a scholarly journal reaches hundreds. It's an ugly situation.[44]

Philip Babcock Gove, editor in chief, *Webster's Third New International Dictionary*. (American Heritage Center, University of Wyoming.)

Top: Noah Webster, age sixty-five. Engraved from a portrait painted by Samuel F. B. Morse in 1823. *Below, left to right:* Chauncey A. Goodrich, editor of the first Merriam-Webster dictionary, 1847; Robert C. Munroe, president of the Merriam company, 1934–50; John P. Bethel, general editor, 1935–52. (Reprinted with permission from Robert Keith Leavitt, *Noah's Ark: New England Yankees and the Endless Quest* [Springfield, Mass.: G. & C. Merriam Company, 1947] © 1947.)

Top: The Gove family (Grace, Philip, Norwood, and Susan) in Oxford in 1939 or 1940 with the noted lexicographer L. F. Powell (center). *Below:* Gove in the navy during World War II. (American Heritage Center photos, University of Wyoming.)

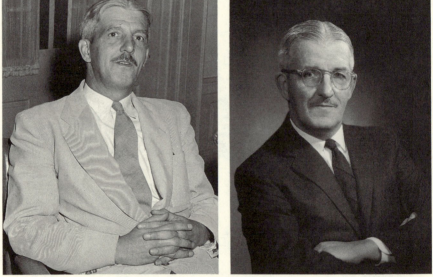

Top: The Merriam-Webster building at 47 Federal Street in Springfield, Massachusetts. From a wood engraving by Rudolph Ruzicka. (Reprinted with permission from Robert Keith Leavitt, *Noah's Ark: New England Yankees and the Endless Quest* [Springfield, Mass.: G. & C. Merriam Company, 1947], © 1947.) *Below, left:* Gove in 1953 several months after succeeding Bethel as general editor; *right:* Gove as editor in chief, the official photograph used for publicity purposes by the Merriam company.

Top: Gove receiving an honorary doctorate degree at Dartmouth College in June 1962 from President John Sloan Dickey. *Below:* Gove, back row second from left, at a meeting of the Editorial Board of Encyclopaedia Britannica, early 1960s. Front row, from the left, Robert Maynard Hutchins, Mortimer J. Adler, William A. Benton. (American Heritage Center photos, University of Wyoming.)

Top, left: Charles R. Sleeth; *right,* Mairé Weir Kay. *Below:* H. Bosley Woolf. (Photos of Miss Kay and Bosley Woolf are courtesy of the Merriam company.)

Top: Edward R. Artin. *Below:* Gove on the farm with his herd.

Cover of the promotional booklet issued by the Merriam company when *Webster's Third* was published in 1961.

12

Commercial Intrusions: Trademarks, Takeover Threats, Competition

In a civilization functioning largely through manufacturing and commerce, trademarks have made a distinct contribution to the common vocabulary.

Introduction to *Webster's Second International Dictionary*

Two unsettling developments added to the company's worries during early 1962. The first was an attack on the Third Edition's treatment of trademarks such as *Frigidaire, Kleenex,* and *Scotch Tape,* which in common parlance were often used generically for refrigerator, facial tissue, and transparent adhesive tape. In the Second Edition, these entries had been capitalized. In the Third Edition, they were not; moreover, in the Third Edition they carried a part-of-speech label, as if they had become part of the common vocabulary. The trademark itself, properly capitalized, was given in the etymology, as in the following: "band-aid *n* [fr. *Band-Aid,* a trademark] : a small adhesive strip with a gauze pad for covering minor wounds."

Corporate attorneys, who believed that trademark protection depended heavily on the owner's proof of vigilance in policing its rights, were alarmed. In their opinion, the treatment in *Webster's Third* had to be challenged lest it be construed as evidence that the product name had passed into the common vocabulary and could be used by competitors. A disclaimer to the contrary in the dictionary did not reassure them. No corporation would take a chance that its trademark might go the way of *cellophane, dry ice, escalator, linoleum,* and *shredded wheat,* to mention a few famous names that had passed into the public domain.[1]

The second challenge came from the American Heritage Compa-

215

ny, which began buying Merriam stock in an effort to wrest control of
the company from its current management. To bolster its case, it
charged in the press that the company was poorly run, hoping thereby
to attract support from other stockholders. The trademark issue was
of greater urgency, the buyout efforts of greater significance for the
future of the company.

THE WORTH OF A NAME

The Merriam company was fully aware of corporate sensitivity to
trademark and copyright issues. It had, after all, suffered a bitter and
costly disappointment itself, the loss of its exclusive rights to the
highly valuable Webster name.[2] The copyright to the 1841 edition of
Webster's *American Dictionary*, which the Merriams had acquired from
Webster's executors, expired in 1889. Because the company had not
taken legal steps to establish an exclusive right to the trade name of
Webster's dictionaries, other publishers began to use the name almost
as soon as the copyright lapsed without making any arrangement with
the Merriam company to do so. By 1904, at least a dozen firms were
using *Webster* in their dictionary titles. Beginning in the late 1920s and
continuing into the 1940s, the World Syndicate Publishing Company
of Cleveland issued twenty-five dictionaries bearing the Webster
name. They appeared under different titles but were sometimes in
fact printed from the same plates; they also contained misrepresentations about the source of the text and the editorial staff. As a result the
World company ran afoul of the Federal Trade Commission (FTC).
On November 14, 1941, the FTC filed a complaint charging the
company with misleading and deceptive trade practices. The Merriam company entered the proceedings as *amicus curiae* in the hope
that the FTC not only would find the World company guilty of deceptive practices but would also order it to stop using the Webster name.

Eight years later, when the FTC rendered its decision, it did indeed find World Publishing guilty of numerous deceptive practices
and ordered it to halt them. But to Merriam's dismay, the FTC
concluded that "to the public, the word 'Webster's' simply means a
dictionary. It does not mean any particular dictionary, nor the dictionary of a particular publishing company."

Thus, the Merriam company won relief from unfair competition, but failed to regain the much more valuable right to the exclusive use of the Webster name. It had succeeded too well in its promotional campaign to identify *Webster* with dictionaries of high quality. Now others were exploiting that identification. With these newest challenges, the company was forced to invest heavily in promoting its trademark, *A Merriam-Webster,* and its distinctive colophon composed of Noah Webster's initials in a wreath of laurel leaves, first used several decades earlier. Both appeared on the title pages and sometimes the covers of the company's books.

The World company, with its right to the use of the Webster name no longer in question, made a fresh and ambitious start under different leadership and a new title. Four years later, in 1953, it brought out a college-level dictionary, *Webster's New World,* which was well received by reviewers and by users. Allen Walker Read wrote that *Webster's New World* deserved high marks for its coverage of the vocabulary, etymologies, pronunciations, and appearance, and he took note of its remarkable transformation. It had "seemed unlikely that a dictionary capable of inspiring confidence and trust could emerge from such a . . . long history of exploiting the public by issuing wretched, poorly edited 'Websters,' with false claims on the title pages." In 1991 yet another major competitor, Random House, published a new dictionary under the Webster flag; it called its new edition the *Random House Webster's College Dictionary.*[3] The Merriam company responded in 1993 by featuring its full corporate name in its new edition, which was entitled: *Merriam-Webster's Collegiate Dictionary,* tenth edition.

Gove's Policy on Trademarks

From Gove's perspective, the treatment of trademarks in the Third Edition largely followed the policy explicitly set forth in the Second Edition. The introduction to *Webster's Second* took note of the contribution of trademarks "to the common vocabulary" and the public's interest in their origin, pronunciation, and meaning. It also clearly acknowledged the trademark owner's interests. It checked every word suspected of being of trademark origin in U.S. Patent Office records and identified all trademark entries in the dictionary. It added a disclaimer: "The inclusion of any word in this Dictionary is not, however, an expression of the publisher's opinion as to whether or not it is subject to proprietary rights but only an expression of their belief that such a word is of sufficiently general interest to warrant its inclusion in a serious work of this kind. Indeed, no definition in this Dictionary is to be regarded as affecting the value of a trade-mark."

The careful checking of trademark records continued during the preparation of the Third Edition. From 1947 until the work on the dictionary was completed, the Merriam company regularly consulted the Washington law firm Longfellow & Rhodes on the trademark status of words being considered for the new edition: Was the trademark unexpired, expired, canceled, or renewed? The company scrupulously inserted standard phrases in its letters to explain its policy. For example: "Terms that we suspect of being trademarks, we submit to you for possible registration sheets. . . . Terms that are registered will be defined in accordance with the established formula." During the summer of 1957, a busy period, such queries were being sent to the attorney once a month.[4]

Terms that were checked during that summer and found to be registered included B.V.D. (underwear), Automat, Carborundum, Cellulose, Scuba, Caterpillar, Aerosol, Ludlow, Synephrin, Phillips (screw), Multilith, Melba toast, Scotch cellophane tape, Popsicle, Kiss (candy), Porcelainize, LP (recording), Krebiozen (cancer medication), Laundromat, Hit Parade, Fig Newton, Blue Cross, and Tommy Gun. No trademark was found for "perfect binder" equipment.

The company policy, as stated in response to routine inquiries, was that the dictionary would enter only those trademarks that had achieved fairly widespread generic use. A more informative explanation appears in correspondence between Gove and Professor Kemp Malone, who had written for advance information on how *thermos bottle* and *vacuum bottle* were to be treated in the Third Edition. Malone explained that this information would be helpful to him in a pending appearance as an expert witness in a court case. He said he intended to cite dictionary entries, including the ones in the Second Edition, and wanted to know what the Third Edition would say. "In my view," he said, "the owners of a trade-mark have a right to consideration – and if they object, the lexicographer should take respectful notice, at least, of their objection." In the Second Edition, *Thermos bottle* was treated as a trademark, but *vacuum bottle* was not. The definition of *Thermos* also noted "*hence, (sometimes not cap.)* the bottle bearing such a trade-mark." This was typical of the handling of a trademark item in that edition.

Gove said company policy precluded his divulging the contents of a forthcoming entry, but he stated his intention as follows:

We plan not to enter into any of our M-W dictionaries a trademark known to us to be such without identifying it in some way as a trademark. We intend however to reflect usage, and if we have evidence that seems to show wide current usage, we feel we must enter it whether or not the registered owner concurs.

For more detail, he referred Malone to page xi of the Second Edition, which included the disclaimer that "no definition in this Dictionary is to be regarded as affecting the validity of any trade-mark." (The term is hyphenated in the Second Edition and is one word in the Third.)[5]

Gove's carefully devised instructions for the Third Edition were intended to reflect the best lexicographical thinking without endangering trademark rights, but business firms saw something else. They objected to the manner in which the rule of showing "wide current usage" was applied. If the citation files showed widespread generic use of a trademark, the Third Edition entry appeared in lowercase as a conventional vocabulary entry. The original Third Edition and Second Edition practices can be contrasted as follows:

[3d] **frigidaire** . . . *n.*-s [fr. *Frigidaire,* a trademark] : a mechanical refrigerator <they have 10 children, a ~, an excellent lavatory – *Southern Lit. Messenger,*> <automobiles, radios, ~ s – J. J. O'Leary>

[2d] **Frigidaire,** *n.* [*frigid* + *air.*] **1.** A trade-mark applied to a type of electric refrigerator; hence [*often not cap.*], the refrigerator bearing this trade-mark. **2.** [*not cap.*] Loosely, any electric refrigerator. *Colloq.*

Within a month after *Webster's Third* was published, letters from companies that were puzzled and worried by the change in treatment began reaching the U.S. Trademark Association in New York. Queries were also arriving at the Merriam company. Gove responded brusquely to one from a New York law firm that sought a discussion of the matter. He denied that the Third Edition entered any trademarks as generic entries:

The entries you raise a question about are not trademarks but generic words. Our definers have been instructed to enter and define them only if there is backing for their generic use. The fact that they do not begin with a capital and that they usually show the possibility of being inflected confirms their generic status, as do the definitions themselves which have genera that would be improper for a trademark. A linotype, for example, is a machine, where *Linotype* is a trademark.

To save space we could have given the etymology simply as "fr. a trademark," but to make a clear distinction between the uncapitalized entry and the capitalized etymon we always show the proper trademark form, as "fr. *Linotype,* a trademark."

Another result of this treatment is to free us from the incompatible dishonesty involved in being compelled to recognize derivatives and extended meanings (*because they exist, although the trademark owners deny their existence*) while at the same time the basic entry is only a trademark.[6] (My emphasis)

Contributing to corporate apprehension was the explanatory statement on page 7a of the Third Edition preface. It included a sentence (italicized in the following quote) that made the implications of the entry itself seem even more threatening. "Words that are believed to be trademarks have been investigated in the files of the United States Patent Office. *Those that were originally trademarks before being taken over generically by usage and becoming lexical are recognized as such.*" Trademark lawyers were not reassured by the inclusion of a disclaimer like the one that had appeared in the Second Edition: ". . . no definition in this dictionary is to be regarded as affecting the validity of any trademark."

Corporate Reaction and the Compromise

In response to the expressions of concern from its members, the Trademark Association agreed to set up a special task force to look into the matter. Gove's letter, especially his view that he had the evidence to sustain his policy if challenged, apparently heightened corporate concerns. The task force discussed several steps: to seek a preliminary injunction, to seek a permanent injunction, or to negotiate a settlement with the publisher.

On January 25, 1962, the task force members – Thacher H. Fisk, president of the Kendall Company, W. G. (Scotty) Reynolds of Dupont, and Louis Kunin, a New York trademark attorney and chairman of the Dictionary Listings Committee – drove to Springfield to meet with the Merriam management. Arriving in a black, chauffeur-driven limousine, they caused a considerable stir among company employees. In his opening remarks, Reynolds reviewed the legal and financial problems that dictionary listings could cause the companies and suggested that the entries be revised to follow the treatment they had been given in the Second Edition. He pointed out that the failure of a company to challenge improper uses of a trademark would result in a loss of trademark protection. Thus, the generic treatment of trademarks in the nation's most authoritative dictionary could not be tolerated.

Victor W. Weidman, Merriam vice-president at the time, and Crawford Lincoln, then assistant to President Gallan, remember the meeting as a tense one, though it was low-key and moderate in tone. Lincoln recalls the opening statement about the value of trademarks and the legal weapons available to protect them – "and Phil, you could just see him bristle." The legal weapons, which had been reviewed during the drive to Springfield, included about a dozen actionable items that the trademark owners might pursue. After considerable discussion, the meeting ended with Gallan's expression of willingness to consider ways to meet the objections of the trademark representatives. Despite the politeness of the discussion on the surface, the underlying message was clear to the Merriam management. Without a successful effort to reach a compromise, the company was in for a long and costly legal battle that might well take the Third Edition out of the market.[7]

The story was already getting media attention. *Advertising Age* reported that "a random check of 65 registered trademarks in the new unabridged shows 44 of them listed as generic." The same issue carried a story stating that attorneys for the makers of Plexiglas had notified the Merriam company that the dictionary had violated a registered trademark.[8]

The *American Press* warned that trademarks "backed by millions of dollars worth of advertising might suddenly become worthless. . . . For the new dictionary, exhibiting a blatant disregard for public acceptance of legal trademarks, spells some of the best known names with lower case." It urged its readers to lead a counterattack to "repel this invasion of the property rights of some of our nation's biggest advertisers."[9]

The Third Edition's practice was attacked as a "frivolous mishandling of trade-marks" in a letter published by *Forbes* magazine. "The new dictionary downgrades practically all of them to lower-case spellings. . . . The owners of these trade-marks . . . will now have a fight on their hands to save what they can of these valuable properties. . . .

A trade-mark is a private property, and . . . its misuse is harmful to all business in a free society."[10]

As Lincoln recalls the negotiations, "We worked with Dorothy Fey, executive director of the United States Trademark Association, and we finally came up with a formula that was adopted for the dictionary. When the dictionary went back to press for the next reprinting, it included a whole raft of changes." These included a revision of the preface, which was approved in early March, and a revision of style for entries that was proposed by Gove later in the month. The Trademark Association's *Bulletin* notified members on May 13, 1962, that the changes would be introduced in the next printing of the dictionary.

More than three hundred entries had to be revised. In the revision, the initial letter of each trademark was capitalized and the full term set in boldface type as a main entry, followed by the italicized label *trademark*. A lightface em dash followed to indicate that the description was not a definition but a usage note. As indicated by the following examples, the revised formula led to a more restricted and less informative entry than had appeared in the Second Edition; it gave no reference to generic uses.

Kleenex . . . *trademark* — used for a cleansing tissue.

Frigidaire . . . *trademark* — used for a mechanical refrigerator.

Missing from the latter entry was the elaboration that had appeared in *Webster's Second:* "hence [*often not cap.*] the refrigerator bearing this trade-mark. **2.** [*not cap.*] Loosely, any electric refrigerator. *Colloq.*"

An exception was made when the trademark was used as a verb. For example: "linotype . . . . [*Linotype*] *vi:* to operate a Linotype machine ~ *vt:* to set by means of a Linotype machine."

It was a discouraging defeat for Gove, who was convinced that his policy was the appropriate one. But the issue was not one of lexicography alone. The corporations succeeded in making it appear to be one of property rights and business survival. There was an additional consequence of the agreement that altered the appearance of the Third Edition, though no one seems to have commented on it in print. Gove's capitalization guidelines were breached. No longer was *God* the only headword to be capitalized. In subsequent printings, hundreds of little gods of corporate productivity, trademarks, were capitalized as well.[11]

The companies were satisfied with the agreement and notification of members, and agreed to Gordon Gallan's request not to turn the episode into a public relations extravaganza.

But though the agreement was kept quiet, the consequences could not be covered up. The Third Edition came under fire for its excessively conservative treatment of words of trademark origin. Sidney Landau called Merriam-Webster dictionaries "the most weaselly nonrecorders of generic meanings of trademark terms." He cited the definition in the *Ninth New Collegiate* of *Band-Aid* as "*trademark* – used for a small adhesive strip with a gauze pad for covering minor wounds," without any reference to a wide range of common figurative uses that warranted treatment as additional senses. He quoted a second sense that appeared in the *American Heritage Dictionary:* "2. Any superficial or temporary solution or remedy." *Webster's New World* (third edition) includes the second sense, as well as *bandaid* as an adjective meaning providing only temporary and superficial relief. "The lexicographer," Landau wrote, "has no intention of depriving a trademark owner of the exclusive right to use a term; he merely argues that his overriding obligation is to dictionary users, and he cannot allow any special interest group to determine what he can or cannot put in his dictionary." This is what Gove had said, too, in his letters to Malone and the trademark lawyer before the corporate delegation came to Springfield.[12]

BUYERS: HOSTILE AND FRIENDLY

In mid-February 1962 the American Heritage Publishing Company of New York publicly acknowledged that it was engaged in a buyout effort. James Parton, company president, announced: "Yes, we have become stockholders in the G. & C. Merriam Company, and we expect to increase our holding. We have offered the stockholders $300 per share, which is three times the highest price previously available."

Parton said that the company "badly needs new guidance. Its sales are up a mere 10 percent in the last five years" compared with the 57 percent average for text and reference books. "Furthermore, Merriam's great scholarly reputation has become tarnished in recent months through its publication of the radically different Third Edition."[13]

He put it more bluntly to a New York newspaper reporter. The Merriam company, he said, was "atrociously managed" and *Webster's Third* was an "affront" to scholarship.[14]

Parton called on other stockholders for support. "Before this Merriam trend away from sound scholarly principles becomes irreparable its owners should insist on new management policies. . . . We believe that American Heritage can greatly strengthen a fine Springfield institution, and assure its continued prosperity in Springfield." The company's local attorney reiterated that there was no intention of moving the company away from Springfield.[15]

Parton's announcement was no surprise to Gordon Gallan. American Heritage had tried to work out a cooperative arrangement with him in 1960 before the Third Edition was published, but he rebuffed the overture. American Heritage then began acquiring stock in the Merriam company. To finance its intended buyout, it offered 140,000 shares of its own stock to the public in October 1961. Gallan also learned from some of the company's shareholders of Parton's efforts to purchase their holdings. There were about a hundred shareholders, including descendants of the Merriam family, board members, and longtime editors.

In replying publicly to Parton's charges, Gallan told the press that the preceding year had been the most successful in the company's history. He called Parton's statement that sales had increased only 10 percent in five years "completely false." He countered Parton's listing of critical reviews in the *New York Times, Atlantic,* and other publications by pointing to favorable reviews in *Time, Editor & Publisher, St. Louis Post-Dispatch, Christian Science Monitor,* and others. He also noted that scholarly reviewers had been "enthusiastically favorable." As for the press criticism, he said, "what Mr. Parton is referring to are the superficial comments of a few journalists who are reluctant to admit that our language has changed rapidly in the last few years."[16]

What did Parton plan to do if he acquired the Merriam company? "We'd take the Third out of print! We'd go back to the Second International and speed ahead on the Fourth. It'll take two or three years, and the company would lose some sales. But if Merriam keeps on the way it's going, they'll ruin their company."[17]

As the original March 15 deadline neared for his offer to buy Merriam stock, Parton announced a week's extension so that American Heritage could complete its direct solicitation of Merriam stock-holders.[18] Even after that deadline passed, he continued to press his case. In midsummer, he made another effort to rouse the stock-holders. He sent each of them a copy of Mario Pei's recent article in the *Saturday Review*, which said that a dictionary had a duty to "define *standards* of *good* and *bad usage*" – a role the Third Edition "had abandoned." He said he agreed with Pei and added that American Heritage "continues to hope that other stockholders will join with us in urging the Company's management to return to the philosophy which made Merriam-Webster dictionaries world-renowned and in-dispensable."[19]

However, the annual report issued by American Heritage the fol-lowing year conceded that the buyout effort "had stalled." Parton reported that he had taken advantage of "an opportunity to sell our Merriam stock at a profit."[20]

Other companies meanwhile had become interested in acquiring Merriam and remaking its dictionary. Among them were the Colum-bia Broadcasting System, whose president, Frank Stanton, was given a tour of the Merriam offices, and Time Inc. Time turned for advice to James Sledd, who had been at Oxford during the 1930s when Hedley Donovan, editor of *Time*, had also been there – as had his close associate at Time Inc., Carl Solberg. Sledd was invited to New York by a staff member, Norman Ross, to give his assessment of the dictionary and what might be done to encourage better English in-struction in schools and better use of English in the United States. Time "had the idea that it might buy the Merriam Company and at once re-publish the dictionary, marking the words they objected to with an asterisk, and adding a supplement of respectable condemna-tion," Sledd noted.[21]

It was not the kind of task Sledd was accustomed to, but he wel-comed it as "the one possible way I have of telling the most powerful journalists in this country that they are wrong." When he arrived in New York, he was taken aside by two staff members who were in obvious awe of their editor and who coached him "on how to address the Great God Donovan."[22] After a lengthy and exasperating discus-sion of *Webster's Third* with Donovan and the assistant managing edi-tor, Sledd agreed to respond in writing to several questions.

The first was, What would Time be getting if it bought the Mer-riam company? Sledd replied:

Well, for one thing you'd be buying the most distinguished series of commercially made and marketed dictionaries in the English-speaking world. You'd be buying an honorable tradition, embodied in one of the few firms that have made an honest contribution to the education (such as it is) of the American people. If you used your brain and your guts, you'd be buying an opportunity to persuade academics not to speak of the Luce empire with a perpetual sneer. . . . You'd be buying access to a lot of lexicographic know-how. You'd inherit the most famous name and the best staff in commercial English lexicography, a staff which you'd have the money to strengthen. And in buying the Merriam files, you'd be buying the one essential to the production of really independent English dictionaries – a priceless and unique body of evidence that makes the Merriam company the envy of its competitors.

Sledd assessed alternative ways in which Time might handle the publicity about its purchase and intentions, the kinds of additional publications that might be developed if the Merriam company were taken over, and his general assessment of the dictionary: "I think the dictionary is a good book, not a great one; that some things in it are definitely wrong; but that it has no real competitor. . . . The prevailing attitude among professionals has been that the hullabaloo in the New York press represents the most abysmal ignorance and stupidity." On the matter of status labels, he said, "I'm quite convinced that . . . Gove was just wrong – led astray by a desire to be completely accurate and objective and perhaps by the influence of some linguists." But, he added, "far too much has been made of this one defect."

Finally, he turned to what could be done to improve the use of English in the United States:

If you want Americans to speak and write better, give them the chance to learn. At the moment, the colleges and universities simply refuse to train teachers adequately: the average graduate student in universities like Chicago, California, and Northwestern doesn't know any system of English grammar, doesn't know any history of the language, can't tell a good sentence from a bad one when they're set before him and can't write worth a damn. Why? Because nobody ever taught him. Freshman English in most colleges and universities is a joke – a device for supporting graduate students so that they can fill up the English department's seminars so that English departments can perform their one surviving function of simple reproduction; and any effort either to strengthen the freshman course or to increase the attention to grammar, rhetoric, and logic is immediately attacked by the lit'ry gentry, who want to talk about the alienation of the artists, fertility spirits, sacrificial kings, and the superiority of poetry to science.

The system turns thousands of incompetents loose in the schools each year, and the refusal of the general public to pay for general education saddles these incompetents with an average of 150 students each. Did you ever try reading 150 essays weekly? There are the two big facts of life: incompetent teachers, impossible teaching loads. . . . make it plain to students and to their parents that society does not need and want a large, literate middle class. One reason students don't bother to learn when they do have a chance is that they don't feel any real social pressure to use their language well.[23]

The Time-Life initiative never advanced very far, and another competitor moved ahead with plans for a friendly acquisition. In September 1964, a year after American Heritage gave up its quest, Encyclopaedia Britannica, Inc., of Chicago announced that it had reached an agreement with G. & C. Merriam to acquire the company for thirty-one dollars a share, double the per-share price originally offered to the stockholders by American Heritage. Britannica, which had purchased thirty thousand shares previously owned by American Heritage, had worked out a friendly takeover that ensured the continuity of the Merriam company in Springfield under its own name and management. Gallan was to stay on as president, and the staff and the publishing program were to remain intact.[24]

About ten days later, however, well in advance of the scheduled meeting at which stockholders were to ratify the agreement, the deal began to unravel. Gallan received an offer from McGraw-Hill, Inc., dated September 22 to buy the company for thirty-six dollars a share, either in cash or in McGraw-Hill stock. The new offer was five dollars a share higher than the Britannica offer, and the option of taking stock instead of cash appealed to stockholders who wanted to postpone the capital gains tax that would have to be paid on a cash sale. A stockholder's suit followed, which led to a court order temporarily blocking the Britannica acquisition.

Britannica responded the day after McGraw-Hill made its offer by proposing to reopen the original agreement and revise the terms to match the McGraw-Hill offer. At the same time it began an aggressive effort to acquire additional Merriam stock. Before the stockholders' meeting took place on October 20, Merriam and Britannica were in full control. The Merriam board voted to turn down a new

McGraw-Hill offer, Gallan signed Britannica's revisions of the original purchase agreement, and Britannica acquired two-thirds of the
Merriam stock, which assured the success of its acquisition effort.
After ratification by its stockholders, Merriam "joined the Britannica
corporate family" on October 26, 1964.[25]

The purchase by Britannica, whose annual sales of $125 million
dwarfed Merriam's, pleased Gove, and he conveyed the news to his
son and daughter-in-law with evident pleasure:

It became official last Monday – lock, stock, and barrel we belong to Encyclopaedia Britannica. But except for a brief lament for the passing of a
venerable and respectable independent organization, I and my colleagues are
enthusiastic about the future. . . .

In return, we will have a broader base for commercial expansion (i.e.
enlarging our market) and for keeping up with the times (i.e. an opportunity
to find out how, what and if computers can contribute to dictionary making –
something that our company by itself cannot face financially.) As far as I
know, my job is not only secure but it is likely to get bigger if I read between
the remarks and expressed intention.[26]

Gove was impressed by Chairman William Benton's strong interest
in the Merriam company and its potential. Benton saw Britannica and
Merriam as natural partners, and he envisioned major gains in dictionary sales overseas through Britannica's well-established foreign operations. Gove was further encouraged when he was later elected a
member of the corporation's editorial board.

THE USAGE PANEL AS COMPETITION

After he was blocked in his bid to take over the Merriam company in
1962, James Parton went ahead with his plans for a new dictionary.
Two years later he appointed William Morris, a Harvard classmate
and an outspoken critic of *Webster's Third*, to be editor. Morris had
worked in the college sales department of the Merriam company in
the 1940s and later as an editor for several other publishers. For
several years he had also been writing a newspaper column syndicated
by the North American Newspaper Alliance (NANA).

His views on *Webster's Third* came through clearly in a column
printed in March 1963 on the eve of the publication of *Webster's*

Seventh New Collegiate Dictionary. He wrote, "The great fight over the Merriam-Webster Third International Dictionary is over – with the Webster editors admitting defeat." The proof, he said, was that *Webster's Seventh New Collegiate* was based on the Second Edition, not the Third. He suggested that the Third had "flopped" like the Edsel automobile. "Nobody seemed to like the Third International but its editors – and now even they seem to have had a change of heart."

Gove, who was editor in chief of the *Seventh Collegiate*, called the article "tommyrot." He said, "It is absolutely not the case that there's been a reversal of policy." The new edition follows the Third, not the Second, on the major lexicographical matters, though it continues "practices and traditions dating from 1898 and contains material designed to be helpful to students" – a reference to the retention of biographical, geographical, and other reference material that had long been a part of all desk dictionaries.[27]

When the new *American Heritage Dictionary* (*AHD*) was introduced to the public in 1969, the publisher (the Houghton Mifflin Company) hailed it as "the new authority on the English language." Morris left little doubt in his preface that the *AHD* sought to assume the role that *Webster's Third* had abandoned as "custodian of the American tradition in language." His dictionary would "faithfully record our language" but would not rest there "like so many others in these permissive times." It would offer "sensible guidance toward grace and precision which intelligent people seek in a dictionary."[28]

The *AHD* was the second major new challenge to the Merriam company that emerged after the publication of *Webster's Third*, but unlike the first – *The Random House Dictionary of the English Language,* unabridged, published in 1966 – it was not an unabridged dictionary.[29] Parton had originally conceived of publishing an unabridged dictionary that would compete directly with *Webster's Third*, but its coverage of the vocabulary and the amount of detail had been reduced after the enormous costs of producing an unabridged on the scale of *Webster's Third* and the time required became fully apparent. What appeared was a large college dictionary.

What American Heritage touted as its distinctive innovation was the creation of a Usage Panel of 105 eminent journalists, editors, literary figures, and college professors to pass judgment on what was acceptable and what was not. It included some fifteen outspoken critics of *Webster's Third* – Dwight Macdonald, Jacques Barzun, Theodore Bernstein (chairman), and others associated with the cluster of publications critical of the Third Edition, the *Saturday Review, New York Times,* and *New Yorker.*

It was a formidable assembly, though hardly representative of educated American speakers and writers – many of whom, contrary to Morris's belief, thought highly of *Webster's Third.* Teachers of English and specialists in the study of language and lexicography were woefully underrepresented on the panel. So were women and blacks, not to mention those residing at some distance from the East Coast. The average age was about sixty-four.

Since the panel was put forward as the arbiter of usage in place of the citations of actual usage that were relied on by Merriam-Webster dictionaries, among others, it merits closer scrutiny. Were its decisions more authoritative or representative of the practices of educated Americans? Does the record of the panel support Morris's belief – and the belief of leading critics of Webster's Third – that *opinions about usage* by prominent people are consistently in agreement or superior to the record of actual usage assessed by experienced editors?

That the *AHD* editors were traditional in their views seems clear from a comparison of their decisions and those of nine other dictionaries and ten usage books. The *AHD* contained 502 usage notes, fewer than half of which contained decisions by the panel, according to a detailed study of the panel by Thomas J. Creswell.[30] He pointed out as well that the panelists had no voice in deciding either of two key questions: which entries warranted a usage note and, of these, which were to be referred to the panel. These decisions were made by the editors, who assumed responsibility for determining the locutions that were "especially dubious and controversial." The panelists, in whom the editor ostensibly placed so much faith, were limited to voting and commenting on the questions submitted to them.[31]

Most of the words submitted to the panel, according to Creswell's compilations, had been treated as standard English by the other books in the sample. Even *Webster's Second,* the most conservative of the nine other dictionaries in the sample, cited a usage restriction in only 49 percent of the instances that worried *AHD,* and only one other dictionary saw problems in more than a third of the instances.[32]

Moreover, he concluded, "it is difficult to see . . . just what constitutes the difference between the two sets of items [those submitted to the panel and the others]. . . . For almost every category of usage problem on which a Panel vote is represented there are examples of usage notes on the same kind of problem on which a vote was not reported."

If Morris expected a strong showing of agreement by members of the panel, he must surely have been disappointed. Even like-minded guardians of the language often found themselves sharply divided. Votes ranged from bare majorities to virtual unanimity. The closest the panel came to unanimity was the vote on *ain't:* 99 percent disapproved of it in writing and 84 percent in speech.

Particularly striking were the differences between the opinions of panelists and those of the editors. The word *shakedown* in the sense of "extortion" is labeled *informal* in the dictionary, although 80 percent of the panel approved its use as a noun without restriction and 67 percent approved its use as a verb phrase *to shake down.* Yet instances in which the panel clearly indicated that its approval was limited to formal use appeared without a label.

Creswell cited other examples that mystified him. He concluded that the "labeling practice in *AHD* is, as has been the case with every aspect of *AHD* handling of usage we have so far examined, characterized by a kind of randomness which raises serious questions about the objectivity of labeling practice and about the usefulness or meaningfulness of the labels themselves. The presence or absence of a label seems as much a function of editorial whim as of any other discernible operating principle."[33]

The wording of the usage questions aroused Creswell's doubts about the objectivity of the process. It seemed intended to elicit a desired answer. "No attempt was made to invite or at least allow for an impartial, unprompted expression of opinion." The reporting of the results was inconsistent. Panel votes were reported in percentages for some questions and not for others with no apparent rationale for the difference in treatment.

After the second edition of the *AHD* was published in 1982, Creswell and Virginia McDavid subjected it to similar scrutiny. They found the panel more representative than its predecessor and the new edition more objective in tone; the "ill-natured comments" by panelists had been eliminated. But the role of the panel had been reduced. The number of entries reporting the panel's conclusions was cut by about half; percentages of approval and disapproval were omitted.

Other shortcomings that had been observed in the earlier edition were still evident. "It seems safe to say," Creswell and McDavid added, "that there is no consistency in relationship between the way an item is treated within an entry and any Usage Panel judgment regarding that item." They found no support for the editor's ringing claims in 1969 and concluded that "the Usage Panel in AHD2 is a marketing gimmick, not a source of serious information about usage."[34]

Was there any public response by *AHD* editors to these devastating criticisms? None, to Creswell's knowledge, perhaps because rejoinders might have attracted attention in the media. In scholarly books and journals, the Creswell and McDavid criticisms were widely cited, but there is no evidence that they hurt the reputation or sales of the *AHD*.

Virginia McDavid later carried the study of usage in the *AHD* a step farther by comparing the panel's judgments with the entries in *Webster's Dictionary of English Usage* (Merriam-Webster, 1989), which was based on the citations in the Merriam files. Her article covered ninety-four items that appeared in the *AHD* (both editions). About half of them were treated alike by the dictionary and the usage book. Each accepted thirty items and rejected eighteen (forty-eight agreements out of ninety-four comparisons). However, Merriam-Webster's *English Usage* found virtually *all* of the other items fully acceptable, whereas the panel accepted only one. In her summing up, McDavid noted that "in about half the items reported on here, the [panel] judges condemned what actual practice reveals as established and standard."[35]

In 1992 the publication of a new edition of *The American Heritage Dictionary*, which was again well received in the media and successful commercially, revived these and related issues, as noted in Chapter 16.

13

At Issue: A Way of Life

I am a friend to neology. It is the only way to give a language copiousness and euphony. . . . Dictionaries are but depositories of words already legitimated by usage.

Thomas Jefferson

By the summer of 1962 Mario Pei had concluded that the key issues in the controversy over *Webster's Third* were not lexicographical, as he had assumed when he wrote his sympathetic review in October 1961, but ideological. The new dictionary was much more than a book about words. It symbolized the further encroachment of a dangerous educational and social philosophy on traditional learning and as such posed a threat to society.[1]

With the benefit of hindsight, Pei had been able to place the Third Edition in the context of a great debate during the 1950s over the teaching of English. The villains under fire were "the teachers of English and the progressive educationists" who were responsible for turning out graduates "who do not know how to spell, punctuate, or capitalize; to divide a thought concept into phrases, sentences and paragraphs; or to express themselves, either in speech or writing, in the sort of English that is meaningful and acceptable." He reminded his readers of Bernard DeVoto's attack in 1948 on cultural anthropologists for trying to apply findings and conclusions about primitive people to the United States in the twentieth century. But, Pei added, "it was only with the appearance of the new third edition . . . late in 1961 that the issues at stake, at least for what concerns language, became clear to the cultured educated layman of America."

Gove read with incredulity the accusation that *Webster's Third* embodied all the sins that had corrupted the use and teaching of English.

He wrote, "Obviously, the appearance of *Webster's Third* . . . did bring into public discussion a number of issues concerning traditional grammar and modern linguists," but far from being clarified by the debate, the issues "have been confused, even more by Pei than by other critics." He found no basis for Pei's sweeping charge other than unsupported accusations by others.[2]

Pei's article developed two allegations by earlier critics that had been strongly disputed by Gove and others. The first was that in the Third Edition "all usage [is] now set on an identical plane"; on this charge Pei inadvertently proved himself wrong. Second, he claimed that the Third Edition's "shift in attitude and point of view in matters of language" had been shaped by "the followers of the American, anthropological, descriptive, structuralist school of linguistics." On this matter, he quoted Dwight Macdonald and Max Marshall, who made a similar accusation in *Science*.

Pei himself failed to demonstrate a link between the dictionary and the doctrine of the structural linguists. Nor did he demonstrate a relationship between the failures of the educational system and the influence of linguistics. The blame lay elsewhere, Gove said. The poor performance of students in speaking and writing could not be blamed on teaching methods based on "cultural anthropology." Quite the opposite. The methods followed by English teachers "reflect almost total ignorance of linguistics and a blind determination to follow outmoded 18th century grammarians" who wanted to teach English as if it were modeled on Latin.[3]

Pei attempted to illustrate the baleful effect of the Third Edition on teaching by presenting an imaginary conversation between a teacher and pupil. It was intended to show a teacher's helplessness when the only recourse was *Webster's Third*, which he portrayed as a book that treated all usage as equally acceptable and nothing as substandard. But even the parody Pei contrived did not support his charges. Contrary to his assumption, the dictionary warns strongly against the first test word in his fable: *learn us* in the sense of "teach" is labeled *chiefly substandard* (qualified as *chiefly* because in Shakespeare's time and in the following two centuries, it was fully acceptable; thus, it can be found in literature of the period and is still heard in dialectical speech).

The misuse of *refraction* for *reflection* is not supported by the Third Edition. A teacher would have no difficulty in showing the difference in meaning between the two by reference to the dictionary. Nor is *teach* for *teacher* condoned. The grammatical errors in the pupil's speech are shocking indeed, but transcripts of meetings and press conferences of highly educated people show that such problems are rather common in speech. The pupil's use of *guys* and *swell* in conversation is no great offense. What Pei's parody shows is that the Third Edition's distinctions between acceptable and unacceptable usages differ from his own, not that it makes no distinctions.

Pei's article aroused strong reader reaction. His reputation as an author and teacher and the standing of the *Saturday Review* gave a considerable boost to the cause of the Third Edition's detractors. This article was the one that James Parton chose to distribute to Merriam stockholders during his campaign to acquire the company. A month later about twenty letters appeared in the *Saturday Review*, some supporting and others attacking Pei. The executive secretary of the National Council of Teachers of English complained that the article misrepresented the NCTE and the dictionary and urged the *Saturday Review* to give space to other assessments of the dictionary and the problems of teaching English.[4]

Two years later, in 1964, Pei returned to the fray with a stronger statement of the ideological gulf. Writing in the *Saturday Review*, he began: "Two voices are raised throughout the land," the "Advocates of Usage" and the "Custodians of Language." Between these two groups, he said, the "main bone of contention and the chief source of criticism" was the Third Edition's restricted use of status labels. "There was far more to the controversy than met the eye," he went on, "for the battle was not merely over language. It was over a whole philosophy of life. Should there be a directing class, qualified as such by reason of intellect, education and general culture, or should there be unbridled democracy with a nose counting process to determine what was good and what was bad?"[5]

Having indicated where he stood on that question, Pei did not try to address the inescapable next issue: How would the kind of "directing class" that he yearned for succeed in controlling the course of language after centuries of experience to the contrary?

RIPOSTES HERE AND THERE

It was the lot of the Third Edition to be dragged into discussions or articles on the misuse of language as an example of linguistics run amok. At the 1962 annual meeting of the Association of American University Presses, Bruce Bliven, editor of the *New Republic,* protested the slovenly pronunciation on radio and television, sloppy usage, and "supposed authorities like Bergen Evans who maintain that whatever is, is right." That led him to *Webster's Third.* "I am not appeased by the fact that, so I am told, I am cited in the new Webster's several times as an authority. Like Groucho Marx, who wouldn't belong to any club that was willing to have him for a member, I don't want a dictionary that cites me as an authority. I want them to cite Shakespeare, Emerson, Thoreau, and Thomas Jefferson."[6]

Bliven may still have been smarting from a rebuke by James Sledd in a reply to a *New Republic* editorial some months earlier in which Sledd challenged him to "explain how an unabridged dictionary can make people talk the way its editors want them to."

Take you, for example. In almost 30 years you didn't learn anything about your own favorite, the Second International. If you had learned anything about it you would have known that its editors set out, like that bolshevik Gove, to record "the usage that now prevails among the educated and cultured people to whom the language is vernacular" and you would have known better than to choose an example like *bimonthly* to bless the Second and damn the Third. . . . Here's the definition of *bi-weekly* in the Second: "Occurring or appearing every two weeks; *fortnightly;* also, *semi-weekly.*" . . . The sense "twice a month" for the word *bimonthly* is new, you say. . . . Drag yourself away from Webster's Second long enough to look at the Oxford. You'll find *bimonthly* in the filthy sense as early as 1864.[7]

Two years after the review by Dwight Macdonald, the *New Yorker* showed that it was still on the lookout for opportunities to twit *Webster's Third.* An article in the "Talk of the Town" told the story of a diplomatic misunderstanding that had arisen over the Spanish word *negociar.* Did it mean "negotiate" or merely "discuss"? News accounts had reported that both Spanish and American dictionaries had been brought into the deliberations to decide the issue. The *New Yorker* writer expressed the hope that the negotiators were consulting *Webster's Second* – "an old fashioned, authoritative dictionary dedicated to judicious hair-splitting," instead of the Third Edition, which "was compiled by a group of modern linguists who bent over backward to be descriptive rather than prescriptive." After extolling the distinctions made in the Second Edition's definition of *negotiate,* the *New Yorker* had to concede that the same distinctions were made in the

Third. It concludes lamely though doggedly that "although the Third Edition still distinguishes between 'discuss' and 'negotiate,' the editors are on record as saying that a dictionary 'should have no artificial notions of correctness or superiority.'" The argument, of course, was about meaning, not about the social status of the word or notions of social correctness.[8]

In June 1962 Sleeth wrote a rebuttal to criticisms that had appeared in the *American Oxonian*. His reply was incorporated in an editorial entitled "Sleeth Bites Back." It was a rare intervention by a Merriam staff member. Responses to critics, after the initial flurry of attacks, were almost always handled by Gove.

Sleeth contrasted the favorable British reviews with those that appeared in the United States, in which the Third Edition had "been subjected to criticism, in terms usually reserved for criminal activities."[9] To the charge that "we did not speak with the expected authority," he replied: "But from what source does a lexicographer derive authority? Only from the persistent voluminous collection and the painstaking evaluation of actual usage. Indeed there is no other source from which his authority could possibly come." Commenting on *Life*'s implicit views of language change, he said, "If language did not change, we would still be forming the past of 'help' and the plural of 'book' by vowel change rather than by suffixation. The first person to say 'helped' and 'books' did not sound any more impressive than a person would sound now in saying 'runned' or 'foots.'"

ETHNIC SENSITIVITIES

While the old familiar issues continued to be reargued, the dictionary was being closely scrutinized by minorities, trade organizations, and other groups of evidence of inaccuracy and bias. In 1965 the handling of religious, racial, and ethnic entries was attacked in *Frontier* magazine by Philip Perlmutter, a writer on civil liberties and interfaith relations who took his cue from Follett, whose article he cited at the outset.

He found the Third Edition's usage notes puzzling and inadequate. The definitions of *kike, dago, nigger, spick, sheeny*, and *coon* are followed by notes that read as follows: "usu[ally] taken to be offensive." This, he said, is a "strange explanation" that suggests the word itself is essentially neutral. "Taking offense implies an innocence on the part of the speaker and a sensitivity, if not fault, on the part of the listener. A connotative onus is placed on the Negro or Jew who takes offense at 'nigger' or 'yid,' leaving the speaker and his words free of any offending characteristics."

Perlmutter also found the qualifying words themselves – "usu[ally]" in some notes and "often" in others – confusing. The phrase "often taken to be offensive" is used with *mick* for Irishman and *jigaboo* for Negro. "How the lexicographers came to the conclusion that Negroes "usu[ally] take offense at 'nigger' and 'often' take offense at 'jigaboo' is anyone's guess," he wrote. "If any generalization can be made, it is that Negroes always take offense at both words because both are always used offensively."

A number of words – including *papist*, *wop*, and *mocky* – are described in the Third Edition as "usu[ally] used disparagingly," which the reviewer considered to be more appropriate, since "the onus is more properly placed on the users of the words." Nevertheless, the term *usu[ally]* is misleading "since racists never use such words respectfully."

Perlmutter pointed out a further puzzling complication: some proper nouns that may be used disparagingly or considered offensive carry neither labels nor usage notes – for example, "jesuit . . . one given to intrigue or equivocation; a crafty person" and "jew . . . a person believed to drive a hard bargain" are treated as standard English.

In sum, the article concludes that *Webster's Third* "is not a record for an educated understanding of racial, religious or ethnic terms as they are written and spoken by the educated or uneducated."[10]

The issue that Perlmutter reopened had angered ethnic and religious minorities for several decades. In the 1920s the *Pocket Oxford Dictionary* and other Oxford dictionaries had come under heavy criticism for entries on racial and religious minorities that carried no cautionary labels or notes. H. W. Fowler, editor of the *Pocket Dictionary*, stood firm: "The dictionary-maker has to record what people say, not what he thinks they can politely say: how will you draw the line between this insult to a nation and such others as 'Dutch courage,' 'French leave' . . . 'a nation of shopkeepers,' and hundreds more. The real question is not whether a phrase is rude, but whether it is current."

Nonetheless, the practice of labeling such derogatory words became accepted in English and American lexicography. Robert Burchfield, who described the problems of the *Pocket Dictionary*, as well as
his own later experiences, concluded that "a special symbol meaning
'regarded as offensive in varying degrees by a person to whom the
word is applied' is long overdue."[11]

R. L. Chapman, who had come to a similar conclusion, introduced
symbols – a pair of delta symbols bracketing the entry – to flag
offensive words in his *New Dictionary of American Slang* and the
abridgment, *American Slang*. Taboo words "*never* to be used" are
marked with solid deltas ◀ ▶ and vulgar words "to be used only when
one is aware of and desires their strong effect" are marked by open
deltas ◁ ▷. He treated "terms of contempt and derision for racial or
other groups" as taboo terms.

In the supplement to the *OED* the notes on derogatory uses of
words include the following: *wop* and the verb *jew down*, "now considered to be *offensive*"; *spig, spic*, "a contemptuous and offensive name
for a Spanish-speaking native of Central or South America, or the
Caribbean"; *yid*, "A (usu. offensive) name for a Jew"; Chink,
"slang . . . (Derogatory)"; *jigaboo*, "coarse *slang* . . . a term that gives
offence."

Gove had set out to avoid offending any minority group. He knew
that the Second Edition had stumbled in its entry for *chinaman* by
failing to include a usage label or note, and it had been forced to make
a correction in later printings. He sought to improve on the Second
Edition's handling of *nigger* and *coon*, which had been treated merely
as colloquial, whereas *mick, spick*, and *yid* were labeled as slang. In the
Third Edition, the note for both *coon* and *nigger* was "usu. taken to be
offensive." He also imposed greater consistency by using this same
phrase for other ethnic terms, such as *kike* and *dago*, which carried
various labels in *Webster's Second*. But he had not thought of putting
the onus on the speaker rather than the hearer.

The sensitivity of minority groups had increased over the years, and
the Merriam company was not the only one to be criticized. Much
stronger objections were received at Oxford during the 1970s, for
example. Copies of the *Pocket Dictionary* were confiscated in Karachi
in protest against the definition of *Pakistan* – "a separate Moslem
State in India" – and a boycott by Arab countries was threatened over
the definition of *Palestinian* – "(native or inhabitant) of Palestine;

(person) seeking to displace Israelis from Palestine." Burchfield later observed that in his experience the focus of controversy had shifted from the inclusion and treatment of sexually explicit words to derogatory religious and ethnic entries. It was only in this area that he had received threats of violence – having been warned once that he would be "bumped off."[12]

Trade associations and professional organizations, which kept a close watch on how dictionaries treated their constituencies, differed in their assessments of the Third Edition. The printing industry expressed disapproval because it feared the effects of the "permissiveness" that Follett had warned against. An industry journal, which quoted Follett's review approvingly, warned that the Third Edition would undermine established standards of style and usage. If the Third Edition is used "as widely as its predecessors have been," it said, it "will have succeeded in codifying the mistakes of thousands of writers and the oversights of thousands of editors and proofreaders."

Funeral directors, however, found "notable improvements" in the Third Edition. They applauded its modernization of funeral terminology, including an entry for *funeral director*, "one whose profession is the management of funeral and burial preparations and observances and who is usually an embalmer; called also mortician and undertaker." The reviewer called attention to a clarification of the distinction between *coffin* and *casket* and said the definition of *embalming* explained modern procedure as well as it did early Egyptian mummification.[13]

THE CHIMERA OF POLITICS

Jacques Barzun joined in the battle belatedly in the spring of 1963, lending the weight of his scholarly reputation and influence to the cause against the Third Edition. He had found the intensity of the debate "gratifying" because it showed that despite signs of "linguistic indifference in daily life, some people at least still feel strongly about language and can be roused to battle." But the dictionary itself infuriated him. He dismissed the Third Edition as a political document – "the longest political pamphlet ever put together by a party." Underlying the definitions, usage notes, and established lexicographical practices, he found messages of profound and disturbing philosophi-

cal portent – "a dogma that far transcends the limits of lexicography."
His indictment was similar in its thrust to those published by his
faculty colleague at Columbia, Mario Pei, but it was harsher.[14]

Barzun prefaced his criticisms by announcing that he wrote with
the full backing of the editorial board of *American Scholar*, the distinguished publication of Phi Beta Kappa, the national academic honorary society. "This was extraordinary," Barzun explained. "Never in my
experience has the Editorial Board desired to reach a position; it
respects without effort the individuality of each member and contributor, and it expects and relishes diversity. What is even more remarkable, *none of those present had given the new dictionary more than a casual
glance*, yet each one felt that he knew how he stood on the issue that
the work presented to the public" (my emphasis).

It is perplexing that Barzun did not see that his statement invited an
entirely contrary interpretation – that it is equally "remarkable" for a
board of scholars to decide on an unprecedented declaration of principle without examining the contents of the work they decried and
without debating contrary views. They acted solely on the basis of
what the dictionary's critics had written, much of which had been
attacked as demonstrably wrong in its facts.

The centerpiece of Barzun's case against the dictionary and its
dogma was his discussion of the entry for *of*. Barzun saw it as an
example of the "scientism of the linguists, which is bound to divide
thinking people still more sharply into adherents and enemies."
Though it might seem farfetched, he said, even the definition of so
simple a word betrayed the "political and moral biases" he had inferred.

[T]he populism and scientism of the new lexicon appear together, for example in the twenty-first use of "of," as an alteration of "have" – "I should of
come." This is given as representing, "especially in written dialogue, a supposed dialectical or substandard speech." . . . Since this usage occurs frequently in speech, as everybody knows, one is bound to wonder whether its
inclusion in a famous dictionary does not confer upon it the lexicographer's
blessing. Certainly there is an implied defense of these of's who are also the
have nots.

Barzun had tracked down this offending usage on page 1565 of a
2,700-page book, following twenty numbered definitions of the preposition *of*. Buried here, he indicated, was the definitive clue to the

dictionary's political bias, its extreme populism. But one is bound to wonder (to borrow his phrase) whether a defense "of these of's" was indeed the editors' intention.

The history of dictionaries points to a different explanation. Gove did not introduce a new dogma in defining *of*; rather, he was following respectable lexicographical precedent. The editors of the *OED*, for example, recorded a similar treatment of *of* in the 1933 supplement, which presented a compilation of words that had been omitted from the original edition or were not yet in widespread use. It reads as follows: "Of, U.S. *dial.* or *colloq.* var. of HAVE v.24c." Three illustrative quotations followed, the first from 1847.

The entry was expanded in the 1976 *OED* supplement, which included a dozen examples of written usage from 1837 to 1977. It read "joc. (being erroneous in Received Standard) or dial. for HAVE *v.* representing unstressed pronunc. of 'have' esp. in such phrases as *could have, might have, must have* and *would have.*"

The *of* entry also exemplified in Barzun's eyes the false "scientism" that pervaded *Webster's Third.* Each sense of the word was introduced in the dictionary by the phrase "used as a function word to indicate . . ." and in each instance the word itself was replaced by a swung dash (~). "This is science," Barzun said.

Barzun interpreted the use of the swung dash as "a subtle attack on The Word, just as it is a blow struck against the sentence." But it was not Gove's innovation. It had been used as early as 1930 in the *Little Oxford Dictionary* and in the 1951 edition of the *Concise Oxford.* The use of symbols for words to save space had been a standard practice of English dictionaries and usage books since the beginning. Cawdrey used them; H. W. Fowler used about seventy abbreviations and symbols in *Modern English Usage,* including the reversed parenthetical marks,)(, placed between words to be compared. The *OED* lists nearly five hundred abbreviations and symbols, excluding those for pronunciation, not because it sought to be mathematical or scientific but because there seemed no other way to cope with the enormous amount of information to be conveyed. The Word didn't die; it proliferated, as each new edition of a dictionary attests.

Barzun attacked linguistics in the manner of Macdonald and others – accusing it of killing grammar and rhetoric in the schools and of denying that there were any standards of good English. He repeated the charge that the Third Edition embodied the "theology" of linguistics. He attacked the formation of neologisms from Latin and Greek roots and the vast list of abbreviations and acronyms included in the dictionary as if they, too, were Gove's innovation rather than the continuation of practices going back a century or more. The rest of the review consisted mostly of attacks on signs of decay in the use of the English language rather than an assessment of the dictionary.[15]

A LINGUIST RESPONDS

Linguists had a score to settle with the journalists and literary colleagues who had used *Webster's Third* as a weapon for attacking their discipline. They believed that their views had been seriously misrepresented in the controversy and, furthermore, that structural linguistics had had little appreciable effect on the Third Edition, except in the treatment of pronunciation – as Gove and others had noted. Albert Marckwardt, for example, wrote, "I find it difficult to find even a hint of structuralism in the handling of the definitions."[16] In 1964 Professor W. N. Francis of Brown University directed a rejoinder at Pei and Barzun and flunked them both for their ignorance of his field.

"A generation has grown up and been educated in lamentable ignorance of the basic facts about language," he wrote. As a result, he said, "I know no respectable academic discipline in which there is such an unbridgeable chasm between the thoughts of the specialist and the beliefs of the public, including some of its most highly educated members." He singled out *Webster's Third*'s most outspoken critics: Barzun, Macdonald, Pei, and Follett.[17]

Turning to Pei's 1962 review of *Webster's Third*, he quoted a paragraph in which Pei attributed eight doctrines to structural linguists. "Every single one of them is wrong," Francis said. "I know of no linguist who would subscribe to any of them, and the work of most of those I know refutes them seriatim and *in toto.*"

Barzun's representation of linguistics in his review of the Third Edition was no less offensive. Francis found the ignorance displayed in the reviews of *Webster's Third* by Pei and Barzun indicative of the odd view that anyone who uses English "competently is an expert. The distinction between operational skill and theoretical knowledge, which is carefully maintained in other disciplines, is here ignored. No one would ask an airline pilot, no matter how skillful, to review an encyclopedic work on aerodynamics."

Webster's Third was not above criticism, Francis added. "Linguists like Sledd and Weinreich have pointed out its shortcomings." But because of reviews like those of Barzun and Pei the discussion was "conducted on irrelevant grounds" and became "mired in a swamp of prejudice and unreason."[18]

WHILE THE THIRD EDITION WAS BEING ATTACKED as a sinister ideological and political document, it was also getting further attention from lexicographers and linguists who were evaluating it seriously as a dictionary. During the mid-1960s, reviews addressing its strengths and shortcomings appeared in such professional and scholarly journals as *American Speech, College English, Quarterly Journal of English,* and *Review of English Studies.* At the same time, Gove was revising and publishing key sections of the Black Books.

14

The Judgment of Peers

By and large, lexicographers and linguists viewed the Third Edition as a major lexicographical achievement. Where they had reservations or criticisms, they expressed their disagreements in the context of the dictionary's aims and accomplishments, recognizing the inevitable limitations of such an undertaking. As Burchfield put it, "The perfect dictionary is a mirage."

Of the two lexicographers quoted below, Burchfield was the more circumspect in his assessment – more respectful than approving, despite his high praise for the up-to-date coverage of the expanded vocabulary and the scholarly qualities of the etymologies. Robert L. Chapman, supervising editor of the Funk & Wagnalls *Standard College Dictionary* (1963), was more admiring, even though he devoted most of his review to his disagreements with Gove. He thought the virtues of the Third Edition were so obvious that they needed no elaboration in a review intended for scholars and practitioners in the field. The other reviewers quoted in the following excerpts were linguists.

Webster's Third . . . is a monumental achievement of exhaustive and highly competent research. It provides the fullest and most accurate description of the current English lexicon. (Harold B. Allen, University of Minnesota)

[A] bold landmark fashioned to meet the needs of the present. . . . The editor and his staff are to be congratulated on bringing to completion an especially arduous task. They have given shape to much that was unformed and have assembled a register of present-day English vocabulary which will be of service for many years to come. The greatness of their achievement will be seen all the more clearly if in future versions a gentler hand is brought to bear on some matters of layout, and if the rich field of words is mapped with even more assiduous attention to the intricate contours of currency, status, and utility. (Robert W. Burchfield, Oxford University Press)

. . . a marvelous achievement, a monument of scholarship and accuracy. (Robert L. Chapman, Funk & Wagnalls)

. . . an honest work, maintaining the principles and the concept of the dictionary characteristic of the previous editions, but carrying them out with greater consistency and basing them upon far more evidence. There have been errors of judgment, more often perhaps with respect to manner of presentation than in the interpretation . . . but this is inevitable in an undertaking of such magnitude. (Albert H. Marckwardt, Princeton University)

As a whole, *Webster's Third* far excels its forebears in both the quantity of information and the accuracy of its judgments. (Raven I. McDavid, Jr., University of Chicago)

In my opinion, the Third New International is still at the forefront of dictionary-making. On every page the rich documentation on which it is based is evident. It is a worthy exemplar of present-day scholarship. . . . the work as a whole deserves unstinting praise. (Allen Walker Read, Columbia University)

. . . a thoroughly professional job, an advance lexicographically over W2, and indispensable for anyone who wishes to be informed of the American language, especially its lexicon, of the middle of the twentieth century. (I. Willis Russell, University of Alabama)

As a completely new, independent, responsibly edited, unabridged dictionary, no other can rival it on precisely its own ground. Its merits are infinitely greater than those of the reviews which have lightly questioned them. Time and the experts will ultimately decide its just rank in the world of English lexicography, whether above, or alongside its predecessor; but meanwhile it can usefully fill a place in the libraries of a generation. (James H. Sledd, Northwestern University)

. . . accurate and clear, and more nearly complete than any other dictionary of English known to me. . . . Some things in the Third do not please me, but it is my privilege to be displeased on occasion, and if so to say so. Such things are, on balance, less than 0.001 per cent of the total content, and I think that all except those whose minds are closed to everything new are in private honesty bound to reach the same conclusion." (Joshua Whatmough, Harvard University)[1]

How the friendly critics diverged in their views on particulars is discussed in the following pages.

THE WORD LIST

The first task of a major revision is to bring the vocabulary up to date, and the Third Edition did so supremely well. On this issue there was virtual unanimity. Even such vociferous critics as Glixon and Macdonald conceded the point. The Merriam citation files, with their rich yield of new words and new senses of old words, came in for considerable commendation. There was a little grumbling about the number of scientific and technical terms, but it didn't amount to much. The dictionary had been served well by the conservative Merriam policy against incorporating a new word into the unabridged dictionary until there was evidence of its use over many years in more than a small locality or among only a very limited group; this practice provided reasonable protection against the inclusion of ephemeral or trendy terms.

DEFINING TECHNIQUE

The most striking assessment of Gove's controversial approach to defining appeared in Chapman's review. Published in 1967, it reflected Chapman's own heavy use of the Third Edition for several years and also took into account the comments of his colleagues. No other review of that period suggests such familiarity with the book and understanding of its objectives and scholarly standards, as well at its less convincing assumptions and practices.

The staff at Funk & Wagnalls had mixed feelings about the reception accorded *Webster's Third*, Chapman pointed out. They could not disguise a certain satisfaction in seeing a competitor put down, but they could not conceal their dismay over much of the criticism. They were quick to point out practices they disagreed with, but as professionals they could appreciate good work when they saw it.

The focus of Chapman's review was on the shortcomings of the Third Edition, but when he came to the topic of defining, he digressed from his agenda to praise *Webster's Third:*

To lexicographers, one of the most impressive and soundly innovative policies of [the Third Edition] . . . is that of defining in strict linear utterances. . . . each modifier is adjacent to what it modifies, each complement coupled in the starkest relations with the verb phrases, and so on. When it works, as it usually does, this style gives the most lucid and satisfying definitions yet written and relieves the readers of the annoying necessity of holding elements in suspension until completing elements are set down. Compared with the stop-and-start syntax, the clumsily embedded modifiers, and the elephantine references of earlier dictionary style, these definitions are clean, clear, and in the best sense modern.[2]

Other reviewers also commented on the strength of the definitions, including I. Willis Russell, who noted that the synonymies "in W3 seem better and word distinctions sharper than those in W2," and the reviewer for *Booklist and Subscription Books Bulletin.* Burchfield took note of the effective use or illustrative quotations from twentieth-century sources to supplement definitions "in a useful, even a delightful way."[3] Some, however, criticized the awkwardness of certain definitions, as Sledd had done in a letter to Gove before the big battles erupted.

SLANG

The treatment of slang was criticized on two closely related grounds: slang labels were not used often enough and they were not applied consistently.

Some reviewers thought that in reducing the number of labels and emphasizing illustrative quotations and usage notes because of their flexibility, Gove was striving for unrealistically fine distinctions. After all, dictionary editors have always made decisions based on limited and ambiguous evidence. Chapman observed, for example, that even if the status of a word was often very difficult to judge in isolation, the attempt should often be made in an effort to assist the reader. He wrote, "In making dictionary policy one must accept peripheral crudeness, minimize it as one can, and try to account for majority uses." Burchfield thought that Gove had been influenced by an "over-literal interpretation of the function of a dictionary as a record of usage rather than a prescriptive guide."[4]

Atcheson Hench, also one of the Third Edition's staunch defenders, thought he saw evidence of inconsistencies in the treatment of usage comments and the handling of slang. He viewed these shortcomings as exceptions to the general excellence of the Third Edition, which he described as "on the whole a magnificent compilation." His purpose in writing the article was to identfy the kinds of things that he hoped "would be different in Webster 4."[5] "Bewildered or mystified" by numerous entries, he found, for example, that four compounds of the word *big,* meaning an important person, were labeled *slang: big bug, big cheese, big chief,* and *big wheel.* Three others were unlabeled: *big boy, big shot,* and *bigwig. Big boy* was followed by a usage comment, "often used ironically, as in <come on, *big boy*>"; and *big shot* was followed by two examples showing it in context, including <he was a *big shot* in gambling circles>.

This challenge to the Third Edition echoed charges made in the past against many dictionaries. Defining slang has been much easier than distinguishing slang words from standard English in the gray boundary area where differences in status are slight.[6] The underlying question is: How does an editor, or a reviewer for that matter, decide when a label is warranted and when it is not? There is no litmus test that lexicographers can apply.

Gove's policy can be summed up simply: in the Third Edition, words are judged to be slang according to what the citations show. The definer examines each citation and decides whether it is in a standard context or requires a label. If most of the citations indicate that the word appears in the context of standard usage, it is left unlabeled. If most of them indicate that the usage is slang (as defined in the guidelines for the Third Edition), it is so labeled. Majority rules. If the citations are about equally balanced, the editor must rely on his or her own judgment. Thus, suppose *bigwig* is much more prevalent in standard usage than *big cheese,* which usually appears in the context of slang. *Bigwig* would not be labeled and *big cheese* would.

An instructive example can be taken from the Merriam files. Gove had been criticized for labeling *cornball* slang and treating *corny* as standard. These critics, who mistakenly assumed that language always follows principles of logic, thought it obvious that these near synonyms from the same root word must have the same status. But that is not what the evidence showed. *Corny* is used much more frequently than *cornball,* and it appears in contexts that suggest it is much more readily accepted among educated users as standard. If *corny* and *cornball* are indeed regarded differently by educated speakers, identical labels would have been a spurious consistency.

These two words appeared in a list compiled by Gove to illustrate

Table 4. *Illustration of labeling for* Webster's Third *based on the number of citations appearing in a standard or slang context (as judged by an editor)*

Word	2d ed. label	Number of standard citations	Number of slang citations	Suggested 3d ed. label
Browned-off	Slang	5	17	Slang
Deadpan	(Not in)	19	1	—
Hijack	Slang	33	13	—
Corny	None	28	15	—
Cornball	(Not in)	1	7	Slang
Look-see (noun)	(Not in)	35	35	Slang[a]

[a]Editor's choice when there is a tie in the citation count.

Source: "Memorandum on Usage Orientation," for Black Books, American Heritage Center.

to the staff how citational evidence could be used to govern usage decisions. A portion of the list is given to Table 4, which shows how each word was treated in the Second Edition (if it appeared there), what the citation files showed, and what the appropriate label would be for the Third Edition.

Corny was not labeled in the Second Edition; most of the citations showed that it was used as standard English. The recommendation was not to label it in the Third. *Cornball* did not appear in the Second; the citation file indicated that it was less frequently used, and almost always in a slang context. The word *look-see* was not in the Second Edition; it appeared to be equally regarded as slang and standard. The decision was up to the editor, who at the time thought the word ought to be considered slang. By the time the final decision was made, however, more evidence was available, the editor had a change of heart, or Gove deleted the label in reading final copy. *Look-see* appears in the Third Edition without a label, but with two supporting illustrative quotations showing its use in a standard context.

A lexicographer who has given considerable thought to the problem, Robert K. Barnhart, has given an excellent example of the fact that labeling remains a "very difficult problem . . . for which there is probably no real solution."

Many years ago, in the late 1930's, my father [Clarence Barnhart] asked several scholars, including Albert Baugh and Sir William Craigie, to mark a small part of a dictionary manuscript for levels of usage. The scholars did not agree. . . . Then in the 1960's he asked . . . George Lane, Randolph Quirk, J. A. W. Bennett, and others to mark up a complete dictionary manuscript of about 175,000 entries. Again there was little agreement among them.

I think it is fair to conclude that language and usage are largely a matter of taste and fashion. An editor who has a file in front of him can give the evidence for usage so far as it is available, and he can add his own judgment which is perhaps what the user is ultimately buying.[7]

The four-volume supplement to the *OED*, in offering its best judgments on the status of collocations using *big*, may also be viewed with puzzlement by some users unaware of the evidence on which the decisions were made: *big boy* is labeled *colloq.*; *Big Daddy* is unlabeled; *big mouth* is unlabeled; *big picture* is *colloq.*; *big wheel* is *slang;* the expression *big of you* is *colloq.*; and *go over big* is *slang.* All of these labels may be appropriate for British usage, but the reasons for the distinctions are no more likely to be obvious to a user than those in *Webster's Third* were apparent to Hench. Consistency, a reasonable and useful criterion for many practices, may be irrelevant or misleading in judging the handling of labels.

What, then, is an appropriate response to Hench's perplexity about the inconsistencies he observed? One can be inferred from Gove's practices and writings. In some instances the words should have been so treated because of clear evidence of differences in usage; in other instances editors arrived at different judgments because they worked from different evidence – or evidence that was inconclusive – or because they interpreted the situation differently; in other instances the editor may have indeed been inconsistent in applying Gove's criteria. Hench was not looking for an answer, however. He said the purpose of his review was to raise "the kinds of things" that he hoped would be handled differently in the Fourth Edition.

WHETHER GOVE USED SLANG LABELS too sparingly may be debatable, but there is no doubt that he used them less frequently than his predecessors. One estimate based on a comparison of samples from the Second and Third Edition suggests that the Third resorted to the slang label less than half as often as the Second.[8]

The Third Edition, by Gove's count, contained about 1,750 words labeled *slang* – a higher number perhaps than one might have guessed from reviewers who gave the impression that the Third Edition had virtually abandoned the label. Nonetheless, judging from Edwin Barber's count, it might have been twice as high had Gove not revised the criteria. From Gove's perspective, of course, the number of words that should be labeled *slang* was the wrong issue. The question was not whether the label was used often enough but whether the reader was properly informed about the status of questionable words – by labels, usage notes, or verbal illustrations, a broader question that has not been thoroughly studied.

Gove sought to clarify how verbal illustrations were used to suggest differences in levels of usage when he replied to a critical editorial in the *New York Herald-Tribune:*

If you look in "Webster's Third" . . . at *pass out,* you will find the quotations, "three men passed out from heat exhaustion," a statement that one would expect to be quite appropriate in nearly any standard context. But there may be some shadow on *pass out* that a user should be made to feel aware of. How better to reveal this than by another quotation reading, "was pretty well plastered, but he rarely got to the state where he passed out"? You call this "egregiously and multitudinously barbarous," which misses the point. The word *plastered* is marked slang in the Third Edition and so the quotation reveals that *pass out* sometimes occurs in a slangy context. Isn't this clear warning that the term, like all terms, should be used only in the right context? And isn't this kind of evidence a help rather than a "horrifying prospect" to a good teacher?[9]

COLLOQUIAL AND OTHER LABELS

There were also strong objections by some linguists and lexicographers to Gove's abandonment of the colloquial label. That the label was frequently misinterpreted by users – perhaps to the point where it was more misleading than helpful – had been widely conceded for years, as noted in Chapter 8. But the willingness of critics to drop *colloquial* did not mean they were ready to ignore the distinction between formal and informal speech. They thought the distinction should be flagged by a more appropriate label. From a pedagogical perspective, Sledd feared that the failure to label questionable entries would complicate the task of teaching and hamper the instruction of young people and foreigners.[10]

Despite the criticisms, Gove held fast to his belief that the distinction between formal and informal was best made by verbal illustrations and usage notes, and he was not without allies. Harold Allen thought *Webster's Third* gave "more precise indications of usage status than were given by such a label as 'colloq.', which was so often misinterpreted as a categorical tag of opprobrium."[11]

Chapman, however, pursued the logic of his criticism a step further and came to a conclusion that invites further examination. As Chapman interpreted the Third Edition, Gove offered a choice between "formal standard English and some variety of nonstandard." This dichotomy, Chapman believed, was less informative than the more frequent three-part classification – formal, informal, slang – though he conceded that the latter did not always work out neatly in practice.

But is this what Gove offered or was he posing a different choice – the choice between two general classes, *standard* English, including both formal and informal styles, and *substandard* English? It seems clear that he was offering the choice between standard and nonstandard. Standard English is not labeled in the Third Edition, neither when it is formal nor when it is informal. For dictionary users, the distinction between these two general types of standard English is indicated by illustrative quotations and usage notes. Each variety is fully acceptable in its own context, but not acceptable in an inappropriate context.

However, substandard English and the other styles that are not standard (nonstandard and slang) are given "stylistic" (or usage) labels to warn readers that an entry deviates in some way from standard English. Labels, being blunt instruments, are best reserved for indicating what is standard and what is not standard.

This interpretation is consistent with John S. Kenyon's important distinction that *formal* and *informal* "are functional varieties of English on the one cultural level, standard English."[12] Kenyon believed that a great misunderstanding had been caused by the failure of language experts to recognize and maintain the distinction between levels and varieties of English. This failure was largely responsible for the widely held misconception that colloquial and informal English are inferior to formal English. The error is exemplified by such groupings as *literary, colloquial,* and *illiterate,* which suggest a hierarchy of correctness, whereas *literary* and *colloquial* are equally correct in the appropriate situation whereas *illiterate* is always substandard.

Gove's implied rationale becomes more useful when one takes into account that standard English includes not only formal and informal expressions, but also professional, technical, literary, and artistic expressions. When used in the appropriate setting, all of these are acceptable varieties of standard speech and writing, but out of place they may be unsuitable, annoying, or offensive. For some reason, perhaps the historical preoccupation with correctness, Americans have been much more worried about the consequences of using informal speech and slang in a formal situation than about using technical jargon or highly formal speech in an informal setting, though it may be equally offensive to the reader or listener or prove embarrassing to the speaker or writer.

Indeed, those who have either taught English composition or have spent years reading term papers and other reports written for college courses find that pompous and vague words and the resort to specialized language are often greater obstacles to clear and effective writing than is the overuse of the informal. Scholarly and technical editors have made the same point, which has also been made in handbooks on writing. Lexicographers, however, have shown much less sensitivity to this aspect of usage than either teachers of composition or editors. Consequently, dictionary users have been left to determine on their own the appropriateness of the very formal or technical words they employ, with whatever guidance can be gleaned from verbal illustrations, if they are provided. There are no warning labels to alert readers to words that are widely viewed as pretentious or virtually meaningless – though a Texas congressman, Maury Maverick, created his own label in the early 1940s, *gobbledygook*, to ridicule bureaucratic, academic, and professional jargon. (*Gobbledygook* is labeled *slang* in *Webster's New World*, third edition, but standard in *Merriam-Webster's Collegiate*, tenth edition, and *The Random House Webster's College Dictionary.*) Maverick attracted attention, but didn't eradicate the practice. The fact remains that there is no substitute for a knowledge of vocabulary and a feeling for language – *sprachgefühl* – a favorite word among Merriam editors and lexicographers generally. Stylistic labels are a weak reed to lean on.

Chapman also tried to clarify what the absence of a label meant (as did Landau more than two decades later). He said that the critics erred in asserting that "the absence of a label stamped a word as approved and fit for use in all contexts." Inclusion of a word in a dictionary did not connote approval, and illustrative quotations and other verbal examples had to be taken into account in deciding when its use was appropriate. Gove had made the same point in his defense of the treatment of *ain't*, but with little success.

ETYMOLOGY

Etymology was the only major feature of the Third Edition that escaped criticism. When it was mentioned, which was not very often, the comments were highly complimentary, especially those by lexicographers. Burchfield, who had assisted in the completion of the *Oxford Dictionary of Etymology* before taking over the *OED* supplement, wrote that "from the samples I have examined, the reassessment of the main etymological works published since O.E.D. has been brilliantly conducted throughout the dictionary. Changes in the orthographies of foreign languages have not gone unnoticed, and the credentials of Latin, late-Latin, and medieval-Latin words, and of OE., ME., ON., &c., forms have been carefully re-examined, usually with conspicuous success. One may also admit that the rapid dissemination of internationalized technical and scientific terms justifies in its usefulness and acumen the introduction of the label 'ISV'" (International Scientific Vocabulary).[13]

Chapman called the introduction of ISV by Charles Sleeth a "keen stroke of policy, likely to be noticed and cheered only by a fellow lexicographer. . . . Anyone who has ever tried to cope with the neo- and neo-neo Latinisms and Grecisms of scientific terminology, fitting them into the orderly set of labels covering the stages of these languages realizes at once the synthesizing brilliance of the conception *ISV*."[14]

John Algeo, who was less impressed, noted some thirty years later that one should distinguish between the usefulness of ISV to the lexicographer and its informativeness to the reader. The term "is handy – it solves certain difficulties for the etymologist. . . . It is useful, honest, informative in a limited way – but basically it is saying that the precise origin of this form is impossible or too troublesome to trace and may not be possible to ascertain with confidence and that the form is widely current in European languages, without being more specific." Algeo thought that since other lexicographers had not adopted the form, ISV had not fully succeeded in solving the problem – but neither had anyone come up with a better solution.[15]

The treatment of pronunciation in *Webster's Third* received a mixed reception, ranging from admiration to exasperation – and since the exasperating features were more obvious, they received disproportionate attention. Edward Artin was widely credited with a prodigious achievement in capturing with unprecedented thoroughness a record of how English was pronounced in the United States in the mid-twentieth century. Raven I. McDavid also welcomed Artin's new pronunciation key as a "happy departure from that used in previous editions," a judgment echoed by Sledd. Sledd added that the Third Edition was thus able to "do fuller justice than its predecessor did to regional variation and to modes of speech less artificial than the 'formal platform speech' of the earlier work."[16]

Though it may have served the experts well, the Third Edition's treatment of pronunciation was too ambitious and detailed for most users. It offered much more than they needed and more than they could cope with – too many alternative pronunciations conveyed by too many new shorthand symbols. Although Artin's system used fewer vowel symbols, most of those it used were new. One sympathetic reviewer shrugged off the criticism with the observation that in practice "the general reader will do what he has always done, of course; he will take the first pronunciation listed and not worry about the rest" – assuming that the average user is always able to follow the shorthand.[17]

Even expert opinion on the pronunciation key was not unanimous. It was divided between those who applauded the new system, such as McDavid, and those who objected to it, such as Robert Sonkin. Sonkin criticized many of Artin's symbols and other innovations that left him with feelings of "frustration and irritation."[18]

The sheer number of variant pronunciations drew the most fire. It seemed that every reviewer found another horrible example to cite.

None of them argued that only a single *correct* pronunciation be shown, as some early detractors had urged; variants had appeared even in the Second Edition. But it was said that the Third Edition had simply gone too far.

The *Booklist* compared the Third and Second Editions and wondered why the Third Edition provided "nine pronunciations . . . for *auld lang syne* instead of three [in the Second]; five for *aunt* instead of two; seven for *idea* instead of three; four for *usurp* instead of two."[19] In his review in *American Speech,* Chapman asked whether eight separate pronunciations for *flightily* were necessary. Sonkin claimed to have counted 132 variants for *a fortiori.*[20]

Burchfield wrote: "A general dictionary . . . seems the wrong place in which to record multiple variant pronunciations (seven pronunciations are given for *perturbation*) and in which to use such clumsy devices as |′⫽(⫽)⫽,⫽| to show that *hatcheryman* is to be pronounced in essentials like the preceding word *hatchery.*" Chapman was also put off by the "strange algebra of 'slanted double hyphens, ditto marks, and plus signs, so that one must go chasing up the columns, picking up one element at a time and holding it in mind until all the bits are found, often at some distance from the word itself. The space saved by ingenuity was too dearly bought."[21]

But unanimity is still lacking on this matter. More than two decades later, Landau spoke up for Artin's work as firmly as McDavid and Sledd had done:

It seems to me that the only synchronic, unabridged dictionary in English should record fully the variant pronunciations documented by regional linguistic atlases and by its own phonological records. . . . I cannot understand why . . . [the Third Edition] should be criticized for providing extraordinarily full pronunciations and also for dropping the obsolete terms listed "under the line" [in the Second Edition].

Of Artin, he wrote, "In spite of some imperfections and overelaborations, the treatment of pronunciation in particular was greatly improved over NID2, and in my estimation, Edward Artin . . . has yet to receive the recognition he deserves."[22]

Edmund S. C. Weiner, coeditor of the second edition of the *OED,* was also highly impressed by Artin's prodigious research on pronunciation, which had proved to be very useful to lexicographers. He did not think it very helpful to the average reader, however, since Artin did not indicate preferences,[23] unlike James Murray, who was also descriptive in his approach.

Though he was also critical of the number of variants, Read was mindful of Artin's dilemma and the difficulty of trying to serve simultaneously the average user and the phonetic specialist. "The average user seeking pronunciations will be better served by the desk-sized dictionaries," he suggested.[24]

On one point, however, there was full agreement. Everyone objected to *Webster's Third*'s effort to reduce costs by placing the pronunciation key only on the inside front and back covers of the Third Edition rather than on every page or every other page. Only one reviewer seems to have pointed out that the *OED* had done the same. Besides the inconvenience, the arrangements led to frequent flipping to the end papers, which greatly increased the wear and tear on the binding. One review suggested that users obtain the Merriam pamphlet on pronunciation and insert it in their dictionary.

Surprisingly, one of the major changes in the treatment of pronunciation went almost unnoticed: the placement of the stress mark before the stressed syllable rather than after it. Since the old practice was widely understood and served its purpose, was a change, logical as it might seem, necessary? One dissenter noted that "although it has the authority of the IPA [International Phonetic Alphabet], [it] seems to me to be a mistake."[25]

MISCELLANY

Spelling

Early critics pounced on the inclusion of variant spellings to support their charge that the Third Edition was permissive. But this was another instance in which they betrayed their unfamiliarity with the Second Edition. Variant spellings were not introduced by Gove, and the extent to which they appeared earlier surprised even those who were familiar with the practice in the Second Edition. One reviewer recalled his incredulity when he read an article in which a leading linguist wrote: "What reader has not experienced at least a momentary blockage upon coming across a *mispelled* word" (my emphasis).

Taken aback by what he had read, he turned to *Webster's Second* and found *mispell* as an acceptable variant to *misspell*. Similarly when he encountered *developement*, he discovered it also was accepted in the Second Edition. (*Mispell* was no longer recognized in the "anything goes" Third Edition, though *developement* continued to be listed as a variant.)[26] Nonetheless, it was argued that variant spellings could go too far. Chapman thought that *Webster's Third*'s listing of *momento* as a variant of *memento* comes close to denying the possibility of error in spelling."

Capitalization

The most idiosyncratic of Gove's innovations, his capitalization style, was universally deplored. Allen, one of his strongest supporters, wrote: "I think rather silly the lower case entry which has to be followed by *usu. cap.*" Burchfield was blunt: "The accompanying labels . . . merely serve to underline the bizarreness of the uncapitalized forms and the cumbersome nature of the explanation."[27]

Chapman argued that the dictionary should reflect prevailing practices and should capitalize entries that were typically capitalized in standard usage. The user was entitled to the best guidance the lexicographer could offer. Read said the decision on capitalization had been carried to "an absurd extreme," as had some other editorial practices.

Lexicographical Theory

On a more substantive matter, many in the academic community were impressed by a commentary written in 1964 by Uriel Weinreich of Columbia University on the backward state of lexicographical theory and the lack of attention devoted to it. Though the article was ostensibly about *Webster's Third*, it was less a critique of the Third Edition than of lexicography generally. Sledd, who had also been troubled by the failure of lexicography to advance theoretically for more than a century, applauded the article, as did Randolph Quirk. As the example chosen to make Weinreich's point, *Webster's Third* was heavily criticized for failing to do what neither researchers nor practitioners had done – and what in large measure remained undone three decades later, though the subject began to attract greater attention.

Noel E. Osselton saw evidence of change by the late 1980s and a "quickening of scholarly interest in lexicographic theory" after a long period in which "incidental sniping" had taken the place of serious criticism.[28]

The Riddle of Intensity

Several academic reviewers speculated about why the controversy had become so widespread and so intense. Among them were Karl W. Dykema, Walter J. Ong, Albert H. Marckwardt, and Raven I. McDavid, Jr. (who had touched on the topic during his examination of the prepublication publicity discussed in Chapter 9).

Dykema thought that the attacks on *Webster's Third* could be attributed largely to cultural lag – the "survival of a medieval linguistic and philosophical attitude in critics who happen to be living in the twentieth century." Twelfth- and thirteenth-century philosophers, he wrote, sought to formalize the structure of Latin in accord with their view of a universal order of nature, and later that view was carried over into English. "Such terms as *subject, predicate, apposition, ablative absolute* appear for the first time though what they purport to describe appeared in Latin from our first records of it. And the study of grammar became an end in itself."[29]

He quoted a twelfth-century definition of grammar by Petrus Heliae that in his view exemplified the doctrine of correctness reflected in the writing of Gove's detractors: "Grammar is the science of correct writing and speaking. This science has as its mission to order in a harmonious manner letters into syllables, syllables into words, words into sentences and to speak them correctly so as to avoid solecisms and barbarisms."[30]

Ong suggested that a psychological factor helped account for the intensity of the attack on the Third Edition. He argued that because of their heavy investment in the mastery of writing, traditionalists felt threatened by the revived importance of speech brought about by new technology. A culture that had come to overvalue writing in the belief that it "reduces restless, unpredictable, evanescent sound to the quiescent order of space *must* control all speech" perceived *Webster's Third* as an element of a larger threat to the status of writing.

Marckwardt found an explanation in the characteristically American longing for authoritarianism in language that Read, Sledd, and others had also pointed to. The persistence of this view, he said, reflected the great failure of the teaching profession to convey to generations of students a decent understanding of the development of the English language. "It is the English teaching profession which should be seriously disturbed by the dictionary controversy. . . . Much of the misunderstanding [about what a dictionary is for and how to use it] . . . can with considerable justice be laid at our door. After all, the embattled critics were once our students."[31]

Marckwardt's theme, the failure of teaching, had also been addressed by Dykema and Allen. Dykema noted that twenty-five years earlier, the president of the Modern Language Association, Edward Prokosch, had described as "treason" the "failure of modern language departments, especially English, to include linguistic study as a part of the graduate program." Allen noted that those who taught speech and English should not forget that they had had J. Donald Adams, Dwight Macdonald, and Wilson Follett in their classes. "During the past three quarters of a century we have largely shunned the responsibility of teaching students the facts of language, of drawing upon the accumulated data in the work of Hermann Paul, Whitney, Sweet, Lounsbury, and Jespersen, and of presenting the linguistic criterions upon which modern lexicography is based."[32]

Nonlexical Material

A few critics touched on the deletion of encyclopedic material, including Kilburn, a staunch defender of the Third Edition, and Chapman, who wrote that they personally preferred a dictionary that also served as a general reference work. They acknowledged nonetheless that limiting the dictionary to lexical entries was a reasonable and legitimate publishing decision. A contrary opinion was expressed in the *Booklist*, which noted the deletion of the encyclopedic material with satisfaction. It pointed out that more than twenty-five years earlier, in a review of the Second Edition, the *Booklist* had urged this step; it had called the inclusion of encyclopedic material superfluous and inappropriate.[33]

The disagreement on the proper scope of the dictionary was characteristic of many of the differences between Gove and knowledge-

able and sympathetic critics. They were matters not of great lexicographical principle but rather of preference and practical
judgment.

THE PERSISTENT CRITIC AND THE SECOND
BATTLE OF *AIN'T*

Against the tide of academic support, Sheridan Baker, a professor of
English at the University of Michigan, continued to attack the Third
Edition almost single-handedly in scholarly publications after other
detractors had had their say. Baker wrote three articles during the
mid-1960s that revived many of the themes propounded by Barzun
and Pei. The first article challenged the evidence on which the entry
for *ain't* was based and questioned Gove's motives, the intentions and
practices of the Third Edition, and the field of linguistics in general.
It stirred a flurry of rejoinders that kept the matter alive for several
months.[34]

Gove was drawn into the debate by Sledd, who had been asked to
review Baker's article when it was submitted to *College English*. Sledd
thought Baker was "flatly wrong in many ways and ought to think
about revising" his work. But he was impressed enough by Baker's
research to urge Gove to tell Baker "precisely what the evidence was
for the entry." Gove replied to Sledd that "your letter compels me to
tell him that there is no large file of evidence being withheld. That's
why, as I have explained to him, the entry in question carefully limits
the use of *ain't* in sense one by 'orally.'" He went on to explain that
"knowledge of some kind of language behavior comes through contact
with its observers and is not always documented because there seems
to be no reason to collect additional evidence."[35]

In the published article, Baker seized on Gove's explanation as
support for his thesis that "*Webster's ain't*, which we have taken as the
sacrosanct product of linguistic science, is really the product of that
osmotic process Dr. Gove has described as the lexicographical
art. . . . Behind Gove's letter we may see something other than rows
of filing cabinets and electronic precision. I at least see something of
the long years of attack on the eighteenth-century rules of grammar."[36]

That Baker found Gove's explanation less than satisfactory is not surprising, since it differs from Gove's invariable defense that decisions on meaning and usage were inferred from citations. But he offered no evidence to support his inference that the case of *ain't* confirmed that Gove was out to advance the views of linguists rather than to describe current usage.

Baker's article was heavily criticized because he sought to prove his thesis by drawing on the survey data on the use of *ain't* that had been gathered for the Linguistic Atlas of the Upper Midwest under the direction of Harold Allen. He accused the author of one report, Virginia G. McDavid, of making numerous errors and suppressing evidence. "True to her calling," he said, she "is out after 'ain't's' in the usage of cultivated speakers." He also attacked the integrity of the survey process itself.

Outraged responses from McDavid and Allen in *College English* pointed out serious errors in Baker's handling of the survey procedures and data. McDavid retorted that "Sheridan Baker is too practical a stylist to sacrifice polemics and name-calling for objectivity and truth. Even so, it took considerable effrontery to use the phrase 'Mrs. McDavid's well suppressed evidence' . . . when the evidence appears in full in table 74 of my thesis."[37]

In a subsequent issue, Baker conceded his errors and added, "I apologize to Mrs. McDavid and Professor Allen." However, he stood firm in his criticism of Gove's rationale for *ain't* and his major arguments against the dictionary and linguists.

In 1965 Baker attacked *Webster's Third* in his presidential address to the Michigan Academy of Science, Arts, and Letters. He began with a disarming acknowledgment that "no one can read many pages of *Webster's Third New International Dictionary* without being impressed." The difficulties of Gove's new defining style "are well offset by entry after entry that is, as he claims, precise and sharp." Then he turned to the attack: "Webster's is partisan, takes quantity for quality, equates the popular with the good, has double standards, has no standards." He attacked the defenders of the dictionary who had argued that even if the Third Edition was mistaken in details it was correct in its theory. The opposite was true, Baker charged. *Webster's Third* was flawed because its theory was essentially anti-intellectual.[38]

At Baker's urging, the academy passed a resolution expressing its dismay over the handling of usage in *Webster's Third* and its disapproval of the omission of encyclopedic material. It called on the Merriam company to revise its editorial policy for the next edition of the *Collegiate Dictionary.*

Baker's third critique of the dictionary appeared seven years later. "The Sociology of Dictionaries and the Sociology of Words" demonstrated his unrelenting opposition to the work itself – and confirmed the persistent intensity of the larger battle between the faculties in English language and literature.[39]

IN JANUARY 1965, Marckwardt was moved to reminisce about better days in the field of English. Equally at home in literature and philology and sympathetic to the research contributions of linguistics, he was one of a small band of academic leaders in the field who had standing in both camps. He noted that at the outset of the century, "relatively speaking, we were a unified profession. Today we are fragmented." In introducing a special issue of *College English* on linguistics, he expressed both his regret and his congratulations on the occasion. He congratulated the journal for giving attention to the subject, but added, "It is unfortunate . . . that such an expository effort directed toward this particular audience should be necessary at all."[40]

PART IV
Sorting It All Out

15

Gove and *Webster's Third*: The Legacy

> If the Webster war has proved little or nothing about dictionaries, it has demonstrated our ineptitude . . . in teaching our students what a dictionary is for, how it is made, and the proper way to use it.
>
> Albert H. Marckwardt, "Dictionaries and the English Language"

Gove spent much of the last decade of his life doggedly defending his principles and explaining his work. He adapted several sections of the Black Books for publication in *American Speech* and other journals, spelling out in about a dozen articles the rationale and editorial guidelines that shaped the Third Edition. From time to time he carried his message to meetings of English teachers and other groups; when he came to town, newspaper reporters continued to seek him out for comments on the Third Edition. In 1967, at the suggestion of a textbook publisher, he took his case to college students in a paperback collection of articles entitled *The Role of the Dictionary*.[1]

In June of that year he stepped down as editor in chief, having reached sixty-five, the retirement age for company executives. He stayed on for five years as a consultant, working full time for three years and half-time for two. His responsibilities were diminished, but his commitment to lexicography did not weaken; nor did his habits change. He faithfully kept regular office hours, making a point of arriving on time and staying until the office closed. He drew up suggestions for the Fourth Edition on the basis of a rigorous reexamination of the Third, trained young editors in reading and marking, and – at the request of his successor, Bosley Woolf – wrote definitions of scatological and racially derogatory terms for *Webster's New*

Collegiate Dictionary, eighth edition. Many more of these terms would be entering the *Collegiate* for the first time – including the taboo word *fuck* that Gallan had deleted from the galleys of the Third Edition. The last of his major articles on *Webster's Third* were completed after he retired. During the retirement years he also wrote book reviews, an essay in a book of collected essays, and an introduction to a facsimile edition of Noah Webster's *Compendious Dictionary* of 1806.

As a consultant, Gove continued to share with Woolf the large office they had jointly occupied for several years. Their desks were side by side, and a long dictionary stand was in front of each. To many of the young staff being recruited and trained by Woolf for the next *Collegiate* dictionary, Gove became an avuncular figure – relaxed, approachable, and helpful – though still rather formidable in manner. No longer "the commander-in-chief, he was able to give us the special attention he had not been able to give new people on *Webster's Third.*"[2] These seemed to be golden years for him. He could work hard without feeling pressured. His dictionary had weathered the storm of criticism, and in the reviews of his peers he had found considerable vindication.

A new president who came on the scene in 1970, David R. Replogle, was impressed by Gove's dedication to Merriam dictionaries and to scholarly standards that were as solid as ever. If some of his bruises from the battles of the early 1960s were still painful, as Replogle believed, there was no evidence of bitterness. Gove continued to express his pride in and satisfaction with what had been accomplished.[3]

Two years later, shortly before his seventieth birthday, Gove requested an extension of his consulting arrangement. Replogle was not convinced, however, of the need for the work that Gove proposed to do and decided against renewing the appointment, much to Gove's chagrin.

WINDING DOWN

Gove's career at Merriam-Webster came to an end in June 1972. Staff members were aware of his great reluctance to retire and sympathized with him in his disappointment. They arranged a farewell party in his honor on the afternoon of his last day at work. It was a happy celebration of his achievements, and Gove was visibly touched. He had refused to give a speech – having already told the editors "all I have to say" – but at the end he changed his mind. His words were well remembered: "I knew I was respected, but I never realized there was so much affection."

Retirement was hard for him to accept. After more than twenty-five years at the Merriam company, Gove missed his office, his associates, and the preoccupation with lexicographical issues. He desperately wanted to be part of the transition to the next unabridged. Woolf, too, was approaching retirement age. The search for a new editor in chief could not be postponed for long if the Fourth Edition was to be published in 1986 or thereabouts. Gove, with his customary self-confidence, believed that he was the best person to complete the review of the Third Edition and the most qualified by experience to identify an editor of the next unabridged.

In early autumn, two staff members visited him in Warren, Hazel Lord, the department secretary, and Grace Kellogg, a longtime editor who remained greatly indebted to Gove for transferring her from an unsatisfying job to one that suited her. They found him a bit discouraged. He did not look well. The farm seemed not to have the same rejuvenating effect it had had in the past. There was also an ominous cloud on the horizon, the rumor of a major real estate development that would remake the landscape of Warren and the neighboring towns of West Brookfield and Brimfield. A Connecticut developer, Carabetta Enterprises, was said to be quietly planning a new town in the vicinity. The prospect of a business boom, jobs, and quick profits for landholders appealed to some insiders, but others who liked the area as it was shuddered at the idea.

As the weeks went by, Carabetta began quietly buying up options on land in the vicinity of Warren. The Goves and other owners of large parcels were put under increasing pressure to support the project. Philip and Grace were strongly opposed to the development plan and sharply critical of the way in which the land purchases were being handled. As the news spread, public pressure mounted for a full disclosure of what the company had in mind. On November 14 Carabetta held a briefing for a small group of property owners in its offices in Warren. Several of those invited refused to attend; they believed that such a meeting should be held in a public building and open to the public. The next night the company met with local officials from Warren, Brimfield, and West Brookfield. The new town, it was explained, would eventually accommodate about 30,000 people on 6,800 acres of land.[4] For Philip and Grace, it was another in a series of environmental threats that they had fought over the years, the most notorious being a proposal to compact Boston's garbage and ship it to Warren in return for Boston's payment of all of Warren's taxes.

Gove did not live to see the outcome of the Carabetta proposal. In the early hours of November 16, 1972 — not long after the second meeting of town officials and the developers had ended — Grace was awakened by a heavy thud from the kitchen. She rushed in and found Philip lying on the floor. He had died of a heart attack, his first, after a career that had been remarkably free of illness; Merriam employees could not recall his missing a day of work because he was sick, though he was treated in 1960 for pernicious anemia. At his own request, there was no funeral and no memorial service. His body, by previous arrangement, was given to the Harvard University Medical School and then was sent to Tewkesbury for burial in Pine Hill Cemetery. About a year later, the Carabetta company abandoned its project.

Gove's death at the age of seventy was reported in newspapers across the country; the controversy over *Webster's Third* had not been forgotten by the press. In *American Speech*, Woolf took note of Gove's distinctive contribution to *Webster's Third*. "It is, in fact, *his* book: he recruited most of its staff, he set its editorial policies, and he read each page of copy before it was sent to the printer." Raven I. McDavid, Jr., took the measure of the man as a scholar and as a courageous defender of his principles: "Out of his travail he grew in stature. . . . He held his ground with dignity; and if he never convinced public entertainers of the logic of his editorial decisions, he demonstrated to scholars the integrity of his work." Woolf noted, too, that Gove had been introduced at a meeting of lexicographers in 1972 as the best-known American lexicographer since Noah Webster, and he added: "The passing years will likely prove him to have been also the most influential."[5]

Grace, in her resolute fashion, carried on her life at the farm independently, maintaining her privacy, discouraging visits from friends, and refusing offers of help from the company and neighbors. From time to time she called Hazel Lord to order copies of Merriam dictionaries to be sent as gifts. She also began assembling Philip's papers and books. After exploring alternative homes for them, she packed up the most important materials and drove them to the American Heritage Center at the University of Wyoming in Laramie. She sold the farm in 1976 and moved to New Hampshire, where she died in late 1981.

DÉJÀ VU AND PLUS ÇA CHANGE

If Gove, like Noah Webster, had lived until his mid-eighties or a few years longer, he would have observed with considerable interest and perhaps occasional incredulity the legacy of the war over *Webster's Third*. Old issues reemerged, and time was kinder to him than were his early judges. Rival publishers, Random House and Houghton Mifflin, put out commercially successful dictionaries – the *Random House*, unabridged, and the *American Heritage* – but neither challenged *Webster's Third* on its own terms.

Ironically, the revised and expanded second edition of the *Random House*, unabridged, ran into trouble with traditionalists because it seemed too much like *Webster's Third*. When it was reviewed in the *New York Times Book Review* on January 3, 1988, it was as if the clock had been turned back to the early 1960s. The reviewer was William Arrowsmith, a distinguished professor of classics at Boston University, writer, translator, and editor; the thrust and style of his criticisms evoked memories of the attacks on *Webster's Third* some twenty-five years earlier, including those in the *New York Times* by editorial writers and book reviewers. Indeed, Arrowsmith viewed "the much (and rightly) abused" *Webster's Third* as the true predecessor of the new edition, despite vast differences between the two in the use of labels and heavy emphasis on encyclopedic material in the *Random House*.

What mattered most to Arrowsmith was the new work's emphasis on description and its faith in quantification. Culturally, he said, this approach "is too often ruthlessly destructive of quality." He was disturbed to find usage exalted as if it were the voice of God, which was revealed only to "a lexicographic pollster like Mr. [Stuart Berg] Flexner," the editor.

The new edition was more permissive than the earlier unabridged, in Arrowsmith's opinion. He decried "the slippage of meanings, and the explosion of cliché, buzzwords, and phrases and the cant of the half-educated. . . . Surely, . . . the lexicographer's descriptive practice, combined with the user's prescriptive expectations, must inevitably make the present appalling plunge of English toward sloppiness, vulgar chic and desperate imprecision more and more precipitate."

The attack on descriptive lexicography did not catch on in the press as it had done in Gove's day, however. Flexner and his book escaped being tagged "permissive." But the review confirmed that *Webster's Third* was still anathema to guardians of the language. A year later, for example, when the British essayist Anthony Burgess was caught misusing the word *compendious* in a review of the *Oxford English Dictionary*, second edition, it was *Webster's Third* that probably came off worst in the badinage, though it was irrelevant to the issue.

Burgess had noted that the original plan for the *OED* called for a work that was "so compendious that the contracting publisher took fright." Edwin M. Yoder, Jr., an American journalist and critic, gleefully pointed out that the meaning intended by Burgess – so large as to be unmanageable – was precisely the opposite of the dictionary meaning, "brief but comprehensive, as of works and authors."[6]

Yoder added that "given enough imitators," Burgess could well destroy the reliability of *compendious*. But as it turned out, it was not Burgess he was after, but the descriptivist dictionaries, especially *Webster's Third*. He described it cavalierly and wrongly as the dictionary from which "all notations of hierarchy and propriety in usage had been expunged." *Webster's Third* had the definition correct, he conceded, but that did not atone for its sins. And the *OED* was no better, since it was equally unwilling to tell the reader what was right and what was not. In the end, the criticism of Burgess was lost in non sequiturs, but the attack on *Webster's Third* stood out with memorable clarity.

A similar case of gratuitous disparagement occurred during the same month in the letters column of the lively British magazine *English Today*. In response to a reader who wanted to know why words such as *history, hereditary,* and *hotel* can be preceded either by *a* or *an*, the editor wrote that usage varies but that *a* is "probably commoner" except among speakers who drop their "aitches." Another reader, who found this response inadequate, wrote a lengthy rejoinder recounting the history of *an*, to which he added:

The query about *an* . . . illustrates how our antigrammarians have enfeebled the advantage history has given us over our sister languages. *Webster's Third* proclaims that the function of a dictionary is not to give an editor's opinion of what a word ought to mean, but only to record the meaning, spelling, and pronunciation of a word as it is actually used. A word becomes standard when large numbers of people, grammatically or not, use it.

Thus, an editor turns himself from being a lexicographer interested in the etymology of a word into a poll taker. . . . So, in defining *an* it gives eight ways in which it is used. First it is used invariably before words beginning with a vowel letter and sound. The other seven are examples of some people's using *an* before consonants.

Aside from its irrelevance to the issue under discussion, the reference to *Webster's Third* misrepresents the entry, which shows three situations, not seven, in which *an* is sometimes used before a consonant. And there is nothing distinctive about them, since they are similar to the variants that appear in *Webster's Second* and the *Oxford English Dictionary*. In this fashion the caricature of the *Webster's Third* is perpetuated.[7]

SECOND THOUGHTS

Although Gove left a pile of three-by-five slips containing detailed criticisms of entries in the Third Edition and suggestions for the Fourth, he apparently did not discuss with his colleagues the kinds of changes he was recommending and why. But clearly he had experienced no change of heart on any major question. Anne Soukhanov, a member of the staff committee for the Fourth Edition, said: "We were thinking about how to go about editing it, to update and improve the original in accord with the original intent. There was no thought of going back to W2 or of becoming prescriptive." Her task was to examine self-explanatory words, those regularly formed compounds and derivatives of words that require no formal definition. (The user is assumed to be able to figure out the meaning from general knowledge of the language and by consulting the definitions of the elements of the compound that appear as dictionary entries. This question had been of considerable concern to Gove during the preparation of the Third Edition.)[8]

From the accounts of family members and associates, it is clear that Gove's preoccupation with planning for the future did not end his brooding over the *Webster's Third* controversy – the press attacks and second thoughts about some of his own decisions. He explicitly

addressed in print his regrets about the wording of his widely misinterpreted 1961 article in *Word Study*, "Linguistics Advances and Lexicography." Other misgivings most likely arose from his omissions –
the steps that he intended to take and did not – and the opportunities
that he failed to sense. In retrospect, these seem more to blame for
the misunderstandings than any lexicographical decisions that he
made, as the following examples indicate.

First, despite his assurances to President Robert Munroe a decade
earlier (see Chapter 4), he did not follow through on his intent to tell
users explicitly that the decisions to drop the encyclopedic material
had been dictated by lack of space. He said in his preface that the
dictionary was limited to "generic words," but that statement was not
specific enough to enable readers and reviewers to grasp the importance of the change, the rationale for it, and the necessity for it.
Nothing of that sort appeared in any Merriam publicity material or in
any of Gove's comments to the press. Nor did he point out that there
was nothing revolutionary in producing a dictionary that dealt with
generic words only. He did not cite the precedent of Johnson's dictionary or the *OED*, which established a tradition that was surely as
respectable as that exemplified by earlier Merriam-Webster dictionaries and other works that sought to serve as general reference
works.

Second, Gove also failed to explain to his readers what he told a
linguistics forum at Georgetown University in 1961 about the limited
purpose of illustrative quotations: they were intended to clarify meaning only, as explained explicitly in his guidelines to editors. What he
wrote in the preface was that a "large number of verbal illustrations . . . has been worked into the defining pattern with a view to
contributing considerably to the user's interest and understanding by
showing a word used in context. . . . More than 14,000 different
authors are quoted for their use of words or for the structural pattern
of their words but not for their opinions or sentiments."[9] But this
hardly amounts to a warning that the ground rules had been completely changed, that the source of a quotation was no longer important, and that quotations were no longer selected to exemplify as far as
possible the best usage by the best writers.

Third, with regard to the most explosive issue – the treatment of
usage – Gove left himself especially vulnerable by neglecting to tell
his readers a key reason for reducing the use of labels. As he ex-

plained to the staff in the Black Books, usage notes and verbal illustrations were to be used in preference to labels when they could be more informative. The Third Edition did not abandon its responsibility to show usage; rather it chose to show it by description and examples rather than by labels. A public debate over Gove's view – was it justified and did it work? – would probably *not* have been decided in Gove's favor, but it might have focused attention on the lexicographical questions rather than on the pseudo-issue of "abrogation of responsibility" and the false accusation that "anything goes" in the Third Edition.[10]

The effect of these oversights was perhaps intensified by Gove's lack of sensitivity to the expectations of his audience and to the problems posed by his new editorial practices. His emphasis on newness in the opening sentences of his preface – "Every line is new," he wrote – could well have offended critics and devoted users of the Second Edition, who might have appreciated greater reassurances about continuity with the established Merriam tradition. Gove did not confront this issue until much later when he had to rebut his critics. By then, the war for the journalistic and public mind had been lost. Similarly, the treatment of pronunciation reflected ambitious linguistic objectives far beyond the needs of the average user; it also showed little understanding of the difficulties imposed by some of Artin's innovations. Gove did not recognize that what was obvious to him and his close associates struck many others as difficult and foreign.

In view of the misrepresentations in the press release, which were rapidly disseminated, there is no assurance that a full and persuasive treatment of these matters in the dictionary itself would have improved the accuracy of the early responses in the media or softened the later attacks by Follett, Macdonald, and others. Moreover, as noted earlier, Gove himself had expressed second thoughts about the ambiguity of his much-quoted article in *Word Study.* He thought it partly to blame for the misinterpretation of the role of linguistics in the making of the Third Edition.

It was his bad luck, moreover, that those in charge of promoting and marketing the dictionary took a naive and shortsighted view of what was appropriate. Thus, Gove had no support where he needed it most – in offsetting his own inexperience in sensing how his words might be misinterpreted by the general public. Where he and the Merriam company failed to explain themselves persuasively, the dictionary's detractors stepped in and introduced their own interpretations.

How would Gove have looked upon the blurring of the sharp distinction between descriptivism and prescriptivism in the writings of grammarians and lexicographers had he lived for another decade? As the British grammarian Sidney Greenbaum put it, "A descriptive grammar is incomplete if it fails to take account of prescriptions." He wrote that experts in the field of English have an obligation not only to describe the language objectively but also to form judgments from the evidence about how to use it. If they don't, the amateurs will step in with their prejudices and their obiter dicta.[11]

From the perspective of lexicography, John Algeo wrote that the scope of descriptivism has been explicitly enlarged to encompass a description of the status of words. In reducing the role of labels, *Webster's Third* "was following the best learned opinion of the time, which ran strongly, indeed enthusiastically, against prescriptivism and hence also against labels that might imply a value judgment. . . . However, users of language do make judgments about whether or not a form is 'correct'; lexicographers, therefore, have an obligation to record, though not adopt, such judgments since they are part of the total meaning of a word."[12]

SMALL WORLD

In 1990 the two dictionaries that were created to supplant *Webster's Third* were under the direction of Merriam alumni who had obtained their early training in Gove's era and who regarded him with great respect and admiration. It was an ironic turn of events that would have amused him immensely.

At the Houghton Mifflin Company, Anne Soukhanov was by this time the executive editor of the third edition of *The American Heritage Dictionary*, which was nearing completion. She credits Gove with having shaped her thinking on many aspects of dictionary making, especially reading and marking. "Everything that I have ever done on my reading and marking program [at Houghton Mifflin] is based on Gove's principles." A new guide that she had just completed for her staff was "based almost entirely" on Gove's basic approach. An advertising slogan she had recently seen reminded her of his injunction against marking headlines for citations: "Let us Malibu you." Using "an *eponymous* term like that as a verb is unusual; it's a contrived use, contrived to get a certain shock effect to get people to read the ad. Gove wouldn't accept that kind of a citation."

She recalled Gove as a good teacher. He was especially patient and helpful when she was having trouble with verb collocations – defining the combination of a verb and adverb or a verb and preposition that takes on a new meaning, one that cannot be inferred readily from the separate meanings of the two words (to *get along*, meaning to be or remain on friendly terms, for example; or to *run down*, meaning to collide with or knock down, as with an automobile). Such phrases warranted a separate entry apart from the base verb. Gove had made a particular effort to distinguish them from other verb phrases in the Third Edition and to drop many verb phrases that had appeared as separate entries in the Second Edition. Troublesome borderline cases made the task very difficult.

Gove's stamina and intense drive – his ability to work without break at his desk, his stubborn determination to push ahead in accord with his own views, his day-and-night reading of proof during the production stage, and his preoccupation with efficiency – which had been criticized by some editors, she found understandable in the light of her own experience. It affected her later career as an executive, as did his "fairness," which she admired. "I think a degree of fanaticism is inevitable for anyone who is going to bring in a tremendous project like that on time and on schedule. Gove really had to budget his time and make the most of it."

Personally, Gove made a strong impression on her. "There was something about him that differentiated him from the pure scholar, and I think it was his common sense. The farm brought everything into perspective. You can't deal with livestock and crops without realizing that a lot of things you are concerned with are minor in the overall scheme of things. It's the same relief I get from living on the Connecticut River in South Hadley [Massachusetts]. What separated him from the pure scholar is that he had this earthbound existence."[13]

At Random House, Robert B. Costello, another Merriam alumnus, had moved up from senior editor for the first and second editions of *The Random House Dictionary*, unabridged, to editor in chief of the company's dictionaries. He had been introduced to lexicography at the Merriam company when he was hired as an editorial assistant in 1960. He was trained in defining by Bosley Woolf – which he called "the best experience I ever had in learning how to write and think." Gove's intellectual rigor also left a deep impression on him.

Costello found Gove aloof and almost shy on the job; he "gave the impression that he was always running away from people." But Costello also recalls that shortly after he received his draft notice, Gove made a special effort to wish him well. It stuck in his mind. "Gove came tearing through the department to shake my hand. He said he expected great things of me."[14]

There was one last twist in the saga. In 1991 Houghton Mifflin hired Costello as an executive editor in the Reference Division while Soukhanov, as executive editor for the third edition of *The American Heritage Dictionary*, took on heavy responsibilities for its promotion, including public appearances across the country, and began a book on new words, among other projects. At Random House, another Merriam graduate – Sol Steinmetz – took over as the chief spokesman for the Random House *Webster's College Dictionary*, completed under Costello's editorship and published in 1991.

A LASTING INFLUENCE

Gove's legacy shows up in modest ways, most of them indirect. As editor in chief, he could be called a company man in the best sense, devoted to his work and loyal to his firm but independent in his professional and scholarly judgments. Like the lexicographers he admired most, he was absorbed in the task of dictionary making. He was not distracted by notions of his own importance, personal ambition, or a hankering for public attention. He made no effort to develop a school or a personal following; his influence on such young editors as Soukhanov and Costello was incidental, not intentional. Most of what he wrote during the heat of the controversy was a defensive reaction to the attacks against the dictionary, not an organized synthesis of his views on the making of dictionaries. He did lay out in scholarly journals the details of his lexicographical policies and practices with an unusual openness – partly, no doubt, in search of vindication but also out of a belief that the record ought to be available. He was devoted to lexicography and the Merriam tradition, and with regard to his personal ambition he lived by what he wrote in his letter to President Gordon Gallan in February 1953 when he said that no higher distinction could come to him than being editor in chief of another edition of *Webster's New International*. He believed, as Bethel had believed, that the editor in chief should be a vice-president of the company to symbolize the interdependence of the business and editorial roles, but the hierarchical title meant little to him compared with the title of editor in chief. It was the merit of his dictionary and the respect of his peers that mattered to him.

Nonetheless, though it was not Gove's intent, lexicography in the United States was surely shaken up by the Third Edition – both by its editorial policies and practices and by the controversy it touched off. The ensuing burst of competition in dictionary making surely owed much to the public debate. Those who were angered by the Third Edition were determined to challenge it. At the same time, the vulnerability of the Merriam company, which rivals sensed, fed the pursuit of commercial opportunity. Another consequence, far removed from the charges of permissiveness and the ideological warfare, was a surge of scholarly interest in dictionaries in both the practice and theory of lexicography. Especially noteworthy was the 1972 International Conference on Lexicography in English, a landmark event that attracted noted foreign as well as American scholars and practitioners.[15] Originally proposed by James Sledd in 1968, the conference was organized and carried out by a distinguished working committee chaired by Raven I. McDavid, Jr. The proceedings, published a year later under the editorship of McDavid and Audrey R. Duckert, were highly valued. The conference, it was said, "set the record straight as to the present status of lexicographical thinking" and encouraged the exchange of views between practitioners of lexicography and others – especially theorists and innovators in related fields.

Sledd, who had been more deeply engaged in the controversy than any scholar outside the Merriam company, proposed on the same occasion the establishment of research centers that would cooperate in the gathering and sharing of descriptive information about language, making full use of the expanding technology for information storage and retrieval. Commercial rivalry, he noted, had served the cause of lexicography and the public interest in dictionaries well enough for nearly a century – from the Webster–Worcester rivalry until the making of *Webster's Second* – while work proceeded on specialized scholarly dictionaries. But the time had come for a more organized collaborative effort under the direction of scholars. "In the later twentieth century, someone must choose whether descriptive English lexicography should still be left to the Cerfs and Bentons, or whether private enterprise should be supplemented in that field, too, by uncommercial cooperative effort."[16]

WHERE GOVE'S INFLUENCE REMAINS MOST PRONOUNCED is at the Merriam-Webster Company, Inc. One of his legacies was the unintentional by-product of his determination to save space. As a result of his stylistic changes and the typographical ingenuity of the R. R. Donnelley company, the book ran some three hundred pages shorter than the Second Edition, though it contained about as much text. Gove's goal had been only to limit the Third Edition to the number of pages in the Second, but he might have saved enough space to accommodate the additional words and senses that would be included in a Fourth Edition.

More important, Gove left his imprint on the future of dictionary making at the Merriam company. Frederick C. Mish, editorial director and editor in chief of *Webster's Ninth New Collegiate Dictionary* (1983) and the tenth edition in 1993, never met Gove but had this to say about his influence: "We still practice Govian lexicography except for minor details. We still are doing single-phrase defining and reading and marking along the same lines he laid down in his instructions. A majority of the staff never knew him, but he is absolutely a living presence in the editorial department of Merriam-Webster. And I don't personally conceive of a time when that will not be so."[17]

16

Concluding Words

I have not always executed my own scheme, or satisfied my own expectations. . . .
[But] I look with pleasure on my book however defective and deliver it to the world
with the spirit of a man that has endeavored well. . . . When it shall be found that
much is omitted, let it not be forgotten that much likewise has been performed.

Samuel Johnson, Preface to the *Dictionary*

Webster's Third New International Dictionary has outlasted its critics
without outliving its usefulness. Updated about every five years with
an addendum of new words and new senses, it has kept abreast of
major changes in vocabulary and dominated the field longer than any
of its predecessors in the Merriam series. Over a period of more than
three decades, no American dictionary of comparable scope has superseded it. By mid-1993, its total sales – domestic and international
– had exceeded 2.5 million copies, far greater than the sales of any
other unabridged dictionary of the English language. Its market was
worldwide: one book in five went to foreign countries. Sales continued to run at about seventy thousand copies a year.[1] The Third
Edition met the market test as well as scholarly scrutiny.

That it escaped the early oblivion its detractors had predicted can
be explained only in part by the periodic updating and the absence of
a persevering competitor with comparable resources. Several other
factors were at work, as the foregoing chapters have pointed out. First,
there was far more favorable publicity about the dictionary from the
outset than its detractors acknowledged, and sales during the first year
were twice as high as those of the Second Edition in any year after it
was published; the assertion that everyone was against the dictionary
simply was not true. Second, great changes had taken place in the

language since the mid-1930s, notably the expansion of the vocabulary and the trend toward informality in expression; it was time for an up-to-date unabridged dictionary, and that message came across in the early publicity, despite the weight of unfavorable commentary. Third, there was a core readership for the unabridged that had no choice but to buy *Webster's Third* (libraries in particular and foreign buyers) since there was no up-to-date dictionary of American English of comparable scope and detail. Fourth, the market for dictionaries continued to expand with the increase in college and graduate school enrollments and with the spread of English throughout the world. Finally, the dominant position of *Collegiate* dictionaries and the company's effective promotion of the Merriam-Webster name helped to sustain the market for the Third Edition.

How much longer can the Third Edition sustain its position in view of the strong competition from Random House and American Heritage? That question invites another: Will there be a *Webster's Fourth?* – a question that continues to pique the curiosity of the lexicographical community. It was on my mind when I began interviewing former staff members and others who had been caught up in the controversy. Opinion was divided. I encountered considerable doubt that a commercial firm would invest in so costly and risky an undertaking, especially in a market that is much more competitive than it was in the early 1930s and 1960s. But it was acknowledged that the failure to make the attempt would also be risky. Not only is the unabridged an important publishing venture in itself, it also enhances and sustains the reputation of the Merriam-Webster *Collegiate*, whose annual sales have averaged more than a million copies for many years. It has been said that the failure of Funk & Wagnalls to keep its unabridged dictionary up-to-date eroded the position of its highly regarded desk dictionary. When my manuscript went to press, the word from Springfield was that a successor of the Third Edition remains on the company agenda. Several years may pass, however, before an official pronouncement is heard or published evidence emerges from 47 Federal Street. Meanwhile there are continuing reminders that the case of *Webster's Third* is not closed.

A CHANGE IN THE CRITICAL CLIMATE

The Third Edition's longevity has been accompanied by a decline in the intensity of the attacks that are still directed against it, though objections to descriptive lexicography have not abated. Follett and Macdonald, the two most active and vociferous critics, are no longer on the scene, and their allies have turned to other matters. Editors and writers who remain hostile toward *Webster's Third* no longer regard it as a pressing threat nor a distinctive one. A collection of essays by the critic John Simon in 1980, for example, illustrates the continuing opposition to the descriptive approach of the Third Edition, but it also displays equal dissatisfaction with lexicography in general. The English language belongs to the elite, in his view, and the watchdog role should be performed by amateur observers of language, not experts. He finds Burchfield's *OED*, Guralnik's *Webster's New World*, and the *Random House* dictionaries all poisoned by the permissiveness that, in his view, permeated *Webster's Third*. He would begin anew.

I propose here a new dictionary. . . . [It] would list under one heading the refined, educated, elitist usage; under another, the popular, demotic, uneducated usage. It would then be up to every one of us to decide what he wants to be, to choose the parlance suited to his aspirations. . . . It would merely confirm a polarization that has already taken place and enable people to be more conscious of where they stand and what they are fighting for. Verbally, of course.[2]

The writings of journalists and writers (sometimes called "language amateurs" by linguists and lexicographers) reflect a range of views. One determined guardian of the tongue, the journalist and television critic Edwin Newman, built a large following for the position of the traditionalists through his highly popular books on usage, beginning with *Strictly Speaking* in 1974. Teachers, such as Arn and Charlene Tibbetts, who hold similar views have helped to keep the prescriptivist view in the debate over usage and dictionaries very much alive. Other commentators more concerned with specifics than ideological pronouncements on the state of the language – William Safire in the *New York Times* and Philip Howard in the *Times* of London – have sought to enliven public discussion of language and usage and raise the level of public understanding.

Most of the controversy about English usage, of course, goes on without reference to *Webster's Third*. Among editors and literary critics, Joseph Epstein has written with civility and understanding in defense of "that best of all lost causes, the battle over good usage" without dragging in Gove's dictionary. He acknowledges that his cause has attracted not only Swift, Johnson, Orwell, and their like, but also "prigs, pedants, intellectual bullies, and snobs." As a guardian of language, he allies himself with Fowler and credits Sir Ernest Gowers with having the "good sense, reasonableness and superior perspective [that] can be a helpful brake on the runaway fanaticism that seems to set in" among some of the purists.[3]

THE MATURING TREATMENT OF USAGE

If usage is neither the special province of dictionaries nor the central focus of lexicography, it has become, unmistakably, a more prominent feature of dictionaries in recent decades. In 1966 *The Random House Dictionary*, unabridged, gave considerable attention to usage notes as well as labels in its effort to make the new dictionary "*fully* descriptive" – a phrase suggesting faith in descriptive lexicography but dissatisfaction with *Webster's Third*.[4] "Since language is a social institution, the lexicographer must give the user an adequate indication of the attitudes of society toward particular words or expressions. . . . He does not need to express approval or disapproval of a disputed usage, but he does need to report the milieu of words as well as their meanings." The usage notes were highly visible typographically, appearing at the end of entries following a dash and the word "Usage" in boldface. In contrast, they had been less frequent, less detailed, and less prominent in *Webster's Third*.

Twenty years later, the second edition of the *Random House*, unabridged, increased the number of usage notes and revised and expanded the earlier ones. The essay on usage took issue with the notion of "absolute correctness that underlies many of the 'rules' of good usage offered by those who regard themselves as arbiters or judges of language." The language of educated speakers "often reveals that the simple right or wrong judgments . . . do not accurately reflect reality."

Two generalizations followed: "First, there is no real agreement about which expressions should be criticized; and second, there is no way to predict what reaction, if any, an item of disputed usage will elicit from a listener or reader. . . . A modern dictionary attempts to report the existence of such criticisms when they exist, but at the same time to make clear that not all careful, educated users of English share in the criticism. . . . Language practices keep changing, and what was favored yesterday may be condemned today. The most elaborate statements cannot do more than set out principles by which a reader or listener may evaluate what is heard and seen."[5]

Over the years usage notes similar in purpose have become increasingly visible features of other American dictionaries intended for the college market.

The year 1992 saw an even greater emphasis on usage in the third edition of *The American Heritage Dictionary,* self-described as more prescriptive than its competitors. Updated and expanded, the new work was marked not only by a rejuvenation of the Usage Panel that had been introduced in the 1969 edition but also by the introduction of a new status label, *Usage Problem,* which serves a purpose that is different from that of a Usage Note.

The phrase *Usage Problem* is listed in the "Guide to the Dictionary" as a status label, along with *slang, informal, nonstandard,* and so on. However, in contrast to the traditional labels, it does not specify what the problem is but rather warns readers that the word poses a problem. It refers them to a Usage Note, which either follows the labeled entry or appears elsewhere, as indicated by a cross-reference. The typical note includes the opinions of the Usage Panel, citation counts taken from computerized texts, illustrative quotations, and the interpretations of the dictionary editors. The example of the word *snuck,* given in an introductory essay on usage by Geoffrey Nunberg, illustrates the editorial rationale.

Take the past tense form *snuck.* It originated as a nonstandard regional variant for *sneaked,* and many people still have a lingering prejudice against it: 67 percent of the Usage Panel disapproves of it. In recent years, however, *snuck* has become increasingly frequent in reputable writing. . . . And while the files show that *sneaked* is by far more prevalent in edited prose by a factor of about 7 to 2, it is no longer possible to label *snuck* as nonstandard, even though many educated users of English continue to consider it informal.[6]

Nunberg strongly criticizes the descriptive approach, as he defines it, and offers a rationale for a prescriptive perspective. In his opinion, the gap between the two camps is greater now than it was in the past – and has, in fact, become "irreconcilable," though he does not develop the case in this brief essay. Others have come to the opposite conclusion, finding the gap between descriptivism and prescriptivism today far smaller than it was in the days of Gove and his detractors, as noted in Chapter 8. Indeed, the usage note on *snuck*, marked by strong restraint in affixing the nonstandard label and a bow in the direction of description with its use of citation counts, seems to have more in common with the views of Bergen Evans than with those of Wilson Follett in the debate over *Webster's Third* in the *Atlantic.*

If, however, the difference between the two positions is essentially a matter of belief about how users of language should react to questionable changes in use rather than lexicographical practice, Nunberg can speak authoritatively about his own convictions and perhaps those of others who share his views. It may well be that disagreement over what lexicographers do and what educated users in the traditional camp think they should do may continue to be substantial.

In the use of citations, the practice of *The American Heritage Dictionary* does not appear to be greatly different from that of rival dictionaries. The new *AHD* prides itself, as do its rivals, on the use of computer technology to gather citations, speed up and improve its research and editorial decisions, and make production more efficient. How often quantitative criteria were used, and for what purposes, is not explained, but the selection of the examples of *snuck* and of *ambiance* suggests that the criteria were of some significance. The editor's introduction points out that the spelling *ambiance* was given preference over *ambience* because *ambiance* appears twice as frequently in its computer database – four thousand citations to two thousand.[7] This example calls to mind Dwight Macdonald's stinging rebuke of Gove when he wrote that "counting cite slips is simply not the way to go about the delicate business of deciding these matters." Nonetheless, it has become firmly entrenched.

The new *AHD* seems to be equally far removed from Follett's brand of prescriptivism. Follett – who had called Gove's unwillingness to reject outright the use of disputed words and constructions an "abrogation of responsibility" – argued that such decisions should be made by dictionary makers, who were experts, and not left to dictionary users. In the new *AHD*, however, words that he damned as "obscenities" escape outright rejection and instead are labeled a *Usage Problem* and treated in usage notes that invite readers to make their own judgments. The following is a sampling of Follett's "obscenities" and their treatment in the *AHD*.

Words from Follett's list labeled a *Usage Problem* in the *AHD* include *alternative* for more than two or as a substitute; *biweekly* in the sense of twice a week; *hopefully* as a sentence modifier.

Words treated only in a Usage Note include *anyplace, everyplace, someplace* for *anywhere; center around* for *center on; different than* instead of *different from; due to* as a compound preposition. The "Guide to the Dictionary" states explicitly under the heading of status labels that "all words not restricted by such a label should be regarded as appropriate for use in all contexts. Presumably that applies to *cohort,* in the sense of a companion or colleague, a usage that especially offended Follett. It is treated in a Usage Note, where it is said to be the predominant sense today. Most members of the Usage Panel (57 percent) nonetheless find it unacceptable.

As a guide to decision making, the panel's role is not clear. It adds another perspective – the collective opinions of one casual sample of educated readers – to the mix of information from other sources, but it is not a decisive factor in the making of editorial decisions. Panel votes also support the view that *opinions about usage* continue to lag behind actual usage tracked by citations, as was indicated in earlier surveys (by Albert Marckwardt and Fred Walcott, for example).

Moreover, the panel votes themselves bear witness to the shift in opinions on usage over the years. There is a clear trend toward the acceptance of words and constructions that were disputed in Gove's day and later. Today, the long-criticized use of *contact* as a verb has become acceptable to 65 percent of the panel. Acceptance of *intrigue* to mean "arouse interest" has risen from 52 to 78 percent and of *aggravate* to mean "irritate" from 43 to 68 percent. Acceptance of *transpire* to mean "happen" has increased from 38 to 58 percent.

On the other hand, the unceasing attacks on *hopefully* as a sentence modifier have made it even less acceptable than it was to the original panel, even though its rejection is based on a purist fiat, not on a violation of the rules of grammar or the usage of educated speakers and writers. The taboo against *hopefully* is perhaps the biggest success of the purists since the avalanche in the press struck down *ain't* after its appearance in *Webster's Third.*[8]

While it may be that the *American Heritage* database reflects citations that have occurred primarily during the past decade or two, many of the words newly reported in the writing of educated speakers had also been found three or four decades ago in the Merriam citation files, which at that time housed the greatest collection of information on the use of English in the United States. Gove may have been overliteral and too narrow in carrying out a descriptive approach, but from today's perspective, it is hard to deny that he was in the mainstream of lexicographical practice in the use of citations and usage comments if not in the use of labels.

WEBSTER'S THIRD AFTER THREE DECADES

It is doubtful that *Webster's Third* would have enjoyed so long a useful life had not a knowledgeable assessment by lexicographers and linguists established it as a major lexicographical achievement, despite its flaws. If it was the media and the literary journalists and scholars who shaped the initial public response to the Third Edition, it has been the lexicographers and linguists who shaped the dictionary's lasting reputation by continuing to give serious attention to the questions it raised. The weight of opinion has been favorable, notwithstanding the criticism of particulars and an occasional dissent. Among the dissenters, Laurence Urdang, managing editor of *The Random House Dictionary*, unabridged edition of 1967, and editor of many major lexicographical works, attributed its longevity more to its coverage of the vocabulary than to lexicographical merit. He criticized the Third Edition sharply for its "Byzantine defining technique and arrangement, which makes using it a painful chore," and its "arcane" pronunciation system. He also said it is not sufficiently descriptive. It "fail[s] to record accurately the way people feel (or felt in the 1950s) about four-letter words, usage, and other lexical matters to which other dictionaries pay such careful attention."[9] But it was the dictionary's strengths that others emphasized.

In a review of British and American dictionaries of the 1970s, Gabriele Stein paid tribute to the Merriam-Webster achievement: It "excelled in the detail and comprehensiveness of its lexical entries, and in so doing it had opened the field for more experimentation and progress in lexicography."[10]

In 1989 John Algeo wrote an assessment of the Third Edition from the vantage point of almost three decades of personal use and a study of the commentaries by others. He concluded that although it was open to criticism on some matters, "it was by far the best dictionary of its time. It was outstanding in thoroughness and accuracy. *Webster's Third* was also one of the most uncompromisingly lexicographical of American dictionaries. It attempted to apply the best standards of mid-twentieth century linguists to dictionary-making and showed little of the encyclopedic tradition that is typical of much of American lexicography. . . . If it tells more about the language than some of its users have wanted to know and is less magisterial in tone than they would have liked, that fact is not to the discredit of *Webster's Third.* No dictionary presents a fuller or more reliable picture of the American vocabulary at mid-century. Augmented by more recent dictionaries in the Merriam-Webster Collegiate series and by supplements like *12,000 Words* . . . [it] remains the greatest dictionary of current American English."[11]

Notes

1. THE BEST OF TIMES AND THE WORST: A PROLOGUE

1. Yakov Malkiel, "The Lexicographer as a Mediator Between Linguistics and Society," in Ladislav Zgusta, ed., *Theory and Method in Lexicography* (Columbia, S.C.: Hornbeam Press, 1980), 54.
2. R. W. Burchfield, "*The Supplement to the Oxford English Dictionary:* The End of the Alphabet," in Richard W. Bailey, ed., *Dictionaries of English: Prospects for the Record of Our Language* (Ann Arbor: University of Michigan Press, 1987), 12.
3. The house was built by Mathew Patrick (originally Fitzpatrick or Gilpatrick), one of three brothers from Northern Ireland who settled in the vicinity in the early 1700s; the farm was worked by his descendants for two centuries until it was sold in 1927.
4. President Gallan sent Gove a warm congratulatory note saluting the achievement and "your part in it" and expressing his thanks for receiving the first copy to have come off the press. Gallan to Gove, Sept. 9, 1961, Philip B. Gove Papers at the American Heritage Center, University of Wyoming (hereafter AHC).
5. Wilson Follett, "Sabotage in Springfield," *Atlantic* (Jan. 1962): 73–7.
6. James Sledd and Wilma R. Ebbitt, *Dictionaries and THAT Dictionary: A Casebook on the Aims of Lexicographers and the Targets of Reviewers* (New York: Scott Foresman, 1962).

2. GOVE'S FORMATIVE YEARS: THE ROAD TO SPRINGFIELD

Parts of this chapter appear in my article, "Philip Gove's Formative Years," *Dictionaries* (Dictionary Society of North America), no. 13 (1991):16–30.
1. John Gove to Florence, Nov. 13, 1898, AHC.
2. Letter from Leyshon to Gove, Nov. 21, 1922, AHC.

3. Gove to Pemberton, Jan. 20, 1956, Merriam-Webster correspondence files (hereafter M-W files).

4. Grace to Philip, July 1, 1944, Gove Family Papers (hereafter GFP).

5. Bowman to Gove, Sept. 11, 1946, AHC. Albert H. Marckwardt was a professor of English at the University of Michigan and coauthor with Fred Walcott of *Facts About English Usage*, a monograph published by the National Council of Teachers of English in 1938. The study indicated that opinions (and textbooks) about English usage were much more conservative than the facts of usage warranted. It reported that numerous disputed usages appeared in standard literary English as well as in colloquial English. On a number of items, however, the evidence for their conclusions was challenged as inadequate.

6. Philip to Grace, June 11, 1936, AHC.

7. Wimsatt to Gove, AHC. The date appears as Jan. 6, 1947, probably an error, since two follow-up letters are dated Feb. 4, 1948, and Apr. 1, 1948. Wimsatt's book, *Philosophic Words*, was published by Yale University Press in 1948.

8. Wimsatt to Gove, Feb. 4, 1948, AHC. Gove's copy of South's *Sermons* was given to the American Heritage Center. Gwin J. Kolb and Ruth A. Kolb list the *Sermons* as one of eleven whole or partial works known to have survived from Johnson's library. Johnson's edition was dated 1692, Gove's 1694. See "The Selection and Use of the Illustrative Quotations in Dr. Johnson's Dictionary," in Howard D. Weinbrot, ed., *New Aspects of Lexicography* (Carbondale: Southern Illinois University Press, 1972), 61–72.

9. Liebert to Gove, Apr. 22, 1955, AHC.

10. Gove to Liebert, May 25, 1955, AHC.

11. Liebert to Gove, June 9, 1955, and telephone interview with Liebert, Jan. 25, 1989. In 1986, fifty years after Gove embarked on his project, Robert DeMaria, Jr., published a study of Johnson's illustrative quotations: *Johnson's Dictionary and the Language of Learning* (Chapel Hill: University of North Carolina Press, 1986). He organized and indexed the material by computer. Apparently he did not know of Gove's cards at the time he wrote the book, but alluded to them in a note in *PMLA*, January 1989, and acquired the cards later after Yale decided against copying them in microform. Allen Reddick's study, *The Making of Johnson's Dictionary* (Cambridge: Cambridge University Press, 1990), which draws on recently discovered manuscript materials, answers many questions about Johnson's work habits that Gove and Wimsatt could only speculate about.

12. Wright to Gove, Feb. 12, 1937, AHC.

13. Gove to Wright, Feb. 27, 1939, AHC.

14. Grace to Philip, June 27, 1939, AHC.

15. Philip to Grace, Aug. 8, 1939, AHC. Dates of letters from the sojourn in England are given as they appear in the AHC inventory. They are not internally consistent, though they seem to be in chronological order, with a few exceptions. Philip didn't date his letters but rather indicated the day of the week. The dates

were supplied later, either by Grace or by someone else apparently from the postmark on the envelope in which the letters arrived, which might have been the same day or a day or two after they were written. It is possible that some of the letters and envelopes were switched.

16. Based on Gove's memoir, "The First Week," *Antioch Review*, 25(1965):349–60.

17. "Notes on Serialization and Competitive Publishing: Johnson's and Bailey's Dictionaries, 1755," *Oxford Bibliographical Society Proceedings and Papers, 1940*, 5:305–22. Among thirteen early dictionaries that Gove later acquired were two editions of Johnson (the fourth of 1773 and the ninth of 1805) and two of Bailey (the 1747 edition of the *Etymological* and a 1736 edition of the *Dictionarium*). His earliest dictionary was the 1623 dictionary of Henry Cockeram in a reprint edition. Gove's dictionaries were given to the American Heritage Center by Grace.

18. DeWitt T. Starnes and Gertrude E. Noyes, *The English Dictionary from Cawdrey to Johnson, 1604–1755* (Chapel Hill: University of North Carolina Press, 1946), 182–4. Starnes and Noyes also devote a chapter to Cawdrey, whose distinctive contribution was simply that he offered readers a list of English words defined by "plaine English wordes." Earlier dictionaries had been bilingual, providing the English meaning of Latin words or words in other languages; none had been devoted to defining English words. By taking this small step forward, Cawdrey earned for himself a small niche in the history of lexicography in the English language. A facsimile reproduction of Cawdrey's book was published in 1966, with an introduction by Robert A. Peters: *A Table Alphabeticall of Hard Usual English Words (1604), the First English Dictionary by Robert A. Cawdrey* (Gainesville, FL: Scholars' Facsimiles & Reprints, 1966, from an original in the Bodleian Library at Oxford, said to be the only surviving copy). See also a new edition of Starnes and Noyes, with an introduction and a select bibliography by Gabriele Stein, published in 1991 by John Benjamins, Philadelphia.

19. Powell to Gove, July 25, Oct. 17, and Nov. 10, 1940, GFP. The other articles published in 1940 are "Dr. Johnson and the Works of the Bishop of Sodor and Man," *Review of English Studies*, 16:455–7; "Early Numbers of *The Morning Chronicle* and *Owen's Weekly Chronicle*" [a bibliographic inquiry], *Library*, 4th series, 20:412–24; "No. 1 of Owen's Weekly Chronicle," *Library*, 4th series, 21:95; "Robert Drury," *Notes and Queries*, 177:150–1.

20. David Fleeman, "A Productive Career," *Our Friend L.F.*, Published in celebration of Dr. Johnson's two hundred and sixty-seventh birthday (New York: The Johnsonians, 1976). Powell served on the Advisory Board for the Yale edition of Johnson's works and collaborated with W. J. Bate in editing Johnson's *Idler* and *Adventurer*.

21. Onions to Gove, Mar. 24, 1940, AHC.

22. Morison to Gove, Nov. 13, 1940, GFP. Earlier, Gove had asked Morison to comment on a draft of an article.

23. Gove to Pegram, June 21, 1940, AHC.
24. The *Modern Language Quarterly* (December 1941) noted that "Mr. Gove's book belongs to the general type of study, now appearing with increasing frequency, which reviews what has been done in a certain field and lays the ground work for additional investigation. . . . This type of research enables the serious student to find out at once what has been done in a field and what needs doing." A review in the *Journal of English and Germanic Philology* (Oct. 1941) concludes: "This is a volume which will prove indispensable to those interested in the forms of prose fiction, or in the novel as an avenue for the expression of geographical, social, political, philosophical or religious knowledge or speculation."
25. Philip to Grace, Sept. 19, 1945, AHC; Oct. 6, 1945, GFP.
26. Letter (and attachments) from Shoemaker to Gove, Apr. 26, 1945, AHC.
27. Gove to G. & C. Merriam, Feb. 12, 1946, AHC.
28. Wright to Bethel, May 27, 1946, AHC; Dobbie to Bethel, May 29, 1946, AHC; Sherburn to Bethel, May 27, 1946, AHC.
29. Bowman to Bethel, May 28, 1946, AHC.

3. THE MERRIAM AND WEBSTER LEGACIES

1. George Philip Krapp, "American Dictionaries," *The English Language in America* (New York: Frederick Ungar, 1966), 1:363; facsimile edition reprinted from the original published by the Century Co. for the Modern Language Association in 1925. Krapp, who has been widely quoted by scholars for his assessment of Webster, recognized Webster's historical importance but was highly critical of much of his work as a lexicographer. Still, it is difficult to concede that in a culture that attributes great importance to being first, the nation's first important lexicographer could be forgotten. Even without taking the dictionaries into account, Webster's place in the history of the United States had been assured by his speller, his writing and lecturing in many fields, and the impact of his controversial personality on his contemporaries.
2. Robert Keith Leavitt, *Noah's Ark: New England Yankees and the Endless Quest* (Springfield, Mass.: G. & C. Merriam, 1947), 7.
3. Krapp, "American Dictionaries," 363. This assessment was echoed in a much more thorough analysis by Joseph Friend, *The Development of American Lexicography, 1798–1864* (The Hague: Mouton, 1967), 35. In a long review essay on Friend's book, Gove judged it to be the best work on the Webster era, ranking it with the works by Starnes and Noyes on early lexicographers and Sledd and Kolb on Johnson's dictionary as the definitive works on the history of English lexicography. *Language*, 45:1(Mar. 1969):157–69.
4. Noah Webster, *A Compendious Dictionary of the English Language*, a facsimile of the first (1806) edition, with an introduction by Philip B. Gove (New York: Crown, 1970). The dictionary's definition of *compendious* is "concise," which

remains its meaning, though it has been used to signify the opposite – by a prominent reviewer of the second edition of the *OED,* for example, in the dispute recounted in Chapter 15.

5. Ibid., Preface, xix. The preface laid out in considerable detail the views on which the larger work would be based.

6. Ibid., xix. His belief that "etymology judiciously traced and displayed" shows the history of ideas was formed more than a decade before his ill-fated ten-year study of etymology.

7. Friend, *Development of American Lexicography,* 36.

8. James A. H. Murray's often-quoted opinion appears in the Romanes Lecture, 1900, at Oxford, *The Evolution of English Lexicography.* Murray used Webster's *American Dictionary* as a guide in estimating the length of the *OED,* according to his biographer. His original estimate was that the *OED,* with its more detailed etymologies and heavy reliance on quotations to illustrate historical changes in meaning, would run four times as long as Webster. As the work progressed he raised the multiple to six times and later to more than eight times. K. M. Elisabeth Murray, *Caught in the Web of Words* (New Haven, Conn.: Yale University Press, 1977), 207, 275.

9. See Friend, *Development of American Lexicography,* 37–8. Friend also sampled the entries from "la to laird" in Johnson and Webster and found that "Webster has 141 entries to Johnson's 84" (39–41).

10. James H. Sledd and Gwin J. Kolb, *Dr. Johnson's Dictionary: Essays in the Biography of a Book* (Chicago: University of Chicago Press, 1955; Midway Reprint, 1974), 198–9.

11. Webster, Preface to *An American Dictionary,* first two pages, unnumbered.

12. Krapp, "American Dictionaries," 363.

13. Allen Walker Read, "The Spread of German Linguistic Learning in New England During the Lifetime of Noah Webster," *American Speech,* 41(Oct. 1966):181.

14. Leavitt, *Noah's Ark,* 48.

15. Friend, *Development of American Lexicography,* 95.

16. See Friend's account of "Round Two" (ibid., 85–6).

17. Leavitt, *Noah's Ark,* 56.

18. Margaret Farrand Thorp, *Neilson of Smith* (New York: Oxford University Press, 1956), 27. See 326–30 for more on Neilson and *Webster's Second.*

19. Letter from Kelsey, Jan. 5, 1988, and interview, Jan. 12, 1988.

20. Twaddell to Bethel, Apr. 20, 1951, AHC.

4. THE NEW EDITOR TAKES HOLD

1. Gove Papers, AHC. The meeting was the first of the Editorial Board in six years. Attending from the editorial staff, in addition to Gove, were Bethel, Edward F.

Oakes (an associate editor since 1934), and W. Freeman Twaddell; Anne M. Driscoll of the editorial staff served as secretary of the board. The business side was represented by Chairman Munroe and R. N. Fuller, who succeeded Munroe as president in 1950; Gordon J. Gallan, the advertising manager; and Walter Thwing, a member of the Board of Directors.

2. Starnes and Noyes, *Cawdrey to Johnson*, 33–4. They credited Cockeram's innovation with greatly extending the work's "scope and usefulness"; they said it "definitely anticipates certain features, such as the brief biographies, common to most English dictionaries of the present day [mid-1940s]."

3. Philip Gove, "The Nonlexical and the Encyclopedic," *Names*, 13(June 1965): 104–5. Merriam editors referred to the material below the line as the "pearl section," from the name for the size of type, which was about five-point, midway between diamond and agate.

4. Ibid., 104. *Lexical* is defined in the Third Edition as "relating to words, word formatives [i.e., the part of the word that gives it appropriate form or inflection] and vocabulary."

5. Ibid., 108.

6. Ibid., 112.

7. Quoted from the original memo to staff, Oct. 29, 1954, 8. The memo was shortened and revised before publication.

8. Ibid., 8.

9. Preface to *Johnson's Dictionary*, in *Johnson's Dictionary: A Modern Selection*, E. L. McAdam, Jr., and George Milne, eds. (New York: Pantheon Books, 1963), 4.

10. Richard Chenevix Trench, *On Some Deficiencies of Our English Dictionaries* (London: Parker & Son, 1857), 45.

11. Gove Papers, AHC. Notes on Nov. 21, 1951, board meeting.

12. Ibid.

13. Ibid.

14. Ibid.

15. The Third Edition took no chances. It used several quotations from respected writers to show the meaning of *journalistic* in context, without a pejorative connotation, and added the phrase "marked by literary quality appropriate to newspapers and magazines."

16. Bethel to Fuller, June 25, 1952, M-W files.

17. Gove to Gallan, Feb. 24, 1953, AHC. Gove's files contain only a copy of the letter, without any notation confirming its delivery or how it was received. Apart from the specifics of Gove's proposal, the memo is interesting as a reflection of the tensions that existed during the last months of R. N. Fuller's brief presidency and the brighter outlook that followed Gallan's appointment. Four decades passed before the editor in chief was named a vice-president. Frederick C. Mish was appointed to the position in early 1993; the executive editor, John M. Morse, was named a vice-president at the same time.

18. Interview with Anne H. Soukhanov, June 22, 1988.
19. Gove to Gallan, June 19, 1952, AHC.
20. Other appointments noted in the report were two assistant editors, Baxter D. Wilson, Ph.D., University of Virginia, and Renate Wolf, Ph.D., Bryn Mawr; they stayed for three and four years, respectively. Later in the year, a third future associate editor, Daniel Cook of the Duke University faculty, was hired; he had obtained a doctorate from the University of California at Berkeley. Cook remained on the staff for five years.
21. Gove to Gallan, Nov. 10, 1952, AHC.

5. THE MEANING OF WORDS: DEFINERS AT WORK

1. For an informative history of *like*, see *Webster's Dictionary of English Usage* (Springfield, Mass.: Merriam-Webster, 1989), 600–4.
2. C. S. Lewis, *Studies in Words* (Cambridge: Cambridge University Press, 1960; 2d ed., 1967; Canto paperback, 1990), 11.
3. James R. Hulbert, *Dictionaries: British and American* (New York: Philosophical Library, 1955), 65–6.
4. Donald W. Lee, "Some Problems about Meanings," Memorandum, Feb. 15, 1955, to which Gove also contributed, AHC. The examples in the text are taken from this memorandum. Hulbert thought the task was enormous but believed "there is no great mystery in this distinction of senses." It was a judgment that lexicographers were able to make on the basis of experience.
5. Interview with Crawford Lincoln, Apr. 6, 1988. Lincoln, who grew up in New Hampshire, attended Yale and majored in English. He was a great admirer of Gove, and the two enjoyed an easy relationship that was built up over lunch and at other informal occasions. Lincoln served as acting president of Merriam-Webster after Gallan's retirement and was later appointed president of the corporation that restored the historic New England village of Sturbridge near Springfield.
6. Robert Burchfield, *The English Language* (Oxford: Oxford University Press, 1986), 105.
7. These examples of semantic tendencies are taken from an unpublished talk by H. Bosley Woolf in November 1965. Woolf also notes the connection between the status of the person with whom a word is customarily linked and the direction of the change in meaning. Thus, *villain*, originally a neutral term for a common person, acquired an unfavorable connotation when used by upper-class speakers and eventually became pejorative.
8. In the late eighteenth century, a formidable exponent of this point of view was John Horne Tooke. Tooke's views were championed by Charles Richardson, a lexicographer who compiled a dictionary much admired for the variety and

quantity of its illustrative quotations. In the face of undeniable evidence of semantic change, Richardson argued that Tooke meant that a word would have only one etymological meaning; it could also have several "applications." See Sledd and Kolb, *Dr. Johnson's Dictionary*, 186–91.

9. Charles Ruhl, *On Monosemy: A Study in Linguistic Semantics* (Albany: State University of New York Press, 1989). His case rests not on etymology but on semantic analysis. According to Ruhl, the standard expectation should be that a word has a single abstract meaning, "the inherent meaning, a word's semantics" (xi), even though many words have multiple meanings. But he acknowledges that the lexicographer's working assumption that a word may have many meanings is reasonable for solving practical problems of dictionary making.

10. Mitford M. Mathews, "Meanings and Etymologies," in Kenneth G. Wilson, R. H. Hendrickson, and Alan Taylor, *Harbrace Guide to Dictionaries* (New York: Harcourt Brace & World, 1963), 128. Mathews was editor of the *Dictionary of Americanisms*.

11. Gove to Sledd, Mar. 1, 1962, M-W files.

12. Sledd to Gove, Feb. 26, 1962, M-W files.

13. Dictionaries conventionally describe function words as words having little or no semantic or lexical meaning. But this should not be taken to indicate that they have "no meaning." John Algeo suggests, for example, "*The* means (roughly speaking) 'I am thinking of a particular referent and I expect you to know which one I have in mind – from clues in the verbal context, the situational context, or our shared familiarity with things.' *a* means 'I don't have a particular referent in mind, or I do have a particular referent in mind, but I don't expect you to know about it." Letter to the author, July 25, 1991.

14. Lee and Gove, "Some Problems about Meanings," 8. The colors were handled by Janet D. Scott, who also did chemistry definitions.

15. Memorandum to staff on editorializing, Apr. 2, 1953.

16. Edward A. Stephenson, "Wine Definitions," *American Speech*, 42 (Feb. 1967), memo to Gove, 78–9; Gove's rejoinder, 80.

17. Murray, *Web of Words*, 178. The devotion of the *OED* volunteers was rekindled for the supplements, as illustrated by a series of articles in 1968 by Marghanita Laski, who submitted 80,000 citations for the supplements. See the *Times Literary Supplement*, Jan. 11, 1968, 37–9, and later issues.

18. Philip Gove, "The Making of a Dictionary," *Language Arts News*, 31(1967):2.

19. Ibid. Inevitably, with so many different editors at work, there were instances in which these guidelines were not followed. Woolf, for example, was struck by the number of citations from the translation of Simone de Beauvoir's *Second Sex*. Personal note, June 15, 1991.

20. Willinsky, in a review of the reading and marking practices of five dictionary publishers, said that Gove's "unfortunate distinction between 'contrived' language and language 'genuinely at work' is a part of this century's marginalization

of literature as a linguistic and cultural force." "Cutting English on the Bias," *American Speech*, 63, (Spring 1988):62. Willinsky's article provides a highly perceptive insight into the assumptions governing the gathering and use of citations in lexicography.

21. "The Story of a Slip," G. & C. Merriam (Springfield, Mass.: 1959), 7. The *OED* omitted the word *appendicitis* from its first printing after J. A. H. Murray was advised in 1891 not to admit "all the crack-jaw medical and surgical words." After Edward VII's coronation was delayed by surgery for the removal of his appendix, the word became common parlance and was accepted in the *OED*. Elisabeth Murray, *Web of Words*, 222.

22. Interview with Robert Burchfield, Aug. 27, 1987. Burchfield visited Springfield in June 1968 and subsequently allotted some staff time to reading and marking, but continued to rely on volunteers, as did his successors. Burchfield and Gove's correspondence had begun earlier in the year. On February 13, 1968, Burchfield wrote to ask Gove's help in providing earlier citations for some words in the *OED* files. His first list contained twenty-two items; Gove was able to supply earlier dates for nine. Several additional lists followed. When Burchfield asked whether there were any conditions attached to Merriam's assistance, Gove replied that there were none: "I feel that it is our duty to make the information available to the *OED*." Burchfield generously acknowledged Gove's cooperation in the supplement.

23. Parts of this section appeared in my article, "Gove's Rationale for Illustrative Quotations in *Webster's Third New International*," *Dictionaries* (Dictionary Society of North America), 11(1989):153–64.

24. Philip Gove, "Subject Orientation within the Definition," Georgetown University Monograph Series on Language and Linguistics, no. 14, 1961, 95–9. Gove used the term *subject orientation* to describe the techniques for showing the word in an appropriate setting. In his article (and the memorandum on which it is based) he included the genus word in a typical definition since it provides an orientation function by providing the first clue to what the definition is about.

25. The guidelines and examples are taken from ibid., 95–107.

26. The counts of quotations are from an internal memo in the files of Bosley Woolf. An earlier one in Gove's files differs slightly on some counts.

6. THE ORIGINS OF WORDS: THE ETYMOLOGIST'S TASK

1. Hulbert, *Dictionaries: British and American*, 64. Mitford M. Mathews called the etymologies in *Webster's Second* the best at the time. E. S. Sheldon's role in the two editions is described by Gove in "The International Scientific Vocabulary in *Webster's Third*," *Journal of English Linguistics*, 2(1968):2. Gove also noted that there was no evidence that Mahn had worked at the Merriam office. Sheldon

augmented his own work by drawing on citations and etymologies prepared for the new dictionary being published at Oxford. Sleeth's lexicographical experience was limited to three summers of work on the *Dictionary of Middle English.*

2. Bopp's contribution was a systematic comparative study of verbs in Germanic, Greek, Latin, Persian, and Sanskrit that supported Jones's insight. Rask wrote an essay on the origins of Old Norse showing its relationship to other Germanic, as well as Hellenic and Italic, tongues. His work led to Jacob Grimm's formulation of the systematic shift in the spelling of consonants that differentiates Germanic languages from Latin and other languages and that became an important tool for etymologists, as noted later in the text. Jacob and his brother Wilhelm (best known to readers for their collection of fairy tales) began a great historical dictionary of the German language well ahead of Murray's work on the *OED*, but it was not published until 1960, long after their deaths.

3. Interview with Charles R. Sleeth, Nov. 17, 1988. This interview is the source of other practices and views attributed to Sleeth, unless reference is made to specific letters from him.

4. Otto Jespersen, *Growth and Structure of the English Language, 1905* (9th ed., 1938) (reprint, New York: Doubleday/Anchor, 1956), 22–3.

5. Skeat set forth "ten canons for etymology," including this principle discussed in *An Etymological Dictionary of the English Language* (Oxford: Clarendon Press 1882), xxviii–xxix, which was the pioneering work in the field.

6. Sleeth interview, Nov. 17, 1988. In a two-fold classification of Indo-European languages, *satem* is the term for the Balto-Slavic and Indo-Iranian tongues and *centum* for the Germanic and other Western European ones.

7. Garland Cannon, "Borrowings from the Japanese Move up to Second Place," *Newsletter of the American Dialect Society,* 24(Jan. 1992):13.

8. John Geipel, *The Viking Legacy: The Scandinavian Influence on the English and Gaelic Languages* (Newton Abbott: David & Charles, 1971), app. 1, "A Selection of Scandinavian Loanwords in Modern Literary English." Estimates of the number of loanwords vary. Baugh and Cable place the total at about 900, plus an equal number that are probable or were influenced by Scandinavian. The Scandinavian influence is also reflected in more than 1,400 place-names in England – mostly in the north and east of England, as shown by their characteristic endings: Derby and Rugby, Althorpe and Bishopthorpe, Braithwaite, and Brimtoft. In Scandinavian, *by* means "farm" or "town," *thorp* means "village," *thwaite* an "isolated piece of land," and *toft* a "piece of ground." Albert C. Baugh and Thomas Cable, *A History of the English Language,* 3d ed. (New York: Prentice-Hall, 1978), 97–104.

9. Jespersen, *Growth and Structure,* 71. The synonyms that follow and the place-names are from Baugh and Cable, *History,* 97.

10. Jespersen, *Growth and Structure,* 104.

11. As a measure of the Latin influence on vocabulary, Jespersen cites estimates that

one of twenty words in the Latin vocabulary appears in English. When French loanwords and others indicating Latin influence are taken into account, the proportion rises to about one in four or five.

12. Sleeth interview, Nov. 17, 1988.

13. Sleeth to McLean, Oct. 16, 1951, M-W files.

14. Philip Gove, "Etymology in Webster's Third New International Dictionary," *Word*, 22(Apr.–Aug.–Dec. 1966):7–82. The published version takes account of changes made during the preparation of final copy for the dictionary. In publishing the article, Gove explained that he was the editor, not the author, of the article. He attributed the authorship to Sleeth, who later expressed his satisfaction at seeing the article in print, and two associates, Henry Kratz, who joined the staff as an etymologist in 1955, and F. Stuart Crawford, who arrived in 1959.

15. Gove, "International Scientific Vocabulary," 5. Gove also cites the entry for New Latin in the *Century Dictionary* of 1889, which goes into more detail. It notes that "New Latin like Middle Latin possesses a huge literature, but the language in this form is now used almost exclusively in theological, philological and scientific works. Its main use is to serve with the Greek vocabulary . . . as the common vocabulary of civilization." The *OED* used the term "Modern Latin."

16. Sleeth interview, Nov. 17, 1988.

17. The word elements appear in the Third Edition as separate entries. The entry for *colloid* identifies it as an ISV term made up of the New Latin *coll-*, a combining form of Greek origin and meaning "glue," and *-oid*. The entry *-pexy* is a combining form taken from New Latin, originating in Greek, and meaning "solidity." About a third of the ISV entries fall in this class of scientific terms that originated in a language other than English.

18. Gove, "Scientific Vocabulary," 10. The term is defined in *Webster's Third* as "a part of the vocabulary of the sciences and other specialized studies that consists of words or other linguistic forms current in two or more languages and differing from New Latin in being adapted to the structure of the individual languages in which they appear."

19. R. H. Hendrickson, who wrote an essay in the 1960s lamenting the survival of questionable etymologies in dictionaries, cited this example as a welcome exception to the general trend. See "Word History," in K. Wilson, R. Hendrickson, and P. Taylor, *Harbrace Guide to Dictionaries*, 118. However, the *schooner* example was a rare occurrence, Sleeth said. By and large, he thought an intelligent inference was better than nothing. Letter to the author, Nov. 15, 1990.

20. The first confirmed reference to "oll korrect" appears in a 1949 dissertation by Robert B. Gunderson. See Ralph T. Eubanks, "The Basic Derivation of 'O.K.,'" *American Speech*, 35 (Oct. 1960):188–91. Read subsequently found the earlier 1839 occurrence of "oll korrect" that is cited in the latest editions of *The American Heritage Dictionary*, 1992) and *The Random House Dictionary* unabridged (1987), as well as in Merriam-Webster dictionaries and *Webster's Word Histories*

(1989), 329–31. The popularity of the term was said to reflect two fads current in the 1830s – the forming of new abbreviations and deliberate misspellings for humorous effect.

21. Sleeth letter to the author, Nov. 15, 1990.

22. Interview with Henry Kratz, Nov. 13, 1989. Kratz came to Springfield after completing his doctorate in German philology at the University of Michigan and teaching there. He left the staff in 1960 to resume his academic career. When interviewed, he was in the Department of German at the University of Tennessee.

23. Interview with Sol Steinmetz, Mar. 19, 1990. The quotations that follow are also taken from this interview. Several months after the Third Edition was completed in 1961, Steinmetz went to work for Clarence Barnhart. Twenty-eight years later, after serving as coeditor of the *Third Barnhart Dictionary of New Words*, he became executive editor of Random House Dictionaries. The editor in chief, Robert B. Costello, had begun his lexicographical career in 1960 on the staff of *Webster's Third*.

24. I. Willis Russell, "Webster's Third New International Dictionary," *English Journal*, 51(May 1962):331–4, 348.

25. The quotation is from John Algeo, *Language*, 65(1989):850. The Barnhart dictionary, published in 1988 by H. W. Wilson, has about 16,000 main entries out of a total of 30,000.

26. Hulbert, who was far from hostile to etymologies, expressed his skepticism with hyperbole, suggesting that only one user in a thousand consults the dictionary for an etymology (*Dictionaries: British and American*, 57). Lexicographer Sidney I. Landau also takes a skeptical view, seeing little need for etymologies in an abridged dictionary, since they are not necessary for an understanding of current meaning. Their greatest usefulness, he believes, lies in the "clues [they provide] to the history of the culture and its relationships to other words." See his *Dictionaries: The Art and Craft of Lexicography* (New York: Scribner's, 1984), 103.

27. Philip Gove, "The History of Dord," *American Speech*, 29:(1954):136–8. What precipitated his action was an article in *American Speech* the previous year, which attributed the appearance of the ghost word *dord* to poor handwriting. The editor who noticed the missing etymology was reputedly Edward Artin (see Chapter 7).

7. THE SOUND OF WORDS AND OTHER MATTERS

1. A summary of Bailey's detailed title page, which calls attention to "accents placed on each Word, directing to their true Pronunciation," appears in Starnes and Noyes, *Cawdrey to Johnson*, 109.

2. Joseph Worcester's opinion, quoted by Sledd and Kolb in *Dr. Johnson's Dictionary*, 175.

3. Arthur J. Bronstein, "Pronunciation in English Language Dictionaries," in Susan Ramsaron, ed., *Studies in the Pronunciation of English: A Commemorative Volume in Honour of A. C. Gimson* (London: Routledge, 1990), 139.

4. The assessment of Webster's pronunciation system appears in Sledd and Kolb, *Dr. Johnson's Dictionary*, 198. Friend goes into considerable detail in the section on pronunciation in his study of Webster, *Development of American Lexicography*, 56–79. Gabriele Stein discusses the treatment of pronunciation in sixteenth-century bilingual and trilingual dictionaries in *The English Dictionary before Cawdrey* (Tubingen: Max Niemeyer, 1985), 313–14.

5. Murray, *Web of Words*, 189.

6. Bronstein, "Pronunciation in English Dictionaries," 142–3.

7. Edward Artin, "Dictionary Treatment of Pronunciation," in Raven I. McDavid, Jr., and Audrey Duckert, eds., *Lexicography in English* (New York: Annals of the New York Academy of Sciences, 1973), 211:126.

8. Letter from Dorothy Artin, Sept. 15, 1988.

9. Gove papers, AHC. Reports on two surveys by Artin and Victor Weidman, vice-president in charge of marketing, and one by Weidman and Sleeth, Feb.–May 1953.

10. Pronunciation symbols in the Third Edition are based on what a reviewer of the manuscript called a *diaphonemic* approach – that is, the only differences in sound to be recorded are those capable of changing a meaning, and every potential difference in meaning in any dialect must be capable of being represented. For example, there must be a pair of contrasting symbols to represent the phonemic contrast in the Middle Atlantic States between *can* in the sense of "be able" and *can* meaning "container."

11. The use of outside consultants by the Merriam company dates back to the War of the Dictionaries, but lexicographers had been calling on outside experts for help since the mid-eighteenth century, and the scope and importance of the activity had increased considerably with the growth of the technical and scientific vocabulary.

12. Letter from Hurd that Gove sent to the board, June 10, 1960. Gove papers, AHC.

13. Letter from Babrick to the author, Aug. 2, 1989.

14. Lincoln interview, Apr. 6, 1988.

8. USAGE AND FINAL TASKS

1. The guidelines on slang were worked out primarily by associate editor Daniel Cook. His article "A Point of Lexicographical Method," *American Speech*, 34(Feb. 1959):20–5, is an entertaining and revealing account of the need for "contextual guides" in the definition of terms that have both standard and slang senses. His example is the history of the word *chicken* as applied to young women

from Defoe's time on. Cook left the Merriam company in 1957 to return to academe.

2. Hulbert, *Dictionaries: British and American*, 83. James B. McMillan, "Five College Dictionaries," *College English*, 10(Jan. 1949):214–21. A professor of English at the University of Alabama, McMillan wrote his dissertation under the direction of Hulbert.

3. Robert L. Chapman, ed., *American Slang* (New York: Harper & Row, 1987). This quotation is part of a longer excerpt that serves as the epigraph to Chapman's preface. This edition is abridged from *The New Dictionary of American Slang* (New York: Harper & Row, 1986).

4. Charles C. Fries, "Usage Levels and Dialect Distribution," *The American College Dictionary* (New York: Random House, 1947), xxv. Nevertheless, the *ACD* did not abandon the colloquial label. Dictionaries published later by Random House and others used the term *informal* in its place.

5. Temporal labels were used to indicate words that had not been in standard use since 1755 (called *obsolete*) and words that had appeared only sporadically since 1755 (called *archaic*). Regional labels were used to indicate words that were usually standard in other countries (*Brit, Austral, Irish*) or in regions of the United States (*North, New Eng*, and so on); the label *dial Brit* was used to indicate a regional variety that was not standard in Britain.

6. Charles C. Fries, *American English Grammar: The Report of an Investigation Financed by the National Council of Teachers of English and Supported by the Modern Language Association and the Linguistic Society of America*, Monograph 10, National Council of Teachers of English (New York: Appleton-Century-Crofts, 1940), 3–5. This study, which was started during the summers of 1926 and 1927, was part of the National Council of Teachers of English series discussed later in this chapter. The quotations cited by Fries are from R. G. White, *Words and Their Uses*, rev. ed. (Boston: Houghton Mifflin, 1899), 14; and Henry Sweet, *New English Grammar*, (Oxford: Clarendon Press, 1891), 1:5.

7. Sterling Leonard, *The Doctrine of Correctness in English Usage, 1700–1800* (Madison: University of Wisconsin, 1929), 231. During this period there were a few advocates of the importance of usage (in the tradition of Horace, John Locke, and others), most notably Joseph Priestley, best known for his discovery of oxygen, but their views were overwhelmed by those of Lowth and his supporters. Though Priestley had little influence on his contemporaries, Leonard regarded him as the precursor of the modern scientific approach to the study of usage.

8. These quotations from Webster's *Dissertations* and *Letter to Dr. Ramsay* are cited in ibid., 236.

9. Ibid., 237.

10. Sterling Leonard and others, *Current English Usage*, National Council of Teachers of English, English Monograph 1 (Chicago: Inland Press, 1932). This study and two follow-up NCTE studies are summarized and assessed by Edward

Finegan in *Attitudes toward English: The History of a War of Words* (New York: Teachers College Press, 1980), 88–108. Leonard's work stirred considerable interest within the teaching community as well as criticism for allegedly concluding more than the data warranted.

11. Finegan, *Attitudes toward English,* 96. The Marckwardt–Walcott study, despite the great superiority of its methods, was criticized for the inadequacy of the data and some of its inferences. Finegan's book includes an assessment of the controversy over *Webster's Third* in the context of the long battle between traditional grammarians and modern linguists.

12. Fries, *American English Grammar,* abridged from 14–15. The centerpiece of this book is the analysis of usage in a sample of 3,000 personal letters, written to government agencies primarily during the 1920s. Its methodology and findings became enormously important to the study of language and to the teaching of English. An excellent summary and assessment of it appear in Finegan, *Attitudes toward English,* 96–105.

13. Gallan to Gove, Dec. 5, 1958, AHC.

14. Gallan to Gove, Dec. 6, 1960, AHC. The Funk & Wagnalls college dictionary was published in 1963.

15. Gove to McDavid, Feb. 18, 1955, M-W files.

16. McDavid to Artin, Apr. 5, 1955, AHC. The complaint about sales tactics was not an isolated one, and it was milder than some written to editorial staff members by friends who had been offended by Merriam salesmen.

17. Gove's progress report, Jan. 10, 1961, Gove papers, AHC.

18. Letter to the author from Babrick, Aug. 2, 1989.

19. Louise Pound, *American Literature,* 7(Mar. 1935):117–18. A very informative discussion of the reaction to the 1909 and 1934 unabridged dictionaries appears in Rosemary M. Laughlin, "The Predecessors of *That* Dictionary," *American Speech,* 42(1967):105–13.

20. *Springfield Republican,* June 26, 1934. Hart had worked on both the 1909 and 1934 editions. The conventional accompanying picture in the newspaper showed A. G. Baker and Robert Munroe, the top company officers, receiving copies of the new work from the editor in chief, Dr. William A. Neilson, who was master of ceremonies for the occasion, and Thomas A. Knott, the general editor.

9. EARLY RETURNS: THE FUSE IS LIT

1. The errors in the *Times* article were not committed by Phillips. They appeared in the press release issued by the Merriam company, as noted later in the chapter.

2. The account of the controversy in Part III is based primarily on four sources: (1) clippings in the Gove papers, AHC, or retained by the family; (2) letters and clippings in the Merriam-Webster files; (3) clippings collected by Raven I. McDavid, Jr., in the Joseph Regenstein Library of the University of Chicago,

Division of Special Collections; and (4) Sledd and Ebbitt, *Dictionaries and THAT Dictionary*, which reprints sixty-two of the news stories, editorials, and reviews that were first printed between September 7, 1961, and the end of May 1962. Comments from Sledd's unpublished papers and from an interview with him are also cited.

3. The comments on the controversy by the *Mason City Globe-Gazette*'s editor, W. Earl Hall, were generally unfavorable. They were first broadcast on his radio program, "One Man's Opinion," over several Iowa stations before appearing in the newspaper. Dogged in his coverage, Hall drew on exchanges of correspondence with Gove and several newspaper editors, including Theodore M. Bernstein of the *New York Times*, the *Times*'s watchdog on usage, to keep the discussion going.

4. Charles McCabe, "Why Ain't 'Slud' in the Dictionary?" *Houston Chronicle*, Apr. 29, 1962.

5. *New Yorker*, Mar. 24, 1962.

6. Herb Caen, *San Francisco Sunday Chronicle*, Sept. 24, 1961; John Ferris, "Dictionary Is Not Just a Book When It Quotes Polly Adler," *New York World-Telegram and Sun*, Sept. 11, 1961.

7. "It Ain't Necessarily Uncouth," *Chicago Daily News*, Sept. 9, 1961.

8. "The Death of Meaning," *Toronto Globe and Mail*, Sept. 8, 1961.

9. The quotation is from the AP wire story from Springfield, Sept. 21. A copy of a typewritten statement dated Sept. 13, which is apparently the same or very similar to the version given to the press, is included in Raven McDavid's papers. McDavid gathered hundreds of clippings from newspapers and other periodicals about the prepublication controversy to prepare an assessment of the early stories about *Webster's Third* for the publishers of *Encyclopaedia Britannica*, who were considering the acquisition of the Merriam company in the early 1960s. Later he presented a paper based on his critique at the 1966 annual meeting of the Modern Language Association; a subsequent version was published in 1971 in the *Journal of English Linguistics* and reprinted in a collection of his essays. See his "False Scents and Cold Trails: The Pre-Publication Criticism of the Merriam Third," in Anivar S. Dil, ed., *Varieties of American English* (Stanford, Calif.: Stanford University Press, 1980), 310–36; reprinted from the *Journal of English Linguistics*, 5(1971):101–21.

10. The quotations from the *Wilmington News* and from McDowell are cited in McDavid, "False Scents," 326.

11. "Why 'Ain't' IS in Our Dictionaries," *Professional Growth for Teachers*, Junior High School Edition, Sept. 1964. Other lexicographers also believe that the absence of a label does not constitute approval of a word, as indicated by the comments of Chapman and Landau cited in Chapter 14.

12. And what is meant by the word *many* – in the expression "used . . . orally by many"? Is it intended to suggest about the same number as the *many* who

disapprove the term? Or fewer, or more? *Merriam-Webster's Collegiate Dictionary,* tenth edition (1993), contributes clarity by providing an extended usage note with numerous examples showing characteristic uses of *ain't.*

13. The interpretation of that evidence became a heated issue three years later in the journal *College English.* Sheridan Baker of the University of Michigan touched off the debate with his article "The Error of Ain't," discussed in Chapter 14.

14. H. W. Fowler, *Modern English Usage* (Oxford: Oxford University Press, 1926), 45, entry "be,7." Fowler gives a cross-reference to this entry at the entry for *ain't.*

15. Frank Tumpane, "All About Ain't," in the *Toronto Telegram,* now defunct; the undated clipping in Gove's family papers seems to have appeared in September 1961. Tumpane quoted Fowler's entry in full.

16. *Binghamton Sunday Press,* Sept. 17, 1961.

17. Jacques Barzun, "Mencken's America Speaking," *Atlantic* (Jan. 1946), reprinted in *A Word or Two Before You Go . . .* " (Middletown, Conn.: Wesleyan University Press, 1986), 161.

18. Gove to Malone, Feb. 13, 1956, M-W files.

19. *Business Week,* Sept. 16, 1961, 89. The article mistakenly describes the Third Edition as the first dictionary to follow a descriptive rather than prescriptive approach to lexicography.

20. *Publisher's Weekly,* Sept. 18, 1961. A week later it printed a letter from an executive of the Dimondstein Book Co., a major distributor, complaining that dealers and customers should have been notified earlier that the Second Edition was going to be superseded. Instead, "Merriam representatives diligently pursued their appointed rounds, and nary a word was mentioned about the forthcoming revision." Jack Mashman, "We Suggest It Might Have been Fairer," Sept. 25, 1961.

21. "Vox Populi, Vox Webster," *Time,* Oct. 6, 1961, 49. *Time* had gone beyond the press release and had done some checking on its own. *Newsweek* used a quotation from Noah Webster – "A living language must keep pace with improvements in knowledge and with the multiplication of ideas" – to introduce its short, inconsequential, but not unfavorable story (Sept. 18). The new edition, the story continued, was keeping a fast pace, "perhaps faster and more razzle-dazzle" than Webster had ever contemplated.

22. "A New 'Webster,'" *Bookseller,* Sept. 9, 1961, 1370–2.

23. Sumner Ives, "Scholarly New Dictionary Addressed to Laymen," *St. Louis Globe-Democrat,* Sept. 24, 1961.

24. "Dig Those Words," *New York Times,* Sept. 10, 1961.

25. McDavid, "False Scents and Cold Trails," 316.

26. Benjamin Jowett's attempt to block James A. H. Murray's use of quotations from newspapers is described in Elisabeth Murray's *Web of Words,* 222–4. James called "this criticism by far the silliest that the Dictionary has elicited. I am certain posterity will agree with me."

27. The copy of the press release cited here is one that had been received by a leading publisher. All of the major facts appear in one news story or another. None of the former members of the editorial or business staffs I queried was able to find a copy of the release; nor was one found in the Merriam files when I asked to see it.

28. Woolf, comment to author, Nov. 24, 1991. Woolf and Sleeth have no recollection of having been consulted.

29. John Allen Reed [pseudonym], "A Big New Dictionary: Its Virtues and Faults," *St. Louis Post-Dispatch*, Dec. 18, 1966. The review, which dealt with the Random House unabridged dictionary, contained several comparisons between the new work and *Webster's Third*.

30. Philip Gove, ed., *The Role of the Dictionary* (Indianapolis, Ind.: Bobbs-Merrill, 1967).

10. THE CONTROVERSY HEATS UP

1. David M. Glixon, "One Hundred Thousand Words More," *Saturday Review*, Sept. 30, 1961, 19–20.

2. "Webster's New Word Book," *New York Times*, Oct. 12, 1961.

3. Sydney J. Harris, "Good English Ain't What We Thought," *Chicago Daily News*, Oct. 20, 1961.

4. Philip Gove, Letter to the editor, *New York Times*, Nov. 5, 1961.

5. "Answers Dictionary Critics," *St. Louis Post-Dispatch*, Nov. 10, 1961.

6. Art Linkletter, Letter to the editor, *New York Times*, Oct. 20, 1961.

7. Evans to Gove, Oct. 18, 1961, M-W files. Evans's book, *Comfortable Words*, was published in 1962. He had just completed a series of fifty half-hour television shows for Westinghouse Broadcasting company, entitled *English for Americans*. The credits at the end of the show had been superimposed over a copy of the Second Edition. Had he known about the new edition he would have much preferred to use it, he told Gove, but the publicity person with whom he talked failed to mention its imminent publication. Gove explained in his reply that the company's policy of prepublication secrecy had made it impossible to take advantage of such promotional opportunities.

8. Gove to Evans, Oct. 23, 1961, M-W files.

9. John Chamberlain, "Bookshelf: Words and What They Mean Now," *Wall Street Journal*, Oct. 12, 1961.

10. Mario Pei, "Ain't Is In, 'Raviolis' Ain't," *New York Times Book Review*, Oct. 22, 1961, 6.

11. Bloch to Gove, Oct. 25, 1961, AHC. Gove circulated this letter to the top editorial staff with the note, "BB quoted at 2 *bad* 5d, 1 *hard* 4a (1), *take over* vt, *valley* 2b and *yourself* 1a." Bloch, a professor of linguistics, had been on the Editorial Advisory Committee of *The American College Dictionary* and editor of *Language*, journal of the Linguistics Society of America.

12. "A Non-Word Deluge," *Life*, Oct. 27, 1961, 4.

13. Gove, Letter to the editor, *Life*, Nov. 17, 1961, 13.

14. Evans to Gove, Nov. 6, 1961, M-W files. He asked Gove to find someone to read an issue of the *Times* for all new words and senses that would bolster his argument in the article he was writing for the *Times*, but Gove replied that he could not spare the staff time.

15. Theodore M. Bernstein, "The Problem of Delinguancy," *Bulletin of the American Society of Newspaper Editors*, Nov. 1, 1961. Bernstein had established a considerable reputation as an authority on usage through his periodic report to the staff, *Winners and Sinners*, which was also widely read and applauded by journalists and editors across the country. The issue of Jan. 4, 1962, carried his directive on the use of *Webster's Third*.

16. Graham Du Shane, "Say It Ain't So!" *Science*, Nov. 10, 1961, 1493.

17. Roy H. Copperud, "English as It's Used Belongs in the Dictionary," *Editor and Publisher*, Nov. 25, 1961, 44.

18. David Horne, "I'd Rather Be Right Than Webster," *Boards and Buckram*, Writings from *Scholarly Books in America*, 1962–1969 (Hanover, N.H.: University Press of New England, 1980), 6.

19. Norman E. Isaacs, "And Now the War on Words," *Louisville Times*, Oct. 18, 1961.

20. Rudolph Flesch, *Long Island Press*, Oct. 31, 1961. The Flesch formula for clear writing – short sentences, emphasis on the active voice, and an informal style enhanced by *personalizing* the text – caught on with the public, but many writers took a dim view of it. E. B. White wrote, "We would as lief Simonize our grandmother as personalize our writing." *Second Tree from the Corner* (New York: Harper, 1954), 166.

21. Millicent Taylor, "The New Dictionary," *Christian Science Monitor*, Nov. 29, 1961.

22. "Finalized?" and "President Strikes Blow for 'Finalize' as English," *New York Times*, Nov. 30, 1961.

23. Rt. Rev. Richard Emrich, "New Dictionary Cheap, Corrupt," *Detroit News*, Feb. 10, 1962. The article, which described the new edition as "a kind of Kinsey Report in linguistics," gave away its lack of firsthand acquaintance with the dictionary by repeating the error that *irregardless* was included "as a proper word."

24. *Webster's Dictionary of English Usage* recounts some of the history of the *-ize* words (568). A classic statement against the *-ize* form appears in Edward Phillips's seventeenth-century dictionary, the *New World of Words:* "Certain kinde of Mulewords propagated of a Latin Sire and a Greek Dam . . . are so monstrously-barbarous . . . that they are not worthy to be mentioned." Quoted in Keith Tracy, "'Finalize': A Case History," *American Speech*, 40(Dec. 1965): 302–4.

25. Ethel Strainchamps, "On New Words and New Meanings," *St. Louis Post-Dispatch*, Dec. 17, 1961.

26. Wes Lawrence, "Breakfast Commentator," *Cleveland Plain Dealer,* Dec. 19, 1961.

11. CALAMITY OR CALUMNY?

1. Merriam editors at the meeting reported that the Third Edition had received "enthusiastic praise" from other attendees. *Springfield Sunday Republican,* Jan. 7, 1962.

2. Gove to Sledd, June 6, 1962, M-W files.

3. Wilson Follett, "Sabotage in Springfield," *Atlantic* (Jan. 1962):73. The quotations that follow are from 64–77.

4. Follett also restated most of the specific objections expressed earlier in other hostile reviews, with the notable exceptions of *ain't* and *finalize,* which are covered by implication in his discussion of questionable words accepted as standard and the use of the term *permissive.*

5. *Richmond News-Leader,* Jan. 3, 1962.

6. *Washington Post,* Jan. 17, 1962.

7. Foster Hailey, "2 Journals Score New Dictionary," *New York Times,* Feb. 8, 1962. Hailey quoted the Merriam sales manager as reporting that the critical articles had not hurt sales and that several reprintings had been ordered. The manager of a chain of bookstores also reported no evidence that the attacks had affected sales.

8. "Logomachy – Debased Verbal Currency," American Bar Association *Journal,* Jan. 1962, 49.

9. Letter to Richard Bentley, editor-in-chief, American Bar Association *Journal,* Jan. 29, 1962, AHC.

10. B. Hunter Smeaton, *Library Journal,* Jan. 15, 1962. In the first part of a two-part review, the *Inland Daily Printer / American Lithographer,* Apr. 1962, 131, quoted Follett extensively. In the second part, the author, Burton Lasky, openly worried that if the Third Edition "is used as widely as its predecessor has been, they will have succeeded in codifying the mistakes of thousands of writers and oversights of thousands of editors and proofreaders."

11. J. Donald Adams, *New York Times Book Review,* Feb. 11, 1962.

12. Garry Wills, "Madness in Their Method," *National Review,* Feb. 13, 1962, 98–9. Wills also complained that a single abbreviation refers to many entries – for example, that "RE . . . means . . . well, nine other things." But here again he was betrayed by his ignorance of his favorite dictionary: the same practice was followed in the Second Edition, where "R.E." was used to signify seven "things," Real Estate, Reformed Episcopal, Royal Engineers, and so on.

13. The *Atlantic* did, however, reprint seven letters to the editor in its March issue commenting on the Follett review, favorably and unfavorably, including one from Gove. A group of Mount Holyoke College students expressed their distress at

learning that the Merriam company had abandoned its responsibility for setting standards. Two strong rejoinders took issue with Follett, one defending the descriptive approach to lexicography and the other rebutting specific comments on grammar and etymology.

14. The first letter from Sledd ("Dear Dr. Gove") was dated Feb. 17, 1962. The second (to "Dear Phil"), dated Feb. 26, included Sledd's criticism of Gove's defining formula (see Chapter 5) and his objections to the omission of the colloquial label. M-W files.

15. Gove to Evans, Mar. 22, 1962, AHC.

16. Evans, "But What's a Dictionary For," *Atlantic* (May 1962):57. The article, which continues to page 62, is the source of the quotations that follow.

17. Noss to G. & C. Merriam Company, May 14, 1962, AHC.

18. Randolph Quirk, *New Statesman*, Mar. 2, 1962, 304. Quirk was the senior author of *A University Grammar of English* (1973) and *A Comprehensive Grammar of English* (1985). Later he was named president of the British Academy. Quirk's review was reprinted in Sledd and Ebbitt, *Dictionaries and THAT Dictionary*, 151–4. The other British reviews appear on 136–9, 144–6, 154–8, 191–3, 194–200, 202–3 of that work.

19. The excerpts are from The *York House Bulletin*, issued by Merriam's British publisher, G. Bell and Sons, York House, London, undated; each review is on a separate sheet, distributed early in 1962.

20. Allen Walker Read, "Dictionary," *The New Encyclopaedia Britannica*, 15th ed. (Chicago: Encyclopaedia Britannica, 1976), 5:713–22. Albert H. Marckwardt is said to have commented that the British look at the pronunciation in a dictionary to see if it records their usage and Americans look to see what the correct pronunciation is.

21. Brooks Atkinson, *New York Times*, Mar. 1, 1962. The story was distributed by the Times News Service and was reprinted in Springfield on March 9 with a three-column photograph of Gove. Atkinson had written Gove on February 12 to propose the interview. Gove replied the next day and on February 15 Atkinson confirmed his plans to come to Springfield. M-W files.

22. Gove to Atkinson, Mar. 3, 1962, M-W files.

23. Macdonald to Gove, Oct. 4, 1961, M-W files.

24. Gove to Macdonald, Oct. 5, 1961; Macdonald to Gove, Oct. 6, 1961; Gove to Macdonald, Oct. 10, 1961, M-W files.

25. Gove to Macdonald, Oct. 25, 1961. Gove wrote again on Oct. 31 to take exception to a "Talk of the Town" item in the *New Yorker* on the word *urban*. The word was not new, he pointed out, but had been around for more than a decade, having appeared in the West in the mid-1930s. (The *OED* shows it occurring in the seventeenth century.) It had been included in the addenda of the 1950 printing of the Second Edition. He added, "It always surprises me to observe the occasions on which people won't use their dictionaries."

26. Sledd to Gove, Mar. 3, 1962. Woolf recalls that a *New Yorker* fact checker, who called to verify several points, put Gove's mind at rest briefly by giving the impression that the review was generally favorable.

27. Dwight Macdonald, "Three Questions for Structural Linguists, Or Webster 3 Revisited," in Sledd and Ebbitt, *Dictionaries and THAT Dictionary*, 257.

28. Evans to Gove, Mar. 31, 1962, M-W files.

29. James Sledd, "Lynching the Lexicographer," in Viola E. Garfield, ed., *Symposium on Language and Culture*, Proceedings of the 1962 Annual Meeting of the American Ethnological Society (Seattle: American Ethnological Society, 1963), 77. Most of the quotations in the section entitled "The Clash of Views" below are from this article (69–75 of the proceedings). Sledd's efforts to get this article published in a magazine of general circulation failed. It appeared in full only in these proceedings, though parts of it were incorporated into Sledd's "Reply to Mr. Macdonald" in Sledd and Ebbitt, *Dictionaries and THAT Dictionary*, 268–74. Even the abridged version in the book reached a small audience, compared with those reached by Follett and Macdonald. Sales of the book totaled 27,494 copies before the work went out of print in late 1975. Letter from Ebbitt to the author, Sept. 18, 1989.

30. Dwight Macdonald, "The String Untuned," *New Yorker*, Mar. 10, 1962, 131.

31. Sledd, "Lynching," 75; *Webster's Second*, Preface, v.

32. *Webster's Second*, Preface, v–vi.

33. Preface to Johnson's dictionary. Trench is quoted on this matter in Chapter 3.

34. Quoted by Sledd from *Letters of Noah Webster*, ed. Harry R. Warfel (New York, 1953), 350, 367.

35. Philip Gove, "Linguistic Advances and Lexicography," *Word Study*, Oct. 1961, 3. *Word Study* was an eight-page publication distributed without charge to high school teachers, college faculty members, and others interested in language. In the fall of 1961 it began its thirty-seventh year of publication. Though it was primarily a marketing tool, it carried a good deal of interesting and useful information on dictionaries. Virtually every issue during the 1950s and 1960s featured byline articles by teachers and prominent linguists and lexicographers – including Kemp Malone, Allen Walker Read, James B. McMillan, and Cabell Greet. Profiles appeared of such influential figures as James A. H. Murray, Benjamin Lee Whorf, and James Joyce.

36. Philip Gove, "English Dictionaries of the Future," in Weinbrot, *New Aspects of Lexicography*, 157.

37. Macdonald, "The String Untuned."

38. Gove papers, AHC.

39. Sledd, "Lynching," 72.

40. Ibid., 71.

41. Macdonald, "The String Untuned," 159–60. Thirty years later, the third edition of the *American Heritage Dictionary*, which described itself as the most prescrip-

tive of American dictionaries then in print, based its treatments of such matters as variant spellings on the counting of citations.

42. Sledd, "Lynching," 83. Something of this sort on a modest scale was attempted a few years later by William Morris, who shared Macdonald's views, with results to be examined in Chapter 15.

43. Ibid., 70.

44. Sledd to Gove, June 11, 1962, M-W files. Sledd also noted that he had offered his "Lynching piece" to Northwestern University Press, University of Chicago Press, and Prentice Hall, but none of them showed any interest in it.

12. COMMERCIAL INTRUSIONS: TRADEMARKS, TAKEOVER THREATS, COMPETITION

1. The examples of lost trademarks are from "Trademarks: The Official Media Guide" (U.S. Trademark Association, 1990), a leaflet that spells out practices that can threaten the viability of trademarks.

2. This account of the case is based on the records in *Federal Trade Commission Decisions*, July 1, 1940, to June 30, 1950 (Washington, D.C.: U. S. Government Printing Office, 1952), 46:223–43.

3. Read's comment appears in "Desk Dictionaries," *Consumer Reports* (Nov. 1963):547–50. The Random House college edition of 1991 also led to a court suit in which the Merriam company charged that the phrase *Webster's College* and the jacket design of the Random House edition (which echoed the Merriam jacket in important aspects) confused book buyers. A New York federal jury found that Random House intentionally copied the Merriam design that had been in use since 1973 and awarded the plaintiffs more than $2 million – $1,774,713 in lost profits and $500,000 in punitive damages. See "$2 Million Award in Word War," *New York Times*, Oct. 23, 1991. Subsequently, the award was doubled. Final settlement was still pending in early 1994.

4. The examples cited are from a letter signed by Kelsey, June 28, 1957, M-W files. Queries were also sent to the attorneys on July 31 and September 19.

5. Gove to Malone, June 30, 1960, M-W files.

6. Gove to Lenore B. Stoughton, Rogers, Hoge & Hills, Oct. 19, 1961, U.S. Trademark Association files. Stoughton's inquiry had been addressed to Gallan, who asked Gove to reply.

7. Interviews with Crawford Lincoln, Apr. 6, 1988, and Victor W. Weidman, Apr. 7, 1988.

8. "New 'Webster's' Ain't Solicitous of Trademarks" and "Plexiglass Still a Trademark: Rohm & Haas," *Advertising Age*, Jan. 15, 1962.

9. "Dangerous Gobbledygook," *American Press*, Feb. 1962, 4.

10. Letter from J. Wendell Sether, *Forbes*, May 15, 1962, 6.

11. Production records indicate that for a printing in late 1962 more than 500 pages

had to be replated, most of them apparently in direct response to the trademark compromise (nearly 1 page out of 5 in the 2,736-page Third Edition). Corrections and revisions were, of course, introduced in virtually every printing, but not on this scale. There were usually fewer than 100, except when the addenda section was introduced and revised. By the end of 1975 – with the dictionary still selling well – the number of printings had reached 27 and the total number of pages revised for corrections and updating since the original print run had reached nearly 2,400, including many that were revised more than once.

12. Landau, *Dictionaries,* 300–1.
13. *Springfield Union,* Feb. 19, 1962.
14. John G. Rogers, *New York Herald-Tribune,* Feb. 20, 1962.
15. *Springfield Union,* Feb. 19, 1962. American Heritage was the publisher of *Horizon* and *American Heritage* magazines, a series of illustrated history books for young readers, and other books. Parton, a New Englander and Harvard graduate, had been an assistant to the president of the *New York Herald-Tribune* before he became founding president of American Heritage in 1954.
16. *Springfield Union,* Feb. 20, 1961. A week before Parton's announcement, Merriam had taken a defensive step, splitting the stock two for one, thereby doubling the number of shares held by the stockholders and reducing the price per share to $150. Later it declared a ten-for-one split.
17. "Dictionaries: The Most Unique," *Newsweek,* Mar. 12, 1962, 105.
18. *Wall Street Journal,* Mar. 13, 1962.
19. Letter from Parton to stockholders, July 19, 1962.
20. *Springfield Union,* Sept. 12, 1963. American Heritage revenues for the year rose 3 cents a share to 85 cents.
21. Sledd to his children, July 18, 1987, accompanying a copy of the letter he sent to *Time* after his visit.
22. Ibid.
23. Sledd to Norman Ross, Time Inc., undated.
24. *New York Times,* Sept. 11, 1964. Britannica had purchased the American Heritage stock for $25 a share. Although the buyout effort failed, Parton's company profited nicely from the investment.
25. The acquisition – which was negotiated by Newton N. Minow, executive vice-president and general counsel – was featured in the Winter 1965 issue of *Know,* the company magazine; the final cost of the acquisition was given as $16,200,000. Minow, former chairman of the Federal Communications Commission, gained public prominence when he labeled television a "vast wasteland."
26. Gove to Norwood and Ruth, Oct. 28, 1964, GFP.
27. "Defeat on Third Edition Is Denied by Merriam Co.," *Springfield Daily News,* Mar. 27, 1963. The dictionary was to be published on April 3. Gove's reply in the Springfield paper was accompanied by the original Morris column distributed by NANA Syndicate. Morris later criticized the *Collegiate* for the kind of "un-

scholarly editing that characterized the 'Third International.'" "Words, Wit, and Wisdom," *Milwaukee Journal,* Dec. 19, 1963.

28. Ironically, it was also the first college dictionary to include the taboo word *fuck* and other obscene words, notwithstanding the fact that its editor had been in the vanguard of attacks on *Webster's Third* for including "many 'gutter' terms which had never before appeared in dictionaries designed for general readership."

29. The big *Random House Dictionary* had been well received, though not with universal approbation, and it found a niche for itself as a general reference work that included not only common words but a full measure of biographical, geographical, literary, and other such information, in addition to "concise" dictionaries of Spanish, French, Italian, and German. Its coverage of the vocabulary was about half that of *Webster's Third* and it offered no illustrative quotations.

30. Thomas J. Creswell, *Usage in Dictionaries and Dictionaries of Usage,* Publication of the American Dialect Society (Tuscaloosa: University of Alabama Press, 1975), 63–4. Creswell and Virginia G. McDavid, who contributed to the planning of the study, later collaborated in preparing the usage notes and the introductory essay on usage for the unabridged *Random House Dictionary of the English Language,* 2d ed. (1987). Both were faculty members at Chicago State University.

31. Creswell listed all 502 entries in an appendix and indicated with an asterisk those on which the panel had been consulted. The 226 questions on which the panel was polled were summarized in detailed tabulations and compared with the treatment of the same entries in other dictionaries. Since more than one vote was taken on 65 items (three on *ain't,* for example: "Ain't I?" "It ain't likely," and "Aren't I?"), the number of votes by the panel totaled 318. Creswell, *Usage,* 21.

32. Ibid., table 22.

33. Ibid., 30.

34. Thomas J. Creswell and Virginia G. McDavid, "The Usage Panel in the *American Heritage Dictionary Second College Edition,*" in William Frawley and Roger Steiner, eds., *Advances in Lexicography,* Part 2 (Edmonton: Boreal Scholarly Publishers, 1986), 95, 83. Creswell and McDavid emphasized that their report dealt only with the functioning of the panel, not with the usage notes generally. They found many usage notes "eminently sensible and accurately descriptive."

35. Virginia G. McDavid, "A Comparison of Usage Panel Judgments in the *American Heritage Dictionary* and Usage Conclusions and Recommendations in *Webster's Dictionary of English Usage,*" Unpublished ms., 9.

13. AT ISSUE: A WAY OF LIFE

1. Mario Pei, "Dictionary as a Battlefront: English Teachers' Dilemma," *Saturday Review,* July 21, 1962, 44–6, 55–6. His original review appeared in the *New York Times Book Review.*

2. Unpublished memorandum, AHC, 1.

3. Ibid.

4. *Saturday Review*, Aug. 18, 1962, 60–2.

5. Mario Pei, "A Loss for Words," *Saturday Review*, Nov. 14, 1964, 82–4.

6. "An 'Authority' Protests Murder of Our Language," *Omaha World Herald*, Sept. 8, 1962.

7. "Correspondence," *New Republic*, May 14, 1962. Sledd also noted a half-dozen other uses of the *bi-* prefix in *Webster's Second*.

8. "Talk of the Town," *New Yorker*, Feb. 8, 1964, 27.

9. *American Oxonian*, Jan. 1963, 26–8. Sleeth's rejoinder was preceded by comments from the editor and excerpts from several hostile reviews. "The fact is," the editor wrote, "that very few major American periodicals carried altogether favorable reviews." Sleeth's letter was dated June 27, 1962. Among other responses by staff members were Woolf's reply to a critical review in the *Richmond Times-Dispatch* (letter to Dr. Lewis F. Ball, book editor, Nov. 22, 1961) and Mairé Weir Kay's rejoinder to *Science*, Apr. 12, 1962. Questions about the Third Edition's sales were answered from time to time by the business staff.

10. Philip Perlmutter, "Prejudice Memorialized," *Frontier*, Sept. 1965, 18. Criticisms of the definition of *Jew* as "a person believed to drive a hard bargain," without a usage note, had appeared in the Jewish press in the spring of 1962, and Jewish leaders around the country had been urged to protest the definition. The treatment of racial terms in *Webster's Ninth New Collegiate* (1983) generally follows the Third Edition policy. *Webster's Dictionary of English Usage* (1989) rarely comments on racial and religious smear terms, but it takes a somewhat stronger stand in one instance. It describes *Jew* as an adjective and the verb *jew down* as "usually considered offensive," and it recommends that "the former should be replaced by 'Jewish,' and the latter avoided altogether."

11. The problems of the *Oxford Pocket Dictionary* are cited by Robert Burchfield in "Dictionaries and Ethnic Sensibilities," in Leonard Michaels and Christopher Ricks, eds., *The State of the Language* (Berkeley and Los Angeles: University of California Press, 1980), 16.

12. Interview with Robert Burchfield, Aug. 27, 1987. The protests against the definitions in the *Pocket Dictionary* are described in "Dictionaries and Ethnic Sensibilities."

13. Burton Lasky, "New Webster's Abdicates Its Duty to Arbitrate Usage," *Inland Printer / American Lithographer*, Apr. 1962, 133. Albert R. Kates, "New Dictionary Recognizes Modern Funeral Technology," *American Funeral Director*, Apr. 1962, 31. The *Lutheran* took a detached view: "You can choose sides in this battle according to your temperament, and not much harm will be done whichever you choose." Elson Ruff, "In Conclusion," Sept. 19, 1962.

14. Jacques Barzun, "What Is a Dictionary?" *American Scholar*, 32(Spring 1963):176–81.

15. Five rejoinders to Barzun's article, including one from Gove, appeared in a later issue, "Controversy: About the Dictionary," *American Scholar*, Autumn 1963, 604–8.

16. Albert H. Marckwardt, "Dictionaries and the English Language," in Gove, *The Role of the Dictionary*, 37, reprinted from *English Journal*, 52 (May 1963):336–45. The importance of usage, Marckwardt noted, had been emphasized by leading scholars since the turn of the century. "The structuralists accept this as a matter of course but they did not invent the idea," he said.

17. W. N. Francis, "Language and Linguistics in the English Program," *College English*, 26(Oct. 1964):13.

18. Ibid., 14.

14. THE JUDGMENT OF PEERS

1. Harold B. Allen, "Webster's Third New International Dictionary: A Symposium," *Quarterly Journal of Speech*, 48(Dec. 1962):432 (other quotations from this issue will be identified as from "A Symposium"); Robert W. Burchfield, "Webster's Third New International Dictionary," *Review of English Studies*, 14(Aug. 1963):320; Robert L. Chapman, "A Working Lexicographer Appraises Webster's Third New International Dictionary," *American Speech*, 42(1967):210; Albert H. Marckwardt, "Dictionaries and the English Language," in Gove, *The Role of the Dictionary*, 37; Raven I. McDavid, Jr., "A Symposium," 437; Allen Walker Read, "A Symposium," 438, 439; I. Willis Russell, "Webster's Third New International Dictionary," *English Journal*, 51(May 1962):348; James Sledd, "The Lexicographer's Uneasy Chair," *College English*, 23(May 1962);687; Joshua Whatmough, "Mr. Webster's New Dictionary: *THIRD* or *SECOND?*" *Education Summary*, Aug. 12, 1962, 5.

2. Chapman, "A Working Lexicographer," 206. He also noted that if followed "unrelentingly" Gove's approach was inferior to ordinary English. Gove, who had not known Chapman, told him later that this review was the best he had seen. Letter from Chapman to the author, July 3, 1991. Chapman turned to a career in teaching at Drew University after the Funk & Wagnalls *Standard* was published but did not abandon lexicography. His latest book is the fifth edition of *Roget's International Thesaurus* (New York: Harper-Collins, 1992).

3. Russell, "Webster's Third," 333. Burchfield, "Webster's Third," 322.

4. Chapman, "A Working Lexicographer," 208. Burchfield, "Webster's Third," 322. Landau agreed "with those who criticized [Webster's Third] for not applying the 'slang' label more liberally." *Dictionaries*, 190, 327 fn. 51. He recognized, however, the wide disagreement among dictionaries in labeling words in the gray area – between slang and standard or between slang and colloquial. Bosley Woolf commented (Mar. 3, 1992) that he was reluctant to use the slang label in the Third Edition. He found "illustrative quotations, carefully chosen, a better means of

showing usage status." He also heartily approved of dropping the colloquial label, though he had no part in the decision.

5. Atcheson L. Hench, "Notes on Reading Webster III," *College English*, 24(May 1963):613–18. Hench, a professor emeritus at the University of Virginia, originally presented his views at a meeting of the National Council of Teachers of English on November 23, 1962.

6. Landau offers a succinct and highly informative treatment of the confusion over this matter in *Dictionaries*, 189–91.

7. Letter from Robert K. Barnhart to the author, Feb. 21, 1991, commenting on my review of the *Third Barnhart Dictionary of New Words* in *Scholarly Publishing* (Jan. 1991):122–27. I had compared differences in labeling practices in recent dictionaries, including the *Third Barnhart Dictionary*, edited by Robert Barnhart and others and published in 1990 by H. W. Wilson.

8. Edwin Barber, "The Treatment of Slang in Webster's Third New International Dictionary," *American Speech* (May 1963):103–16. Barber drew a sample of words from the *Dictionary of American Slang* (1960), identified the ones that appeared in both Merriam editions, and counted the number of slang labels used in each edition for the same words. He interpreted the difference as the best measure of changes in Merriam editorial policy from 1934 to 1961. Gove noted an obvious conceptual error: Barber had not taken into account changes in the status of words in the sample between 1934 and 1961; that is, Barber assumed that all of the words judged to be slang in 1934 would have been considered slang in 1961.

9. Philip Gove, "Different Than Us," *New York Herald-Tribune*, May 27, 1962.

10. Sledd, "The Lexicographer's Uneasy Chair," 685. Chapman and Burchfield took the same position, and Quirk, in his review, called the omission "regrettable."

11. Allen, "A Symposium," 432.

12. John S. Kenyon, "Cultural Levels and Functional Varieties of English," *College English*, 10(Oct. 1948):31–6. Reprinted in Allen, *Readings in Applied English Linguistics*, 2d ed. (New York: Appleton-Century-Crofts, 1964). He noted that these varieties also exist within substandard English, which can be either formal or informal. Allen called this article "the most significant single statement about English usage yet published." *Applied English Linguistics*, 272.

13. Burchfield, "Webster's Third," 322–3.

14. Chapman, "A Working Lexicographer," 210. Russell also found the etymologies "a substantial improvement" over those in the Second Edition, drew attention to the ISV innovation, and praised the effective use of "origin unknown," "perh." and "prob.," which "add to one's confidence that speculation is kept to a minimum and usually labelled." "Webster's Third," 333.

15. Algeo to the author, Feb. 25, 1990.

16. Sledd, "The Lexicographer's Uneasy Chair," 686. Sledd also expressed sympa-

thy for Artin's predicament – having to write "at a particularly difficult time, when phonological theory is so unsettled that rival groups among the linguists can scarcely communicate with each other." McDavid's comment appeared in "A Symposium," 436.

17. Patrick E. Kilburn, "Ruckus in the Reference Room," *Union College Symposium* (Spring 1962):6. Sumner Ives had noted earlier that since a word may be pronounced differently in different parts of the country by speakers of equal education, the dictionary user should select the pronunciation that "fits most naturally into his own pattern of speech" and avoid those that appear to him to be an affectation. Ives, "A Review of *Webster's Third,*" *Word Study* (Dec. 1961):6.

18. McDavid, "A Symposium" 435–6, and Robert Sonkin, ibid., 439–40.

19. *Booklist,* 59(July 1, 1963):873.

20. Sonkin, "A Symposium," 440. It should be noted that these variants were not all listed separately. The bits of punctuation information (letters and symbols) took up only about one line in the entry. The number 132 was presumably calculated from the possible combinations offered by the sequence of alternative forms. Only a very determined user or a specialist would even try to scan the line, and only the mathematically inclined would try to perform the calculation.

21. Burchfield, "Webster's Third," 320; and Chapman, "A Working Lexicographer," 207. Years later Bosley Woolf said that he had agreed with these criticisms of pronunciation in *Webster's Third.* For the eighth edition of *Webster's Collegiate,* which he edited, Woolf pointed out that Artin did "what would have been essentially OK" for the Third Edition.

22. Landau, *Dictionaries,* 95–96, and 65.

23. Interview with Edmund S. C. Weiner, Aug. 27, 1987. For its second edition, the *OED* followed the IPA.

24. Allen Walker Read, "*That* Dictionary or *The* Dictionary," *Consumer Reports* (Oct. 1963):492.

25. Sonkin, "A Symposium," 440. "Premature" might have been more appropriate than "mistake." Three decades later, the second edition of the *OED* incorporated not only the placement of the stress mark before the stressed syllable but also the rest of the IPA system without critical repercussions.

26. John B. Newman, "A Symposium," 337.

27. Allen, "A Symposium," 432; Burchfield, "A Review of *Webster's Third,*" 320.

28. Uriel Weinreich, "Webster's Third: A Critique of Its Semantics," *International Journal of American Linguistics,* 30(1964):405–9. Weinreich commended Merriam's technological, managerial, and commercial know-how but distanced himself from the controversy in which it "embroiled itself – and unfortunately all of us as linguists." Osselton's comments appear in "The History of Academic Dictionary Criticism with Reference to Major Dictionaries," in Franz Joseph Housman et al., eds., *Dictionaries: An International Encyclopedia of Lexicography* (Berlin: de Gruyter, 1989) 1:229. For another view of the uncertainty of experts

over the functions of lexicography ("applied science") and lexicology ("applied research"), see Yakov Malkeil's comments in "The Lexicographer as Mediator," 54.

29. Karl W. Dykema, "Cultural Lag and Reviewers of Webster III," *AAUP Bulletin*, 49(Winter 1963):364–9; reprinted in Gove, *Role of the Dictionary*, 43–50. Dykema was dean of the College of Arts and Sciences at Youngstown University.

30. Dykema in Gove, *Role of the Dictionary*, 45.

31. Walter J. Ong, "Hostility, Literacy, and Webster III," *College English*, 26(November 1964):106–11. Ong was professor of English at St. Louis University. Marckwardt, "Dictionaries and the English Language," 38.

32. Allen, "A Symposium," 432. The earlier quotation from Prokosch is from Dykema, "Cultural Lag."

33. *Booklist*, 59(July 1, 1963):873.

34. Sheridan Baker, "The Error of *Ain't*," *College English*, 26(Nov. 1964):91–104.

35. Sledd to Gove, Jan. 14, 1964; Gove to Sledd, Jan. 20, 1964, M-W files.

36. Baker, "The Error of *Ain't*," 93.

37. Virginia G. McDavid, "More on *Ain't*," immediately following Baker's article. Jean Malmstrom, another researcher whose work was criticized, replied in a later issue (on page 402), denying the motives imputed to her but conceding some factual errors that Baker had detected. Other respondents included Arthur Norman and Archibald Hill.

38. Sheridan Baker, "The Art and Science of Letters: *Webster's Third New International Dictionary*," *Papers of the Michigan Academy of Science, Arts and Letters* (1965, 1964 meeting):521, 534.

39. Sheridan Baker, "The Sociology of Dictionaries and the Sociology of Words," in Weinbrot, *New Aspects of Lexicography*, 138–51.

40. Marckwardt, "Linguistics Issue: An Introduction," *College English*, 26(January 1965):249. His comments appeared two months after "The Error of *Ain't*," but were wholly unrelated to it.

15. GOVE AND *WEBSTER'S THIRD:* THE LEGACY

1. A bibliography of Gove's writings appears at the end of an article by Bosley Woolf, "Philip Babcock Gove," *American Speech*, 45(Fall–Winter 1970):165–7. It lists more than fifty books, articles, and reviews written by Gove, as well as nine dictionaries that he edited. *The Role of the Dictionary* was a title in the Bobbs-Merrill series in composition and rhetoric and included three articles by Gove on the dictionary's function, repetition in defining, and usage.

2. Interview with Anne Soukhanov, June 22, 1988.

3. Telephone interview with David Replogle, June 24, 1988. Replogle found much to criticize in what he viewed as the narrow outlook of previous Merriam man-

agements – their tightfisted pay practices, excessively cautious approach to investment, and unequal treatment of business and editorial staffs. When he learned that vacation policy was more generous at Britannica, he changed Merriam policy to conform to it.

4. Sylvia Buck, librarian at the Warren public library, made available the newspaper accounts in the library files. The first local story was published in the Warren *Courier*, Nov. 16.

5. Woolf, "Philip Babcock Gove," 164. Raven I. McDavid, Jr., "Philip B. Gove, 1902–1972," *Newsletter of the American Dialect Society*, 5(June 1973):8, 10. Owing to a backlog in *American Speech*, Woolf's article was not published until 1983; the issue in which it appeared was dated 1970, two years before Gove's death.

6. Edwin M. Yoder, Jr., "Fighting Fit or Overweight? Look It Up Sir and Repent," *International Herald Tribune*, Apr. 7, 1989.

7. "An," *English Today* (Apr. 1989):58–9.

8. His staff memo on self-explanatory words for the Black Books ran to thirty pages as he tried to steer a course between eliminating unnecessary definitions and observing William Dwight Whitney's injunction in the front matter of the *Century Dictionary* of 1889, which he quoted with approval: "When a full account of the language is sought, every omission of a genuine English form, even when practically necessary, is so far a defect; and it is therefore better to err on the side of broad inclusiveness than of narrow exclusiveness."

9. In "Subject Orientation within the Definition," Gove wrote that "it doesn't matter who is quoted . . . the quotation is illustrating a word, not citing an author."

10. In 1964 Gove also lamented his failure to explain his use of the label *often attrib* to indicate "a noun that is often used as an adjective equivalent . . . (as in *air passage, cabbage soup*)." He had recognized that the label ("new to lexicography") would be scrutinized and he "would have some explaining to do," but he conceded that the brief mention of the label in explanatory note 6 was not an explanation. Since almost any noun "can be used attributively sometimes," the *often attrib* label was reserved for those given widespread attributive use. It was introduced to combat the classification of such nouns as adjectives, which he thought was done too often in the Second Edition. He was responding to a critical article that appeared in *American Speech*. See John Dawkins, "Noun Attributives in 'Webster's Third New International Dictionary,'" *American Speech*, 39(Feb. 1964):33–41; Philip B. Gove, "'Noun Often Attributive' and 'Adjective,'" *American Speech*, 39(Oct. 1964):163–75.

11. Sidney Greenbaum, *Good English and the Grammarian* (London: Longman, 1988), 36. He uses the agitation against *hopefully* as an example of the need for an expert to speak out. "The rage against the disjunct use of *hopefully* has . . . no grammatical justification" (12). "It is normal in English for adverbs to convey the speaker's comment; we could replace *hopefully* . . . by many other adverbs that

express the speaker's opinion; for example, *happily, frankly, fortunately, predictably, obviously.*" Greenbaum succeeded Randolph Quirk as the director of the Survey of English Usage at University College, London.

12. John Algeo, "American Lexicography," in Franz Joseph Hausman et al., eds., *Dictionaries: An International Encyclopedia of Lexicography* (Berlin: de Gruyter, 1990), 2:1996.

13. Soukhanov interview, June 22, 1988.

14. Interview with Robert Costello, Mar. 19, 1990.

15. Organized by Raven I. McDavid, Jr., and Audrey R. Duckert, the conference was held June 5–7, 1972, in New York City. The proceedings were published in the *Annals of the New York Academy of Sciences* 211 (1973). The origins of the conference are described in McDavid's opening remarks. Gove did not participate in the planning or appear on the program, although two of his colleagues gave papers, Woolf on defining and Artin on pronunciation.

16. Sledd introduced his proposals at a Modern Language Association meeting in 1968. The paper, "Dollars and Dictionaries," was published in Weinbrot, *New Aspects of Lexicography,* 119–37.

17. Interview with Frederick C. Mish, Aug. 3, 1989. Mish also noted that though some editors would like to restore encyclopedic material, "I think the shape of the Merriam-Webster unabridged dictionary is determined as far as I can see into the future. . . . With all the electronic innovations, there may be room for something different, and the inclusion of encyclopedic matter may become feasible. But as a printed book I don't think the members of the public are prepared to pay what is necessary to keep it up to date."

16. CONCLUDING WORDS

1. The total of 2.5 million copies was a company estimate in July 1993. Company policy has been not to disclose total sales figures, but in 1973 the *Wall Street Journal* reported that sales had exceeded 500,000 copies and were growing at the rate of 60,000 a year (Richard Martin, "The Word Watchers," *Wall Street Journal* Nov. 28, 1973). *Publishers Weekly,* May 18, 1992, reported that annual sales were about 70,000 copies.

2. John Simon, *Paradigms Lost: Reflections on Literacy and Its Decline* (New York: Clarkson Potter, 1980; Penguin paperback, 1981), 199.

3. In the history of efforts at language reform and standardization in the United States, *Webster's Third* plays a much smaller role than it does in lexicography. In the larger controversy over language, the effort of language reformers and purists in the cause of good usage has had "an overwhelming lack of success," according to Dennis Baron. But that failure has been "no deterrent" to their persistence. Baron, *Grammar and Good Taste,* 239–40. For an opposing view, see Arn Tibbetts and Charlene Tibbetts, *What's Happening to American English?*

(New York: Scribner's, 1979). Arn Tibbetts, a professor of English at the University of Illinois, where he could keep an eye on the activities of the NCTE, which had its headquarters there, echoed Barzun, Baker, et al. in his attacks on the new grammarians. During the 1960s he was in the thick of the dictionary debate; he called the Third Edition "an inelegant, five-and-dime store approach to language . . . as democratic and mechanical as a bean picker." "The Real Issues in the Great Language Controversy," 1966. Quoted in Finegan, *Attitudes toward English*, 8.

4. The introductory essay, "Usage, Dialects, and Functional Varieties," by Raven I. McDavid, Jr., notes: "Despite some yearnings for authorities who would prescribe how people should use their language, the tendency in the English-speaking world is toward teaching based on objective description of the language. This does not mean an abandonment of standards" (xxii).

5. Thomas J. Creswell and Virginia McDavid, "Usage: Change and Variation," *The Random House Dictionary of the English Language*, 2d ed. (1987), xxiv. See the discussions of usage and Creswell's and McDavid's studies of usage questions in Chapter 12.

6. Geoffrey Nunberg, "Usage in the *American Heritage Dictionary:* The Place of Criticism," *American Heritage Dictionary of the English Language*, 3d ed. (Boston: Houghton Mifflin, 1992), xxvii. The Usage Note itself is longer and includes quotations from Garrison Keillor, Anne Tyler, the *New Republic*, and others. The third edition of the *AHD* also greatly revised and expanded its treatment of etymology with an appendix on Indo-European roots and 400 highly readable word histories inserted with selected entries throughout the volume.

7. Anne H. Soukhanov, Introduction to *AHD*, 3d ed., vi.

8. Nunberg, "Usage," xxvii–xxix. For the third edition, the panel was enlarged to 173 members and made more representative of different age groups, ethnic groups, gender, and geographical areas. To what extent do such changes in the voting pattern reflect a change in the composition of the panel and to what extent do they reflect a change in nation-wide usage? The dictionary acknowledges this question and leaves it to the reader's conjecture. A thorough assessment of this change in usage and its treatment is beyond the scope of this book. Finegan's 1980 book, *Attitudes Toward English*, remains the best broad and persuasive account of developments that occurred before the events discussed in this chapter.

9. Laurence Urdang's assessment appeared in the Book Club Catalogue section of his quarterly publication, *Verbatim*, during the years 1987–9.

10. Gabriele Stein, "Best of British and American Lexicography," *Dictionaries*, 1(1979):1. She lamented, however, that because of the abuse heaped on *Webster's Third*, publishing houses may "shrink from trying out the newly opened-up ground" (2).

11. Algeo, "American Lexicography," 2:1996–7.

Index